Exploring tl Philosophy of Death and Dying

Exploring the Philosophy of Death and Dying: Classical and Contemporary Perspectives is the first book to offer students the full breadth of philosophical issues that are raised by the end of life. Included are many of the essential voices that have contributed to the philosophy of death and dying throughout history and in contemporary research. The 38 chapters in its nine sections contain both classic texts (by authors such as Epicurus, Hume, Nietzsche, and Schopenhauer) and new short argumentative essays, specially commissioned for this volume, by world-leading contemporary experts.

Exploring the Philosophy of Death and Dying introduces students to both theoretical issues (whether we can survive death, whether death is truly bad for us, whether immortality would be desirable, etc.) and urgent practical issues (the ethics of suicide, the value of grief, the appropriate medical criteria for declaring death, etc.) raised by human mortality, enabling instructors to adapt it to a wide array of institutions and student audiences.

As a pedagogical benefit, PowerPoints, discussion questions, and test questions for each chapter are included as online ancillary materials.

Michael Cholbi is Chair in Philosophy at the University of Edinburgh and the founder of the International Association for the Philosophy of Death and Dying. His publications include *Suicide: The Philosophical Dimensions* (2011), *Immortality and the Philosophy of Death* (2015), and *Grief: A Philosophical Guide* (2021).

Travis Timmerman is Assistant Professor of Philosophy at Seton Hall University and executive committee member of the International Association for the Philosophy of Death and Dying. He specializes in the philosophy of death, normative ethics, and applied ethics. He has been the recipient of a National Endowment of the Humanities grant and co-recipient of an Immortality Project grant for his work in ethics and death respectively.

"The areas of death, immortality, meaning in life, and related issues are hot topics in contemporary philosophy. Once the domain only of European philosophers, especially the existentialists, in the last few decades Anglo-American analytic philosophers have jumped in. This book is an excellent introduction to the best work on these interrelated issues. The editors have done an outstanding job of selecting authors who know their stuff and write very accessibly. This book would be perfect for an undergraduate class, and it would also be invaluable to anyone interested in learning the lay of the philosophical land in this lively area of historical and contemporary interest. The book shows how philosophy engages with issues of deep human interest."

John Martin Fischer, Distinguished Professor
of Philosophy, University of California, Riverside

"This splendid collection is distinctive in many ways. The essays address issues that really matter to us, such as whether it is bad to die, and if so, why, whether we might survive death, and whether the inevitability of death undermines meaning in our lives. Although most of the essays were written by contemporary philosophers for this collection, there are also judicious selections from classic writings in the history of philosophy, including works by ancient Greek and Roman philosophers and works from Eastern traditions as well. Those who are haunted in one way or another by the specter of death, as most of us are, will find much careful argument, as well as some genuine wisdom in these pages."

Jeff McMahan, White's Professor
of Moral Philosophy, University of Oxford

Exploring the Philosophy of Death and Dying

Classical and Contemporary Perspectives

Edited by
Michael Cholbi and Travis Timmerman

Routledge
Taylor & Francis Group

NEW YORK AND LONDON

First published 2021
by Routledge
52 Vanderbilt Avenue, New York, NY 10017

and by Routledge
2 Park Square, Milton Park, Abingdon, Oxon, OX14 4RN

Routledge is an imprint of the Taylor & Francis Group, an informa business

Library of Congress Cataloging-in-Publication Data

A catalog record for this title has been requested

ISBN: 978-1-138-39357-8 (hbk)
ISBN: 978-1-138-39358-5 (pbk)
ISBN: 978-1-003-10605-0 (ebk)

Typeset in Bembo
by SPi Global, India

Access the Support Material: www.routledge.com/9781138393585

Contents

Contributors

Roman Altshuler is Assistant Professor in the Department of Philosophy at Kutztown University and Lecturer in the Department of Philosophy at Princeton University. He has published primarily on agency, narrative identity, and the implications of death for what matters in life. He is the co-editor (along with Michael Sigrist) of *Time and the Philosophy of Action* (2016).

David Beglin is the Law and Philosophy Fellow at UCLA. He works primarily in ethics, moral psychology, and agency theory.

Kathy Behrendt is Associate Professor in Philosophy at Wilfrid Laurier University. She has published in the areas of: personal identity theory; the metaphysics and value of death; narrative views of the self; illness; memory, trauma, and the works of W.G. Sebald.

David Benatar is Professor of Philosophy at the University of Cape Town. His books include *Better Never to Have Been* (2006) and *The Human Predicament* (2017).

Ben Bradley is Sutton Professor of Philosophy at Syracuse University. He has published primarily on death and well-being. His books include *Well-Being and Death* (2009) and *Well-Being* (2015).

Stephen Cave is Executive Director of the Leverhulme Centre for the Future of Intelligence at the University of Cambridge, UK. He writes on a wide range of topics at the intersections of philosophy, science and society. His works include *Immortality* (2012), a New Scientist book of the year.

Michael Cholbi holds a chair in Philosophy at the University of Edinburgh. His books include *Suicide: The Philosophical Dimensions* (2011), *Immortality and the Philosophy of Death* (2015), and *Grief: A Philosophical Guide* (2021).

Kirsten Egerstrom is a tenure-track Instructor of Philosophy and Discipline Lead for Philosophy at Whatcom Community College. Additionally, she is a Research Associate with the Faculty of Humanities at the University of Johannesburg, South Africa. Her current research focuses on the topic of meaningfulness in life—i.e., what makes human lives meaningful or meaningless.

Neil Feit is Distinguished Teaching Professor at the State University of New York at Fredonia. He has published work on the nature of harm and related issues in ethics, and also on several topics in epistemology and the philosophy of mind. His books include *Belief about the Self* (2008) and *Attitudes De Se* (2013).

Cody Gilmore is Professor of Philosophy at University of California, Davis. He specializes in analytic metaphysics and writes mainly on mereology, theories of location, and the nature of properties, relations, and propositions.

August Gorman is a values and public policy Postdoctoral Research Fellow at the University Center for Human Values and the Center for Health and Wellbeing at Princeton University. They have published primarily on agency and responsibility, mental health ethics, and the desirability of immortality.

Michael Hauskeller is Professor of Philosophy at the University of Liverpool. He has published widely on a broad range of topics. His most recent books are *Mythologies of Transhumanism* (2016) and *The Meaning of Life and Death* (2019).

David Hershenov is Professor of philosophy and Co-Director of the Romanell Center for Clinical Ethics and the Philosophy of Medicine at the University at Buffalo. His research interests are in issues as the intersection of personal identity and bioethics.

Rose Hershenov is Adjunct Professor of philosophy at Niagara University. Her research interests are primarily in the metaphysics and ethics of embryology.

Jens Johansson is Professor of Practical Philosophy at Uppsala University, Sweden. He has published a number of essays on the evil of death, the nature of harm, and personal identity, and co-edited *The Oxford Handbook of Philosophy of Death* (2013, with Ben Bradley and Fred Feldman).

Frederik Kaufman is Professor in the Department of Philosophy & Religion at Ithaca College. He has published articles primarily on contemporary moral problems. His books include *Life's Hardest Questions: An Introduction to Moral Philosophy* (2008).

John P. Lizza is Professor of Philosophy at Kutztown University. His books include *Persons, Humanity, and the Definition of Death* (2006) and *Defining the Beginning and End of Life: Readings on Personal Identity and Bioethics* (2009).

Todd May is Class of 1941 Memorial Professor of the Humanities at Clemson University. His work concerns both ethics and Continental philosophy. He is the author, most recently, of *Kenneth Lonergan: Filmmaker and Philosopher* (2020) and *A Decent Life: Morality for the Rest of Us* (2019).

Thaddeus Metz is Professor of Philosophy at the University of Pretoria in South Africa. He is known for his work on philosophical approaches to the meaning of life, with his books on this topic including *Meaning in Life: An Analytic Study* (2013) and *God, Soul and the Meaning of Life* (2019).

Benjamin Mitchell-Yellin is Assistant Professor of Philosophy in the Department of Psychology & Philosophy at Sam Houston State University. He has published primarily on issues in ethics, agency, race, and death. He is the co-author, with John Martin Fischer, of the book *Near-Death Experiences: Understanding Visions of the Afterlife* (2016).

Michael Nair-Collins is Associate Professor of Behavioral Sciences and Social Medicine at Florida State University College of Medicine. He has published primarily on the metaphysics and biology of death and brain death. His publications have appeared in, among others, *Journal of Medical Ethics* and *Hastings Center Report*.

Philip Reed is Professor of Philosophy at Canisius College. His primary research areas are ethics and moral psychology. He is the co-editor of *Hume's Moral Philosophy and Contemporary Psychology* (2018).

Patrick Stokes is Associate Professor of Philosophy at Deakin University. His recent books include *Digital Death: A Philosophy of Online Immortality* (2020) and *The Naked Self: Kierkegaard and Personal Identity* (2015).

James Stacey Taylor is Professor of Philosophy at The College of New Jersey. His publications include *Death, Posthumous Harm, and Bioethics* (2012) and the edited collection *The Ethics and Metaphysics of Death* (2013).

Travis Timmerman is Assistant Professor of Philosophy at Seton Hall University and an executive committee member of the International Association for the Philosophy of Death and Dying. He specializes in the philosophy of death, normative ethics, and applied ethics.

Jukka Varelius is a Research Fellow at the Department of Philosophy, Contemporary History, and Political Science at the University of Turku, Finland. He has published primarily on questions of applied ethics. His books include *New Directions in the Ethics of Assisted Suicide and Euthanasia* (2015, co-edited with Michael Cholbi) and *Adaptation and Autonomy: Adaptive Preferences in Enhancing and Ending Life* (2013, co-edited with Juha Räikkä).

Acknowledgements

Travis Timmerman would like to thank Dana Bersch for his input on the Nietzsche intro-duction, Erica O'Neil for her help writing the introduction to The Four Noble Truths, Tyler Paytas for his input on the Seneca introduction, and Andrew Clapham and Adam Taylor for their input on introductions for chapters that unfortunately had to be cut. He would also like to thank Kurt Blankschaen, Monis Rose, and Amanda Timmerman for reading and providing feedback on every introduction. Finally, he would like to thank Peter A. Graham, Eric Moore, and Matt Rohal for suggestions on poems to include in the text.

Michael Cholbi would like to thank innumerable students in his Confrontations with the Reaper courses over the years, whose input illustrated the need for this anthology and shaped its contents. He is also grateful to the membership of the International Association for the Philosophy of Death and Dying (IAPDD), for creating a community in which philosophical work on death and dying can thrive.

Introduction

Michael Cholbi and Travis Timmerman

Death is obviously a fascinating and important subject. It's one that raises a plethora of philosophical questions, philosophical questions that are of the utmost importance because (spoiler alert) all of us are going to someday die. Yet, in spite of its philosophically robust nature and universal relevance, death is a topic rarely discussed in day-to-day life. This is not surprising. After all, the perceived morbidity of the topic makes it difficult to organically work into polite conversation.

BILL: Hey Ted, did you catch the Lakers game last night?
TED: I sure did. Lebron James was on fire, wasn't he? Also, when you die do you think you become a corpse or simply cease to exist?
BILL: [...]
TED: [...]
BILL: I have to go.

Joking aside, when death *is* discussed, the discussion is usually prompted by some tragic situation. On a more personal scale, a loved one may be suicidal, or diagnosed with a terminal illness, or on their death bed, or have recently died. Or perhaps one of these things may be true of you. On a more public scale, news can be dominated by the casualties of war, natural disasters, acts of terrorism, and even a global pandemic. These tragic events may prompt some discussions about death, but these conditions are, to put it mildly, suboptimal. These are simply tragic times, during which people are grieving, mourning, processing theirs and others' losses, and often striving to do what they can to prevent the situation from getting worse. They're often (rightly) trying to minimize the pain for others, and themselves.

The ideal time to think through philosophical issues about death are not during times of duress, but rather when a person is in a position to be as level-headed as possible. This requires creating a space to discuss philosophical issues pertaining to death in an everyday context. There is already widespread desire to create such a space, as evidenced by the rise of so-called *Death Cafés*. Death Cafés are a recent phenomenon where people meet to "eat cake, drink tea and discuss death," and are created with the explicit aim of talking about death (see https://deathcafe.com/). They are not grief support groups or counseling sessions, but rather are created with the intent to get people talking about death in non-tragic contexts. Death Cafés are a welcome development, though they are far from sufficient to remedy this problem.

This is where philosophy comes in and proves to be uniquely valuable. Philosophers of death have been using the methodological tools provided by philosophy to ask, and answer, a wide array of questions pertaining to death for a few thousand years. These questions, and their answers, have been consistently subjected to scrutiny and revised accordingly. The result is hard-earned progress. Philosophical discussions about death among philosophical experts will not only help structure the shape of the dialogue, but (more importantly) it will provide invaluable insight into the answers to each of these questions, and raise the level of the discourse in doing so.

One reason we put this book together was to help create a space where people can have extended, rigorous, philosophical discussions about death in the classroom. From our own experience teaching *Philosophy of*

Death at our respective universities, this has proven to be *the* most fruitful context for such discussions. The academic classroom will provide a space where you can examine deep and probing questions about death at length. This will no doubt include questions that have been on your mind a while and will also introduce you to new issues or problems surrounding death that you've never even thought of before. Classes on the philosophy of death help advance students' and instructors' understanding of the issues surrounding death and, if all goes well, the class may even advance the field itself.

This text provides a general non-technical overview of an eclectic range of questions about death from a diverse group of philosophers and philosophical traditions. It contains a mix of classical texts and cutting-edge contemporary essays that advance the field, yet are written to be maximally accessible. As such, it may profitably be read by everyone, from students with no prior background in the field, to those who are experts in the literature.

We've divided the text into nine different sections revolving around the following nine general questions.

I. When do we die?
II. Can we survive our death?
III. Can death be good or bad for us?
IV. Can Lucretius' asymmetry problem be solved?
V. Would immortality be good for us?
VI. What is the best attitude to take towards our mortality?
VII. How should we react to the deaths of others?
VIII. Is suicide rationally or morally defensible?
IX. How, if at all, does death affect the meaning of our lives?

Within each section are three to five chapters that address the general question of the section, as well as more precise questions that fall within the scope of the more general question. One to three of the chapters within each section are classic texts that are historically significant and typically instrumental to the development of the current literature. The other chapters in each section are written by contemporary philosophers who themselves have made seminal contributions to the philosophy of death. Each of their original chapters address the issue at hand with philosophical rigor and yet are written to be maximally accessible. These works thus provide the ideal, representative, introduction to the philosophy of death, while simultaneously advancing the field.

Each section is preceded by its own brief introduction, which details the contents of each of the chapters within that section. We have also included a list of four additional recommended readings at the end of each section introduction in case some specific question(s) pique your interest enough to research it beyond this text. As will become clear from reading this text, no single book on the philosophy of death could be exhaustive. Rather than strive for the impossible, we have provided a gateway into the field, one that will help you become acquainted with some of the most important ancient and modern texts about death. Reading them will help you familiarize yourself with the origins of the field, and with the cutting edge work that is being done right now. None of the chapters, however, are the final word on the subject. There is much more progress to be made. Help us make it.

Part I When Do We Die?

A Death-Scene

....One long look, that sore reproved me
For the woe I could not bear,
One mute look of suffering moved me
To repent my useless prayer:

And, with sudden check, the heaving
Of distraction passed away;
Not a sign of further grieving
Stirred my soul that awful day.

Paled, at length, the sweet sun setting;
Sunk to peace the twilight breeze:
Summer dews fell softly, wetting
Glen, and glade, and silent trees.

Then his eyes began to weary,
Weighed beneath a mortal sleep;
And their orbs grew strangely dreary,
Clouded, even as they would weep.

But they wept not, but they changed not,
Never moved, and never closed;
Troubled still, and still they ranged not,
Wandered not, nor yet reposed!

So I knew that he was dying,
Stooped, and raised his languid head;
Felt no breath, and heard no sighing,
So I knew that he was dead.

—**Emily Brontë**

Introduction to Part I

When Do We Die?

This first section covers one of the most deceptively complicated questions in the philosophy of death literature. When do we die? The answer may seem obvious. If Victor is vaporized by a nuclear bomb at noon, then he died at noon. That is straightforward enough. But what if someone's body is biologically dead, but their consciousness continues in some form? Is *the person* dead now? Or what if they're brain dead, but the human organism that is their body is still alive? Is *the person* dead now? Or, what if someone is permanently cryogenically frozen, or if each of the living cells that comprise them are separated from one another, permanently ending their consciousness, but not killing any of the living cells that made them up? Or, what if they die, but are seemingly resurrected at a later date? These cases, and others, reveal that it's far from obvious what makes it the case that a person is dead. In this section, you will get to read one landmark legal document that sets out to define death and three contemporary philosophers' take on the question of when someone dies.

You will first get to read a very important historical document, *Defining Death: Medical, Legal and Ethical Issues in the Determination of Death*. It was written by the President's Commission for the Study of Ethical Problems in Medicine and Biomedical and Behavioral Research, appointed by Jimmy Carter, and published in 1981. After considering various criteria for death, and their philosophical and legal merits, the commission ultimately argued that an individual has died when they have "sustained either (1) irreversible cessation of circulatory and respiratory functions, or (2) irreversible cessation of all functions of the entire brain."

This definition is controversial, to say the least. In the next chapter, John Lizza first provides a brief history of how public definitions of death changed from just being (1) to include (2) as well. That is, he reviews how "brain death" came to be introduced into law and then he reviews the considerations in its favor. After that, Lizza acknowledges that this competing view is a good account of death from a purely biological point of view. However, he argues that insofar as we are looking to understand death in a social and cultural context, we also have to account for metaphysical, moral, and social considerations in addition the biological factors. Taking *all* of these considerations into account, Lizza defends the idea that we should accept "brain death" as being sufficient for death.

This chapter is followed by Michael Nair-Collins', in which he argues for the contrary conclusion that "brain death" is not death in any sense of the term. The "brain death" view of death, he argues, is a product of a certain theory about personal identity that is based on the false assumption that humans are fundamentally different from non-human animals. But we're not, he argues, so the criterion of death that applies to humans should apply to non-human animals as well. That criterion, in a nutshell, is that death occurs when entropy overwhelms homeostasis. In other words, death occurs when the amount of "unavailable" energy in a system overwhelms the steady internal, physical, and chemical conditions maintained by living systems. Nair-Collins then reviews a bit of history, arguing that the abovementioned Presidential Commission defining death adopted "brain death" as a sufficient criterion for death for practical purposes, as it allowed them to declare *brain* dead comatose patients on ventilators as dead. Such patients who were organ donors could then have their organs harvested for donation. Nair-Collins ends by reviewing competing accounts of the metaphysical and moral status of "living unconscious patients." He argues that since these accounts of life and death reflect fundamental and personally meaningful commitments, a pluralism of views should be accepted in society for moral reasons (even though only one such view is actually true).

In the final chapter of this section, Cody Gilmore raises, and attempts to solve, the

Paradox of Cryptobiosis. Cryptobiosis refers to the "state of an organism when it shows no visible signs of life, and when its metabolic activity becomes hardly measurable, or reversibly to a standstill." Gilmore asks us to imagine a tardigrade (a tiny insect-like creature) who is alive, enters a state of cryptobiosis where their metabolisms have ceased, and then comes out of that state, returning to function as they did before. Now consider the tardigrade while it's in cryptobiosis. It seems plausibly true that it's not alive or dead while in that state, and it seems plausibly true that everything is either alive or dead. The paradox arises because these seemingly true propositions are mutually inconsistent, so one of them must be false. Gilmore goes on to defend a positive view of what it is to be alive, viz. activism and dead, viz. neutral incapacitation. These views collectively entail that it's not true that everything is either alive or dead. Gilmore thus concludes that the paradox can be solved by rejecting the claim that everything is either alive or dead. The tardigrade in cryptobiosis is an example of something that is neither.

If you're interested in reading more about when death occurs, check out the following:

1. Michael Nair-Collins, Sydney R. Green, and Angelina R. Sutin's "Abandoning the Dead Donor Rule? A National Survey of Public Views on Death and Organ Donation" (2015) *Journal of Medical Ethics* 41 (4):297–302.
2. Cody Gilmore's "When Do Things Die?" in *The Oxford Handbook of Philosophy of Death* (2013) edited by Ben Bradley, Fred Feldman, and Jens Johansson, New York: Oxford University Press.
3. Fred Feldman's book *Confrontations with the Reaper: A Philosophical Study of the Nature and Value of Death* (1992) New York: Oxford University Press.
4. Peter Singer's book *Rethinking Life and Death* (1996) New York: St. Martin's Griffin Press.

Defining Death

A Report on the Medical, Legal and Ethical Issues in the Determination of Death (excerpt)

President's Commission for the Study of Ethical Problems in Medicine and Biomedical and Behavioral Research

Defining Death: A Report on the Medical, Legal and Ethical Issues in the Determination of Death (1981)

Summary of Conclusions and Recommended Statute

The enabling legislation for the President's Commission directs it to study "the ethical and legal implications of the matter of defining death, including the advisability of developing a uniform definition of death." In performing its mandate, the Commission has reached conclusions on a series of questions which are the subject of this Report. In summary, the central conclusions are:

1. That recent developments in medical treatment necessitate a restatement of the standards traditionally recognized for determining that death has occurred.
2. That such a restatement ought preferably to be a matter of statutory law.
3. That such a statute ought to remain a matter for state law, with federal action at this time being limited to areas under current federal jurisdiction.
4. That the statutory law ought to be uniform among the several states.
5. That the "definition" contained in the statute ought to address general physiological standards rather than medical criteria and tests, which will change with advances in biomedical knowledge and refinements in technique.
6. That death is a unitary phenomenon which can be accurately demonstrated either on the traditional grounds of irreversible cessation of heart and lung functions or on the basis of irreversible loss of all functions of the entire brain.
7. That any statutory "definition" should be kept separate and distinct from provisions governing the donation of cadaver organs and from any legal rules on decisions to terminate life-sustaining treatment.

To embody these conclusions in statutory form the Commission worked with the three organizations which had proposed model legislation on the subject, the American Bar Association, the American Medical Association, and the National Conference of Commissioners on Uniform State Laws. These groups have now endorsed the following statute, in place of their previous proposals:

Uniform Determination of Death Act An individual who has sustained either (1) irreversible cessation of circulatory and respiratory functions, or (2) irreversible cessation of all functions of the entire brain, including the brain stem, is dead. A determination of death must be made in accordance with accepted medical standards.

The Commission recommends the adoption of this statute in all jurisdictions in the United States.

Introduction

Death is the one great certainty. The subject of powerful social and religious rituals and moving literature, it is contemplated by philosophers, probed by biologists, and combatted by physicians. Death, taboo in some cultures, preoccupies others. In this Report the President's Commission explores only a small corner of this boundless topic. The question addressed here is not inherently difficult or complicated. Simply, it is whether the law ought to recognize new means for establishing that the death of a human being has occurred. The accepted standard for determining death has been the permanent absence of respiration and circulation. A question arises about continued reliance on the traditional standard because advances in medical technique now permit physicians to generate breathing and heartbeat when the capacity to breathe spontaneously has been irretrievably lost. Prior to the advent of current technology, breathing ceased and death was obvious. Now, however, certain organic processes in these bodies can be maintained through artificial means, although they will never recover the capacity for spontaneous breathing or sustained integration of bodily functions, for consciousness, or for other human experiences. Such artificially-maintained bodies present a new category for the law (and for society), to which the application of traditional means for determining death is neither clear nor fully satisfactory. The Commission's mandate is to study and recommend ways in which the traditional legal standards can be updated in order to provide clear and principled guidance for determining whether such bodies are alive or dead.

CHAPTER I Why "Update" Death?

For most of the past several centuries, the medical determination of death was very close to the popular one. If a person fell unconscious or was found so, someone (often but not always a physician) would feel for the pulse, listen for breathing, hold a mirror before the nose to test for condensation, and look to see if the pupils were fixed. Although these criteria have been used to determine death since antiquity, they have not always been universally accepted.

Developing Confidence in the Heart–Lung Criteria

In the eighteenth century, macabre tales of "corpses" reviving during funerals and exhumed skeletons found to have clawed at coffin lids led to widespread fear of premature burial. Coffins were developed with elaborate escape mechanisms and speaking tubes to the world above, mortuaries employed guards to monitor the newly dead for signs of life, and legislatures passed laws requiring a delay before burial. The medical press also paid a great deal of attention to the matter. In *The Uncertainty of the Signs of Death and the Danger of Precipitate Interments* in 1740, Jean-Jacques Winslow advanced the thesis that putrefaction was the only sure sign of death. In the years following, many physicians published articles agreeing with him. This position had, however, notable logistic and public health disadvantages. It also disparaged, sometimes with unfair vigor, the skills of physicians as diagnosticians of death. In reply, the French surgeon Louis published in 1752 his influential *Letters on the Certainty of the Signs of Death*. The debate dissipated in the nineteenth century because of the gradual improvement in the competence of physicians and a concomitant increase in the public's confidence in them.

… The invention of the stethoscope in the mid-nineteenth century enabled physicians to detect heartbeat with heightened sensitivity. The use of this instrument by a well-trained physician, together with other clinical measures, laid to rest public fears of premature burial. The twentieth century brought even more sophisticated technological means to determine death, particularly the electrocardiograph (ECG), which is more sensitive than the stethoscope in detecting cardiac functioning.

The Interrelationships of Brain, Heart, and Lung Functions

The brain has three general anatomic divisions: the cerebrum, with its outer shell called the cortex; the cerebellum; and the brainstem, composed of the midbrain, the pons, and the medulla oblongata. Traditionally, the cerebrum has been referred to as the "higher brain" because it has primary control of consciousness, thought, memory and feeling. The brainstem has been called the "lower brain," since it controls spontaneous, vegetative functions such as swallowing, yawning and sleep-wake cycles. It is important to note that these generalizations are not entirely accurate. Neuroscientists generally agree that such "higher brain" functions as cognition or consciousness probably are not mediated strictly by the cerebral cortex; rather, they probably result from complex interrelations between brain stem and cortex.

Respiration is controlled in the brainstem, particularly the medulla. Neural impulses originating in the respiratory centers of the medulla stimulate the diaphragm and intercostal muscles, which cause the lungs to fill with air. Ordinarily, these respiratory centers adjust the rate of breathing to maintain the correct levels of carbon dioxide and oxygen. In certain circumstances, such as heavy exercise, sighing, coughing or sneezing, other areas of the brain modulate the activities of the respiratory centers or even briefly take direct control of respiration.

Destruction of the brain's respiratory center stops respiration, which in turn deprives the heart of needed oxygen, causing it too to cease functioning. The traditional signs of life—respiration and heartbeat—disappear: the person is dead. The "vital signs" traditionally used in diagnosing death thus reflect the direct interdependence of respiration, circulation and the brain. The artificial respirator and concomitant life-support systems have changed this simple picture. Normally, respiration ceases when the functions of the diaphragm and intercostal muscles are impaired…

However, an artificial respirator (also called a ventilator) can be used to compensate for the inability of the thoracic muscles to fill the lungs with air… The respirators are equipped with devices to regulate the rate and depth of "breathing," which are normally controlled by the respiratory centers in the medulla… provided that the lungs themselves have not been extensively damaged, gas exchange can continue and appropriate levels of oxygen and carbon dioxide can be maintained in the circulating blood.

Unlike the respiratory system, which depends on the neural impulses from the brain, the heart can pump blood without external control. Impulses from brain centers modulate the inherent rate and force of the heartbeat but are not required for the heart to contract at a level of function that is ordinarily adequate. Thus, when artificial respiration provides adequate oxygenation and associated medical treatments regulate essential plasma components and blood pressure, an intact heart will continue to beat, despite loss of brain functions. At present, however, no machine can take over the functions of the heart except for a very limited time and in limited circumstances (e.g., a heart-lung machine used during surgery). Therefore, when a severe injury to the heart or major blood vessels prevents the circulation of the crucial blood supply to the brain, the loss of brain functioning is inevitable because no oxygen reaches the brain.

Loss of Various Brain Functions

… severe injuries to the brain cause an accumulation of fluid and swelling in the brain tissue, a condition called cerebral edema. In severe cases of edema, the pressure within the closed cavity increases until it exceeds the systolic blood pressure, resulting in a total loss of blood now to both the upper and lower portions of the brain. If deprived of blood flow for at least 10–15 minutes, the brain, including the brainstem, will completely cease functioning…

Once deprived of adequate supplies of oxygen and glucose, brain neurons will irreversibly lose all activity and ability to function. In adults, oxygen and/or glucose deprivation for more than a few minutes causes some neuron loss. Thus, even in the absence of direct trauma and edema, brain functions can be lost if circulation to the brain is impaired. If blood flow is cut off, brain tissues completely self-digest (autolyze) over the ensuing days. When the brain lacks all functions, consciousness is, of course, lost. While some spinal reflexes often persist in such bodies (since circulation to the spine is separate from that of the brain), all reflexes controlled by the brainstem as well as cognitive, affective and integrating functions are absent. Respiration and circulation in these bodies may be generated by a ventilator together with intensive medical management. In adults who have experienced irreversible cessation of the functions of the entire brain, this mechanically generated functioning can continue only a limited time because the heart usually stops beating within two to ten days.

… When brainstem functions remain, but the major components of the cerebrum are irreversibly destroyed, the patient is in what is usually called a "persistent vegetative state" or "persistent noncognitive state." Such persons may exhibit spontaneous, involuntary movements such as yawns or facial grimaces, their eyes may be open and they may be capable of breathing without assistance. Without higher brain functions, however, any apparent wakefulness does not represent awareness of self or environment (thus, the condition is often described as "awake but unaware"). The case of Karen Ann Quinlan has made this condition familiar to the general public. With necessary medical and nursing care—including feeding through intravenous or nasogastric tubes, and antibiotics for recurrent pulmonary infections—such patients can survive months or years, often without a respirator.

Conclusion: The Need for Reliable Policy

Medical interventions can often provide great benefit in avoiding irreversible harm to a patient's injured heart, lungs, or brain by carrying a patient through a period of acute need. These techniques have, however, thrown new light on the interrelationship of these crucial organ systems. This has created complex issues for public policy as well. For medical and legal purposes, partial brain impairment must be distinguished from complete and irreversible loss of brain functions or "whole brain death." The President's Commission, as subsequent chapters explain more fully, regards the cessation of the vital functions of the entire brain—and not merely portions thereof, such as those responsible for cognitive functions—as the only proper neurologic basis for declaring death. This conclusion accords with the overwhelming consensus of medical and legal experts and the public.

CHAPTER 3 Understanding the "Meaning" of Death

It now seems clear that a medical consensus about clinical practices and their scientific basis has emerged: certain states of brain activity and inactivity, together with their neurophysiological consequences, can be reliably detected and used to diagnose death. To the medical community, a sound basis exists for declaring death even in the presence of mechanically assisted "vital signs." …

The "Whole Brain" Formulations

One characteristic of living things which is absent in the dead is the body's capacity to organize and regulate itself. In animals, the neural apparatus is the dominant locus of these functions. In higher animals and man, regulation of both maintenance of the internal environment (homeostasis) and interaction with the external environment occurs primarily within the cranium. External threats, such as heat or infection, or internal ones, such as liver failure or endogenous lung disease, can stress the body enough to overwhelm its ability to maintain organization and regulation. If the stress passes a certain level, the organism as a whole is defeated and death occurs.

The Concepts: The functioning of many organs—such as the liver, kidneys, and skin—and their integration are "vital" to individual health in the sense that if any one ceases and that function is not restored or artificially re-placed, the organism as a whole cannot long survive. All elements in the system are mutually interdependent, so that the loss of any part leads to the breakdown of the whole and, eventually, to the cessation of functions in every part.

Three organs—the heart, lungs and brain—assume special significance, however, because their interrelationship is very close and the irreversible cessation of anyone very quickly stops the other two and consequently halts the integrated functioning of the organism as a whole. Because they were easily measured, circulation and respiration were traditionally the basic "vital signs." But breathing and heartbeat are not life itself. They are simply used as signs, as one window for viewing a deeper and more complex reality: a triangle of interrelated systems with the brain at its apex. As the biomedical scientists who appeared before the Commission made clear, the traditional means of diagnosing death actually detected an irreversible cessation of integrated functioning among the interdependent bodily systems. When artificial means of support mask this loss of integration as measured by the old methods, brain-oriented criteria and tests provide a new window on the same phenomenon. On this view, death is that moment at which the body's physiological system ceases to constitute an integrated whole. Even if life continues in individual cells or organs, life of the organism as a whole requires complex integration, and without the latter, a person cannot properly be regarded as alive. This

distinction between systemic, integrated functioning and physiological activity in cells or individual organs is important for two reasons. First, a person is considered dead under this concept even if oxygenation and metabolism persist in some cells or organs. There would be no need to wait until all metabolism had ceased in every body part before recognizing that death has occurred. More importantly, this concept would reduce the significance of continued respiration and heartbeat for the definition of death. This view holds that continued breathing and circulation are not in themselves tantamount to life. Since life is a matter of integrating the functioning of major organ systems, breathing and circulation are necessary but not sufficient to establish that an individual is alive. When an individual's breathing and circulation lack neurologic integration, he or she is dead.

The alternative "whole brain" explanation of death differs from the one just described primarily in the vigor of its insistence that the traditional "vital signs" of heartbeat and respiration were merely surrogate signs with no significance in themselves. On this view, the heart and lungs are not important as basic prerequisites to continued life but rather because the irreversible cessation of their functions shows that the brain had ceased functioning. Other signs customarily employed by physicians in diagnosing death, such as unresponsiveness and absence of pupillary light response, are also indicative of loss of the functions of the whole brain.

This view gives the brain primacy not merely as the sponsor of consciousness (since even unconscious persons may be alive), but also as the complex organizer and regulator of bodily functions. (Indeed, the "regulatory" role of the brain in the organism can be understood in terms of thermodynamics and information theory 3.) Only the brain can direct the entire organism. Artificial support for the heart and lungs, which is required only when the brain can no longer control them, cannot maintain the usual synchronized integration of the body. Now that other traditional indicators of cessation of brain functions (i.e., absence of breathing), can be obscured by medical interventions, one needs, according to this view, new standards for determining death—that is, more reliable tests for the complete cessation of brain functions.

Critique: Both of these "whole brain" formulations—the "integrated functions" and the "primary organ" views—are subject to several criticisms. Since both of these conceptions of death give an important place to the integrating or regulating capacity of the whole brain, it can be asked whether that characteristic is as distinctive as they would suggest. Other organ systems are also required for life to continue— for example, the skin to conserve fluid, the liver to detoxify the blood.

The view that the brain's functions are more central to "life" than those of the skin, the liver, and so on, is admittedly arbitrary in the sense of representing a choice. The view is not, however, arbitrary in the sense of lacking reasons. As discussed previously, the centrality accorded the brain reflects both its overarching role as "regulator" or "integrator" of other bodily systems and the immediate and devastating consequences of its loss for the organism as a whole. Furthermore, the Commission believes that this choice overwhelmingly reflects the views of experts and the lay public alike…

Policy Consequences: Those holding to the "whole brain" view—and this view seems at least implicit in most of the testimony and writing reviewed by the Commission— believe that when respirators are in use, respiration and circulation lose significance for the diagnosis of death. In a body without a functioning brain these two functions, it is argued, become mere artifacts of the mechanical life supports. The lungs breathe and the heart circulates blood only because the respirator (and attendant medical interventions) cause them to do so, not because of any comprehensive integrated functioning. This is "breathing" and "circulation" only in an analogous sense: the function and its results are similar, but the source, cause, and purpose are different between those individuals with and those without functioning brains. For patients who are not artificially maintained,

breathing and heartbeat were, and are, reliable signs either of systemic integration and/or of continued brain functioning (depending on which approach one takes to the "whole brain" concept).

The "Higher Brain" Formulations

The two "higher brain" formulations of brain-oriented definitions of death discussed here are premised on the fact that loss of cerebral functions strips the patient of his psychological capacities and properties. A patient whose brain has permanently stopped functioning will, by definition, have lost those brain functions which sponsor consciousness, feeling, and thought. Thus the higher brain rationales support classifying as dead bodies which meet "whole brain" standards, as discussed in the preceding section. The converse is not true, however. If there are parts of the brain which have no role in sponsoring consciousness, the higher brain formulation would regard their continued functioning as compatible with death.

The Concepts: Philosophers and theologians have attempted to describe the attributes a living being must have to be a person. "Personhood" consists of the complex of activities (or of capacities to engage in them) such as thinking, reasoning, feeling, human intercourse which make the human different from, or superior to, animals or things. One higher brain formulation would define death as the loss of what is essential to a person. Those advocating the personhood definition often relate these characteristics to brain functioning. Without brain activity, people are incapable of these essential activities. A breathing body, the argument goes, is not in itself a person; and, without functioning brains, patients are merely breathing bodies. Hence personhood ends when the brain suffers irreversible loss of function.

For other philosophers, a certain concept of "personal identity" supports a brain-oriented definition of death. According to this argument, a patient literally ceases to exist as an individual when his or her brain ceases functioning, even if the patient's body is biologically alive. Actual decapitation creates a similar situation: the body might continue to function for a short time, but it would no longer be the "same" person. The persistent identity of a person as an individual from one moment to the next is taken to be dependent on the continuation of certain mental processes which arise from brain functioning. When the brain processes cease (whether due to decapitation or to "brain death") the person's identity also lapses. The mere continuation of biological activity in the body is irrelevant to the determination of death, it is argued, because after the brain has ceased functioning the body is no longer identical with the person.

Critique: Theoretical and practical objections to these arguments led the Commission to rely on them only as confirmatory of other views in formulating a definition of death. First, crucial to the personhood argument is acceptance of one particular concept of those things that are essential to being a person, while there is no general agreement on this very fundamental point among philosophers, much less physicians or the general public. Opinions about what is essential to personhood vary greatly from person to person in our society—to say nothing of intercultural variations…

Equally problematic for the "higher brain" formulations, patients in whom only the neocortex or subcortical areas have been damaged may retain or regain spontaneous respiration and circulation. Karen Quinlan is a well-known example of a person who apparently suffered permanent damage to the higher centers of the brain but whose lower brain continues to function. Five years after being removed from the respirator that supported her breathing for nearly a year, she remains in a persistent vegetative state but with heart and lungs that function without mechanical assistance. Yet the implication of the personhood and personal identity arguments is that Karen Quinlan, who retains brainstem function and breathes spontaneously, is just as dead as a corpse in the traditional sense. The Commission rejects this conclusion and the further implication that such patients could be buried or otherwise treated as dead persons.

The Non-Brain Formulations

The Concepts: The various physiological concepts of death so far discussed rely in some fashion on brain functioning. By contrast, a literal reading of the traditional cardiopulmonary criteria would require cessation of the flow of bodily "fluids," including air and blood, for death to be declared. This standard is meant to apply whether or not these flows coincide with any other bodily processes, neurological or otherwise. Its support derives from interpretations of religious literature and cultural practices of certain religious and ethnic groups, including some Orthodox Jews and Native Americans.

Another theological formulation of death is, by contrast, not necessarily related to any physiologic phenomenon. The view is traditional in many faiths that death occurs the moment the soul leaves the body. Whether this happens when the patient loses psychological capacities, loses all brain functions, or at some other point, varies according to the teachings of each faith and according to particular interpretations of the scriptures recognized as authoritative.

Critique: The conclusions of the "bodily fluids" view lack a physiologic basis in modern biomedicine. While this view accords with the traditional criteria of death, as noted above, it does not necessarily carry over to the new conditions of the intensive care unit—which are what prompts the re-examination of the definition of death. The flow of bodily fluids could conceivably be maintained by machines in the absence of almost all other life processes; the result would be viewed by most as a perfused corpse, totally unresponsive to its environment. Although the argument concerning the soul could be interpreted as providing a standard for secular action, those who adhere to the concept today apparently acknowledge the need for a more public and verifiable standard of death. Indeed, a statute incorporating a brain-based standard is accepted by theologians of all backgrounds.

2 Defining Death in a Technological World

Why Brain Death Is Death

John P. Lizza

Advances in medical technology have enabled life to be sustained and extended in unprecedented ways. With these advances have come new ethical and conceptual challenges, perhaps none more challenging than how we fix the beginning and end of our lives. Although the issue of when human life begins has taken center stage in the public debate over abortion, the issue of when our lives end has not generated the same degree of public focus. Nonetheless, the question is essentially the same at both ends of our lives. How are the bounds of our lives being determined? What does it mean for our lives to begin and end?

Traditionally, death was determined on the basis of observation of the cessation of circulation and respiration. However, over the last fifty years, we have moved to accept a brain-based or neurological criterion for determining death. In the United States and in much of the world, we legally accept the irreversible loss of all brain functions as a new way of determining our death. However, the justification for this move has been controversial from the start. In this chapter, I begin with a brief history of how what is commonly referred to as "brain death" (total brain failure) was introduced into law and the two main reasons that historically have been given for its acceptance. One of these reasons assumes that defining death is a strictly biological matter and that the acceptance of a neurological criterion can be justified on biological grounds alone. The other reason holds that metaphysical, moral, and social considerations beyond simply biological ones are relevant to defining death and that those considerations justify acceptance of the neurological criterion. Although the first of these reasons

has become the "received view," it has been forcefully challenged by those who reject any neurological criterion for determining death and accept only the traditional criterion of irreversible loss of circulation and respiration as the criterion for determining death. In their view, we can continue to live, albeit on artificial support, despite the complete loss of all brain function. In this chapter, I will argue that this criticism of the received view has merit, if our death is understood in strictly biological terms. However, since we are looking to define death in a social and cultural context rather than in a textbook for biology, I hope to show that there is good reason for rejecting the idea that our death in this context can be understood in strictly biological terms and that metaphysical, moral, and social considerations are relevant to determining when we die. I will argue that these considerations strongly support accepting brain death as death and in fact have probably been the reason all along that many of us have accepted and should continue to accept brain death as death.

I.

A neurological criterion for determining death was first formally proposed in 1968 by the Ad Hoc Committee of the Harvard Medical School to Examine the Definition of Death. In addition to the traditional, standard criterion of the irreversible loss of circulatory and respiratory functions, the Committee proposed "irreversible coma" (a permanently non-functioning brain) as a new criterion for determining death. In 1970 Kansas became the first state to legally adopt the recommendation of the Harvard Committee. However, since other states did not adopt the new criterion, there was the curious problem that someone could be legally dead in Kansas but alive, for example, in the neighboring state of Missouri. It seems odd that someone could turn from being dead to alive by simply being driven across a state border.

In 1981, the President's Commission for the Study of Ethical Problems in Medicine and Biomedical and Behavioral Research addressed this problem by proposing the Uniform Determination of Death Act (UDDA), which holds, "An individual who has sustained either (1) irreversible cessation of circulatory and respiratory functions, or (2) irreversible cessation of all functions of the entire brain, including the brainstem, is dead" (President's Commission 1981, 2). By 1994 every state and the District of Columbia in the United States had either judicially or legislatively adopted the provisions of the act.[1] New Jersey is exceptional in having enacted a "conscience clause" that allows individuals who reject the neurological criterion on religious grounds to have only the traditional criterion of cessation of circulation and respiration apply.[2] Such a legal provision may provide some early acknowledgment that a legal definition of death goes beyond strictly biological or medical considerations and is bound up with religious and metaphysical considerations. The work of the 1981 Commission was highly influential in leading to the acceptance of a neurological criterion for determining death in many other countries around the world.

When the Harvard Committee issued its report, it contained little in the way of an explanation or justification for the new criterion. Indeed, the chair of the committee, Henry Beecher, shifted back and forth between two different explanations for why "irreversible coma" is equivalent to death (Pernick 1999, 12). The first explanation was that the brain is essential to the physiological integration of the human organism. Without brain function, the organism is no longer physiologically integrated and therefore has died. In this view,

the brain is seen as the control center for the functioning of the organism as a whole. The second explanation appealed to the significance of consciousness in our lives. Without brain function, our psychophysical integration is irreversibly lost. We lack consciousness, emotions, personality, and every other mental capacity that makes us who we are. Without any brain function, our lives are over.[3]

The President's Commission was clearer in its explanation for why brain death is death. It endorsed the strictly biological definition of death as "the permanent cessation of the integrated functioning of the organism as a whole" (President's Commission 1981, 55). The Commission writes:

> On this view, death is that moment at which the body's physiological system ceases to constitute an integrated whole. Even if life continues in individual cells or organs, life of the organism as a whole requires complex integration and without the latter, a person cannot properly be regarded as alive.
>
> (President's Commission, 33)

At the time the Commission proposed the UDDA, it was assumed that the cessation of all brain functions quickly led to the cessation of circulation and respiration and thus what temporarily remained after the cessation of all brain functions was more a collection of organic parts than an integrated organism as a whole. However, this assumption has been seriously challenged by critics of the neurological criterion (Byrne *et al.* 1982/83, 2000; Halevy and Brody 1993; Seifert 1993; Shewmon 1997, 1998b, 2004; Taylor 1997; Truog 1997; Brody 1999; Nair-Collins 2015). Pointing to cases of "post-mortem" pregnancy in which pregnant women who have lost all brain functions are artificially sustained for weeks or months to allow the fetus to gestate and be removed by Caesarian section[4] and the extraordinary case reported by D. Alan Shewmon (1998a) in which a boy with no brain function was artificially sustained for over twenty years, the critics argue that such individuals are still integrated organisms as a whole despite the loss of all brain functions and thus have not died. Artificially sustained human bodies that have lost all brain function may exhibit a range of integrated biological functions. For example, oxygen will continue to be processed across the alveolar membrane and distributed to cells throughout the body. The body will continue to process nutrition and eliminate waste. Homeostasis, including energy balance and temperature regulation, is maintained. The body can heal if wounded and respond to fever and stress. Sexual maturation and proportional growth may occur. In short, these critics claim that a functioning brain is not necessary for a human organism to be integrated as a whole and therefore total brain failure is not an adequate criterion for determining death. They argue for a return to using only the traditional criterion of irreversible loss of circulation and respiration for determining death.

In 2008, largely in response to the mounting biological evidence challenging brain death as death, the President's Council on Bioethics revisited the question of whether brain death is death. The Council agreed with the critics that in view of the highly integrated functioning that may continue among the various parts of an artificially sustained, brain-dead human body, it is implausible to hold, as the 1981 President's Commission held, that what remains is simply a disintegrated collection of internal organic parts. However, a majority of members of the Council nonetheless accepted total brain failure as a criterion for determining death. They went on to define the existence of the human organism as a whole, not in terms of the internal integration of its parts, but in terms of the organism's interaction and integration with its environment in a life-sustaining way. According to the Council, individuals with total brain failure are dead, because artificially sustained whole-brain dead human bodies lack the spontaneous "drive" and "felt need" to breathe and interact consciously with the world. They have irreversibly lost the capacity to engage in commerce with the surrounding world to secure their sustenance.[5] In short,

by redefining organic integration in terms of having a spontaneous "drive" and "felt need" to interact with the environment in a life-sustaining way and holding that brain function is necessary for this "drive" and "felt need," the Council defended acceptance of total brain failure as a neurological criterion for determining death.

However, it is unclear whether this justification for brain death fares any better. Critics of brain death like Shewmon (2009) question why the integration of the organism as a whole is now being defined in terms of its ability to autonomously interact with its environment in a life-sustaining way without artificial assistance, rather than in terms of its internal organic integration with or without assistance. Why isn't the presence of so much integrated biological functioning in a body with total brain failure evidence that the body is alive, not dead? Why aren't the myriad integrated biological functions (e.g., homeostasis, energy balance, temperature regulation, wound healing, immune defense, digestion, elimination of waste, gestation, etc.) evidence of the "spontaneous drive" and "felt need" of the organism to respond in a life-sustaining way? In short, the critics maintain that such integrated biological activity indicates that the organism as a whole is still alive.

A second criticism of the Council's view (Lizza 2016) is that it is not justified on biological grounds alone and that, in fact, it relies on the metaphysical notion of the soul as the animating principle of the body. The crucial concept invoked by the Council in its defense of brain death is that without brain function the organism has lost its "spontaneous drive" and "felt need" to interact with the environment in a life-sustaining way. However, "spontaneous drive" and "felt need" are not concepts found in modern biology textbooks at all and therefore cannot explain in modern biological terms what it means for an organism to be integrated internally and externally with its environment. Instead, these concepts are stand-ins for the metaphysical notion of the soul. Under the guise of biological talk of a "spontaneous drive" and "felt need," the Council actually defends brain death as death on grounds that the body has lost its vital or animating principle, i.e., its soul.[6]

II.

If death should be understood in strictly biological terms and acceptance of brain death as death cannot be justified on strictly biological grounds, should we turn back the clock and return to using only the irreversible loss of circulation and respiration as the criterion for determining death? No. The reason why is because the assumption that the legal definition of death must be understood in strictly biological terms is mistaken. The reason why this assumption is mistaken is shown by the "Decapitation Gambit" (Lizza 2011).

The "Decapitation Gambit" holds that to reject brain death as death would entail the absurd implication that artificially sustained, decapitated human bodies are living human beings and should be counted among the living "we." This implication follows because the brain would play the same role in the integration of the artificially sustained, decapitated body as it plays in the integration of the artificially sustained human body with total brain failure, i.e., no role at all. If the organic integration in an artificially sustained, brain-dead body is sufficient for one of us to still be alive, then that same degree of organic integration in an artificially sustained, decapitated body would be sufficient for one of us to still be alive. However, this implication is absurd. Thus, if physical decapitation would entail our death, then physiological decapitation, evident in cases involving total brain failure, entails our death.

The President's Commission was keenly aware of how artificial substitutes, such as kidney dialysis and ventilators, can be used to restore the integrated functioning of the organism. However, the Commission also contrasted such situations with the hypothetical case of artificially sustaining a decapitated human body to prevent the outpouring of blood and to generate respiration. "Continuation of bodily functions in

that case," the Commission (1981, 36) writes, "would not have restored the requisites of human life." Indeed, as Shewmon (2010, 7) has admitted, the same degree of organic integration may be present in an artificially sustained decapitated body and in a brain-dead body. However, such biological functioning is insufficient for the continuation of a human life. Headless human bodies are not human beings as a whole in any sense relevant to a statutory definition of death and thus should not be counted among the living "we." Thus, if the artificially sustained, decapitated human body is not a living human being, neither is an artificially sustained brain-dead body.

If simple decapitation is not enough to convince one to accept brain death as death, consider the following complexity. Suppose that at the same time that the individual's decapitated body was artificially sustained, the individual's decapitated head was successfully transplanted to another body, as Dr. White (1971) did in his horrible experimentation of transplanting the heads of monkeys. Suppose further that the individual regained consciousness, as also happened in White's experiments with the monkeys.[7] In this case, we should agree with Bernard Gert, Charles Culver, and K. Danner Clouser (2006, 292) that a death has not occurred because of the importance that consciousness plays in the life of human beings and perhaps other higher-order organisms. Assuming that the human being cannot be in two places at once, the psychophysical integration of the human being would continue with the transplanted head and not with the artificially sustained headless body. Suppose further that the original, artificially sustained, decapitated body were destroyed. Again, no one would have died. The human being would continue to exist. Even if the artificially sustained, decapitated body is a living organism of some sort and dies, it would not be the death of any human being. However, if no one dies in that event, then the continuation of the integrated biological functions of the brainless body or brain-dead body cannot be sufficient for the continuation of a human life.

The "Decapitation Gambit" challenges the assumption that death can be understood in strictly biological terms as the "cessation of the functioning of an organism as a whole." Even if this were a defensible *biological* definition of death, it would not be the relevant sense of what it means for one of us to die in the social and cultural context in which we need to formulate a statutory definition of death. In other words, rejecting brain death as death does not fit with our interests and purposes in devising a statutory definition of death because it has the absurd implication that artificially sustained decapitated yet integrated human organisms should be counted among the living "we." We accept decapitation as death because it coheres with our moral, social, and cultural systems of thought, which provide the framework for why we are interested in defining death in the first place. Artificially sustained, decapitated bodies and, by analogy, artificially sustained brain-dead bodies do not fit into those systems of thought. No such purpose or interest is served by treating them as living human beings.

While we do have a biological nature, technology has intervened in that nature to create new phenomena that challenge our ordinary concepts of life and death. If our heads could be transplanted to other bodies and our consciousness preserved, others would continue to recognize, relate to, and value us as the same human being. We would retain our place as a locus of value in a network of conscious social relations and thus would not have died. What tracks our existence in this case would be the persistence of our psychophysical integration in a social and cultural context. While such a continuation of psychophysical integration would not have its normal cause, there would be a new way in which this integration could be maintained. In short, there would be new ways in which we could live. Accordingly, there are new ways in which our psychophysical integration can irreversibly cease and thus new ways in which we can die. I am suggesting that brain death is such a new way in which we die. What remains after brain death is just that: our remains. Whereas in the past, these remains took the form of an inanimate corpse, technology has made it possible for our remains to now take the form of an artificially sustained, living body of some sort devoid of any possibility for consciousness or any other experience. Without the potential for consciousness and any other mental function, we are no longer human beings in any sense that is relevant to formulating a statutory definition of death.

III.

It may be objected that the view that I have just advocated conflates the factual or biological issue of whether a human being is dead with the ethical or legal issue of how a human being should be treated. Just because there is no ethical or legal reason to treat the brain-dead body as a living human being does not mean that it is not a living human being. Death, it may be claimed, is a biological concept and means the same thing for all biological organisms. Thus, ethical or legal considerations should not have any bearing on whether someone is dead or alive. The biology of death should inform our reasoning about who gets counted among the living, rather than an ethical consideration informing whether someone is dead or alive.

This objection, however, misses its mark for several reasons. First, Justice Stevens is correct in his *Cruzan* (1990) dissent, when he states that "there is a serious issue of whether the mere persistence of bodies is 'life' as that word is commonly understood, or as it is used both in the Constitution and Declaration of Independence." Stevens does not frame the question of whether Nancy Cruzan, an individual in a permanent vegetative state, was alive in strictly biological terms, since he is interested in the life and death of human beings in a legal context. In this context, we are understood to be more than simply biological beings. We are understood to be moral and social beings with rights and privileges. Stevens is raising the issue of whether a being with amentia (no mental functions and no potential for mental functions) counts as a living human being in the social and legal context.[8] Framing the issue of when someone is dead or alive in strictly biological terms appears to rule out the essential psychological, moral, and social dimension of human beings from the start and thereby distorts the purpose of seeking an answer in the legal context to the question in the first place. Moreover, as I have pointed out above, restricting an account of what it means for one of us to die to only biological considerations has strongly counterintuitive results in actual and hypothetical cases. Many people would not identify themselves with artificially sustained, decapitated or brainless organisms, even though the strictly biological account of life and death has this absurd implication. Accordingly, there is no legal reason for accepting it.

Second, defining death in a legal context involves drawing a line between which beings get counted among the living "we" and which do not. It would be a mistake to think that this line drawing can be done on the basis of biological considerations alone. Indeed, which biological facts or features we deem relevant has to be understood within the context of our interests, purposes, and values. As Daniel Callahan pointed out many years ago in his discussion of when human life begins

> Biological data, however great the details and subtlety of scientific investigation, do not carry with them self-evident interpretations. There are no labels pasted by God or nature on zygotes, primitive streaks, or fetuses that say "human" or "non-human." Any interpretation of known facts is going to be the result not only of our particular interests as we go about establishing criteria for interpretation, but also of the kind of language and type of analytic-conceptual devices that we bring to bear to solve the problems we set for ourselves. This is only to say, at the very outset, that a purely scientific answer to the question of the beginning of human life is not possible. "Science" itself is a human construct—a set of methods, terms, and perspectives—and any use of science to answer one particular question, particularly when the answer has moral

implications, will be a human use, that it, a use subject to human definitions, distinctions, and decisions. The language of science is a human artifact; the word "life" is a word devised by human beings in order to refer to certain phenomena which can be observed in nature. Scientific method can classify and analyze the phenomena and draw certain "scientific" conclusions (e.g., establish empirical correlations, causal relationships, etc.). But the conclusions it draws will be a result of humanly devised conceptual schemes used to approach the phenomena in the first place.
>
> (Callahan 1988, 32)

Callahan's remarks apply equally well to how we fix the end of life. We need to interpret the biology in light of what it means to be the kind of being that we are in the practical context of determining death.

Third, the crucial concept invoked in the strictly biological account of death, i.e., what it means for an organism to "irreversibly lose its integration as a whole," is vague.[9] Maureen Condic (2016), for example, claims that the emergent functions that critics of brain death like Shewmon point to as indicative of the persistence of the human organism as a whole in an artificially sustained brain-dead body (e.g., homeostasis, energy balance, temperature regulation, wound healing, immune defense, gestation, etc.) can be duplicated in a laboratory setting. She argues that the artificially sustained brain-dead body is a mere aggregation of "coordinated" living human cells, tissues, and organs but that the aggregation lacks the level of organization to be an integrated human organism as a whole. Because many biological functions can now be maintained artificially, she (Condic 2016, 263) concludes "The challenge in defining death is to determine when the biological system is self-regulated in the service of the whole and when it merely reflects the intrinsic properties of cellular parts." Since functional criteria alone cannot distinguish an aggregation of coordinated organic parts from a whole organism. She believes that we must resort to some concept of the nature of the organism or being to resolve the issue.

At this point, she (Condic 2016, 264) invokes the Aristotelian concept of a human being as a rational animal whose life is "rooted in the soul, understood as the unifying, vivifying, organizing principle of a living being." She then claims that human life persists if either mental function or global, autonomous integrations of vital functions persist and that this disjunction is not satisfied when a human being is brain dead.

I will not comment on the merits of Condic's specific appeal to an Aristotelian view of our nature. I only wish to point out how, if Condic is right that what it means for an organism to exist "as a whole" is biologically vague, then we need to go beyond strictly biological considerations to resolve the issue of what it means for one of us to die. Moreover, we should not expect there to be some univocal biological definition of death for all organisms, since the definition of death will depend on the kind of organism that lives and dies. Indeed, Hans Jonas (1974, 136) got it right very early in the debate over the definition of death when he wrote that how we define death ultimately depends on "a definition of man and what life is human." However, the definition of what life is human is a philosophical issue that goes beyond biology. It must be addressed in a context in which there are various interests, values, and laws, as well as a diversity of metaphysical and cultural beliefs, that frame any acceptable answer to the question.

An analogy may be useful to understanding this last point. A river is "a large natural stream of water emptying into an ocean, lake, or other body of water, and usually fed along its course by converging tributaries" (American Heritage Dictionary of the English Language). However, this naturalistic definition is not much help if we need to define the boundaries of a river for some legal purpose, such as a dispute over a treaty where the boundary of access to land may be fixed by a river and the river actually moves over time. In this context, other, non-naturalistic considerations would bear on how the river is defined. It is not that the water and the course of the river are not essential to the river. Not just anything can count as a river. Defining the river in the legal

context is not simply a social construction. It is just that the naturalistic definition of a river is insufficient to determine answers in a legal context for where a river may begin or end or what its boundaries are for the purposes of settling a treaty dispute. My claim is that technology has intervened in our natural life history. It has changed the course of our lives, enabling life associated with our being to be extended in unprecedented ways. Just as the boundaries of a river may move due to natural or artificial causes, the boundaries of our lives have been altered by technological intervention. We can live in ways that were previously impossible. My suggestion is that we can now die in ways that were previously impossible. Like the boundaries of a river, whether we live or die is not fixed by naturalistic considerations alone. Although life and death are biological in nature, this biological nature is insufficient to determine the boundaries of our being in the social and legal context. However, it is equally true that the boundaries of our lives are not simply socially constructed. Brain death is death because it results in the destruction of our psychophysical integration. Without the potential for consciousness and any other mental function, we as biological, social, and cultural beings cease to exist.

Notes

1. For the specific state statutes, regulations, and case law that have recognized the criteria for determining death in the Uniform Determination of Death Act, see Charles M. Kester (1994, footnotes 44–46).
2. Section 26:6A-5 of the New Jersey Declaration of Death Act reads:
   Death not declared in violation of individual's religious beliefs. The death of an individual shall not be declared upon the basis of neurological criteria pursuant to sections 3 and 4 of this act when the licensed physician authorized to declare death, has reason to believe, on the basis of information in the individual's available medical records, or information provided by a member of the individual's family or any other

person knowledgeable about the individual's personal religious beliefs that such a declaration would violate the personal religious beliefs of the individual. In these cases, death shall be declared, and the time of death fixed, solely upon the basis of cardio-respiratory criteria pursuant to section 2 of this act, L.1991, c90, s5 (www.braindeath.org/law/newjersey/htm).

See also Orlick 1991. For an interesting commentary on this conscience clause, see (Veatch 1999).

3. Indeed, the Committee's labeling the criterion as "irreversible coma" reflected this ambiguity in explanation, as the term "irreversible coma" had been used by some in the past to describe the condition of individuals in deep coma or persistent vegetative state, conditions in which some brain functions persist (Joynt 1984).

4. See, for example (Field *et al.* 1988); (Bernstein *et al.* 1989); (Anstötz 1993); (Powner and Bernstein 2003).

5. The President's Council on Bioethics (2008, 61) states:

> The work of the organism, expressed in its commerce with the surrounding world, depends on three fundamental capacities:
>
> 1. Openness to the world, that is, receptivity to stimuli and signals from the surrounding environment.
> 2. The ability to act upon the world to obtain selectively what it needs.
> 3. The basic felt need that drives the organism to act as it must, to obtain what it needs and what its openness reveals to be available.
>
> Appreciating these capacities as mutually supporting aspects of the organism's vital work will help us understand why an individual with total brain failure should be declared dead, even when ventilator-supported "breathing" masks the presence of "death."

6. I argue for this interpretation of the Council's view more fully in Lizza (2016).

7. It is unclear what type of consciousness the monkeys regained in White's experiment. However, White reports that they were aware, responsive, and able to track objects visually.

8. Human organisms with diminished mental functions are still psychophysically integrated. The arguments presented in this chapter thus do not rule them out of the class of the living "we." The 1981 President's Commission's concern that a consciousness-related definition of death might classify the severely senile or cognitively disabled as "dead" is therefore completely unfounded.

9. Shewmon (2010, 6) also admits that what it means for an organism to exist "as a whole" is vague.

References

Ad Hoc Committee of the Harvard Medical School to Examine the Definition of Brain Death. 1968. A Definition of Irreversible Coma. *Journal of the American Medical Association* 205 (6): 337–340.

Anstötz, A. 1993. Should a Brain-Dead Pregnant Woman Carry Her Child to Full Term? The Case of the "Erlanger Baby". *Bioethics* 7 (4): 340–350.

Bernstein, I., M. Watson, G. M. Simmons, M. Catalano, G. Davis, and R. Collins. 1989. Maternal Brain Death and Prolonged Fetal Survival. *Obstetrics and Gynecology* 74 (3): 434–437.

Brody, B. 1999. How Much of the Brain Must Be Dead? In *The Definition of Death: Contemporary Controversies*, edited by S. J. Youngner, R. M. Arnold, and R. Schapiro, 71–82. Baltimore, MD: Johns Hopkins University Press.

Byrne, P. A., S. O'Reilly, P. Quay, and P. W. Salsich, Jr. 1982/83. Brain Death—The Patient, the Physician, and Society. *Gonzaga Law Review* 18 (3): 429–516. Reprinted in *Beyond Brain Death: The Case against Brain Based Criteria for Human Death* (2000), edited by M. Potts, P. A. Byrne, and R. G. Nilges. Dordrecht: Kluwer.

Callahan, D. 1988. The Beginning of Human Life. In *What Is a Person?*, edited by M. Goodman, 29–55. Clifton, NJ: The Humana Press.

Cruzan, N. B., by her Parents and Co-Guardians, *Lester L. Cruzan et ux. v. Director, Missouri Department of Health et al.*, 1990. 497 US 26.

Condic, M. L. 2016. Determination of Death: A Scientific Perspective on Biological Integration. *Journal of Medicine and Philosophy* 41: 257–278.

Field, D. R., E. A. Gates, R. K. Creasy, K. R. Jonsen, and R. K. Laros. 1988. Maternal Brain Death during Pregnancy. *Journal of the American Medical Association* 260 (6): 816–822.

Gert, B., C. Culver, and D. K. Clouser. 2006. *Bioethics: A Systematic Approach*. Oxford: Oxford University Press.

Halevy, A. and B. Brody. 1993. Brain Death: Reconciling Definitions, Criteria, and Tests. *Annals of Internal Medicine* 119: 519–525.

Jonas, H. 1974. Against the Stream: Comments on the Definition and Redefinition of Death. In *Philosophical Essays: From Ancient Creed to Technological Man*, edited by H. Jonas. Englewood Cliffs, NJ: Prentice-Hall.

Joynt, R. J. 1984. A New Look at Death. *Journal of the American Medical Association* 252: 682.

Kester, C. M. 1994. Is There a Person in That Body? An Argument for the Priority of Persons and the Need for a New Legal Paradigm. *Georgetown Law Journal* 82: 1643–1687.

Lizza, J. 2016. Elvis Ain't Dead Until We Say So. In *Death and Mortality—From Individual to Communal Perspectives, Studies across Disciplines in the Humanities and Social Sciences 19*, edited by O. Hakola, S. Heinämaa, and S. Pihlström, 48–60. Helsinki: Helsinki Collegium for Advanced Studies.

Lizza, J. P. 2011. Where's Waldo? The "Decapitation Gambit" and the Definition of Death. *Journal of Medical Ethics* 37 (12): 743–746.

Nair-Collins, M. 2015. Taking Science Seriously in the Debate on Death and Organ Transplantation. *Hastings Center Report* 45: 38–48.

Orlick, R. S. 1991. Brain Death, Religious Freedom, and Public Policy: New Jersey's Landmark Legislative Initiative. *Kennedy Institute of Ethics Journal* 1: 275–288.

Pernick, M. S. 1999. Brain Death in a Cultural Context. In *The Definition of Death: Contemporary Controversies*, edited by S. J. Youngner, R. M. Arnold, and R. Schapiro, 3–33. Baltimore, MD: Johns Hopkins University Press.

Powner, D. J. and I. M. Bernstein. 2003. Extended Somatic Support for Pregnant Women after Brain Death. *Critical Care Medicine* 31 (4): 1241–1249.

President's Commission for the Study of Ethical Problems in Medicine and Biomedical and Behavioral Research. 1981. *Defining Death: Medical, Ethical, and Legal Issues in the Determination of Death*. Washington, DC: U.S. Government Printing Office.

President's Council on Bioethics. 2008. *Controversies in the Determination of Death*. Washington, DC: U.S. Government Printing Office. www.bioethics.gov.

Seifert, J. 1993. Is "Brain Death" Actually Death? *The Monist* 76 (2): 175–202.

Shewmon, D. A. 1997. Recovery from "Brain Death": A Neurologist's Apologia. *Linacre Quarterly* 64 (1): 31–96.

Shewmon, D. A. 1998a. Chronic "Brain Death": Meta-analysis and Conceptual Consequences. *Neurology* 51 (6): 1538–1545.

Shewmon, D. A. 1998b. "Brainstem Death," "Brain Death," and Death: A Critical Reevaluation of the Purported Evidence. *Issues in Law and Medicine* 14 (2): 125–146.

Shewmon, D. A. 2004. The "Critical Organ" for the "Organism as a Whole": Lessons from the Lowly Spinal Cord. In *Brain Death and Disorders of Consciousness*, edited by C. Machado and D. A. Shewmon, 23–41. New York: Kluwer.

Shewmon, D. A. 2009. Brain Death: Can It Be Resuscitated? *Hastings Center Report* 39 (2): 18–24.

Shewmon, D. A. 2010. Constructing the Death Elephant: A Synthetic Paradigm Shift for the Definition, Criteria, and Tests for Death. *Journal of Medicine and Philosophy* 35 (3): 256–298.

Taylor, R. M. 1997. Re-examining the Definition and Criteria of Death. *Seminars in Neurology* 17: 265–270.

Truog, R. D. 1997. Is It Time to Abandon Brain Death? *Hastings Center Report* 27 (1): 29–37.

Veatch, R. M. 1999. The Conscience Clause: How Much Individual Choice in Defining Death Can Our Society Tolerate? In *The Definition of Death: Contemporary Controversies*, edited by S. J. Youngner, R. M. Arnold, and R. Schapiro, 137–160. Baltimore, MD: Johns Hopkins University Press.

White, R. J., L. R. Wolin, L. C. Massopust et al. 1971. Cephalic Exchange Transplantation in the Monkey. *Surgery* 71: 35–39.

3

We Die When Entropy Overwhelms Homeostasis

Michael Nair-Collins

Introduction

Death is a natural, biological phenomenon, and the death of a human is no different, metaphysically or biologically, from the death of other organisms. When the organism no longer resists entropy, when its ability to preserve physiologic stability is lost, when the organism has transitioned from consuming energy and actively maintaining homeostasis to disintegration and decay, then the organism has died.

In this chapter I develop and defend the thesis that we die when entropy overwhelms homeostasis. I explain the concept of "brain death" and why it is not death, in spite of the medical community's scientifically baseless insistence to the contrary. I review the higher-brain theory of death, explaining it as an application of a metaphysical theory of personal identity or related concepts to the context of severe brain injury involving cessation of consciousness. I argue that a pluralism of views about the metaphysical and moral status of such patients should be accepted in society. Finally, I argue that contemporary death determination practices are conceptually confused and create significant ethical concerns.

Evolution, Entropy, Death

Like everything else in the universe, humans are products of, and beholden to, fundamental physical forces and processes. On Earth, the tremendous diversity of life forms results from evolution by natural selection, a result of random genetic mutation and differential adaptation to the environment relative to conspecifics, creating differential abilities to survive and procreate, which in turn drives selection for organisms better adapted to their environmental niche. The process of evolutionary change and species differentiation tends to be gradual and iterative, building on existing mechanisms rather than creating new ones. This is why there are conserved biochemical pathways, anatomical homologies, common behavioral patterns, and even similar patterns of social relationships across species.

Furthermore, while humans communicate, are capable of learning and problem-solving, and exhibit complex social relationships, many nonhumans also have these abilities. Humanity exists on a continuum with other creatures, not in a position of stark difference or superiority.

This is important because it is often assumed that humans are fundamentally different from other creatures so that what it means for "one of us" to die is somehow different from what it means for "one of them" to die; that death for a human is ontologically different than death for a rabbit. This idea is at the root of the higher-brain concept of death and, derivatively, the whole-brain concept as well: That humanity is fundamentally different from other creatures, therefore death for humans is "the irreversible loss of that which is essentially significant to the nature of [humanity]" (Veatch 1975, 23).

This conceit of human difference and superiority is as old as humanity itself, and it is both scientifically and ethically baseless. We are products of physical forces and evolution; we evolved in similar ways as other creatures; our evolutionary forebears lived and died for billions of years before hominids arrived. Other creatures experience pain and fear, have lives that can go well or ill for them, and they die—just like humans. And the universe cares no more for my death than for that of a cockroach. So let us investigate death as it is: a biological phenomenon with an ancient evolutionary history.

The human body is composed of approximately 100 trillion cells, all of which are bathed in fluid, known as extracellular fluid. This fluid is in constant motion, circulated in blood and passing across capillaries. Because of the constant mixing and movement, this fluid has a homogenous composition throughout the body. Thus, it is known as the internal environment, or *internal milieu*. It is the environment within which all of our cells live and function (Hall 2016).

One fascinating aspect of the extracellular fluid is that it appears to approximate the chemical composition of the primordial seas during the Paleozoic era, when organisms first began to migrate from the seas to land (Banfalvi 1991). This suggests that early organisms developed the ability to carry the life-sustaining environment of the primordial seas within them, enabling them to exit the sea and venture onto land. Intriguingly, it is as if we all carry the primordial seas within us in the form of extracellular fluid.

Extracellular fluid contains water, ions, oxygen, glucose, lipids, and many other factors, all of which are actively maintained within certain parameters by multiple organs, tissues, and cells, operating in a mutually interdependent fashion. Consider, for example, ions in extracellular fluid: hydrogen and bicarbonate, sodium, potassium, magnesium, calcium, chloride, and phosphate. Their concentrations must be actively maintained within specific boundaries, or cells (and by extension the organism) will not survive. These concentrations are maintained by complex interactions between the kidneys, lungs, hypothalamus, pituitary, pancreas, adrenal glands, parathyroid glands, bone, liver, intestines, and red blood cells. Regulation and storage of energy is maintained by the stomach, pancreas, gallbladder, liver, small intestine, enteric nervous system, muscle, and the production of the basic energy source of the body, adenosine

triphosphate (ATP), the final step of which occurs in the mitochondria of all cells. There are many other physiologic variables that must be maintained within specific limits which, again, is a function of multiple organs, tissues, and cells, operating in a mutually interdependent fashion (Hall 2016).

The process of maintaining physiologic stability within the organism, and especially the chemical composition of the extracellular fluid, is known as *homeostasis* (Hall 2016). This is the core concept underlying the science of physiology.

A related concept, drawn from gerontology (the scientific study of aging), is *homeostenosis*. This term derives from "homeostasis" and "stenosis"—which means to narrow (as in coronary artery stenosis). The idea is that as we age, the capacity of the organism to recover from threats and stresses—or the ability to preserve homeostasis—diminishes (or, "stenoses"). For example, a trip and fall in an otherwise healthy 30-year-old person would not pose much of a threat; whereas a trip and fall in a 90-year-old person, especially one who is frail, is a significant threat to health and life. The same threat or stressor—a fall—has a differential impact due to homeostenosis (Khan et al. 2017).

Finally, the second law of thermodynamics is a fundamental physical law which states, roughly, that things tend toward chemical and thermal equilibrium with their surroundings; another term for this is *entropy*. The second law of thermodynamics explains things like passive diffusion, where molecules cross a permeable membrane from the direction of higher concentration to lower, without any infusion of energy. Entropy explains why a hot cup of coffee and a cold cup of water, on the same table in the same room, will change temperature in opposite directions. They're both going to reach room temperature, following their natural path towards thermal equilibrium.

Unlike the cup of coffee, I hope to avoid reaching room temperature anytime soon; because that would mean that I am dead. Living organisms resist entropy—we resist equilibrium with our immediate environment, perhaps most obviously in the case of thermal regulation as alluded to just a moment ago. We do so by maintaining homeostasis, an energy-demanding process. For a different example, the sodium-potassium pump, which maintains concentrations of sodium and potassium on either side of the cell wall, requires energy in the form of ATP because it pumps these ions against their electrochemical gradient, thereby maintaining the electrical and chemical difference (or non-equilibrium) across the cell wall; this is a precondition for most cellular functions.

Putting these ideas together, we get the following conceptions of life and death. Multicellular living organisms are collectives of many cells, trillions in the human case, which work together to maintain the cellular environmental conditions necessary for their continued existence and functioning, especially by preserving the chemical composition of the extracellular fluid. Living organisms are localized pockets of anti-entropy, achieved by the mutually interdependent functions of organs, tissues, and cells, all of which both require and contribute to homeostasis. This is what it means to live. But the inexorable force of entropy will, sooner or later, prevail.

Death, therefore, is a thermodynamic point of no return. It is the event that separates the processes of homeostasis and anti-entropy from disintegration and decay. Alternatively, following the homeostenosis theory of aging to its natural conclusion, death occurs when the organism's homeostatic reserves are spent: It can no longer preserve internal stability nor resist entropy.

Some clarifications are in order. First, this theory explains death as an instantaneous event—a threshold—not as a process. Dying is a process; death is an event; being dead is a state. Second, knowing *that* an individual is dead does not entail knowing *when* the event of death occurred. It is usually easy to know *that* an organism is dead. Thus we infer that the event of death has occurred. But specifying the exact timing of the thermodynamic point of no return in precise mathematical language is an extremely complex, and as yet unfinished task.

Third, it is plausible that this theory does not comport with "ordinary language," nor with a commonsense concept of death. This is irrelevant to the project we are undertaking.

By analogy, consider that water is H_2O; that heat is mean molecular kinetic energy; that rust is combustion; that lightning is electromagnetic discharge. These scientific identifications are not beholden to anyone's intuitions nor to commonsense concepts. Instead, we should evaluate scientific theories or definitions by the following criteria: How well does the theory cohere with other well-accepted scientific beliefs about the world? Does the theory draw on similar ontological posits or theoretical frameworks found in other, well-accepted scientific domains, or does it require positing wholly new kinds of entities or forces? Does it explain or predict empirical phenomena?

From this perspective, the theory of death as a thermodynamic threshold draws on or is implied by fundamental posits of physiology, gerontology, thermodynamics, and evolutionary biology. It is part of a larger, coherent story of the world based in well-accepted mechanistic principles from physics, chemistry, and biology. We are a part of the natural world, and our lives and deaths can and should be explained in the same terms as we explain the rest of the natural world.

Whole-Brain Death

In the United States, the Uniform Determination of Death Act defines death for legal purposes as the irreversible cessation of circulatory and respiratory functions, or, irreversible cessation of all functions of the entire brain, including the brain stem (President's Commission 1981). The latter clause defines the condition commonly referred to as "brain death," or "whole-brain death," since it requires the cessation of functioning of the whole brain, setting it apart from the higher-brain theory of death discussed below.

The concept of brain death was developed around the 1960s in response to ethical and legal concerns (Nair-Collins 2015).

Specifically: Would removing mechanical ventilation from patients who lacked a respiratory drive be homicide (since stopping ventilation would result in death)? Is it a just use of resources to maintain the lives of patients who were ostensibly irreversibly unconscious? Would maintaining the lives of these patients create needless emotional and financial burdens on their families? And finally, could these patients be vital organ donors? Lack of blood flow, or ischemia, quickly damages organs, so organs taken from truly dead bodies are not viable for transplant. Yet "brain dead" patients, so long as they are supported with mechanical ventilation, have continued circulation and oxygenation, and apart from severe brain injury, are often otherwise healthy, making them seemingly ideal organ donors. But surgically removing vital organs from a living body is lethal, obviously. Would it nonetheless be permissible to remove their organs while on the ventilator and with a beating heart?

The solution arrived at for all of the above concerns was simple, ingenious, and profoundly mistaken: *Redefine death itself*, so that physicians would be permitted to declare a subclass of comatose patients to be dead bodies while they remained on the ventilator (Ad Hoc Committee of the Harvard Medical School to Determine the Definition of Brain Death 1968). No scientific evidence was presented for why this subclass of comatose patients were corpses. No physiological changes occurred that would justify their reclassification from living human patients to corpses. And no input from their families was either sought or allowed. Instead, these living patients were simply reclassified as dead bodies because of the perception that doing so made certain ethical, social, and legal problems more tractable. In particular, it allowed medicine to (falsely) declare that vital organ procurement does not kill the donor, thus protecting surgeons from charges of homicide while preventing public outcry against organ transplantation.

In spite of its broad acceptance within medicine and law, brain death is deeply problematic. First, it is not a reliable diagnosis:

many patients who are labeled "brain dead" have some preserved brain function, usually of the hypothalamus; and there are a number of other concerns regarding the credibility of brain death diagnostic practices (Nair-Collins and Miller 2019). But the bigger problem is that brain death is not death.

Patients declared "brain dead" are capable of maintaining homeostasis and resisting entropy; they have not crossed the thermodynamic threshold into entropy and disintegration. Such patients can gestate fetuses and deliver healthy babies; can grow, sexually mature, and remain alive with life support for years; can heal wounds and develop a fever in response to infection; can absorb and digest nutrients through the gut and produce waste; along with many other biological functions. In fact, if the patient survives the initial, acute phase of the injury, they transition to a chronic, stable phase in which they can be discharged from the hospital on home ventilation. Such patients may be even more physiologically stable, with more homeostatic capacity than other unconscious and dying patients, whom no one would claim are biologically dead (Shewmon 2001; Nair-Collins and Miller 2017).

One might think that it is the ventilator and other medical interventions that are responsible for supporting the aforementioned functions. This is both true and irrelevant. The ventilator is life-sustaining technology, without which the patient would die. But it only provides support: it is impossible for a ventilator, which merely blows air in and out of the lungs, to cause gas exchange (a cellular function), or for the ventilator to cause the heart to beat, or for the ventilator to preserve homeostasis of the extracellular fluid (Nair-Collins and Miller 2017). The ventilator blows air in and out. The living organism does all the rest. This is as true for the "brain dead" patient as it is for any other patient on a ventilator. Of course, the patient *would die* without the ventilator. This is not in dispute. But the fact that a patient *would die* if life-sustaining treatment were removed does not show that the patient is *already dead*; indeed, it shows precisely the opposite.

Finally, the major attempt to justify brain death as biological death is based on the claim that the brain is the central integrator without which the organism as a whole can no longer preserve homeostasis (President's Council 1981). This is an empirically false claim, as discussed above. The preservation of homeostasis cannot be localized to any particular organ, including the brain. It is the result of multiple, mutually interdependent functions of organs, tissues, and cells throughout the body, all of which require, and contribute to, the maintenance of homeostasis.

The science underlying brain death is profoundly flawed; more accurately, there is no science underlying brain death. Brain death is not biological death.

Higher-Brain Theory of Death

Altered Carbon is a dystopian cyberpunk novel adapted into an internet television series (Altered Carbon 2018). In its futuristic setting, technology has been developed that allows a person's mind to be uploaded into a disk known as a "stack." The stack is implanted into the skull of a human body, can be removed, stored, backed up, and implanted into a different body. Revealingly, the bodies that stacks inhabit are referred to as "sleeves"; these sleeves can be donned and removed at will. The allegory here is that our bodies are mere clothing, which can be discarded or replaced, but they are not essential aspects of who we are as human persons. Instead, the functional activities of the stack—consciousness, sensations and perceptions, memories, love, regrets, sorrows—these things constitute the human person. These things constitute who and what we truly are.

Takeshi Kovacs, a lead character, was a member of an elite fighting force, engaged in rebellion against the imperialist, plutocratic new world order (not quite so "new"—this is a dystopic allegory for the modern global order). The uprising was defeated, Takeshi's body was killed, and his stack was deactivated. Two hundred and fifty years later, a narcissistic, amoral plutocrat purchased his stack and implanted it into a new sleeve, "reawakening" Takeshi after centuries of unconsciousness.

Though disoriented, being in a new body and learning that centuries have passed, Takeshi quickly adjusts. His memories and character traits remain, particularly his love for his little sister and memories of their traumatic, yet bonding childhood; his deep and abiding love for his romantic interest; and his exceptional intellect and intuition. He also has vivid recollections of the failed rebellion which, along with the belief that everyone he loves is dead, lead to a predictable nihilism in his outlook on this new world in which he has been unwillingly thrust.

His (first) body was shot to death hundreds of years ago. His mind is clearly intact. Is Takeshi alive or dead? Is he the same person now as he was when he was fighting for the rebellion, centuries ago?

I suspect that most people reading this would say that, in some meaningful sense, Takeshi is alive and the same person now as he was then. Because of the continuity of his sense of self through memories, and his retained personality traits, Takeshi lives on even though he "wears a new sleeve." Indeed, this basic ontological assumption about Takeshi's continued personal identity is a fundamental assumption of the entire narrative. The writers, actors, and audiences of this work would not be able to make sense of any part of the story without this basic assumption.

This reveals something important: The concept of continued personal identity as rooted in psychological continuity and not necessarily in bodily continuity is a deeply rooted cultural assumption. *It just makes sense*, to most of us, intuitively and immediately. And for good reason: There is a long tradition in Western philosophy that develops and defends the idea of personal identity in precisely these terms (e.g., Parfit 1984).

Now consider an alternative plotline. Instead of killing his body, the soldiers destroyed Takeshi's stack. His "empty" sleeve was placed on life support, and publicly displayed in an exhibit by the ruling class, as a warning to would-be pursuers of freedom and equality.

Is Takeshi alive or dead? I suspect most people will reach a different conclusion in this scenario: Takeshi is dead. Everything that made him "who he was" is gone forever. Although he left behind a living body, Takeshi Kovacs himself was killed.

In a nutshell, this is the basic suite of ideas underlying the higher-brain theory of death. So long as our capacity for consciousness is preserved, we remain alive. When that capacity is lost, we are dead—even if a biologically living body is left behind.

While there are several variations of the higher-brain theory of death, there are features common to all of them. First, the higher-brain theory is not a theory of biological, organismic death. Higher-brain theorists are explicit about this. For example, John Lizza argues for a "semantic bifurcation," with "death" taking on two distinct meanings: the death of the organism, and the death of the human person or human being (Lizza 2018). Robert Veatch argues that death for humans occurs at "the irreversible loss of that which is essentially significant to the nature of [humanity]" (Veatch 1975, 23)—not necessarily when the biological organism dies. And Jeff McMahan is similarly explicit that his version of the higher-brain theory defines "death" as a technical term of art (McMahan 2002, 425), whose meaning is different from the ordinary, biological concept of death; in this way he offers something similar to Lizza's semantic bifurcation.

Second, on all versions of the higher-brain theory, this non-biological concept of death is in some way a function of the cessation of consciousness or of the capacity for consciousness. Third, all higher-brain theorists acknowledge that the body or organism is biologically alive in brain death.

Therefore, by their own lights, higher-brain theorists are literally talking about something else. They are having a different conversation than the debate about biological death and whether brain death is biological death. In essence, higher-brain theorists are developing or expanding metaphysical and moral concepts such as personal identity, personhood,

and similar ideas, and applying them to a new social context, a context in which unconscious patients can be kept alive for extended periods, when in the past, they would have died. Advances in medicine created the new possibility of living but unconscious humans, able to survive potentially indefinitely with life-sustaining therapy, but without recovering the capacity for consciousness. As a scientific matter, they are clearly alive. But, though they are alive, there are also interesting and important questions to be addressed about their moral and metaphysical status. The higher-brain theory offers one perspective on this, drawing from the Western cultural and intellectual tradition; we will learn of a few more perspectives on their moral and metaphysical status shortly.

It is unfortunate that higher-brain theorists choose to use the word "dead" in this bifurcated way. Indisputably, "dead" has a biological meaning, whatever else it might mean. "Dead" is used to describe a cockroach and a tree and a human, all in the same biological sense. Using "dead" to mean something entirely different and non-biological, and intended to apply only to humans, seems to unnecessarily muddy the discourse about what is already a complex intersection of difficult philosophical and scientific topics. Unless its meaning is explicitly distinguished from the other, biological side of the semantic bifurcation, use of the term "dead" to mean something like "cessation of personal identity in a living human body" creates needless confusion.

Death Determination Practices

When do we die? According to standard medical practices, supported by law, we die either at the cessation of cardiopulmonary function, or the cessation of neurological function (i.e., brain death). The mainstream medical view is that brain death and cardiac death are, biologically, one and the same: That brain death is biological death, even though it may not appear that way to the non-expert observer (Russell et al. 2019). According to the higher-brain theory, the mainstream medical view is both right and wrong. It is wrong, because brain death is not biological death. However, the higher-brain theory also holds that human death is not a matter of biology, or not solely a matter of biology. Instead it is a function of consciousness in some way. Assuming the patient is truly unconscious, and assuming that this is irreversible (both very strong assumptions), then the human person or human being has ceased to exist, leaving behind an "empty shell" of a living body. And so the brain dead patient *is* dead—just not biologically.

The higher-brain theorists are correct that brain death is not biological death. Even bracketing the arguments I've offered above, recall that the transition to brain death was never justified on scientific grounds. No physiologic reasons were given for why this subset of comatose patients should be targeted for "death by redefinition"; no scientific or theoretical advances were offered to justify their reclassification from very ill but living patients, to corpses. Instead, brain death was supposed to make certain ethical, legal, and social problems more tractable. Whether it did or didn't, that has nothing to do with science and biology. The medical profession, and specifically the neurology and intensive care community, is damaging its credibility by continuing to insist that brain death is biological death. For example, the idea that a "brain dead" pregnant woman gestating a fetus over a period of many weeks, then delivering a healthy baby, has really been a corpse, a biologically dead body, a cadaver that is dead in the same way that cadavers in an anatomy lab are dead the entire time, is just beyond belief. Insisting on such manifestly false claims can only damage the credibility of those professional societies that endorse them, such as the American Academy of Neurology (Russell et al. 2019).

The current situation in death determination is unnecessarily convoluted and opaque. The brain dead patient is legally dead, biologically alive, and with a moral and metaphysical status that is reasonably disputed or uncertain. The higher-brain camp sees these patients as no longer human beings or persons; that which is fundamentally significant to the

nature of humanity is already lost, on their view. Because of this position on the metaphysics of human identity, they take the moral position that, even though the body is alive, it is no longer part of the human moral community, it is no longer "one of us," and it has the moral (but not biological) status of a corpse.

But the view of human identity that undergirds the higher-brain theory of death is not the only reasonable view on these matters. In fact, there are many competing views, backed by their own reasons and evidence, philosophical arguments, cultural and religious traditions, and so on. Some people see a living unconscious human as a full moral person, because they take moral status to be inherent in every human from conception to natural death as a result of religious commitments. Others might see the patient as having full moral status because they take the essence of human identity to reside, *not* in psychological states, but in continued biological life. Others yet see our lives as stories, as narratives, which can continue even after consciousness is lost, because the key characters in our life story still relate to us, still care for us, we still exist within a social nexus, and our life's drama carries on.

From an Eastern cultural perspective, one might see the essence of personal identity in circulating *chi*, which does not require the presence of consciousness. Also from this perspective, one might see personhood as relational and existing within a web or network of obligations, as part of a community first and an individual only derivatively; in which case, similar to narrative identity, one would see the unconscious patient as still a member of the community, worth being cared for and indeed playing a role in the community precisely as one needing and deserving of care, and thus still "one of us," still a human being.

The feminist perspective of the ethics of care offers a similar perspective and argument, where the embodied relationship of care, often between mother and child, is itself held to be a source of independent moral value. The moral status of the one-caring and the cared-for are derivative on that embodied, caring relationship, which itself partly defines the human and personal identities of those involved. From the perspective of disability studies, the living unconscious human body is a full-fledged moral person, with severe physical and cognitive disability, on the far end of the spectrum of disorders of consciousness. From the perspective of standard bioethical concepts of end of life planning and advance directives, I've argued that "brain dead" patients are relevantly similar in moral status to patients with severe, end-stage dementia and retain all the rights to precedent autonomy, bodily integrity, etc., that patients with severe dementia have (Nair-Collins 2017). Thus, the metaphysical and moral status of the living unconscious patient is surely not settled and there are reasonable arguments to be made for a variety of views.

It is important to reflect on how fundamental and personally meaningful these deep philosophical and religious matters are, especially around times of tragedy or grief. Beliefs about our ultimate nature(s), as human persons, as animals, as social beings, as moral beings, as spiritual beings—these are derived from large-scale metaphysical, religious, and moral worldviews. They are rooted in thousands of years of cultural tradition, religious practice, philosophical analysis, and aesthetic, spiritual, and religious reflection. They are not arbitrary or capricious, and there are good reasons supporting a variety of views about "who we are," about our ultimate nature, or about the nature of the universe and humanity's place within it. No single fundamental metaphysical or religious worldview, from which views of personal identity and related concepts are derived, holds sway as "the" objectively correct worldview which all rational people would be forced, by virtue of reason and evidence alone, to endorse. Instead, reasonable people with access to all the same evidence and arguments can reasonably disagree about some of these foundational philosophical questions, including about the nature of the self, personhood, and human identity.

That's an important point. It doesn't mean that there is no truth about these issues and I'm not endorsing any kind of relativism.

Instead, it means that these questions are so deep, so conceptually and epistemologically foundational, and so personally meaningful, that a certain amount of epistemic and moral humility is warranted, on all of our parts. Furthermore, respect for persons demands that we allow each other (within limits) to try to live our best life and die our best death, according to *our* conceptions of the meaning of life and existence, the role of spirituality or some divinity, the nature of personhood or the self, and so on, and not to have someone else's conceptions imposed upon us.

And that is precisely what is wrong with contemporary death determination practices. The social and legal status of "corpse" is compulsorily and coercively imposed onto the living unconscious patient, based either on a false biological claim or on one among many reasonable views on the moral and metaphysical status of these patients. In effect, no other view on the moral and metaphysical status of the biologically living patient is permitted: The living patient must be, and is, treated as a corpse, regardless of the patient's or family's views, or the views of their community. No pluralism of fundamental worldviews or theories of personhood, human identity, or moral status is accepted when it comes to brain death. In this regard, brain death is like the pro-life/anti-choice view in abortion: Both think that *their* view of personhood as applied to each particular context (a fetus, or a "brain dead" patient) is not only objectively correct, but that their view should be implemented via the coercive force of law, so that other views of the metaphysical and moral status of the entity in question will not be tolerated. Brain death, like the pro-life view on abortion, is an anti-choice stance.

Many people want to donate organs after death, but find biological life morally relevant in and of itself, and would consider being killed by organ procurement a grave moral and religious violation. They are grossly misled into doing exactly what they wanted to avoid. More generally, people considering organ donation are not even offered the simple respect of accurate information in order to make an informed choice. In particular, this includes the clearly relevant fact that heart-beating organ procurement is biologically lethal, so that they can choose for themselves, based on their values, their understanding of the nature of the good, or their notion of the self or personhood. In a similar fashion, some people, usually parents whose children have suffered this horrible injury, seek continued care for their child. These parents most certainly do not agree with the higher-brain theorists, in concluding that their biologically living, profoundly disabled child, is not a human being, is not "one of us," or has the moral status of a corpse. But our medicolegal system nonetheless seeks to force the removal of life-sustaining treatment anyway, again, because the imposition of the social and legal status of "corpse" onto these living human bodies is compulsory, not optional. This is what I mean when I say that a single, rationally contestable theory of human identity is forced onto us all—and this practice has serious, real-world, life and death consequences that both disrespect and harm people.

To conclude, in a diverse, multicultural, global world, a pluralism of views on the metaphysical and moral status of living, unconscious patients should be accepted. The higher-brain view is certainly one reasonable view. But it is not the only one, and it should not be imposed onto all, by way of compulsory cessation of life-sustaining treatment from living patients, or by way of false or misleading information about the lethality of heart-beating organ procurement. On the other hand, whatever else we may be, we are also biological creatures, products of an ancient evolutionary history. As biological organisms, we die when entropy overwhelms homeostasis.

References

Ad Hoc Committee of the Harvard Medical School to Examine the Definition of Brain Death (1968). "A definition of irreversible coma." *Journal of the American Medical Association* 205:337–340.

Altered Carbon. Netflix Original Series, 2018.

Banfalvi, G (1991). "Evolution of osmolyte systems," *Biochemical Education* 19(3):136–139.

Hall JE (2016). *Guyton and Hall Textbook of Medical Physiology*, 13th ed. Philadelphia: Elsevier.

Khan SS, Singer, BD, and Vaughan, DE (2017). "Molecular and physiological manifestations and measurement of aging in humans," *Aging Cell* 16:624–633.

Lizza JP (2018). "Defining death: beyond biology," *Diametros* 55:1–19.

McMahan J (2002). *The Ethics of Killing: Problems at the Margins of Life*. Oxford: Oxford University Press.

Nair-Collins M (2015). "Clinical and ethical perspectives on brain death," *Medicolegal and Bioethics* 5:69–80.

Nair-Collins M, Miller, FG (2017). "Do the 'brain dead' merely appear to be alive?," *Journal of Medical Ethics* 43:747–753.

Nair-Collins M (2017). "Can the brain-dead be harmed or wronged? On the moral status of brain death and its implications for organ transplantation," *Kennedy Institute of Ethics Journal* 27(4):525–559.

Nair-Collins M and Miller FG (2019). "Commentary: False positives in the diagnosis of brain death," *Cambridge Quarterly of Healthcare Ethics* 26:648–656.

Parfit D (1984). *Reasons and Persons*. Oxford: Oxford University Press.

President's Commission for the Study of Ethical Problems in Medicine and Biomedical and Biobehavioral Research (1981). *Defining Death: Medical, Legal, and Ethical Issues in the Determination of Death*. Washington, DC: U.S. Government Printing Office.

Russell JA, Epstein LG, and Greer DM, et al. (2019). "Brain death, the determination of brain death, and member guidance for brain death accommodation requests. AAN position statement," *Neurology* 92(5):228–232.

Shewmon DA (2001). "The brain and somatic integration: Insights into the standard biological rationale for equating 'brain death' with death," *Journal of Medicine and Philosophy* 26:457–478.

Veatch RM (1975). "The whole-brain-oriented concept of death: An outmoded philosophical formulation," *Journal of Thanatology* 3:13–30.

4 What It Is to Die

Cody Gilmore

I. The Paradox of Cryptobiosis

The term **cryptobiosis** was coined by the biochemist David Keilin for "the state of an organism when it shows no visible signs of life and when its metabolic activity becomes hardly measurable, or comes reversibly to a standstill" (1959: 166). Cryptobiosis can be achieved artificially, as when a human embryo is frozen in a lab, later to be thawed and implanted, or naturally, as when a tardigrade (a tiny insect-like animal with eight legs and a multi-lobed brain) dehydrates and later, in response to normal environmental changes, rehydrates and returns to an active state.

Consider a cryptobiotic tardigrade—call it Grady—that will return to an active, obviously living state in a few months. Let's assume that the metabolisms in cryptobiotic organisms have not merely slowed, as in dormancy or hibernation, but ceased (more on this later). Then we can ask: What is Grady's status now, while cryptobiotic? Is Grady alive? Dead? Both? Somewhere in between?

These questions about Grady give rise to a **paradox**, a set of propositions each of which is plausibly true, or at least tempting, when considered on its own, but which are collectively inconsistent: it is impossible for them all to be true together. The propositions are:

1. Grady is not alive.
2. Grady is not dead.
3. Everything is either alive or dead (call this **Exhaustivism**).

This is the **Paradox of Cryptobiosis**. To see why this obviously inconsistent set counts as a *paradox*, we need to see why each proposition

is at least tempting on its own. (1) might seem plausible, on the grounds that Grady is not undergoing any of the processes that are constitutive of life: for example, Grady is not moving, growing, reproducing, eating, or metabolizing. And (2) might seem plausible, on the grounds that if a thing is not badly damaged and will be alive in the future, then it is not dead now. Finally, one might take it to be obvious that "dead" means the same thing as "not alive," hence that Exhaustivism is true by definition. So, all three propositions have something going for them (and some of the arguments for them will be improved upon later). But since they're inconsistent, at least one of them must be false.

A *solution* to the paradox will correctly identify the false proposition(s), and will justify its verdicts. Paradoxes are important not because they evoke a feeling of mystery, but because they offer an opportunity to identify and correct a mistaken belief (or tendency to believe), and thereby to learn something. We begin with a tendency to believe each of the relevant propositions and without any clear awareness of their inconsistency. By the end, if all goes well, we know that the propositions are inconsistent, and we know which ones are false.

My goal here is to defend accounts of what it is be alive, and what it is to die, that solve the Paradox of Cryptobiosis. I will argue that (1) and (2) are true and that Exhaustivism is false: Grady is neither alive nor dead. To a first approximation, to be alive is to be undergoing certain vital processes, and to die is to cease to be capable of undergoing those processes, in a sense of "capable" that, in Section IX, I attempt to clarify without reductively defining. This opens up space for things, such as Grady, that are not undergoing the relevant processes, and so are not alive, but have not lost the capacity to do so, and so have not died and are not dead.

II. Applications to Human Death?

Thinking carefully about what it is to be alive and what it is to die, in abstract and general terms, can be useful in making progress on more concrete, practical issues.

Consider the case of a 20-year-old car accident victim who has suffered "brain death" (complete and irreversible loss of function of the entire brain, including the brain stem), but many of whose physiological processes continue, with some artificial support, and many of whose organs are in excellent condition and could be used for transplantation. For example, although the patient's brain stem no longer regulates breathing, a ventilator blows air into her lungs, which remain healthy and continue to perform the complex task of oxygenating her blood; her heart continues to beat without any artificial stimulation; her body successfully fights off infection; its wounds heal.

This patient is legally dead in the United States. But that is a question of law, which is separable from the biological question, "Is she alive or is she dead?" Ordinarily, we assume that there is no third alternative. But a careful examination of the properties of being alive and being dead, which attempts to be fully general and so pays attention to non-human as well as human cases, may call that assumption into question. Perhaps there is reason to think that the patient is neither alive nor dead. Even if not, the highly abstract project pursued here promises to give us a clearer "big picture" of the theoretical landscape.

The current project may also shed light on questions about the moral significance of being alive and being dead. It may be tempting to assume that if someone has volunteered to be an organ donor, then it becomes morally permissible to procure their organs when they cease to be alive. But presumably it would be no less wrong to procure organs from a non-living, cryptobiotic patient (were such a case to arise) than from a still living patient. If so, then the distinction between being alive and not carries less moral significance than we may be tempted to assume. Perhaps the morally important distinction, then, is between being dead and not? Although I will not pursue this question here, a clearer understanding of what it is to be dead will obviously be helpful in addressing it.

III. What It Is To Be Alive: Activism Stated

Let's return to the topic of cryptobiosis. Three rival views about the status of cryptobiotic organisms have been defended in the scientific and philosophical literature:

Still-Alive: cryptobiotic things are alive (Luper 2009: 44).
Already-Dead: cryptobiotic things are dead (Wilson 1999: 101).
Neither-Nor: cryptobiotic things are neither alive nor dead (Wreen 1987; Feldman 1992: 60–62; Persson 1995: 500; Clegg 2001: 615; Belshaw 2009: 9; DeGrazia 2014: 83).

In this section, I present Activism, an account of what it is to be alive. In Section IV, I will use this account to argue that cryptobiotic organisms are neither alive nor dead.

Being alive, I will assume, is a property that is shared by things across the biological spectrum. Bacteria, human skin cells, trees, cats, and human beings can all be alive, in the same sense of "alive." Further, being alive is an **internal** property in the sense, roughly, that whether or not a cell or organism counts as alive at a given time t is purely a matter of what is going on within the boundaries of the organism at t, together perhaps with facts about the laws of physics and facts about what is going on inside the organism throughout any arbitrarily brief chunk of time whose midpoint is t (without the facts about how things are throughout a chunk of time around t, we might not have enough to determine the facts about, say, the motions of an organism's constituent particles at t. If its particles aren't moving in certain specified ways, it may fail to count as alive. But to determine how its particles are moving at t, we may need facts about their locations before and after t).

Since being alive is internal, there is no possible situation in which two organisms are atom-for-atom duplicates throughout a given, say, tenth of second with t as its midpoint and are governed by the same laws of physics, but in which one of them is alive at t and the other is not (henceforth by "laws" I will mean laws of physics). Not all properties are internal. *Being in the path of a falling boulder* is not internal. There is a possible situation in which two people, A and B, are atom-for-atom duplicates but A is in the path of a falling boulder at t and B is not. *Having existed for more than two days* is not internal. There is a possible situation in which two water molecules, C and D, are duplicates at a time t, but C has existed for more than two days, whereas D has not, because it was created in a chemical reaction just one day ago. Whether or not something has the property *having existed for more than two days* at a time t is a matter of the thing's history prior to t, not a matter of what is going on within its boundaries at t. But many familiar properties are internal. Being 2 kg in mass is internal. Having a temperature of 98.6°F is internal. So is being alive.

That much is mostly common ground. **Activism** is somewhat more informative and controversial. We can think of Activism as a partially filled-in template, rather than a fully fleshed out account of what it is to be alive. Stated in simple terms, the idea is roughly this: for a thing to be alive is for that thing to be using matter and energy from its environment to maintain itself. A more careful formulation of Activism is this: there are internal conditions (properties), Cs, and processes (process types), Ps, meeting the constraint *that the Ps are causal processes whereby a thing can acquire matter and energy from its environment and use this matter and energy to maintain and repair itself, thereby retaining a fairly stable large-scale structure*

despite gradual and nearly continuous turnover in its constituent matter, but otherwise left open, such that for a thing alive is for it in one of the Cs and to be actively undergoing a mix of the Ps appropriate to that condition.

The reason for mentioning both *conditions* and *processes appropriate to those conditions* is to make room for the view that cells or organisms with different structures (for example, a bacterium and a human being, or an early human embryo and an adult human being) need to be undergoing different processes in order to count as being alive. One might want to say that (i) if a thing is in a condition characteristic of an adult human being, then it can't count as being alive without brain function, but that (ii) if a thing is in a condition characteristic of a normal early human embryo (with no brain), it can count as being alive without brain function. Our formulation of Activism allows for this (see Persson (2002) for a helpful discussion of human death that takes early embryos into account).

Let's abbreviate Activism as follows: for a thing to be alive is for it to be undergoing *the relevant vital processes*. I've said little about those processes. But it is plausible that, in all *actual* cases at least, and probably in any possible situation governed by the actual laws, if an organism or cell is not **metabolizing**, then it is not undergoing the relevant processes and so according to Activism is not alive (Dennett 1995: 127; Boden 1999).

What is it to metabolize? Roughly, it is to have molecular parts within cells that are undergoing certain chemical reactions—reactions in which energy is extracted from fuel and used to power various processes and activities, including the construction of organic material and the elimination of wastes. According to biologist James Clegg, "a metabolism must consist of systematically controlled pathways of enzymatic reactions, governed in rate and direction, integrated and under the control of the cells in which they are found" (2001: 615). For now, the point is this: where these systematically controlled sequences of chemical reactions are absent, the relevant vital processes are absent.

IV. Cryptobiotic Things Are Neither Alive Nor Dead

With Activism in place, we are in a position to argue that cryptobiotic organisms are neither alive nor dead.

First, we can argue that they are not dead. Cryptobiotic things are mostly intact and undamaged. They can resume their vital processes relatively easily, without first being repaired. Their internal condition ensures that they are capable of undergoing the relevant vital processes, and that they have a disposition to resume those processes in response to appropriate stimuli. But if all of this is true of something, then it is not dead.

Next, we argue that they are not alive. Call this the No Metabolism Argument, which we set out in standard form:

Premise 1: Cryptobiotic things are not metabolizing.
Premise 2: Things that are not metabolizing are not undergoing the relevant vital processes.
Premise 3: Things that are not undergoing those processes are not alive.
Conclusion: Cryptobiotic things—such as Grady—are not alive.

Working backward, Premises 3 and 2 were discussed in Section III. Premise 3 follows from Activism, our account of what it is to be alive. Premise 2 can be supported by enumerative induction, among other things. We have observed many things to be undergoing the relevant processes and metabolizing, but we have never observed something to be doing the former but not the latter. Finally, Premise 1 has been defended in different ways by biologists such as Keilin (1959), Clegg (2001: 615), and David Wharton. Wharton writes that

> One of the most sensitive techniques for detecting metabolism is to feed an organism radiolabelled glucose and look for CO_2 production. This method is capable of detecting metabolism that is 0.01% of normal levels. Metabolism cannot be detected in anhydrobiotic [cryptobiotic due to dehydration] nematodes using this technique.
> (2015: R1114)

This does not establish the absence of metabolism with absolute certainty, but it makes it a reasonable position to hold pending further evidence.

It follows from the conclusions of the two arguments given above that cryptobiotic things are neither alive nor dead, i.e., that Neither-Nor is true.

V. The Capacitist Objection to the No Metabolism Argument

The argument above can be resisted by replacing Activism with **Capacitism**. A careful formulation of Capacitism would be parallel to our longer formulation of Activism, but we will work with a shorter version: for a thing to be alive is for it to be undergoing *or capable of undergoing* the relevant vital processes, in a sense of "capable" discussed below (see Luper (2009: 44–45) and, for a similar view, van Inwagen (1990: 146–149)). Activists and Capacitists can agree about which vital processes are relevant (for which internal conditions). For simplicity, I will assume that they *do* agree about this. What they disagree about is whether being *capable* of undergoing those processes is sufficient for being alive. Capacitists say "Yes"; Activists say "No."

Cryptobiotic organisms are not metabolizing, or so I will assume. But they are *capable* of metabolizing and undergoing any other processes that might be relevant, as shown by the fact that they return to normal activity so easily. So, according to Capacitism, these organisms are alive. Capacitists therefore deny Premise 3 of the No Metabolism argument, along with its conclusion. They say that crypobiotic organisms are still alive. They think that the solution to the Paradox of Cryptobiosis is to deny proposition (1) and say that our tardigrade Grady is still alive, since it has the relevant capacities.

VI. The Activist Reply

I now offer a brief defense of Activism. We can start by noting that some biologists have sided with Activism against Capacitism, at least with regard to cryptobiotic organisms. John Maynard Smith writes:

> A freeze-dried insect is not alive: it was alive, and may be alive again in the future. Energy must be supplied in either the form of suitable chemical compounds or as sunlight, and in either case atoms are continuously entering and leaving the structure of the organism.
>
> (1986: 2)

Clegg goes further and endorses Neither-Nor:

> an organism in anhydrobiosis lacks all the dynamic features characteristic of living organisms, notably due to the lack of an ongoing metabolism to transduce energy and carry out biosynthesis. In that sense it is not "alive," yet neither is it "dead" since suitable rehydration produces an obviously living organism... there are three states of biological organization: alive; dead; and cryptobiotic.
>
> (2001: 615)

However, the dispute between Activism and Capacitism is not purely empirical. It cannot be settled in any direct way just by consulting the scientific data. Activists and Capacitists can agree about all this data. They can agree about the biochemistry of metabolism and about what is occurring at the biochemical level in cryptobiotic organisms. What they disagree about here is whether those organisms, which are not undergoing the relevant processes but have the capacity to do so, count as being alive. Maynard Smith and Clegg simply *presuppose* that the correct answer is "No." I happen to agree. But Maynard Smith and Clegg don't give any *argument* for this answer that has the potential to rationally persuade our target audience—namely, those (such as Luper and van Inwagen) who are informed of the relevant data and still accept Capacitism or remain undecided about it.

Can we do better? Here is a try. It is far from being a knock-down argument, but it may carry some weight. First, it is a necessary truth that a thing is alive at a time t if and only if it is *living* at t. Second, to be living is relevantly similar to many other less controversial biological properties, such as to be *digesting*, to be *photosynthesizing*, and to be *breathing*. Third, these latter properties all require biological activity, not merely the capacity for such activity. It is impossible for a thing to be digesting or photosynthesizing or breathing at a given time without undergoing the relevant active processes at that time. So, by analogy, it is plausible that to be living, a thing must be undergoing the active processes relevant to living. But in that case, given my first premise, it follows that undergoing active processes, not merely being *capable* of undergoing them, is a necessary condition for being *alive*. So, contrary to what Capacitism says, cryptobiotic organisms are *not* alive.

VII. The Exhaustivist Argument for Capacitism

Are there any arguments in *favor* of Capacitism? One such argument relies on some premise such as **Exhaustivism**: everything is either alive or dead. The argument continues: since cryptobiotic things are not dead (as indicated by the easy resumption of their vital processes), they must be alive, and the most plausible account of life that allows for this is Capacitism. This is the Exhaustivist Argument for Capacitism.

The problem with the Exhaustivist Argument is that Exhaustivism is false. It's not as if being alive and being dead are *contradictories*, like being green and being non-green, so that everything must have one or the other. Rather, they are *contraries*, like being green and being red. Nothing can have both, but many things (for example, yellow things) have neither. Many things—rocks, toasters—are neither alive nor dead.

This shows both that Exhaustivism is false and that "dead" does not mean the same thing as "not alive." To be dead, a thing needs to have died, and to have died, a thing needs to have been alive or cryptobiotic, which toasters never have been. Being dead is a partly historical property and therefore not internal. An atom-for-atom duplicate of a dead thing need not be dead. In principle, with sufficiently advanced nanotechnology, scientists could manufacture an atom-for-atom duplicate of a dead bacterium. The bacterium was alive, then died, and is now dead. The duplicate was never alive, never died, and so is not now dead. And yet the two things are perfect duplicates. They have exactly the same internal properties.

One might try to fix the Exhaustivist Argument by replacing Exhaustivism with something like **Exhaustivism***: if a thing is alive at one time, t, then for any other time t^*, that thing is either alive at t^* or dead at t^*. Toasters, rocks, etc., aren't counterexamples to this principle, since no toaster is alive at any time. But Exhaustivism* is vulnerable to counterexamples as well (I leave these as exercises for the reader). In any event, such principles are dubious from the outset. Given that toasters are neither alive nor dead, there is nothing weird about this status.

We should pause to note that this solves the Paradox of Cryptobiosis. Propositions (1) and (2) are true, as I've argued, and so Exhaustivism must be false. But now we know that Exhaustivism should *also* be rejected for reasons that have nothing to do with cryptobiosis. Since being dead is a historical property that requires having died, all non-biological objects (such as rocks and toasters) are neither alive nor dead, despite the fact that they are not cryptobiotic. Exhaustivism never should have been tempting in the first place.

VIII. What Is It to Die? Cessation and Neutral Incapacitation

What is it to die? One constraint that any answer must respect is **Becoming-Dead**: necessarily, a thing dies at a time t if and only if the thing becomes dead at t. So far, so good. But it would be better to say something more informative, by spelling out the relationship

between what it is to die and what it is to be alive. The simplest plausible account is **Cessation**: for a thing to die is just for it to cease to be alive. Unfortunately, Cessation is in tension with Neither-Nor.

To see the tension, suppose that Greta is a tardigrade that is undergoing the relevant processes, and is clearly alive, throughout some interval leading up to t_1; that Greta ceases to undergo those processes, and becomes cryptobiotic, at t_1; that Greta is cryptobiotic from t_1 to t_3, when Greta's vital processes resume; and that Greta is alive from t_3 to t_4, at which moment Greta is crushed by a falling rock. At t_4, Greta ceases to be capable of undergoing the relevant vital processes (the notion of a capacity is discussed in the next section).

Let t_2 be a time between t_1 and t_3. According to Neither-Nor, since Greta is cryptobiotic at t_2, Greta is not *dead* at t_2 or at any time during the $t_1 - t_3$ interval. So Greta did not *become* dead at t_1. So—by Becoming—Dead above—Greta did not *die* at t_1. However, again given Neither-Nor, Greta did cease to be *alive* at t_1, when the relevant vital processes ceased. So Greta is a counterexample to Cessation. Greta ceased to be alive, but did not die, at t_1 (Feldman 1992: 60–62). Cessation is false.

A natural alternative, which can be accepted by Activists and Capacitists alike, is **Neutral Incapacitation** (NI): for a thing to die is for it to cease to be either undergoing or capable of undergoing the relevant vital processes (a similar view is defended by Persson 1995). More carefully: there are internal conditions, the Cs, and processes, the Ps, meeting the constraints given in the previous section, such that for a thing to die at t is for the thing to be in one of the Cs throughout some interval leading up to t, and for the thing to cease, at t, to be either *undergoing* or *capable of undergoing* the mix of Ps appropriate to that condition. Both Activists and Capacitists agree that Greta dies upon being crushed, not upon entering cryptobiosis. NI gives both camps a common explanation of why this is. Only when crushed does Greta cease to either undergo or be capable of undergoing the relevant processes.[1]

IX. What Is It to Be *Capable* of Undergoing the Relevant Processes?

The basic idea behind NI is that there are certain processes associated with life, and if a given organism ceases to undergo these processes but remains capable of undergoing them, the organism may or may not cease to be *alive*, but it doesn't then *die*. Instead, it dies when and only when it ceases to be capable of undergoing them (a similar idea lies behind many accounts of death. Consider the Uniform Determination of Death Act: "An individual who has sustained either (i) **irreversible** cessation of circulatory and respiratory functions, or (i) **irreversible** cessation of all functions of the entire brain, including the brain stem, is dead" (1981: 73, boldface added). Compare that to a parallel statement framed in terms of capacities: an individual (i) who has ceased to engage in circulatory and respiratory functions and who **is not capable of** engaging in these functions again, or (ii) who has ceased to engage in all functions of the entire brain, including the brain stem, and who **is not capable of** engaging in them again, is dead. It is an interesting question whether these two statements disagree, and if so how).

Given how much weight we are placing on the notion of a capacity, we should ask: "What is it to be capable of undergoing the relevant processes?" Here are three tempting answers; each can be plugged in to NI to yield a more informative account of what it is to die (Feldman 1992, Persson 1995, and Belshaw 2009: 31–38 cover similar ground).

A1: Technological possibility. For a thing x to be capable at t of undergoing the relevant processes is for it to be technologically possible, at t, to cause x to undergo those processes.

A2: Physical possibility, holding fixed everything about the actual past and present. For a thing x to be capable at t of undergoing the relevant processes is for there to be nothing about the past or present that, together with the laws, rules out x's undergoing those processes at some later time.

A3: Physical possibility, holding fixed only x's current internal properties. For a thing x to be capable at t of undergoing the relevant processes is for there to be nothing about x or x's internal properties at t that, together with the laws, rules out x's undergoing those processes at some later time (see Persson 1995: 506).

A1 can be rejected on the grounds that it conflicts with the fact that *being capable of undergoing the relevant processes* is an internal property. Suppose that, in 2020, I fall into an icy lake and my vital processes come to a halt. Further, suppose that these processes can be restarted, but only with the help of post-1970s technology. Suppose also that exactly the same thing happened to my great-grandfather, in 1920. Suppose that he and I were atom-for-atom duplicates from the moment we fell into the lake until five minutes after we were pulled out. Then, according to A1, I still have the capacity to undergo the relevant processes when I am pulled out of the lake (because of the availability of the necessary technology) but my great-grandfather does not (the technology not being available in his day). And yet we have exactly the same internal properties at the given times. So, according to A1, the relevant capacity is not an internal property. Since that capacity *is* internal, A1 is false.

Relatedly, when A1 is plugged into NI, it yields the result that my great-grandfather dies while he is in the lake but I do not. But that can't be right, given our perfect internal similarity throughout the process. Whether an organism dies at a time t is, in the relevant sense, internal (Hershenov 2003). It is purely a matter of what is going on in the organism throughout any arbitrarily brief chunk of time with t as its midpoint. So the version of NI associated with A1 should be rejected as well.

A2 can be ruled out for similar reasons. Let O be some cryptobiotic organism located on a ledge near the base of a sheer granite cliff. Suppose that, at t_1, O is not undergoing the relevant processes, but nothing about the past or present, together with the laws, rules out O's undergoing those processes in the future. Now suppose that, at t_2, an atom of uranium, embedded within the cliff face about 300 ft above O, non-deterministically decays. Prior to t_2, nothing about the universe or the laws guaranteed that the atom would decay at t_2. But it did decay then. Its decaying triggered several other small changes in the surrounding rock, which were just enough to dislodge a house-sized block of granite which had been precariously attached to the wall. Once the atom decayed, the total state of the universe, together with the laws, guaranteed that the block would fall, hit the ledge below, and pulverize O so completely that O would never undergo the relevant processes again. So it was at t_2 that it became physically impossible, in the relevant sense, for O ever to undergo the relevant processes again. However, the block did not actually hit O until t_4, a few seconds later.

Now consider a time t_3 during the block's fall, and suppose that O has exactly the same internal properties at t_3 that it had at t_1. Given that the capacity to undergo the relevant processes is internal, it follows that O has that capacity at both t_1 and t_3 or at neither time. A2 conflicts with this. According to A2, O has the capacity at t_1, when it remained open that O might undergo the relevant processes again in the future, but O does not have the capacity at t_3, after it has been settled by changes in O's surroundings that O will never undergo the processes again, but before O is damaged by the block. So A2 should be rejected (this argument presupposes the falsehood of determinism, the thesis that the internal state of the universe at any one time, together with the laws, guarantees everything about the internal state of the universe at all later times. Exercise: show that A2 is false on the assumption that determinism is true).

Relatedly, when A2 is plugged in to NI, it yields the result that O dies at t_2, when the far-away uranium atom decays (despite the fact O does not undergo any internal damage at that time). This shows that we should reject

the relevant version of NI as well (Feldman 1992: 65; Gilmore 2013: 20).

A3 faces a different problem. Let Beta be a bacterium. At t_1, Beta is actively alive. At t_2, Beta is frozen and cryptobiotic. At t_3, Beta suffers internal damage while frozen: its cell membrane remains intact, but its chromosome is broken up into several parts, as are many of its ribosomes and proteins. Before Beta suffered this damage, it was true that if Beta were thawed and otherwise left alone, it would have resumed normal activity. After the damage, at t_4, this is no longer true. What is true instead is that if Beta were thawed and otherwise left alone, it would decompose. Given all this, it seems that Beta died at t_3, when it was damaged, and that, at t_4, Beta is dead and not capable of undergoing the relevant vital processes.

However, I strongly suspect that A3 conflicts with these verdicts. According to A3, in order for it to be true that

(i) Beta is not capable, at t_4, of undergoing those processes,

   it must be true that

(ii) Beta's internal condition at t_4, together with the laws, rules out Beta's undergoing those processes at any later time.

I say that (i) *is* true. But (ii) seems extremely unlikely. Granted, Beta is in bad shape internally at t_4. Left alone, Beta will not return to an active state. But presumably, with the intervention of sufficiently advanced nanotechnology, Beta could be repaired, and the damage to Beta's constituent molecules could be reversed—all without the violation of any laws (Gilmore 2007: 25; 2013: 23–26).

When a car, parked with the engine off, is damaged and loses the capacity to run, it does not then become physically impossible for the car ever to run again. The car can be repaired and made to run again. I can't prove that the same is true of organisms in cases like Beta's, but it would be very surprising if it weren't. Organisms are more complex, so when they "break" and lose the relevant capacities, they are harder to repair. But it doesn't follow—and it seems highly unlikely—that in *all* cases, when they lose the relevant capacity, it becomes *physically impossible* for them to return to activity. So my view is that A3 is almost certainly false.

Likewise for the version of NI that results from plugging in A3 (here I depart from Feldman (1992) and Persson (1995), who take the equivalent of NI, spelled out in terms of A3, to adequately address problems about cryptobiosis). If what I've said about Beta is right, then the "A3 version" of NI yields the (I think false) result that Beta does not die at t_3, when it suffers the specified damage.

I've said what the relevant capacity is *not*. I haven't said what it *is*. Unfortunately I don't have a reductive account to offer. But all accounts have to stop somewhere. And even where no further reductive account is given, one can still clarify—by, among other things, offering examples, constraints, and analogies. To that I now turn.

Examples: The relevant capacity is had by all actively living things and also by cryptobiotic things, but not by clearly dead things (Lenin) or non-biological objects (rocks). Constraints: the relevant capacity, whatever it is, should turn out to be: (i) internal, (ii) a property that, when lost, is at least *difficult* to regain without advanced technological help, and (iii) a property that a thing can lose even though it remains physically possible, at least with the help of advanced technology, for the thing to be actively alive in the future. Analogies: consider a cryptobiotic organism; it is capable of undergoing the relevant processes but is not currently undergoing them. It is like a car or computer that is turned off, but in perfect working order. If the organism is damaged and loses the relevant capacity, in the manner of Beta, it is like a car or computer that is broken and won't turn on. These things all lack the disposition to become active in response to the appropriate stimuli, and it is extremely improbable that they will ever become active again unless they are first *repaired*. Such repairs may be difficult. For most organisms, even the most "freshly incapacitated," the needed repairs may exceed the reach of any future human technology. But that's a far cry from being physically impossible.

X. Conclusion

In Section II it was suggested that a "brain dead" patient might turn out to be neither alive nor dead. But now we can see that, while cryptobiotic organisms are neither alive nor dead, "brain dead" human beings are quite different: they are either alive or dead (though Activism and NI do not say which). The key feature of cryptobiotic organisms that allows them to be neither alive nor dead is that they have an *unexercised* capacity to undergo certain vital processes. Typical "brain dead" patients do not. When it comes to the relevant processes, they are doing everything they are capable of doing. They are capable of metabolizing, circulating their blood, oxygenating their blood, and so on, and they are in fact doing those things. They are not integrating and controlling these processes with their brains, they are not consciously thinking or experiencing anything, and indeed, they are not even capable of doing any of that. So, if there is an argument to be made that these individuals are not dead, it will have to be made by appeal to the processes that these patients are actively undergoing. If this argument is successful, it will show not only that these individuals are *not dead*, but further, that they are *alive*.[2]

Notes

1. For the record, I reject NI, though for reasons that are not relevant here. For counterexamples to NI and the necessary repairs, see Gilmore (2013) and Gilmore (2016).
2. Thanks to Michael Cholbi and Travis Timmerman for helpful comments.

References

Belshaw, C. 2009. *Annihilation: The Sense and Significance of Death*. Montreal: McGill-Queen's.

Boden, M. A. 1999. "Is Metabolism Necessary?," *British Journal for the Philosophy of Science* 50 (2): 231–248.

Clegg, J. S. 2001. "Cryptobiosis: A Peculiar State of Biological Organization," *Comparative Biochemistry and Physiology Part B* 128: 613–624.

DeGrazia, D. 2014. "The Nature of Human Death," in S. Luper (ed.), *The Cambridge Companion to Life and Death*. Cambridge: Cambridge University Press, pp. 80–97.

Dennett, D. 1995. *Darwin's Dangerous Idea*. New York: Simon & Schuster.

Feldman, F. 1992. *Confrontations with the Reaper: A Philosophical Study of the Nature and Value of Death*. Oxford: Oxford University Press.

Gilmore, C. 2007. "Defining 'Dead' in Terms of 'Lives' and 'Dies'", *Philosophia* 35: 219–231.

Gilmore, C., 2013. "When Do Things Die?" in B. Bradley, F. Feldman and J. Johansson (eds), *The Oxford Handbook of Philosophy of Death*. Oxford: Oxford University Press.

Gilmore, C. 2016. "The Metaphysics of Mortals: Death, Immortality, and Personal Time," *Philosophical Studies* 173: 3271–3299.

Hershenov, D. 2003. "The Problematic Role of 'Irreversibility' in the Definition of Death," *Bioethics* 17: 89–100.

Keilin, D. 1959. "The Problem of Anabiosis or Latent Life: History and Current Concept,"
Proceedings B of the Royal Society of London 150: 149–191.

Luper, S. 2009. *The Philosophy of Death*. Cambridge: Cambridge University Press.

Maynard Smith, J. 1986. *The Problems of Biology*. Oxford: Oxford University Press.

Persson, I. 1995. "What Is Mysterious about Death?," *Southern Journal of Philosophy* 33: 499–508.

Persson, I. 2002, "Human Death—A View from the Beginning of Life," *Bioethics*, 16: 20–32.

President's Commission for the Study of Ethical Problems in Medicine and Biomedical and Behavioral Research. 1981. *Defining Death*. Washington, DC: Government Printing Office.

van Inwagen, P. 1990. *Material Beings*. Ithaca, NY: Cornell University Press.

Wharton, D. 2015. "Anhydrobiosis," *Current Biology Magazine* 25, R1114–R1116.

Wilson, J. 1999. *Biological Individuality*. Cambridge: Cambridge University Press.

Wreen, M. J. 1987. "The Definition of Death," *Public Affairs Quarterly* 1 (4): 87–99.

Part II Can We Survive Our Death?

Death, be Not Proud
(Holy Sonnet 10)

Death, be not proud, though some have
    called thee
Mighty and dreadful, for thou art not so;
For those whom thou think'st thou dost
    overthrow
Die not, poor Death, nor yet canst thou
    kill me.
From rest and sleep, which but thy
    pictures be,
Much pleasure; then from thee much
    more must flow,
And soonest our best men with thee
    do go,
Rest of their bones, and soul's delivery.
Thou art slave to fate, chance, kings, and
    desperate men,
And dost with poison, war, and sickness
    dwell,
And poppy or charms can make us sleep
    as well
And better than thy stroke; why swell'st
    thou then?
One short sleep past, we wake eternally
And death shall be no more; Death,
    thou shalt die.

—John Donne

Introduction to Part II

Can you survive your death? Many people believe they will and many more at least hope they will. But this raises the question of what must happen in order for *you* to survive. If, for example, you're identical to your body (or, more precisely, your brain) and your brain is destroyed upon death, then it seems impossible for you to survive your death. Unless, of course, it were somehow possible to bring *your* brain (not a clone of your brain) back into existence. In this section, you will get to read one literary take and two contemporary takes on this question, all of them unique in their own right.

The first chapter is an excerpt from various parts of Miguel de Unamuno's (1912) masterpiece the *Tragic Sense of Life*. Unamuno was a great Spanish Catholic and his *Tragic Sense of Life* is, among other things, about the tension (and apparent mutual dependence) between faith and reason. It is about humans' longing for a kind of personal immortality, one where the person literally continues living on indefinitely, and not merely metaphorically living on in the hearts and minds of those who come after them. It is about the relationship between meaning in life and our (im)mortality. It is also about so much more than that.

The excerpts that you will read focus on some of Unamuno's central claims about immortality. He begins with a claim that he doesn't want to know whether his death brings about the permanent cessation of his existence. If he learned it did, then he'd despair and if he learned it didn't, then resignation would follow. Yet he faces a sort of trilemma. If he cannot know one way or the other, then the result is "resignation in despair or despair in resignation, a separate designation or a resigned despair." In short, he faces "conflict," a conflict that permeates the entire work.

Unamuno proceeds to share a number of fascinating, perhaps insightful, observations about immortality. He expresses skepticism at those who claim *not* to want immortality. He poetically expresses his deep insuppressible desire for personal immortality. He discusses what he takes to be vain manifestations of this desire. Most importantly, he suggests that this desire or immortality "finds no consolation in reason," as the question about immortality supposedly "falls outside reason." Yet, he claims, "Faith in immortality is irrational." Neither are sufficient to handle human's longing for personal immortality. As Don Miguel de Unamuno put it, this is Unamuno's "inner deadlock." Reason, supposedly, "can rise no higher than skepticism, and, unable to become vital, dies sterile; his faith, exacting anti-rational affirmations and unable therefore to be apprehended by the logical mind, remains incommunicable."

In the second chapter of the section, Stephen Cave considers three different ways we might be thought to survive our death, and argues that all three face profound philosophical challenges. The first way someone might be thought to survive their death is by being resurrected after dying. Cave argues, however, that this faces three serious problems. If the same atoms were used to make up two different people at two different times, who would be resurrected with that atom? Moreover, could the person who doesn't get that atom still come back? Second, if we're resurrected using the atoms that make up our body right before we died, then how (in typical cases) could the post-resurrected person be happy and healthy? Maybe the resurrectionist will hold that it doesn't need to be the exact same atoms that make up your body, nor do you need to be put in the state you were in right before death in order to come back. But then it looks like God could make duplicates of you. But how could that be? At most, there can be only one of you! Instead, as already mentioned, one might claim that we're a soul and so no physical parts are needed for us to survive our death. Cave argues that the problem with this view is the evidence suggests that our mind is completely dependent on our brain and body. Finally, Cave considers whether we could survive death through our "legacy," but ultimately concludes that it wouldn't truly be *us* surviving, at least not in the ordinary sense that a person identical to us lives on after our bodily death.

In the final chapter of the section, David and Rose Hershenov consider whether it

is possible to survive your death on various accounts of personal identity. They grant that it seems easier for us to survive our deaths if we're immaterial souls rather than living members of the species Homo-sapiens, but suggest that our body is, in a sense, an essential part of who we are. They first consider the historical conceptions of soul theories of personal identity, then Lockean conceptions, and then materialism. In doing so, they review the merits of each view, as well as the possibility we could survive our death given the truth of these accounts of personal identity. After that, they defend a kind of hylomorphism, which (generally speaking) is the view that the human being is the result of its body "being organized" by its soul. According to the view, we're not identical to our soul (just like a statue is not identical to its shape) nor are we identical to our body (just like a statue is not identical to the clay it's made of), but are distinct from each. The Hershenovs consider the merits of different, more precise, versions of hylomorphism before explaining how it's indeed possible to survive your death if hylomorphism is true.

If you're interested in reading more about personal identity and death, check out the following:

1. Peter Van Inwagen's "The Possibility of Resurrection" (1978) *International Journal for Philosophy of Religion* 9 (2):114–121.
2. Dean Zimmerman's "Personal Identity and the Survival of Death" in *The Oxford Handbook of Philosophy of Death* (2013) edited by Ben Bradley, Fred Feldman, and Jens Johansson. New York: Oxford University Press.
3. Stephen Caves' book *Immortality: The Quest to Live Forever and How it Drives Civilization* (2012) New York: Crown Publishers.
4. Tamar Szabó Gendler's "Personal Identity and Metaphysics" in *The Oxford Handbook of Philosophy of Mind* (2009) edited by Ansgar Beckermann, Brian P. McLaughlin, and Sven Walter. New York: Oxford University Press.

5 The Tragic Sense of Life (excerpts)

Miguel de Unamuno

The Tragic Sense of Life (1912), trans. J.E. Crawford Flitch (Macmillan and Co., 1921)

II

Whence do I come and whence comes the world in which and by which I live? Whither do I go and whither goes everything that environs me? What does it all mean? Such are the questions that man asks as soon as he frees himself from the brutalizing necessity of labouring for his material sustenance. And if we look closely, we shall see that beneath these questions lies the wish to know not so much the "why" as the "wherefore," not the cause but the end. Cicero's definition of philosophy is well known—"the knowledge of things divine and human and of the causes in which these things are contained"; but in reality these causes are, for us, ends. And what is the Supreme Cause, God, but the Supreme End? The "why" interests us only in view of the "wherefore." We wish to know whence we came only in order the better to be able to ascertain whither we are going.

★★★

Why do I wish to know whence I come and whither I go, whence comes and whither goes everything that environs me, and what is the meaning of it all? For I do not wish to die utterly, and I wish to know whether I am to die or not definitely. If I do not die, what is my destiny? and if I die, then nothing has any meaning for me. And there are three solutions: (*a*) I know that I shall die utterly, and then irremediable despair, or (*b*) I know that I shall not die utterly, and then resignation, or (*c*) I cannot know either one or the other, and

then resignation in despair or despair in resignation, a desperate resignation or a resigned despair, and hence conflict.

★★★

For the present let us remain keenly suspecting that the longing not to die, the hunger for personal immortality, the effort whereby we tend to persist indefinitely in our own being, which is, according to the tragic Jew, our very essence, that this is the affective basis of all knowledge and the personal inward starting-point of all human philosophy, wrought by a man and for men. And we shall see how the solution of this inward affective problem, a solution which may be but the despairing renunciation of the attempt at a solution, is that which colours all the rest of philosophy. Underlying even the so-called problem of knowledge there is simply this human feeling, just as underlying the enquiry into the "why," the cause, there is simply the search for the "wherefore," the end. All the rest is either to deceive oneself or to wish to deceive others; and to wish to deceive others in order to deceive oneself.

And this personal and affective starting-point of all philosophy and all religion is the tragic sense of life. Let us now proceed to consider this.

III

Let us pause to consider this immortal yearning for immortality...

First of all let us recall once again—and it will not be for the last time—that saying of Spinoza that every being endeavours to persist in itself, and that this endeavour is its actual essence, and implies indefinite time, and that the soul, in fine, sometimes with a clear and distinct idea, sometimes confusedly, tends to persist in its being with indefinite duration, and is aware of its persistency (*Ethic*, Part III., Props. VI.-X.).

It is impossible for us, in effect, to conceive of ourselves as not existing, and no effort is capable of enabling consciousness to realize absolute unconsciousness, its own annihilation. Try, reader, to imagine to yourself, when you are wide awake, the condition of your soul when you are in a deep sleep; try to fill your consciousness with the representation of no-consciousness, and you will see the impossibility of it. The effort to comprehend it causes the most tormenting dizziness. We cannot conceive ourselves as not existing.

The visible universe, the universe that is created by the instinct of self-preservation, becomes all too narrow for me. It is like a cramped cell, against the bars of which my soul beats its wings in vain. Its lack of air stifles me. More, more, and always more! I want to be myself, and yet without ceasing to be myself to be others as well, to merge myself into the totality of things visible and invisible, to extend myself into the illimitable of space and to prolong myself into the infinite of time. Not to be all and for ever is as if not to be—at least, let me be my whole self, and be so for ever and ever. And to be the whole of myself is to be everybody else. Either all or nothing!

All or nothing! And what other meaning can the Shakespearean "To be or not to be" have, or that passage in *Coriolanus* where it is said of Marcius "He wants nothing of a god but eternity"? Eternity, eternity!—that is the supreme desire! The thirst of eternity is what is called love among men, and whosoever loves another wishes to eternalize himself in him. Nothing is real that is not eternal.

***

The tragic Portuguese Jew of Amsterdam wrote that the free man thinks of nothing less than of death; but this free man is a dead man, free from the impulse of life, for want of love, the slave of his liberty. This thought that I must die and the enigma of what will come after death is the very palpitation of my consciousness. When I contemplate the green serenity of the fields or look into the depths of clear eyes through which shines a fellow-soul, my consciousness dilates, I feel the diastole of the soul and am bathed in the flood of the life that flows about me, and I believe in my future; but instantly the voice of mystery whispers to me, "Thou shalt cease to be!" the angel of Death touches me with his wing, and the systole of the soul floods the depths of my spirit with the blood of divinity.

Like Pascal, I do not understand those who assert that they care not a farthing for these things, and this indifference "in a matter that touches themselves, their eternity, their all, exasperates me rather than moves me to compassion, astonishes and shocks me," and he who feels thus "is for me," as for Pascal, whose are the words just quoted, "a monster."

***

Although this meditation upon mortality may soon induce in us a sense of anguish, it fortifies us in the end. Retire, reader, into yourself and imagine a slow dissolution of yourself—the light dimming about you—all things becoming dumb and soundless, enveloping you in silence—the objects that you handle crumbling away between your hands—the ground slipping from under your feet—your very memory vanishing as if in a swoon—everything melting away from you into nothingness and you yourself also melting away—the very consciousness of nothingness, merely as the phantom harbourage of a shadow, not even remaining to you.

I have heard it related of a poor harvester who died in a hospital bed, that when the priest went to anoint his hands with the oil of extreme unction, he refused to open his right hand, which clutched a few dirty coins, not considering that very soon neither his hand nor he himself would be his own any more.

And so we close and clench, not our hand, but our heart, seeking to clutch the world in it.

A friend confessed to me that, foreseeing while in the full vigour of physical health the near approach of a violent death, he proposed to concentrate his life and spend the few days which he calculated still remained to him in writing a book. Vanity of vanities!

If at the death of the body which sustains me, and which I call mine to distinguish it from the self that is I, my consciousness returns to the absolute unconsciousness from which it sprang, and if a like fate befalls all my brothers in humanity, then is our toil-worn human race nothing but a fatidical procession of phantoms, going from nothingness to nothingness, and humanitarianism the most inhuman thing known.

★★★

The problem is tragic and eternal, and the more we seek to escape from it, the more it thrusts itself upon us. Four-and-twenty centuries ago, in his dialogue on the immortality of the soul, the serene Plato—but was he serene?—spoke of the uncertainty of our dream of being immortal and of the *risk* that the dream might be vain, and from his own soul there escaped this profound cry—Glorious is the risk!—καλος γαρ ο κινδυνος, glorious is the risk that we are able to run of our souls never dying—a sentence that was the germ of Pascal's famous argument of the wager.

Faced with this risk, I am presented with arguments designed to eliminate it, arguments demonstrating the absurdity of the belief in the immortality of the soul; but these arguments fail to make any impression upon me, for they are reasons and nothing more than reasons, and it is not with reasons that the heart is appeased. I do not want to die—no; I neither want to die nor do I want to want to die; I want to live for ever and ever and ever. I want this "I" to live—this poor "I" that I am and that I feel myself to be here and now, and therefore the problem of the duration of my soul, of my own soul, tortures me.

★★★

When doubts invade us and cloud our faith in the immortality of the soul, a vigorous and painful impulse is given to the anxiety to perpetuate our name and fame, to grasp at least a shadow of immortality. And hence this tremendous struggle to singularize ourselves, to survive in some way in the memory of others and of posterity. It is this struggle, a thousand times more terrible than the struggle for life, that gives its tone, colour, and character to our society, in which the medieval faith in the immortal soul is passing away. Each one seeks to affirm himself, if only in appearance.

Once the needs of hunger are satisfied—and they are soon satisfied—the vanity, the necessity—for it is a necessity—arises of imposing ourselves upon and surviving in others. Man habitually sacrifices his life to his purse, but he sacrifices his purse to his vanity. He boasts even of his weaknesses and his misfortunes, for want of anything better to boast of, and is like a child who, in order to attract attention, struts about with a bandaged finger. And vanity, what is it but eagerness for survival?

VI

We have seen that the vital longing for human immortality finds no consolation in reason and that reason leaves us without incentive or consolation in life and life itself without real finality. But here, in the depths of the abyss, the despair of the heart and of the will and the scepticism of reason meet face to face and embrace like brothers. And we shall see it is from this embrace, a tragic—that is to say, an intimately loving—embrace, that the wellspring of life will flow, a life serious and terrible. Scepticism, uncertainty—the position to which reason, by practising its analysis upon itself, upon its own validity, at last arrives—is the foundation upon which the heart's despair must build up its hope.

Disillusioned, we had to abandon the position of those who seek to give consolation the force of rational and logical truth, pretending to prove the rationality, or at any rate the non-irrationality, of consolation; and we had to abandon likewise the position of those who seek to give rational truth the force of consolation and of a motive for life. Neither the one nor the other of these positions satisfied us. The one is at variance with our reason, the other with our feeling. These two powers can never conclude peace and we must needs live by their war. We must make of this war, of war itself, the very condition of our spiritual life.

★★★

In the concrete vital problem that concerns us, reason takes up no position whatever. In truth, it does something worse than deny the immortality of the soul—for that at any rate would be one solution—it refuses even to recognize the problem as our vital desire presents it to us. In the rational and logical sense of the term problem, there is no such problem. This question of the immortality of the soul, of the persistence of the individual consciousness, is not rational, it falls outside reason. As a problem, and whatever solution it may receive, it is irrational. Rationally even the very propounding of the problem lacks sense. The immortality of the soul is as unconceivable as, in all strictness, is its absolute mortality. For the purpose of explaining the world and existence—and such is the task of reason—it is not necessary that we should suppose that our soul is either mortal or immortal. The mere enunciation of the problem is, therefore, an irrationality.

★★★

Faith in immortality is irrational. And, notwithstanding, faith, life, and reason have mutual need of one another. This vital longing is not properly a problem, cannot assume a logical status, cannot be formulated in propositions susceptible of rational discussion; but it announces itself in us as hunger announces itself. Neither can the wolf that throws itself with the fury of hunger upon its prey or with the fury of instinct upon the she-wolf, enunciate its impulse rationally and as a logical problem. Reason and faith are two enemies, neither

of which can maintain itself without the other. The irrational demands to be rationalized and reason only can operate on the irrational. They are compelled to seek mutual support and association. But association in struggle, for struggle is a mode of association.

★★★

Veracity, the homage I owe to what I believe to be rational, to what logically we call truth, moves me to affirm, in this case, that the immortality of the individual soul is a contradiction in terms, that it is something, not only irrational, but contra-rational; but sincerity leads me to affirm also my refusal to resign myself to this previous affirmation and my protest against its validity. What I feel is a truth, at any rate as much a truth as what I see, touch, hear, or what is demonstrated to me—nay, I believe it is more of a truth—and sincerity obliges me not to hide what I feel.

★★★

The absolute and complete certainty, on the one hand, that death is a complete, definite, irrevocable annihilation of personal consciousness, a certainty of the same order as the certainty that the three angles of a triangle are equal to two right angles, or, on the other hand, the absolute and complete certainty that our personal consciousness is prolonged beyond death in these present or in other conditions, and above all including in itself that strange and adventitious addition of eternal rewards and punishments—both of these certainties alike would make life impossible for us. In the most secret chamber of the spirit of him who believes himself convinced that death puts an end to his personal consciousness, his memory, for ever, and all unknown to him perhaps, there lurks a shadow, a vague shadow, a shadow of shadow, of uncertainty, and while he says within himself, "Well, let us live this life that passes away, for there is no other!" the silence of this secret chamber speaks to him and murmurs, "Who knows!…" He may not think he hears it, but he hears it nevertheless. And likewise in some secret place of the soul of the believer who most firmly holds the belief in a future life, there is a muffled voice, a voice of uncertainty, which whispers in the ear of his spirit, "Who knows!..." These voices are like the humming of a mosquito when the south-west wind roars through the trees in the wood; we cannot distinguish this faint humming, yet nevertheless, merged in the clamour of the storm, it reaches the ear. Otherwise, without this uncertainty, how could we live?

X

...Once again I must repeat that the longing for the immortality of the soul, for the permanence, in some form or another, of our personal and individual consciousness, is as much of the essence of religion as is the longing that there may be a God. The one does not exist apart from the other, the reason being that fundamentally they are one and the same thing. But as soon as we attempt to give a concrete and rational form to this longing for immortality and permanence, to define it to ourselves, we encounter even more difficulties than we encountered in our attempt to rationalize God.

***

Yes, the prudent, the rational, and, some will say, the pious, attitude, is not to seek to penetrate into mysteries that are hidden from our knowledge, not to insist upon shaping a plastic representation of eternal glory, such as that of the *Divina Commedia*. True faith, true Christian piety, we shall be told, consists in resting upon the confidence that God, by the grace of Christ, will, in some way or another, make us live in Him, in His Son; that, as our destiny is in His almighty hands, we should surrender ourselves to Him, in the full assurance that He will do with us what is best for the ultimate end of life, of spirit and of the universe. Such is the teaching that has traversed many centuries, and was notably prominent in the period between Luther and Kant.

And nevertheless men have not ceased endeavouring to imagine to themselves what this eternal life may be, nor will they cease their endeavours so long as they are men and not merely thinking machines. There are books of theology—or of what passes for theology—full of disquisitions upon the conditions under which the blessed dead live in paradise, upon their mode of enjoyment, upon the properties of the glorious body, for without some form of body the soul cannot be conceived.

And to this same necessity, the real necessity of forming to ourselves a concrete representation of what this other life may be, must in great part be referred the indestructible vitality of doctrines such as those of spiritualism, metempsychosis, the transmigration of souls from star to star, and the like; doctrines which as often as they are pronounced to be defeated and dead, are found to have come to life again, clothed in some more or less new form. And it is merely supine to be content to ignore them and not to seek to discover their permanent and living essence. Man will never willingly abandon his attempt to form a concrete representation of the other life.

But is an eternal and endless life after death indeed thinkable? How can we conceive the life of a disembodied spirit? How can we conceive such a spirit? How can we conceive a pure consciousness, without a corporal organism? Descartes divided the world into thought and extension, a dualism which was imposed upon him by the Christian dogma of the immortality of the soul. But is extension, is matter, that which thinks and is spiritualized, or is thought that which is extended and materialized? The weightiest questions of metaphysics arise practically out of our desire to arrive at an understanding of the possibility of our immortality—from this fact they derive their value and cease to be merely the idle discussions of fruitless curiosity.

***

How can a human soul live and enjoy God eternally without losing its individual

personality—that is to say, without losing itself? What is it to enjoy God? What is
eternity as opposed to time? Does the soul
change or does it not change in the other life?
If it does not change, how does it live? And
if it changes, how does it preserve its individuality through so vast a period of time? For
though the other life may exclude space, it
cannot exclude time, as Cournot observes in
the work quoted above.

If there is life in heaven there is change. ...
In any case, it is impossible for us to conceive
life without change, change of growth or of
diminution, of sadness or of joy, of love or of
hate.

In effect, an eternal life is unthinkable and
an eternal life of absolute felicity, of beatific
vision, is more unthinkable still.

***

Yes, but what I work at, will not that too
be lost in the end? And if it be lost, wherefore should I work at it? Yes, yes, it may be
that to accomplish my work—and what is my
work?—without thinking about myself, is to
love God. And what is it to love God?

And on the other hand, in loving God
in myself, am I not loving myself more than
God, am I not loving myself in God?

What we really long for after death is to
go on living this life, this same mortal life, but
without its ills, without its tedium, and without death.

6 Can We Survive Our Deaths?

Stephen Cave

At first look, it might seem odd to ask whether we can survive our own deaths. If we were reading an account of a battle or a disaster, we would expect the report to divide the people who were present into those who had died and those who had survived, with everyone falling into one or other of these categories and none remaining. We would be surprised to read that some had died but survived nonetheless. Yet at the same time, the idea that people do survive their own deaths is widespread, featuring in many cultures today and throughout history. This contradiction shows that the notion of 'survival' can have very different meanings. Determining whether we really can in any sense survive death requires not only unpacking these meanings, but also understanding what it is to be human.

In this chapter, I will introduce three broad categories of belief about how people might survive their deaths: through resurrection, as a soul, and by leaving some kind of legacy.[1] Each of these three beliefs has its own attractions and is consequently widespread in many civilizations across the globe. I show that each depends on a particular notion of what a human being is—what is sometimes called personal ontology.[2] Despite many brilliant people having tried to defend them, I show that each of these beliefs has deep, unresolved problems.

Human Life, Human Death

To both the casual observer and the highly trained biologist, it seems obvious that humans are a kind of organism; more specifically, a kind of animal. Like other animals, we eat and excrete, breathe, and move about—sometimes in search of mates with which to reproduce. Even more specifically, since Carl Linnaeus published his *Systema Naturæ* in 1735,[3] humans have been classified as a form of primate, and it is now known that we share all but a few percent of our genes with chimpanzees.[4]

One of the most obvious facts about animals, as obvious as the fact that they are born, is that they die.[5] Evidence suggests that humans have long found this fact upsetting: for example, the oldest surviving epic, that of the Sumerian king Gilgamesh, is the story of a man raging against mortality, and there have been many such myths since.[6] There is a growing body of work known as 'terror management theory' which suggests that people find the thought of their mortality so devastating that they are strongly compelled to pursue strategies (or believe stories) that promise escape from death's grip.[7] Indeed, most of the inventions that comprise civilization can be seen in this light: agriculture provides humans with necessary food, militaries keep them safe, medicines ward off disease, and so forth.

Alongside these technologies designed to postpone death, there have also been many that have aimed to banish it altogether. A large number of cultures tell stories about elixirs of life, or fountains of youth, or alchemical systems that have been claimed to stop ageing and disease.[8] In the Epic of Gilgamesh, for example, the hero finds an underwater plant with the power of rejuvenation—but it is stolen by a snake, which sheds its skin as it slithers away. The rise of the empirical methods in Western Europe and North America in recent centuries have seen claims for many such wonders made in the name of science.[9]

In the twenty-first century, such claims are as popular as ever, with the ingredients of today's elixirs ranging from gene therapy to nanoscience.[10]

We might reasonably hope that biomedical science will find ways to delay ageing or counter its effects, thereby extending lifespans by years or even decades. But progress is slow, and, so far, anything like a real elixir of life has eluded the scientists as surely as it did Gilgamesh. For humans, as for other animals, death remains one of life's few certainties. But as we noted, humans are not good at accepting that they must cease to exist. Although Plan A for survival is not dying, if that cannot be achieved, then a Plan B is required: one that involves surviving death. For a creature so obviously of flesh and blood, this poses the conundrum we noted earlier: that death and survival seem like opposites. Flesh and blood quickly rot away, leaving nothing that looks like a person. To resolve this conundrum requires some imaginative metaphysics.

Resurrection

The first approach we will examine is resurrection, which means coming back to life. We will deal with resurrection first because of what it has in common with survival Plan A, staying alive: which is the notion that humans are basically these flesh-and-blood objects we encounter every day. Though sometimes thought of as the 'bodily' view of personal identity,[11] most advocates of this view today would rather use terms such as 'organism' or 'animal' to describe the kind of thing humans are: the term 'body' carries some unfortunate metaphysical baggage, having long been used to describe the non-thinking part of the mind/body duality; and the term 'organism' better captures the extent to which a human is a dynamic system, continually changing in small ways while remaining the same individual.[12]

The obvious problem with believing that humans are basically organisms is, as we noted above, the fact that organisms die and rot away. But when we consider nature's cycles, death does not always appear to be the end. In winter, flowers seem to die, and in spring they seem to return to life—a phenomenon celebrated around the world in festivals such as Easter. But for Christians, of course, Easter is not only a symbolic celebration of rebirth—it is a very explicit celebration of resurrection as a route to immortality.[13] According to the Bible, Jesus Christ, after lying dead for three days, physically returned to life and came out of his tomb. He even went to his disciples and ate fried fish in front of their eyes in order to prove that he was really "flesh and blood."[14]

For Christians, the fact that Jesus physically conquered death means that all believers can hope to do just the same. Although many Christians put more faith in an immortal soul, which we consider next, it remains orthodox belief, not only for Christians, but also for Jews and Muslims, that they will *physically* rise again. Thus, half of the world's population—some three and a half billion people—officially subscribe to the physical resurrection of the bodies they have known in this life. In reality, however, the figure is much smaller. One 2006 survey showed that, although 80% belong to one of the three Abrahamic religions, only just over 35% of Americans believe they will be bodily resurrected.[15]

As with all these putative routes to surviving death, the idea of resurrection also has a technological version: cryonics, the belief that when a person dies, they (or their corpse) can be preserved at very low temperatures, then thawed, repaired, and revived when medicine has made sufficient advances.[16] Like the pursuit of an elixir of life, the attempt to raise the dead also has a long history in science: recall that Mary Shelley was satirizing this ambition two hundred years ago in her novel *Frankenstein*.[17] However, whether one believes that an omnipotent god or omnipotent scientists will bring it about, the notion of resurrection faces deep challenges. I will discuss three: what I will call the Cannibal Problem, the Transformation Problem, and the Duplication Problem.

Remember that resurrection-based views of survival take a bodily or organism-based view of what human beings are. Once a human dies, decay quickly sets in. Although corpses might remain recognizable for days or weeks (depending on the conditions), inside the rot starts fast, and whole organs, including the brain, lose their complex, delicate structures and turn to mush. When people imagine resurrection, they imagine something like the body rising as it was when it died. But this is difficult, of course, if that body has rotted away or been burnt. Some theologians have therefore suggested that God would reassemble the body from those parts (atoms or whatever) that constituted the person when they died. Indeed, it is this recreation of the person as they were, from the same parts, that is taken to guarantee that the deceased and the resurrected really are one and the same person.[18]

But imagine that some of those parts had in the meantime become part of another person. For example, because that other person had consumed plants that had grown on the soil fertilized by the rotting body; or, in the case of the cannibal, through direct consumption of the corpse. If the same atom was part of two different people at the moment of their respective deaths, who would get it on the day of resurrection? And what would happen to the other person? This is the Cannibal Problem. Theologians have thought hard about this problem, and come up with many innovative solutions, but none that are widely considered plausible.[19] The best response would be to avoid the problem altogether by preserving the body exactly as it was at the moment of death—as many have tried, from the mummifiers of ancient Egypt, to cryonics practitioners today.

This leads, however, to the next problem. Preserving the body exactly as it was at the moment of death might help avoid the Cannibal Problem. But 'as it was at the moment of death' is unlikely to be an attractive state—perhaps old, withered, wounded or riddled with cancer. Few people imagine being resurrected to live again in such a condition. Instead, they hope that their bodies will be transformed, as promised by St Paul: "For this perishable body must put on

imperishability, and this mortal body must put on immortality."[20] But the resurrectionist has therefore run into a contradiction: on the one hand, their survival depends upon exactly the same atoms being reassembled just as they were before they died; yet, on the other hand, the post-resurrection person is supposed to be a different creature altogether, whole and healthy, and made of invincible stuff clearly very different to ordinary human matter. This is the Transformation Problem.

Now the resurrectionist might say that what is required to recreate the person is not exactly the same atoms (which leads to the Cannibal problem), nor is it even the exact recreation of the body or organism (which might lead towards the Transformation Problem). Rather, it might be the recreation of some crucial component of the person, such as their brain, as it was at some suitable moment before death, in any suitable vessel (a body perhaps thirty years younger). Such a feat might seem within the power of either God or futuristic scientists. But it is susceptible to the most serious of all the problems: if the original atoms were not required, then if God or science could recreate one such new you, they could recreate many. This is the Duplication Problem.

The Duplication Problem raises many challenges. Identity is taken to be a logically one-to-one relationship: having multiple versions of you appear at the same time breaks the rules of logic,[21] and not even an omnipotent God can do that. To illustrate: imagine you are promised you could be resurrected a century hence through this recreation of your brain in a new body. But the scientists accidentally do it five times. Which one of these new beings would you be? Why one and not another? You could not be all five.[22] Which might lead us to think that you would be none: they would all be (merely) elaborate copies.

Over the centuries, these problems have caused followers of all three Abrahamic religions to seek alternative means for surviving death. The next strategy we will consider is particularly attractive for appearing to solve the problems resurrection poses.

The Soul

The deep problem with the Resurrection approach is that it admits that death is real: the human person ends.[23] Of course, it tells a story in which that human begins again. As we have seen, however, it is difficult to make this story philosophically credible. The Soul approach avoids this problem: it says the real you is not this body that dies and rots, but instead something immaterial. Therefore what appears to be the end of the human person is merely the death of the material part: the important part continues to live on.[24] This is, of course, an attractive view, and one held by the overwhelming majority of people on earth.

Like the Resurrection view, the Soul view might initially seem at odds with the basic facts of our material, organic existence. But also like the Resurrection view, the Soul view has some intuitive plausibility. First, many people have thought they could imagine their mind or consciousness detaching from their body to explore this realm or another. Second, life itself has long seemed a mystery in need of an explanation, and the soul has been posited as the vital spark that distinguishes the animate from the inanimate. Third, consciousness seems to be a greater mystery still, and consequently there is a long tradition in both Eastern and Western philosophy of identifying it with the immaterial soul.

Although people often talk of 'having' a soul, we should more properly think of 'being' one. When bodily death comes and the soul departs, you have to be clear which way you are going: whether you are identical with the body left behind, or the soul departing. To say that humans possess souls and that they can therefore survive death is therefore to make a strong claim about what humans fundamentally are: i.e. that they are their souls, and that the rest is peripheral and can be left behind. There is then a further question about how much can be left behind, and how much must continue for this to constitute survival. Hindu and Buddhist traditions, which emphasize reincarnation (i.e. the soul entering a new body), take a thin view: that a kind of pared-down consciousness must survive. Western traditions take a thicker view: visions of the soul in Heaven (or elsewhere) tend to have the full mind of the original person, with all their memories, quirks, etc. Indeed, the notion that a person might be punished after death for their sins in life would seem highly unjust if the post-mortem person did not have the same dispositions, moral sense, etc., of the sinner.

The case for the existence of the immortal soul therefore rests upon the mind (whether in a thick or thin sense) being independent of the body, and dependent instead upon some spiritual soul-substance that can survive the death of the human organism. Many critics have raised questions about this view over many centuries, questions such as: What is this soul-substance? Does it have parts? How does it interact with the body? How do we know where it is? Or which one is yours?[25] And so on. Such questions prompted US President Thomas Jefferson to write that he would

> prefer swallowing one incomprehensibility rather than two. It requires one effort only to admit the single incomprehensibility of matter endowed with thought, and two to believe, first that of an existence called spirit, of which we have neither evidence nor idea, and then secondly how that spirit, which has neither extension nor solidity, can put material organs into motion.[26]

But the biggest problem for the idea that we can survive death as an immaterial soul is that the soul is supposed to preserve a person's essence or mind, yet all evidence suggests that a person's essence or mind is completely dependent on their body. As Voltaire put it:

> as God has connected the ability to have ideas to a part of the brain, he can preserve this faculty only if he preserves this part of the brain; for preserving this faculty without the part would be as impossible as preserving a man's laugh or a bird's song after the death of the man or the bird.[27]

Since then, a good deal of further evidence has accumulated to support this view.

In the previous century, the capacities of medicine to keep alive people with brain damage, and of science to systematically study such cases, have increased enormously. Consequently, there is now a wealth of data on how injuries to particular parts of the brain can eliminate or substantially alter core aspects of the mind.[28] It is well documented that specific brain injuries can, for example, destroy a person's capacities for particular emotions, their memories, their respect for social or moral norms and or ability to make decisions.[29] My own father died of brain cancer, and underwent profound changes to his personality as the tumor grew. All these aspects of the mind have been attributed to the soul. The essence of the challenge then is this: for the soul to do what is hoped, it must be able to preserve such mental attributes when the whole brain is destroyed by bodily death; why then can it not preserve these attributes when only a small portion of the brain is destroyed by accident or cancer?[30]

The prospects for defending a thick notion of the soul-as-mind seem hopeless. But what about the thinner notion of a kind of bare consciousness that survives bodily death? Again, the evidence speaks against. Every day, all around the world, people have their consciousness extinguished by a syringe full of chemicals—a general anesthetic. If consciousness is dependent on the soul, rather than on chemical activity in the brain, how can it be shut down by anesthetic? If the soul can sustain consciousness after the death of the whole body, why can it not sustain consciousness in the face of small changes to brain activity? These questions have no satisfactory answers.

Legacy

The first approach to surviving death that we examined, Resurrection, was premised on the view that humans are fundamentally organisms that must physically rise again, whereas the second view, Soul, posited an immaterial essence quite separate from the body. As we

have seen, however, both have serious problems. This third view takes a quite different approach: instead of suggesting that we are each one single thing—whether body or soul—it suggests that each of us is more like a bundle of disparate elements, and that these elements might dissipate upon death, but that we might survive nonetheless, in a way at least, through this "Legacy." Although there might be fewer philosophers and theologians ardently defending this view, like the other two, it has had many adherents throughout history.

In the Western canon, the mold was set by Achilles, greatest of the Greek heroes, who weighed his options on the battlefield of Troy:

> I carry two sorts of destiny towards the day of my death. If I stay here and fight beside the city of the Trojans, I shall not return home, but my glory shall be everlasting; whereas if I return home to the beloved land of my father, my glory will be gone, but there will be long life left for me.[31]

Famously, he chose the former—and, in doing so, he stepped out of the realm of nature and into the realm of legend, where he still thrives today. For the ancient Greeks, this was the key to immortality: to escape the course of nature with its death and decay, and carve out a space in the symbolic realm of culture, which might survive from generation to generation indefinitely.[32]

Socrates discussed this view with his teacher, the wise-woman Diotima, who said:

> Think of the ambition of men, and you will wonder at the senselessness of their ways, unless you consider how they are stirred by the love of an immortality of fame. They are ready to run all risks greater far than they would have run for their children, and to spend money and undergo any sort of toil and even to die, for the sake of leaving behind them a name which shall be eternal.[33]

But although the pursuit of renown might explain their actions, is this pursuit really any less senseless?

Certainly, the cultural realm can transcend generations—as Achilles proved—and so give an impression of transcending bodily death. In the words of Zygmunt Bauman: death

> is the ultimate condition of cultural creativity as such. It makes permanence into a task, into an urgent task, into a paramount task—a fount and a measure of all tasks—and so it makes culture, that huge and never stopping factory of permanence.[34]

But leaving a cultural legacy is not obviously the same as surviving. For legacy to count as survival, we would have to believe, firstly, that a person such as you or I is essentially a bundle of different elements—beliefs, memories, images, etc.—and, secondly, that a person could survive bodily death if enough of that bundle continues, even if it is dissipated. So, for example, the bundle of thoughts or whatever else that is Achilles was once centered on his physical body; once that died, however, Achilles continued to exist, but spread around between statues, copies of the *Iliad*, and so forth.

A handful of philosophers have made the case for a theory of personal identity that would permit survival as a radically dispersed bundle. Mark Johnston, for example, has suggested that good people can survive death in a way that the selfish cannot, because good folk identify with—and so become—"the onward rush of humanity."[35] Of course, that was not Achilles' approach, he who filled rivers with bloody corpses. Patrick Stokes has suggested that people can in a sense survive through their digital legacy—their social media posts and other online activity.[36] Indeed, there are now commercial services offering just such a digital immortality,[37] and millions of people are now able to use modern technology to leave a legacy vastly beyond what previous generations might have aspired to.

The proponent of the Legacy view might admit that, on the surface, this does not look much like survival as we ordinarily think of it. For Achilles, it does not seem to be much of a life, being spread between various marble statues and old books. Nor do those statues and books, spread across the world, look anything much like a person. However, a Legacy supporter might say: this criticism implicitly assumes that there really is a core of the self, that each of us, prior to bodily death, is more than a collection of disparate properties—but this assumption is mistaken since there is no such coherent core of the self. In which case the post-mortem Achilles is less different to the pre-mortem one than it might at first seem.[38]

Still, many philosophers argue, for example, that there cannot be memories, desires, etc., without there being someone doing the remembering and desiring. Desires cannot float about in bundles or any other way. But if there is a person doing your remembering and desiring, then surely you are that person. In which case you are not a collection of memories, desires, impressions etc., but rather the person with the memories, desires, impressions etc. Perhaps most to the point, the life of posterity does not sound like the kind of life one could meaningfully look forward to enjoying, or indeed experiencing at all. It is not credible to think that there is a being called Achilles who is continuous with the original Greek hero and who is now experiencing the world by virtue of being represented in statues and books, as these are not the kinds of objects that have experiences.

It seems, therefore, that the Legacy view cannot provide a route to surviving death in the ordinary sense that there will be a person after your biological demise who is identical with you now and whose adventures you could rationally look forward to experiencing. Considerations such as these led the unquestionably famous Woody Allen to say, "I don't want to live on in the hearts of my countrymen; I want to live on in my apartment."[39]

But at the same time, some philosophers argue that legacy can still be more than merely a consolation. Samuel Scheffler, for example, has argued that much of what matters to us is bound up with a different sense of 'afterlife'—the life of other ordinary human people who will come after us.[40] We realize this, he suggests, when we consider how despondent we would be if we learned that the world would end 30 days after our own deaths. Given how much of what matters to us is in fact independent of our personal survival, he argues, we should be less concerned about biological death, and more concerned with the 'collective afterlife' of humanity and our contribution to it.

Conclusion

We noted above that there is a good deal of evidence that we are powerfully compelled to believe stories that tell us death is not the end. But wishing does not make it so. We have now seen that all three of the major ways in which people have imagined surviving death have, shall we say, grave problems. The apparent contradiction in the notion of surviving death appears to be real, and lacking resolution. For humans, as for other organisms, death is for each the end of their individual, personal existence. What this means for how we live our lives—how we find solace, how we find meaning, how we appreciate being, rather than fear not-being—that would be the topic for another essay.

Notes

1. Stephen Cave, *Immortality: The Quest to Live Forever and How It Drives Civilization* (New York: Crown, 2012).
2. Eric T. Olson, *What Are We? A Study in Personal Ontology* (New York: Oxford University Press, 2007).
3. Carolus Linnaeus, *Systema Naturae* (Nieuwkoop: B. de Graff, 1964).
4. Wen-Hsiung Li and Matthew A. Saunders, "The Chimpanzee and Us," *Nature* 437 (August 31, 2005): 50.
5. Of the millions of extant species of animal, there might be one or two for which this is not the case, such as the hydra, a simple one-centimeter-long polyp: but certainly it is true of all vertebrates.
6. Anonymous, *The Epic of Gilgamesh*, trans. Andrew George (London: Penguin Books, 1999).
7. Sheldon Solomon, Jeff Greenberg, and Tom Pyszczynski, *The Worm at the Core: On the Role of Death in Life* (New York: Random House, 2015).
8. Gerald J. Gruman, *A History of Ideas about the Prolongation of Life* (New York: Arno Press, 1966).
9. David Boyd Haycock, *Mortal Coil: A Short History of Living Longer* (New Haven, CT: Yale University Press, 2008).
10. The Immortality Institute, *The Scientific Conquest of Death* (Buenos Aires: Libros en Red, 2004).
11. Harold W. Noonan, *Personal Identity*, 2nd ed (London; New York: Routledge, 2003).
12. Eric T. Olson, *The Human Animal* (New York: Oxford University Press, 1997).
13. Cave, *Immortality: The Quest to Live Forever and How It Drives Civilization*, Chapter 3.
14. *Holy Bible: King James Version*, Oxford World's Classics (Oxford: Oxford University Press, 1997), Luke 24: 42-43.
15. "Most Americans Don't Believe in the Resurrection," *Religion News Blog*, 2006, www.religionnewsblog.com/14273/most-americans-dont-believe-in-the-resurrection.
16. Robert C.W. Ettinger, *The Prospect of Immortality* (Palo Alto, CA: Ria University Press, 2005).
17. Mary Shelley, *Frankenstein, or, The Modern Prometheus* (London: Penguin Books, 2002).
18. Caroline W. Bynum, *The Resurrection of the Body in Western Christianity: 200–1336* (New York: Columbia University Press, 1995).
19. Bynum. Note the Cannibal Problem is largely a problem for views (such as the Christian view) that posit all people being resurrected simultaneously. It need not be an obstacle to only one person being resurrected.
20. *Holy Bible: King James Version* 1 Corinthians 15:54.
21. Derek Parfit, *Reasons and Persons* (Oxford: Clarendon Press, 1984).
22. Simon Blackburn, "Has Kant Refuted Parfit?," in *Reading Parfit*, ed. Jonathan Dancy (Oxford: Blackwell, 1997), 180–201.
23. Eric T. Olson, "Life After Death and the Devastation of the Grave," in *The Myth of an Afterlife*, ed. M. Martin and K. Augustine (Lanham, MD: Rowman & Littlefield, 2012).
24. Stewart Goetz and Charles Taliaferro, *A Brief History of the Soul*, Brief Histories of Philosophy (Malden, MA: Wiley-Blackwell, 2011).
25. Corliss Lamont, John Dewey, and Half-Moon Foundation, *The Illusion of Immortality* (New York: Continuum, 1990), Chapter 3; Olson,

What Are We? A Study in Personal Ontology, Chapter 7.

26. Thomas W. Clark, *Encountering Naturalism: A Worldview and Its Uses* (Somerville, MA: Center for Naturalism, 2007).

27. Voltaire, "The Soul, Identity and Immortality," in *Immortality*, ed. Paul Edwards (New York: Prometheus Books, 1997), 141–47.

28. Oliver Sacks, *The Man Who Mistook His Wife for a Hat and Other Clinical Tales* (New York: Summit Books, 1985).

29. Antonio R. Damasio, *Descartes' Error: Emotion, Reason, and the Human Brain* (New York: Putnam, 1994).

30. Stephen Cave, "What Science Really Says About the Soul," *Skeptic* 18, no. 2 (2013): 16–18.

31. Homer, *The Iliad*, trans. Caroline Alexander (London: Vintage, 2015), ll. 9.410–416.

32. Gregory Nagy, "Poetic Visions of Immortality for the Hero," in *Homer's The Iliad*, ed. Harold Bloom (New York: Chelsea House, 1987), 111–34.

33. Plato, *Symposium*, trans. Benjamin Jowett, 2015.

34. Zygmunt Bauman, *Mortality, Immortality and Other Life Strategies* (Cambridge: Polity Press, 1992), 4.

35. Mark Johnston, *Surviving Death* (Princeton, NJ: Princeton University Press, 2010).

36. Patrick Stokes, "Ghosts in the Machine: Do the Dead Live on in Facebook?," *Philosophy & Technology* 25, no. 3 (2012): 363–379, https://doi.org/10.1007/s13347-011-0050-7.

37. Such as http://eterni.me/

38. Johnston, *Surviving Death*.

39. Woody Allen and Linda Sunshine, *The Illustrated Woody Allen Reader* (New York: Knopf, 1993).

40. Samuel Scheffler, *Death and the Afterlife*, ed. Niko Kolodny, The Berkeley Tanner Lectures (Oxford and New York: Oxford University Press, 2013).

Bibliography

Allen, Woody, and Linda Sunshine. *The Illustrated Woody Allen Reader*. New York: Knopf, 1993.

Anonymous. *The Epic of Gilgamesh*. Translated by Andrew George. London: Penguin Books, 1999.

Bauman, Zygmunt. *Mortality, Immortality and Other Life Strategies*. Cambridge: Polity Press, 1992.

Blackburn, Simon. "Has Kant Refuted Parfit?" In *Reading Parfit*, edited by Jonathan Dancy, 180–201. Oxford: Blackwell, 1997.

Bynum, Caroline W. *The Resurrection of the Body in Western Christianity: 200–1336*. New York: Columbia University Press, 1995.

Cave, Stephen. *Immortality: The Quest to Live Forever and How It Drives Civilization*. New York: Crown, 2012.

Cave, Stephen. "What Science Really Says About the Soul." *Skeptic* 18, no. 2 (2013): 16–18.

Clark, Thomas W. *Encountering Naturalism: A Worldview and Its Uses*. Somerville, MA: Center for Naturalism, 2007.

Damasio, Antonio R. *Descartes' Error: Emotion, Reason, and the Human Brain*. New York: Putnam, 1994.

Ettinger, Robert C. W. *The Prospect of Immortality*. Palo Alto, CA: Ria University Press, 2005.

Goetz, Stewart, and Charles Taliaferro. *A Brief History of the Soul. Brief Histories of Philosophy*. Malden, MA: Wiley-Blackwell, 2011.

Gruman, Gerald J. *A History of Ideas about the Prolongation of Life*. New York: Arno Press, 1966.

Haycock, David Boyd. *Mortal Coil: A Short History of Living Longer*. Hartford, CT: Yale University Press, 2008.

Holy Bible: King James Version. Oxford World's Classics. Oxford: Oxford University Press, 1997.

Homer. *The Iliad*. Translated by Caroline Alexander. London: Vintage, 2015.

The Immortality Institute. *The Scientific Conquest of Death*. Buenos Aires: Libros en Red, 2004.

Johnston, Mark. *Surviving Death*. Princeton, NJ: Princeton University Press, 2010.

Lamont, Corliss, John Dewey, and Half-Moon Foundation. *The Illusion of Immortality*. New York: Continuum, 1990.

Li, Wen-Hsiung, and Matthew A. Saunders. "The Chimpanzee and US." *Nature* 437 (August 31, 2005): 50.

Linnaeus, Carolus. *Systema Naturae*. Nieuwkoop: B. de Graff, 1964.

"Most Americans Don't Believe in the Resurrection." *Religion News Blog*, 2006. www.religionnewsblog.com/14273/most-americans-dont-believe-in-the-resurrection.

Nagy, Gregory. "Poetic Visions of Immortality for the Herop." In *Homer's The Iliad*, edited by Harold Bloom, 111–134. Broomall, PA: Chelsea House, 1987.

Noonan, Harold W. *Personal Identity*. 2nd edn. London and New York: Routledge, 2003.

Olson, Eric T. *The Human Animal*. New York: Oxford University Press, 1997.

Olson, Eric T. *What Are We? A Study in Personal Ontology*. New York: Oxford University Press, 2007.

Olson, Eric T. "Life After Death and the Devastation of the Grave." In *The Myth of Afterlife*, edited by M. Martin and K. Augustine. Lanham, MD: Rowman & Littlefield, 2012.

Parfit, Derek. *Reasons and Persons*. Oxford: Clarendon, Press, 1984.

Plato, Benjamin Jowett, Hayden Pelliccia. "Modern Library of the World's Best Books." In *Symposium: The Benjamin Jowett Translation*, Trans.: Benjamin Jowett, Hayden Pelliccia Modern Library, 1996.

Sacks, Oliver. *The Man Who Mistook His Wife for a Hat and Other Clinical Tales*. New York: Summit Books, 1985.

Scheffler, Samuel. "Death and the Afterlife." In *The Berkeley Tanner Lectures*, edited by Niko Kolodny. Oxford and New York: Oxford University Press, 2013.

Shelley, Mary. *Frankenstein, or, The Modern Prometheus*. New York: Penguin Books, 2002.

Solomon, Sheldon, Jeff Greenberg, and Tom Pyszczynski. *The Worm at the Core: On the Role of Death in Life*. New York: Random House, 2015.

Stokes, Patrick. "Ghosts in the Machine: Do the Dead Live on in Facebook?" *Philosophy & Technology* 25, no. 3 (2012): 363–379. https://doi.org/10.1007/s13347-011-0050-7.

Voltaire. "The Soul, Identity and Immortality." In *Immortality*, edited by Paul Edwards, 141–147. New York: Prometheus Books, 1997.

7 The Possibility of an Afterlife

David Hershenov and Rose Hershenov

I. Introduction

To answer the question of whether we can survive our deaths we must first ascertain what kind of entity we are, i.e., get clear about our essence. It is conceivable that if what we are fundamentally is a certain kind of *material* being, then having such a nature makes it impossible for us to exist posthumously. That said, it is still the case that some theories of what we are seem more plausible than others for reasons independent of whether they can promise us an afterlife. We think that is true of views like Aristotle's that construe us as essentially living animals. The view that we are each identical to a living member of the species Homo-sapiens seems more compelling than other materialist accounts that construe us persons as each intimately related to, but distinct from a human animal. Alas, it would be easier for us to provide an account of how we can exist posthumously if we shared Plato and Descartes' views that we are identical to an immaterial soul that just ceases to be related to the body at death. Their position that we are each a soul which is neither identical to nor a part of an animal body renders it less mysterious how we could persist after our bodies are destroyed. The worry that some philosophers have about our view is that given our animal bodies are destroyed at death, or soon afterwards, then even God can't restore us to life. Nevertheless, we believe a metaphysically plausible case can be made for a view of resurrection in which the deceased human animal is restored to life.

We will restrict our inquiry to Western metaphysics, where the historically leading answers to the question "What am I?" differ over (i) whether we persons are identical to human animals and (ii) whether we are ensouled or consist completely of matter. The best-known account, John Locke's, maintains that we are each distinct from our animal but that this is compatible with our person either having an immaterial soul or being fully material. Some modern Lockean-inspired accounts of personhood envision us replacing our frail, dying, organic bodies with healthier bodies, perhaps even longer-lasting bionic ones. Such views of an afterlife don't have their fate tied to God's existence, so they will appeal to atheists and agnostics. Proponents of soul theories posit a God who created the soul or sustains it in the afterlife, thus inheriting whatever weaknesses or strengths that are to be found in theistic views.

II. Souls and Divinely Sustained Afterlives

There are different versions of soul theories. The best-known, call it "pure dualism," is that you are identical to your soul. You stand in an intimate relation to your body, but your body is not a part of you. Therefore, you are not extended in space. An alternative version, "compound dualism," is that you are a compound of two substances, a soul and a body.[1] You are not your soul. You literally possess bodily organs as parts and thus have a mass and physical location.

There are various reasons to accept some sort of soul theory. One has to do with the difficulty that rival materialist accounts have in explaining how our brains produce thought. Philosophers from Leibniz to McGinn have trouble "conceiving of how technicolor phenomenology can arise from soggy grey matter."[2] Strawson claims that making sense of how thought emerges from non-thinking atoms is like trying to explain how the abstract arises from the concrete or the extended from the unextended.[3] Moreover, if beliefs and desires are stored in the brain, that would appear to imply they had volume and mass. That seems like a category mistake akin to claiming that abstract numbers are colored. How can the thought that "Proust is more subtle than L'Amour" be neurologically realized or indicated by neurons firing?[4] Materialist accounts also have trouble explaining the unity of our experience. The sights, sounds, and smells presented to you at dinner tonight will be experienced as a unity. But if different parts of the brain are responsible for different aspect of the entire experience, how could such a complex entity produce a *unified* experience? The simple (partless) composition of the soul seems better able to account for the unity of experience.[5]

The simplicity of the soul is also a reason for thinking **that** persons survive death. Complex entities can be destroyed, i.e., disintegrate into their parts. But a soul has no parts into which it can be decomposed. So the simple soul seems a good candidate for survival. It may be that the soul doesn't literally die as it is not a living entity instantiating life processes such as metabolism and homeostasis. So death of the ensouled needs to be reconstrued as the soul ceasing to stand in a certain relationship to a living body when that body dies, i.e., ceasing irreversibly to instantiate life processes.

It is easier to conceive of an afterlife of the person construed according to the tenets of pure dualism than compound dualism, despite the latter satisfying our sense of being extended and embodied. Compound dualists deny the pure dualist's claim that you are your soul, instead insisting that the soul is merely one of your parts, albeit the essential part, while your body is but a contingent part, which means that your existence doesn't require that you always have a body. So, the compound dualist has it that at death

you would leave your body behind and come to be composed of a single immaterial part, your soul. One problem plaguing the compound dualist's conception of the afterlife is that it is hard to understand how something can have just a single part. If it is not a conceptual truth, it is certainly typically the case that composition involves two or more parts. If x is a proper part of y then it seems that y must have another part that doesn't overlap x. But according to compound dualism, the relationship between you and your soul in the afterlife would involve you becoming a purely immaterial entity intimately involved with but distinct from your soul. Your immaterial soul is your only part. Thus, you would be an immaterial being consisting of a distinct immaterial entity and no other parts. Eric Olson complains that the view "suffers from a sort of ontological double vision" that makes him "lose [his] grip on what it is for one thing to be part of another."[6] Your posthumous survival is much easier to understand if the passing into the afterlife just involved you, a soul, ceasing to be in a certain causal relationship with what was your body, whose parts were never your parts.

We stressed that it is difficult to conceive of how material beings can think. However, it is not easy comprehending how an immaterial (partless) entity produces complex thoughts or any thoughts. Defenders of the soul respond that there is nothing to explain because the soul is simple, partless.[7] Its nature is to think just as the simple (partless) electron's nature is to have a negative charge. When an entity is simple it has no parts that would enter into an explanation of how it does what it does.

But mysteries still abound even on the pure dualist account. Our paradigm of causation is something along the line of one billiard ball colliding with and moving another; so we assume causes and effects require contact between spatially adjacent entities. Therefore, it is difficult to grasp how a soul and body can causally interact when they are not both in space. Moreover, how does your soul think without the support of the brain? Thought certainly seems *dependent* upon the brain even if it is the soul and not the brain that is the thinking person, i.e., the subject of thought. Injuring the brain can bring about a state of unconsciousness, not a person still remaining conscious who is just unable to use a damaged brain to move her body or receive sensations. Most soul theorists today believe the soul is dependent upon the brain, roughly akin to the lightbulb and the socket.[8] That explains why damage to the brain impairs our thought despite the soul being the subject of thought. However, even if the soul can think when its ties to the brain are compromised, how does the detached soul communicate with other souls? Would you not be a lonely soul?[9] So the problem isn't just the traditional interactionist puzzle of how the immaterial and nonextended soul causally interacts with the extended and material brain and body, but how does one soul in the afterlife communicate with other souls. It would seem that we must rely upon God to causally connect you to other souls, including Himself.[10] Therefore, the possibility of an afterlife seems no more plausible than the existence of God.

III. Lockean Persons and the Afterlife

The prospect of our soul surviving without our idiosyncratic psychology of memories, desires, and beliefs may seem hardly any more attractive than existing posthumously as a corpse. Imagine that we lose our memories due to dementia and then death occurs. Our posthumous soul may be capable of thought, but any thoughts then would have little to do with our ante-mortem thoughts, none of which it could recollect. A good number of people would not think that they survive if all their memories and desires were lost; and many more would not care for such a future, even if it was theirs, as it would involve them acquiring completely new memories, desires, intentions, and beliefs. Furthermore, the traditional religious conception of an afterlife is tied to the idea of a final judgment, rewards for the virtuous and punishment for the evil. If the person in the afterlife had no psychological connections to their ante-mortem self, rewards and punishments would seem unjust.

Locke famously claimed that "person" is a forensic notion, which means a person is someone who can be held morally responsible for what she does. Persons are entities that are accountable for their past actions and thus must be self-conscious. They have to remember the past to be identical to the person who lived at that time and to be responsible for his earlier deeds. So Locke conjectured that persons extend as far back in time as their psychology extends. *If one can't remember any events of a certain time then one was not a person present at that time.*

Locke claimed that if Socrates when awake couldn't remember his dreams than that wouldn't be him dreaming but someone else he called "Sleeping Socrates."[11]

Unlike Plato and Descartes, Locke distinguished persons from souls. The same thinking soul could support different persons, so you and your psychology could switch souls. A different soul could come to support your consciousness which consists of your beliefs, memories, desires, etc. Locke trusted that God would ensure that your person would be paired with your soul in the afterlife, so a different soul would not be punished for what you did. Leibniz believed that God was also needed to posthumously restore people's lost mental states "so consequently they will always know what they are, otherwise, they not be susceptible of reward or punishment."[12]

IV. Transhumanist Persons and an Atheistic Afterlife

Locke believed it likely that the person's thought was sustained by an immaterial thinking soul, but he left it open whether there was a material substance involved with the production of the person's mental life. Most modern Neo-Lockeans believe persons are material beings i.e., composed only of material parts. They also differ from Locke in that they don't distinguish the person from an underlying thinking substance, which thus avoids the problematic consequence of Locke positing there were two thinkers (the soul and the person) when it seems like there is just one. The soul/person relationship is quite obscure. However, the modern-day neo-Lockean materialist does distinguish persons from their animal. They insist that if you switch your cerebrum with someone else's, then you would have switched bodies, leaving your original animal behind. What they take to be crucial for your persistence and location is that your psychology continue and they assume that the cerebrum is responsible for that.

Body switching gives rise to the possibility that an afterlife would not require God, just a replacement for your dead body. Transhumanists hope for a Godless afterlife.[13] It may be that our psychology can be sustained by an inorganic or a better organic body when our body dies. The former might involve living brain cells replaced with more durable metallic machinery while the latter consists of the thought-producing part of our brain being removed from our skull and transplanted into a healthier body. The former is, in principle, quite plausible. If we are naturally undergoing replacement of our brain's organic matter over time, but still persist because our psychology is *functionally* unchanged by the turnover in matter, why couldn't we undergo replacements of our organic matter with more durable inorganic parts, perhaps bionic parts made of silicon, that leave our psychology (functionally) unchanged? This new body would, even if it not immortal, last far longer than our organic body.

Our transplantation into a new organic body or our body being transformed into an inorganic one would involve us truly dying in the process and, consequently, we would literally survive our deaths and have posthumous experiences. We would strictly die in the two scenarios because we cease to instantiate life processes that are necessary for the bodily integration characteristic of life. So even if we are not identical to a living body, if we persons have a body that is alive with bodily parts involved in metabolism and homeostasis, then we can die when we cease to possess a living body.

That would occur when we are reduced to the size of our cerebrum (an organ, not an organism) or have our organic parts replaced with inorganic ones. An organ is not engaged in the metabolic self-sustaining activities of an organism, but is dependent upon the life processes of the organism to retain its structures and powers. It is even more obvious that a bionic body without cellular parts would not be engaged in the biological processes constitutive of life. In both cases we no longer instantiate (bodily) life processes. When living entities lose the capacity to engage in metabolic and homeostatic activities they die. But we would not cease to exist if our thought continues to be realized in an inorganic brain or a cerebrum moving between bodies. So even if we are not identical to an organism, having shared a living body with an organism means that we can die when we cease to have parts involved in those life processes which made that body alive.

Since persons are neither souls nor bodies on the Lockean account, this leads to puzzles about the relationship of the human person to their human animal bodies. Persons can't be the same as their bodies for they can leave them behind when transplanted or they can survive the destruction of their organic body and its replacement with a new bionic body. But before the person is transplanted or the organic body replaced, she was the same size and in the same place as the organism. Living persons are atom for atom the same as their animal. They share an organic brain If the person can use that brain to think, the co-located animal should also be able to use the same brain to produce thought. So the conundrum is: why can't the animal think if the person can think? This leads to two thinkers where we would like there to be just one. Metaphysical puzzles abound. We suspect they are sufficient to render the possibility of a Godless afterlife as conceived by Lockean-inspired transhumanists to be untenable. First, why are two physically indistinguishable beings (persons and animals) members of different kinds? What could make one a person that is essentially a psychological being and not a living being, while the other, physically indistinguishable entity is essentially a living animal that has its psychological traits just contingently? In other words, why can animals survive the loss of their mental life with the onset of a persistent vegetative state but persons cannot when they are atom for atom the same? A second puzzle is how would the person know whether she is the person rather than the animal?[14] Any evidence that she has to think she is the person, the animal would have as well. So she has no reason to think that she is not the animal who is mistaken in believing herself to be a person. Finally, the co-located animal and person may not even have the same interests and therefore both couldn't autonomously agree to the replacement of their body. It would be a premature death for the animal to obtain an inorganic body but would be a way for the person to survive much longer. These problems go away if the human person is identical to the human animal rather than distinct and sharing parts.

V. Material Animals and the Afterlife

A rival of Lockean approaches to personal identity is animalism, which identifies human persons and human animals. They are not two distinct but overlapping thinking entities, but one and the same entity referred to with different terms. This is akin to "Michael Jordan" and "Air Jordan" picking out the same human being. Human persons are animals with certain sophisticated psychological abilities such as self-consciousness or rationality. That animal existed before it acquired personhood and could exist after it is lost and lapses into an irreversible coma. No new entity came into existence with the onset of any kind of mental life; the animal just became a thinking person. Being a person is like being a student. You may be identical to a student, but you are not essentially a student. You can cease to be a student without going out of existence. Likewise **a human animal** can cease to be a person without going out of existence. Animals go out of existence when they die or, alternatively, when their corpse undergoes too much decomposition.

If one is essentially an animal, then one is essentially a body. If one is essentially a *living* animal, then one exists only when one is alive. So how could one survive death? We have said the animal goes out of existence at death – or sometime afterwards with too much decomposition. To avoid having to determine which is our end, imagine that you die in an explosion that leaves not a corpse but scattered remains.

You might think that God could just put you back together. Peter van Inwagen disagrees.[15] What God would do by reassembling your parts is make a duplicate of you who might mistakenly think he is you. To help see why, imagine that a child's sandcastle is destroyed by an ocean wave and her parents put it back together. Would that be the original sandcastle? It seems not to be the original because the parts (grains of sand) are not where they are because the child put them there but because the parents did. So, by analogy, it may be that even God can't reassemble the same organism that dies and decays by configuring the very same atomic parts in the manner that they were before death, but would instead have brought into existence a duplicate. The parts are not where they are because of earlier life processes. They fail to be "immanently caused," that is, the later parts of the reassembled human animal body are not where they due to the causal powers of their body's previous biological states. They are where they are because of God's intentions and interventions. This renders the person a duplicate of the deceased, just as the reassembled sand castle is a duplicate and not the original restored to existence.

van Inwagen is a materialist about human beings, but a Christian. His solution to how the human animal gets to Heaven (or Hell) involves God whisking away and preserving the freshly dead corpse and replacing it with a duplicate. So we don't bury Grandma's body, only have the illusion of doing so.[16] This metaphysical solution has led God to be described as a "body snatcher"[17] and the suggestion that he is engaged in deception, a trait not typically associated with a morally perfect divine being.[18]

Unlike others, we aren't *morally* troubled by van Inwagen's solution, just skeptical of the metaphysics. Since deception involves intentionally producing a false belief in another, we don't think God's "body snatching" meets that standard. If van Inwagen is correct, then Grandma's body can't be reassembled and Grandma so restored to life, but she still exists later in Heaven or Hell. So Grandma can't be in the grave. It is our metaphysical ignorance, not God's deception, that prevents us from realizing that it can't be Grandma or her corpse that we bury. In fact, it seems morally worse to whisk away Grandma's fresh corpse without a replacement. We would never be sure that Grandma had died rather than is alive and missing. A faux corpse enables us to begin the grieving process.

Our metaphysical worry is that if death involves the loss of the life processes that produce the biological integration constitutive of life, then even a fresh corpse may have to be reassembled (somewhat) for its parts to instantiate life. But reassembly involves a duplicate, not the original person. So our worry is that the body snatching either occurs too early or too late. If life processes have stopped but can be restarted, the person God has taken away is not dead. But resurrection is of the dead, according to the Nicene Creed. If the person is dead, then the bodily integration constitutive of life has been lost and resurrection would really be the creation of a living duplicate, not the restoration of life.

Given the problems plaguing van Inwagen's account, one might want to explore the reassembly version. There are plenty of artifacts designed for disassembly and reassembly—tools, guns, musical instruments, etc. Maybe organisms are more like them than our sandcastle. Moreover, consider that it doesn't seem important where our matter was before it first became arranged as zygote. It could have been scattered in an egg and a sperm or just contained in test tube in a lab. As long as that matter came together in the zygotic form, that would be our origins. Perhaps the same is true for the resurrection. As long as the matter at our restoration was roughly the same and arranged similarly to the matter right before our death, then that would be us even in the absence of immanent causation.[19]

However, the problem that would remain involves the possibility that the parts of the buried end up back in the food chain and someone in the future is composed at their death of the same parts in the same configuration as someone who died much earlier. Who would then be resurrected by reassembly of those parts? Would the last to die with the parts be the first reassembled and when his parts are metabolically removed, the other person is resurrected? But what would account for this time indexing? Even if God could prevent the parts of the deceased from composing a duplicate later, the mere possibility of this suggests that there is something missing the reassembly conception of personal identity.

VI. Hylomorphic Animals and the Afterlife

van Inwagen's soulless animalism is not the only version of animalism. He favors a type of animalism that has been called "Latter Day Animalism" because Aristotle and Aquinas were the "Original Animalists."[20] The Original Animalists believed we were essentially animals, but differ from the latter-day animalist in that the former thought we were essentially rational. So we have essentially both psychological (rationality) and animal (living) properties. That makes the account a hybrid view.

The original animalists also assumed a soul or form was responsible for configuring our matter in such a way that the result was a rational animal. This hylomorphic soul is very different from the souls conceived of by Plato and Descartes, who are best interpreted as pure dualists. They understood the soul to be the person. The person is literally their mind, an immaterial thinking substance that could exist apart from the body. The person or soul is causally related to a distinct substance, the body. The body is not literally a part of the person. Hylomorphism, on the contrary, doesn't consider us to be our soul any more than it considers the statue to be identical to its shape. The statue is a result of clay (matter) being given a certain shape (form). Likewise, the human being is the result of its body (matter) being organized by its soul (form). The hylomorphic soul is the crucial component of us that is responsible for configuring the matter that results in us being both an animal and a rational one. So, on this view, you have a soul and a mind but they are distinct from each other and from you.

Unlike Cartesian and other soul theories, hylomorphism can easily explain the need for resurrection as you are not your soul but the result of the soul configuring matter. So the view fits well with Christian doctrine where Cartesian souls seem to not provide a rationale for the resurrection. Another attractive aspect of the hylomorphic position is that you did not require the same matter, only the same soul. Any matter configured by your soul would result in your body coming back to life. The soul configured matter ante-mortem and will do so again post-mortem. There is no need for the matter to be the same. So the reassembly problems are avoided as the reassembled will be individuated by having the same ante-mortem and post-mortem soul rather than the same matter.

One hylomorphic version of the afterlife shares some of the problems plaguing the conception of the afterlife associated with compound dualism. This strand of hylomorphism, known as "Survivalism," maintains that you exist after death and prior to the resurrection with your soul as your only part. It is again a sort of ontological double vision to think of yourself as an immaterial being with only a single part that is also immaterial. It is easier to imagine that you're identical to a soul in the sense Descartes and Plato had in mind. It is also a strange conception of an animal that can exist bodiless between death and resurrection. Defenders of the view think that the detached soul retains the capacity to configure matter into a living body and that suffices for being an animal. But a bodiless animal is a very queer animal.

An alternative view, one which we think can be more rightly ascribed to Aquinas, is that it is your soul but not you that exists between death and resurrection. This view is called "Corruptionism" because the human being's body or animal has corrupted and thus the human being doesn't exist in the interim period between death and resurrection. This account has a glaring moral problem and some less obvious metaphysical problems than the survivalist account. The moral problem is that the soul is being punished in Hell or is being painfully reformed in Purgatory for what the human being did prior to death. The agent then was the human being, not the soul. So it seems unfair. Even if the moral objections to such an afterlife can be explained away, there remain metaphysical puzzles. If the detached soul can think and act posthumously, why couldn't it do so prior to death? Why wasn't it an additional thinker, embodied in the human being?

We would prefer a hylomorphism that construes the human being as embodied in the period between death and resurrection.[21] The puzzle then is to explain why there is a need for resurrection if the dead are already embodied in Purgatory. Perhaps Dante's fanciful descriptions could be of help. The bodily form we need for the purging of Purgatory is different from the mode of body we need when ready to be eternally in God's presence. That would make the subject posthumously punished the same as the one who did the actions in question. It would also prevent a soul from being an additional thinker, rather than something whose contribution enables the human being to think but is not itself a thinker.

VII. Conclusion

We have taken a dim view of a secular afterlife in the Lockean tradition. New organic or inorganic bodies render the relationship between the human being and animal very puzzling and problematic. The secular may be better off hoping scientists enable them to continue to avoid death rather than return from it. Pure dualism doesn't have that problem, but it isn't easy to conceive of ourselves as not being where our animal bodies are located. However, it doesn't seem that we can get to an afterlife without God's assistance. Even if we are animals and future scientists trace and reassemble our matter, Star-Trek style, given the puzzles of reassembly, there is the worry that the result would be a duplicate rather than our animal's resurrection. However, God may be able to guarantee that our animal is resurrected. So it seems that our hopes in an afterlife will depend upon the existence of a God that will enable us animals, ensouled or not, to live again.

Notes

1. We borrow these labels from Eric Olson, "A Compound of Two Substances" in *Soul, Body and Survival*, ed. Kevin Corcoran (Ithaca: Cornell University Press, 2001), 73–88.
2. Colin McGinn, "Can We Solve the Mind--Body Problem?," *Mind* 98, no. 391 (July 1989): 249.
3. Galen Strawson, "Realistic Monism: Why Physicalism Entails Panpsychism" in *Consciousness and Its Place in Nature: Does Physicalism Entail*, ed. Anthony Freeman (Exeter: Imprint Academic, 2006), 3–31.
4. Alvin Plantinga, "Materialism and Christian Belief" in *Persons: Human and Divine*, ed. Peter van Inwagen and Dean Zimmerman (Oxford: Clarendon Press, 2007), 140.
5. William Hasker, "Persons and the Unity of Consciousness" in *The Waning of Materialism*, ed. Robert Koons and George Bealer (Oxford: Oxford University Press, 2010), 175–190.
6. Olson, "Compound of Two Substances," 87.
7. Alvin Plantinga, "Against Materialism," *Faith and Philosophy* 23, no. 1 (2006): 3–32.
8. Richard Swinburne, *The Evolution of the Soul* (Oxford: Oxford University Press, 1986), 310–311.
9. Jaegwon Kim, "Lonely Souls" in *Soul, Body and Survival*, ed. Kevin Corcoran (Ithaca: Cornell University Press, 2001), 30–43.
10. Soul theorists typically rely upon God for the soul's creation. And even the emergent dualists who claim that the soul emerges when there is sufficient neurological complexity, still rely upon God's miraculous intervention to support the soul in the Afterlife after the brain is destroyed.

11. John Locke, *An Essay on Human Understanding*, ed. Peter Nidditch (Oxford: Oxford University Press, 1975), 342. Contemporary Neo-Lockeans modify Locke's position and allow that continuities of other mental states like beliefs and desires can avoid the embarrassing gaps in our existence that would seem to follow from Locke's account.
12. Gottfried Leibniz, *Discourses on Metaphysics* (Manchester: Manchester University Press, 1953), 61–62.
13. Nick Bostrom, "A History of Transhumanist Thought," *Journal of Evolution and Technology* 14, no. 1 (April 2005): 1–25.
14. Eric Olson, *The Human Animal: Personal Identity without Psychology* (Oxford: Oxford University Press, 1997).
15. Peter Van Inwagen, "The Possibility of Resurrection," *International Journal of Philosophy of Religion* 9, no. 2 (1978): 121.
16. Van Inwagen added a postscript twenty years after publishing his "Possibility of Resurrection" where he expressed regrets about writing earlier that this was only way God could accomplish material resurrection. But he still insists that his aim was to provide a story that readers could recognize as metaphysically possible, even if wasn't right about the specific mechanism of resurrection. However, we want to deny the possibility of any such mechanism given that death is analyzed as involving the loss of integration and van Inwagen's own claim that identity preserving integration can't be restored once it is lost.
17. Dean Zimmerman, "Materialism and Survival" in *Philosophy of Religion: The Big Questions*, ed. E. Stump and M. Murray (Oxford: Blackwell, 1999), 379–386.
18. William Hasker, "Materialism and the Resurrection: Are the Prospects Improving?," *European Journal for Philosophy of Religion* 3, no. 1 (2011): 85.
19. God would then have to save our life from whatever internal conditions would soon kill our resurrected body.
20. Patrick Toner, "Hylemorphism, Remnant Persons, and Personhood," *Canadian Journal of Philosophy* 44, no. 1 (2014): 76–96.
21. Rose Hershenov and David Hershenov, "Purgatory" in *Handbook of the Afterlife*, ed. Benjamin Matheson and Yujin Nagasawa (London: Palgrave Macmillan, 2017), 215–233.

Part III Can Death Be Good or Bad for Us? If So, When Is It Good or Bad for Us?

Ozymandias

I met a traveller from an antique land,
Who said—"Two vast and trunkless legs
of stone
Stand in the desert… Near them, on the
sand,
Half sunk a shattered visage lies, whose
frown,
And wrinkled lip, and sneer of cold
command,
Tell that its sculptor well those passions
read
Which yet survive, stamped on these life-
less things,
The hand that mocked them, and the
heart that fed;
And on the pedestal, these words appear:
My name is Ozymandias, King of Kings;
Look on my Works, ye Mighty, and
despair!
Nothing beside remains. Round the
decay
Of that colossal Wreck, boundless and
bare
The lone and level sands stretch far away."
—**Percy Bysshe Shelley**

Introduction to Part III

Suppose that you permanently cease to exist once you die. Could such a death be bad for you? You might think the answer to this question is an obvious "Yes!," as people fear such deaths and go to great lengths to prolong the day they go out of existence. Perhaps nothing seems more obvious than that such a death could be bad. But the answer to this question is not as straightforward as you may think. In

this chapter, you will get to read an excerpt from the most important ancient philosopher who argued death cannot be bad for us, as well as three contemporary philosophers' take on the question.

The first chapter is an excerpt from a letter that the ancient Greek philosopher Epicurus (341–270 B.C.E.) wrote to Menoeceus. Epicurus believed that death could not be bad for us and tries to convince Menoeceus of this, writing the following:

> Become accustomed to the belief that death is nothing to us. For all good and evil consists in sensation, but death is deprivation of sensation. So death, the most terrifying of ills, is nothing to us, since as long as we exist death is not with us; but when death comes, then we do not exist.

This wording is a bit cryptic and admits of multiple interpretations. In his chapter, Jens Johansson will consider two such interpretations and assess the argumentative merits of each interpretation. On one reading, Epicurus is making the Timing Argument. That is, he is arguing that every event that is bad for us is bad for us at some time, and that there is no time that death is bad for us (since we don't exist when we're dead, and are not dead when we exist). Consequently, death cannot be bad for us. On a second novel interpretation, Epicurus is making the Future Well-Being Argument. That is, he is arguing that every event that is bad for a person is detrimental to one's well-being after the event has occurred, but death is not detrimental to one's well-being after it has occurred, so death cannot be bad for the person who dies. Johansson argues that the second interpretation has some advantages over the first, but both arguments are ultimately unsound.

In the next chapter James Stacey Taylor offers a contemporary defense of Epicurus and aims to formulate a sound version of his Timing Argument. Taylor considers two versions of Epicurus' Timing Argument, arguing that at least one of these versions is sound. Taylor first considers the "Existent Variant" of the argument according to which events (or states of affairs) can harm a person only if they occur prior to, or during, the time a person exists. In other words, anything that is bad for you must have happened before you existed or while you existed. Taylor then considers a "Hedonic Variant" of the argument, which presupposes that only events (or states of affairs) that affect a person's experiences can have any effect on their well-being. In other words, only something that affects your experiences can affect how well or poorly your life is going for you. Since the "Existent Variant" of the argument assumes the truth of the "Hedonic Variant," Taylor defends the latter version. He argues death cannot affect our experiences in the relevant way, and so it cannot be bad for us. Since we're all going to die, Taylor believes this is good news, and we should welcome it.

In the next chapter, Neil Feit tackles Epicurus' aforementioned Timing Argument. Deprivationists, and anyone who accepts that death can be bad for the person who dies, has to answer the question "When is death bad for the person who dies?" After expounding on the relevant notion of harm, and reviewing the Timing Argument, Feit defends subsequentism. More precisely, he argues that death is bad for the person who dies after they're dead during the times at which, had they not died when they did, they would have been alive and living a good life. He ends the chapter by arguing against alternative responses to the Timing Argument.

In the final chapter of the section, Kirsten Egerstrom focuses on the most popular view that rivals Epicureanism, viz. deprivationism. According to the deprivationist, your death is bad for you to the extent that, and because, it prevents you from living additional life that is, on the whole, good. Egerstrom discusses a surprising implication of deprivationism identified by Jeff McMahan. Deprivationism entails that you can change how bad a person's death was for them after they died by changing what kind of life they would have had were they still alive. To illustrate, Egerstrom asks you to suppose your friend loved reading books from the Jack Reacher series before she died. Once she is dead, let's suppose, you convince the author (James Dover Grant) to stop writing the series, so your deceased friend isn't missing out on any new Jack Reacher novels. McMahan has argued that such attempts to make a person's death less bad are "self-defeating." In contrast, Egerstrom argues that this is a perfectly reasonable thing to do if you care about your deceased friend's well-being and so long as you can do so without frustrating the interests of living people.

If you're interested in reading more about whether death can be bad for us, check out the following:

1. Thomas Nagel's "Death" (1970) *Noûs* 4 (1): 73–80.
2. F. M. Kamm's "The Badness of Death and What to Do about It (if Anything)" in *Saving People from the Harm of Death* (2019) edited by Espen Gamlun and Carl Tollef Solberg, New York: Oxford University Press.
3. Ben Bradley's book *Well-Being and Death* (2009) New York: Oxford Uni-versity Press.
4. David Hershenov's "A More Palatable Epicureanism" (2007) *American Philosophical Quarterly* 44 (2): 171–180.

8 Letter to Menoeceus

Epicurus

Letter to Menoeceus by Epicurus, trans. Robert Drew Hicks

Greeting.

Let no one be slow to seek wisdom when he is young nor weary in the search thereof when he is grown old. For no age is too early or too late for the health of the soul. And to say that the season for studying philosophy has not yet come, or that it is past and gone, is like saying that the season for happiness is not yet or that it is now no more. Therefore, both old and young ought to seek wisdom, the former in order that, as age comes over him, he may be young in good things because of the grace of what has been, and the latter in order that, while he is young, he may at the same time be old, because he has no fear of the things which are to come. So we must exercise ourselves in the things which bring happiness, since, if that be present, we have everything, and, if that be absent, all our actions are directed toward attaining it.

Those things which without ceasing I have declared to you, those do, and exercise yourself in those, holding them to be the elements of right life. First believe that God is a living being immortal and happy, according to the notion of a god indicated by the common sense of humankind; and so of him anything that is at agrees not with about him whatever may uphold both his happiness and his immortality. For truly there are gods, and knowledge of them is evident; but they are not such as the multitude believe, seeing that people do not steadfastly maintain the notions they form respecting them. Not the person who denies the gods worshipped by the multitude, but he who affirms of the gods what the multitude believes about them is truly impious. For the utterances of the multitude about the gods are not true preconceptions but false assumptions; hence it is that the greatest evils happen to the wicked and the greatest blessings happen to the good from the hand of the gods, seeing that they are always favorable to their own good qualities and take pleasure in people like to themselves, but reject as alien whatever is not of their kind.

Accustom yourself to believe that death is nothing to us, for good and evil imply awareness, and death is the privation of all awareness; therefore a right understanding that death is nothing to us makes the mortality of life enjoyable, not by adding to life an unlimited time, but by taking away the yearning after immortality. For life has no terror; for those who thoroughly apprehend that there are no terrors for them in ceasing to live. Foolish, therefore, is the person who says that he fears death, not because it will pain when it comes, but because it pains in the prospect. Whatever causes no annoyance when it is present, causes only a groundless pain in the expectation. Death, therefore, the most awful of evils, is nothing to us, seeing that, when we are, death is not come, and, when death is come, we are not. It is nothing, then, either to the living or to the dead, for with the living it is not and the dead exist no longer. But in the world, at one time people shun death as the greatest of all evils, and at another time choose it as a respite from the evils in life. The wise person does not deprecate life nor does he fear the cessation of life. The thought of life is no offense to him, nor is the cessation of life regarded as an evil. And even as people choose of food not merely and simply the larger portion, but the more pleasant, so the wise seek to enjoy the time which is most pleasant and not merely that which is longest. And he who admonishes the young to live well and the old to make a good end speaks foolishly, not merely because of the desirability of life, but because the same exercise at once teaches to live well and to die well. Much worse is he who says that it were good not to be born, but when once one is born to pass with all speed through the gates of Hades. For if he truly believes this, why does he not depart from life? It were easy for him to do so, if once he were firmly convinced. If he speaks only in mockery, his words are foolishness, for those who hear believe him not.

We must remember that the future is neither wholly ours nor wholly not ours, so that neither must we count upon it as quite certain to come nor despair of it as quite certain not to come.

We must also reflect that of desires some are natural, others are groundless; and that of the natural some are necessary as well as natural, and some natural only. And of the necessary desires some are necessary if we are to be happy, some if the body is to be rid of uneasiness, some if we are even to live. He who has a clear and certain understanding of these things will direct every preference and aversion toward securing health of body and tranquillity of mind, seeing that this is the sum and end of a happy life. For the end of all our actions is to be free from pain and fear, and, when once we have attained all this, the tempest of the soul is laid; seeing that the living creature has no need to go in search of something that is lacking, nor to look anything else by which the good of the soul and of the body will be fulfilled. When we are pained pleasure, then, and then only, do we feel the need of pleasure. For this reason we call pleasure the alpha and omega of a happy life. Pleasure is our first and kindred good. It is the starting-point of every choice and of every aversion, and to it we come back, inasmuch as we make feeling the rule by which to judge of every good thing. And since pleasure is our first and native good, for that reason we

do not choose every pleasure whatever, but often pass over many pleasures when a greater annoyance ensues from them. And often we consider pains superior to pleasures when submission to the pains for a long time brings us as a consequence a greater pleasure. While therefore all pleasure because it is naturally akin to us is good, not all pleasure is worthy of choice, just as all pain is an evil and yet not all pain is to be shunned. It is, however, by measuring one against another, and by looking at the conveniences and inconveniences, that all these matters must be judged. Sometimes we treat the good as an evil, and the evil, on the contrary, as a good. Again, we regard independence of outward things as a great good, not so as in all cases to use little, but so as to be contented with little if we have not much, being honestly persuaded that they have the sweetest enjoyment of luxury who stand least in need of it, and that whatever is natural is easily procured and only the vain and worthless hard to win. Plain fare gives as much pleasure as a costly diet, when one the pain of want has been removed, while bread and water confer the highest possible pleasure when they are brought to hungry lips. To habituate one's self, therefore, to simple and inexpensive diet supplies all that is needful for health, and enables a person to meet the necessary requirements of life without shrinking and it places us in a better condition when we approach at intervals a costly fare and renders us fearless of fortune.

When we say, then, that pleasure is the end and aim, we do not mean the pleasures of the prodigal or the pleasures of sensuality, as we are understood to do by some through ignorance, prejudice, or willful misrepresentation. By pleasure we mean the absence of pain in the body and of trouble in the soul. It is not an unbroken succession of drinking-bouts and of merrymaking, not sexual love, not the enjoyment of the fish and other delicacies of a luxurious table, which produce a pleasant life; it is sober reasoning, searching out the grounds of every choice and avoidance, and banishing those beliefs through which the greatest disturbances take possession of the soul. Of all this the end is prudence. For this reason prudence is a more precious thing even than the other virtues, for a life of pleasure which is not also a life of prudence, honor, and justice; nor lead a life of prudence, honor, and justice, which is not also a life of pleasure. For the virtues have grown into one with a pleasant life, and a pleasant life is inseparable from them.

Who, then, is superior in your judgment to such a person? He holds a holy belief concerning the gods, and is altogether free from the fear of death. He has diligently considered the end fixed by nature, and understands how easily the limit of good things can be reached and attained, and how either the duration or the intensity of evils is but slight. Destiny which some introduce as sovereign over all things, he laughs to scorn, affirming rather that some things happen of necessity, others by chance, others through our own agency. For he sees that necessity destroys responsibility and that chance or fortune is inconstant; whereas our own actions are free, and it is to them that praise and blame naturally attach. It were better, indeed, to accept the legends of the gods than to bow beneath destiny which the natural philosophers have imposed. The one holds out some faint hope that we may escape if we honor the gods, while the necessity of the naturalists is deaf to all entreaties. Nor does he hold chance to be a god, as the world in general does, for in the acts of a god there is no disorder; nor to be a cause, though an uncertain one, for he believes that no good or evil is dispensed by chance to people so as to make life happy, though it supplies the starting-point of great good and great evil. He believes that the misfortune of the wise is better than the prosperity of the fool. It is better, in short, that what is well judged in action should not owe its successful issue to the aid of chance.

Exercise yourself in these and kindred precepts day and night, both by yourself and with him who is like to you; then never, either in waking or in dream, will you be disturbed, but will live as a god among people. For people lose all appearance of mortality by living in the midst of immortal blessings.

9 Two Arguments for Epicureanism

Jens Johansson

I. Introduction

In this chapter, I am not going to discuss what Epicurus might have meant by the following famous words:

> Become accustomed to the belief that death is nothing to us. For all good and evil consists in sensation, but death is deprivation of sensation. So death, the most terrifying of ills, is nothing to us, since as long as we exist death is not with us; but when death comes, then we do not exist.
>
> (Epicurus 1940: 31)

Instead, I shall discuss two arguments that are at least suggested or inspired by this passage, whether or not they are what Epicurus actually had in mind. Proponents of either argument *could* use his words to express the basic idea behind it.

The two arguments purport to show that, contrary to common sense and the vast majority of philosophers, death doesn't harm—isn't bad for—the one who dies. Call this thesis *Epicureanism* (again, without assuming that Epicurus himself accepted it), and call its denial *anti-Epicureanism*. Everyone agrees that the *process of dying* can be painful, and therefore harmful, for the person undergoing it. What Epicureans deny, and anti-Epicureans affirm, is that the *event* of death—which puts an *end* to the process of dying, and more generally to the person's life—can harm her.

One of the arguments, the *Timing Argument*, figures prominently in the contemporary literature on the evil of death. Although its premises might look unassailable at first glance, it is usually—and I think rightly—rejected. However, reflection on it will smoothly lead us to the other argument, the *Future Well-Being Argument*. To my knowledge, this argument hasn't been presented before, but in some respects it's an improvement over the Timing Argument. Nonetheless, I shall argue that the Future Well-Being Argument, too, should be rejected. Insofar as Epicurus did provide a convincing argument in the above passage, then, it wasn't by putting forward either of these two arguments.

II. What Makes an Event Harmful?

Before turning to the two arguments, we shall take note of something that will be significant at several points in this chapter. A guiding thought in our discussion should be that if death is harmful, then it's harmful in the same way other events are harmful, such as breaking one's leg or losing one's job. That is, if death is bad, it must be *made* bad by whatever it is that makes other events bad. Denying that death is harmful in the way other events are harmful is only one step away from denying that it's harmful at all (even if you believe that death has a distinctive kind of harmfulness, you shouldn't take that to be its *only* kind of harmfulness).

Consequently, anti-Epicureans have typically based their view on a much more general theory of harm. They've displayed a particular fondness for this account:

The Counterfactual Account of Harm
What makes an event bad, or harmful, for a person is that she would've been on balance

better off – her total lifetime well-being level would've been higher – if the event hadn't taken place.

(Bradley 2009; Feit 2016; Feldman 1991; Luper 2009)

Suppose you break your leg. Suppose for simplicity also that hedonism about well-being is true (as Epicurus thought): the more pleasure and the less pain you experience, the better off you are. Suppose, moreover, that your life would've contained a greater total balance of pleasure over pain had you not broken your leg. On these suppositions, the Counterfactual Account of Harm yields that breaking your leg harms you. And in the same way, it yields that death, too, can harm the one who dies. For in many cases, the person who dies would've been on balance better off if her death hadn't occurred.

In a way, then, the enthusiasm for the Counterfactual Account of Harm among anti-Epicureans isn't surprising. But in another way, it is. For in the more general debate on the nature of harm—a debate that isn't specifically concerned with the harm of death—the Counterfactual Account of Harm is considerably more controversial. Two problems with it are worth noting here.

The first problem concerns *creation*. Consider this case:

Mary's Misery

Mary is created. Otherwise, she would've never existed at all. Unfortunately, her life is altogether miserable.

Being created apparently harms Mary. But what would've been the case if she hadn't been created, and thus never existed at all? Plausibly, she wouldn't have occupied any well-being level, including a zero (neutral) level. For having a level of *well-being* in a scenario arguably requires having *being* in that scenario. After all, it isn't true that, say, the winner of the 2013 US presidential race occupies a well-being level, for there will never be any such individual (since there was no such race in 2013). And

if Mary had never existed, she would've been just as unreal. It's not true, then, that Mary would've occupied a higher well-being level if she hadn't been created.[1] The Counterfactual Account of Harm thus implies, implausibly, that being created is *not* bad for Mary—despite the far from enviable situation it puts her in.

The second problem involves *preemption*. Consider this case:

Arthur's Arm

I break Arthur's arm. If I hadn't, I would have torn it off—making his well-being level even lower. One of my available options, however, was to simply leave Arthur and his arms alone.[2]

Intuitively, my action harms Arthur. This judgment, too, is incompatible with the Counterfactual Account of Harm. For my action makes Arthur better off, not worse off, than he would've otherwise been.

I don't mean to suggest that these problems are any cause for celebration for the *Epicurean*. For what they indicate is that there are harms that the Counterfactual Account of Harm fails to identify.[3] So, the problems cannot provide any reason to think that death is harmless. Their relevance to our discussion is more indirect, as we shall see. For the moment, we should note that while Mary's Misery and Arthur's Arm threaten the Counterfactual Account of Harm, they leave intact one attractive thought behind it. This is the thought that harmful events are somehow detrimental to—have a negative impact on—the person's lifetime well-being. What Mary's Misery and Arthur's Arm indicate is that the relevant notion of being detrimental to the person's lifetime well-being is slightly broader than the one captured by the Counterfactual Account of Harm. Spelling out this broader notion with more precision is a task I cannot pursue here (for two reasons: (a) space limitations, and (b) I don't really know how to do it). However, the points just made will still be helpful in what follows.

III. The Timing Argument

It's time to turn to the Timing Argument. The main idea here is that your death isn't bad for you since it's *never* bad for you. Suppose someone said that even if there's no *time* at which your death *interests* you or *amuses* you, your death can nonetheless interest or amuse you. We'd find that statement ludicrous (and not only for the curious choice of subject matter): such "timeless" interest or amusement cannot be taken seriously. According to the Timing Argument, something similar holds for death's harmfulness: your death cannot harm you since there's no *time* at which it harms you.

Here's one way of formulating the argument more carefully (Bradley 2009: 73; Johansson 2013: 255):

> **The Timing Argument**
> Premise 1: Any event that is bad for a person is bad for her at some time.
> Premise 2: There's no time at which a person's death is bad for her.
> Conclusion: A person's death is not bad for her.

Premise 1 is a natural claim to make, considering that ordinary harms are bad for their victims at particular times. If you break your leg, or someone breaks your heart, this seems to be bad for you when you're in pain as a result, and when you're unable to do various enjoyable things that you might have otherwise been doing. Similar remarks apply to other paradigmatic harms, such as losing your job, losing your friends, or losing your mind.

According to Premise 2, however, similar remarks do *not* apply to what is often seen as the most paradigmatic harm of all: losing your *life*. That is, the event of your death is bad for you neither before, during, or after its occurrence. While *worrying* obsessively about your future death can evidently be bad for you while you're still alive, your *death itself* can hardly be bad for you before it has even taken place.[4] (Compare: if you break your leg now, how could this have been bad for you *yesterday*, while your leg was still entirely intact?)

And assuming your death marks the end of your existence, once you die you'll no longer be there to be harmed. Once you're dead and gone, so is the possibility for anything—including your death—to be bad for you.

From these two premises, the Epicurean conclusion follows: death is harmless.

IV. Harm-at-a-Time

In order to evaluate the Timing Argument, we first need to address a clarificatory question. What is it for an event to harm a person *at a certain time* (as opposed to the more familiar phenomenon of simply harming her—that is, without temporal qualification)?

In the debate on the Timing Argument, harm-at-a-time is usually understood as a purely counterfactual matter, as follows:

> **The Counterfactual Account of Harm-at-a-Time**
> What makes an event bad, or harmful, for a person at a certain time is that she would've been better off at that time—her well-being level at that time would've been higher—if the event hadn't occurred.

To illustrate, suppose again that you break your leg now. On the Counterfactual Account of Harm-at-a-Time, this will be bad for you tomorrow, say, just in case your well-being level tomorrow will be lower than it would've been if you hadn't broken your leg. For instance, perhaps you would've had a greater balance of pleasure over pain tomorrow if you hadn't broken your leg.

The popularity of this account of harm-at-a-time is probably due to the popularity among anti-Epicureans of the structurally similar Counterfactual Account of Harm. As we've seen, though, the latter account is not an ideal source of inspiration. In fact, cases like Mary's Misery and Arthur's Arm (Section II) create trouble not only for that account, but also for the Counterfactual Account of Harm-at-a-Time. This is for two reasons.

First, the Counterfactual Account of Harm-at-a-Time makes it too easy to refute

Premise 1—the claim that any harmful event is bad for its victim at some time. Again, in Mary's Misery, being created apparently harms Mary. Yet there's no time at which she would've been better off (or, for that matter, worse off or equally well off) if she hadn't been created. Similarly, in Arthur's Arm, my breaking Arthur's arm apparently harms him. Yet there need be no time at which he would've been better off if I hadn't broken his arm. So, assuming the Counterfactual Account of Harm-at-a-Time, Mary's Misery and Arthur's Arm provide straightforward counterexamples to Premise 1. This shows no defect in Premise 1; instead, it shows that it's too uncharitable to the Epicurean to assume the Counterfactual Account of Harm-at-a-Time.

Second, Mary's Misery and Arthur's Arm also provide direct counterexamples to the Counterfactual Account of Harm-at-a-Time itself. It seems perfectly appropriate to say that being created is bad for Mary at every time at which she is unhappy. Likewise, it seems perfectly appropriate to say that my breaking Arthur's arm is bad for him when he has a low well-being level as a result.

What's the lesson of all this? It is analogous to the one I suggested with regard to the Counterfactual Account of Harm in Section II. The lesson now is that harm-at-a-time should be taken to consist in being *detrimental to your well-being at the relevant time*—where this is understood in some slightly broader sense than the one captured by the Counterfactual Account of Harm-at-a-Time. There's no need here to spell out such a broader sense in more detail. The important thing to note is that we should still require the person to occupy *some* well-being level (positive, negative, or neutral) at the time at which the relevant event is bad for her. Clearly, both Mary and Arthur do so.

But what about a *dead* person? We're now ready to evaluate the premises of the Timing Argument.

V. Posthumous Well-Being

Most anti-Epicureans have concentrated their efforts on criticizing Premise 2—the claim that a person's death isn't bad for her at any time. On the most plausible version of this approach, your death is bad for you *after* your death. Advocates of this view—often called *subsequentism*—grant that you will not occupy a *positive* or *negative* well-being level when you're dead. But, they contend, once you die you'll occupy a well-being level of *zero*. If this is right, your death will be relevantly detrimental to your well-being at various times after your death (for instance, because you would or could have had a positive, and thereby higher, well-being level at those times if you hadn't died). Fortunately for subsequentists, their view is consistent with denying that a *never*existing individual has a well-being level (see Section II).

However, maybe Epicureans can resist subsequentism (Luper 2009; Carlson & Johansson 2018). They might begin their counterattack by asking a perhaps unexpected question. Does the Michelangelo sculpture *David* currently occupy a level of zero on a financial scale, making it poorer than most people and richer than some (those whose debts exceed their assets)? Intuitively, the answer is No. Rather, *David* has no financial status whatsoever now (or, for that matter, at any other time). But what's the explanation for this? A plausible explanation, the Epicurean might say, is that *David* doesn't currently even have the *capacity* for having a positive or negative financial status. It's currently incapable of having financial assets or debts, much like it's incapable of walking or talking.

This explanation requires a relatively weak conception of capacity.[5] On a more demanding conception, a normal living person might be said to currently lack a capacity for occupying a positive or negative financial level if a powerful demon, say, is dedicated to prevent her from doing so. She still seems to currently occupy a level of zero. However, the Epicurean will claim that the relevant conception of capacity is much weaker, and that even on it, *David* lacks a capacity for positive or negative financial status. Even without any demons lurking around, *David* is not an apt bank customer or business partner.

Presumably, this has something to do with the object's internal structure—and, more specifically, with whether that structure is at least somewhat fit to produce mental features. Marble might be marvelous, but not in this way.

If this explanation is on the right track, the Epicurean might continue, analogous reasoning should also apply in the case of well-being as well. Hence, *David* also fails to currently occupy any level on the well-being scale—including zero—for the reason that *David* doesn't currently have the right kind of capacity for having positive or negative well-being. For example, it's currently not capable, even in a fairly weak sense, of experiencing pleasure and pain.

Now what about a dead person, such as David Bowie? Well, intuitively Bowie, too, occupies no financial level now (although, unlike *David*, he did so at many times in the past). The same explanation apparently holds here as for *David*: the reason Bowie occupies no financial level now is that he is nowadays not capable, even in a fairly weak sense, of occupying a positive or negative financial level. Crucially, moreover, Bowie is nowadays not capable, even in a fairly weak sense, of having positive or negative well-being. We can conclude, the Epicurean will say, that Bowie no longer occupies any well-being level (although, unlike *David*, he did so at many times in the past).

This is a sensible, albeit sketchy, criticism of subsequentism. Thus, the Epicurean might well be right to affirm Premise 2. Why, though, have so many anti-Epicureans been so anxious to undermine Premise 2? This isn't because they find intuitively attractive, or otherwise independently plausible, the claim that we occupy a well-being level after death (or that death harms us at some earlier time). Rather, it's because they find the remaining anti-Epicurean option even worse: to deny Premise 1 – the claim that any harmful event harms its victim at some time. However, let's examine whether Premise 1 is worthy of this respectful attitude.

VI. Timeless Badness

Recall two things we've already noted. First, it's problematic to take death to harm its victim at some time. Second, the claim that death is harmless is counterintuitive, and incompatible with plausible accounts of harm. Given these two points, why should we accept that *all* harmful events are bad for us at times? What justifies accepting Premise 1, rather than the claim that *nearly* all harmful events are bad for us at times, but death is not?

Perhaps it would be illegitimate to *reject* Premise 1 on the grounds that death is a counterexample to it. That might be to assume the point at issue: that death is harmful. But this is not what I'm doing. I'm asking why we should *accept* Premise 1. Unless we already believe that death is harmless, why should we agree that *no* event is timelessly harmful?

Of course, Premise 1 might be considered more elegant than the "nearly all" claim. "All" is more clean and beautiful than "nearly all." However, this doesn't justify Premise 1. Compare: the claim that *all* people's deaths leave behind a corpse is more elegant than the claim that *nearly* all people's deaths leave behind a corpse. Yet we should accept the latter claim and deny the former.

Is it somehow arbitrary or unprincipled to take death's badness, unlike the badness of other events, to be timeless? There's a good reason for denying that all people's deaths leave behind a corpse: some die in extraordinarily violent circumstances, such as explosions. By contrast, it might be claimed, there's no good reason for regarding death as a timeless harm. However, this complaint is evidence of poor memory. We've already seen a good and principled reason for denying that death harms us at times: a dead individual has no capacity for positive or negative well-being. At least *Epicureans* should agree that this is a good reason: if it isn't, perhaps Premise 2 should be resisted after all (furthermore, I'll suggest in Section VIII that if this is indeed a good reason, then even Epicureans should deny Premise 1).

Maybe the problem with regarding death's badness as timeless is instead that it violates a certain condition laid out earlier. In Section II, we noted that if death is bad, then it is *made* bad by whatever it is that makes other events bad. It might be suggested that the idea that death's badness is timeless commits us to explaining the badness of death only in some way that doesn't also apply to other events. This would indeed be an undesirable asymmetry. However, taking death's badness to be timeless doesn't commit us to such an asymmetry (Johansson 2013). As already indicated, there are a number of general accounts on harm, which explain the badness of death and the badness of other events in the same way (Section II). In particular, I've suggested that what makes an event harmful is that it's detrimental to the person's lifetime well-being. This applies to both death and other harmful events, such as breaking your leg. The claim that death isn't harmful at any *time*, though still harmful, is fully compatible with this view.

VII. The Future Well-Being Argument

Epicureans might be unpersuaded by what I just said. Indeed, they might claim that I've now unwittingly pointed to a novel argument for Epicureanism.

What makes an event harmful, the Epicurean might suggest, is not that it's detrimental to the person's *lifetime* well-being. In particular, how well off the person is (or would or could have been) *before* the event is irrelevant. Instead, the relevant factor is that the event is detrimental to the individual's *future* well-being—future, that is, relative to the time at which the event occurs. In other words:

The Future Well-Being Account of Harm

What makes an event bad, or harmful, for a person is that it's detrimental to her well-being *after* the occurrence of the event.

Three remarks are in order. First, what matters on this view is the person's well-being in the future (relative to the time of the event) *as a whole*. The idea isn't the absurdity that all that matters is the person's well-being immediately after the event's occurrence. For example, the Future Well-Being Account of Harm is supposed to allow that even if catching a serious illness causes you no trouble immediately afterwards, it still harms you—say, by making the remainder of your life much worse than it would've otherwise been.

Second, the Future Well-Being Account of Harm shouldn't be taken to allow that an event can harm someone by preventing her from occupying *any* well-being level afterwards. Without this restriction, the principle is useless for the Epicurean.

Third, some might think that the Future Well-Being Account of Harm isn't in conflict with "lifetime" accounts. For perhaps any event that is detrimental to your future well-being is automatically also detrimental to your lifetime well-being, and vice versa. By the time an event happens, it might be too late for it to be detrimental to your *earlier* well-being. However, the Future Well-Being Account of Harm is still in conflict with "lifetime" accounts. Unlike them, it says that your well-being before the event is not part of what *explains* the event's badness—not part of what *makes* it bad.

On the basis of this account, the Epicurean could now suggest the following argument:

The Future Well-Being Argument

Premise 1	Any event that is bad for a person is detrimental to her well-being after the occurrence of the event.
Premise 2	A person's death is not detrimental to her well-being after her death.
Conclusion	A person's death is not bad for her.

Premise 1 is, of course, based on the Future Well-Being Account of Harm. Premise 2 is based on the claim, already discussed (Section V), that a person doesn't occupy any well-being level after her death.

This novel Epicurean strategy has certain advantages over the Timing Argument. For one thing, the Timing Argument would be defeated if it could be shown, after all, that your death is bad for you *before* it occurs. That would do nothing to undermine the Future Well-Being Argument. For another, this novel Epicurean strategy, based as it is on the Future Well-Being Account of Harm, makes it clearer how reflection of *why* harmful events are harmful might lead us to Epicureanism.

How plausible is the Future Well-Being Account of Harm? Some anti-Epicureans might regard it as inferior to more traditional accounts—those that appeal to the person's *lifetime* well-being—precisely on the grounds that it rules out the badness of death. But it's not as if the Epicurean begs any questions by invoking the Future Well-Being Account of Harm. After all, its "future-directedness" is likely to make it attractive to subsequentists. Moreover, there are independent reasons to prefer it over "lifetime" accounts. On a common view, for example, harming crucially involves a *causal* element—and causation is purely future-directed. An event can cause you to have a certain well-being level *later*, but not to have had a certain well-being level *earlier*. Furthermore, the Future Well-Being Account of Harm might sit well with the intuition that some sort of temporal partiality is reasonable: the future matters more than the past. Perhaps because of considerations such as these, the Future Well-Being Account of Harm might also be taken to provide a more attractive explanation of the badness of ordinary harms, such as breaking your leg or losing your job. What happens before these events take place, one might think, isn't plausibly part of what makes them bad.

This novel Epicurean approach, then, has some nice features. But enough flattery—it should still be rejected.

VIII. The Capacity Problem

We can put the Epicurean in an uncomfortable position by focusing on the following case:

Bianca's Brain

A doctor does a lot of damage to Bianca's brain, so that she permanently loses her capacity for having positive or negative well-being (though she continues to live for several years). If the doctor had left Bianca alone—which he could easily have done—she would've had a happy future.

What should we say about the doctor's action? Unfortunately for the Epicurean, whatever we say will either be implausible or undermine the Future Well-Being Argument.

One thing we might say is that (a) the doctor's action harms Bianca, and (b) it isn't detrimental to her well-being after the time of action. The motivation for (b) is, of course, that in order to have a well-being level at a time, you need a capacity at that time for positive or negative well-being (Section V). However, the combination of (a) and (b) undermines the Future Well-Being Argument: the doctor's action will be a counterexample to Premise 1.

Alternatively, we could say that (a) the doctor's action harms Bianca, and (c) it *is* detrimental to her well-being after the time of action. Claim (c) implies that you *can* occupy a well-being level at a time *without* having a capacity for positive or negative well-being at that time. This apparently leaves the Epicurean without any justification for denying that we occupy a well-being level after death. So, the combination of (a) and (c) undermines the Epicurean's support for Premise 2.

Yet another thing we could say is that (d) the doctor's action does *not* harm Bianca—perhaps precisely *because* (b) it isn't detrimental to her well-being after the time of action. However, (d) has little credibility. Surely depriving someone of future happiness, in this active, direct, and unnecessary way, harms her.

The Epicurean might try to argue here that eliminating Bianca's capacity for positive or negative well-being makes her cease to exist. Thus, it's more or less the same as causing her *death*. Therefore, my dismissive judgment on (d) merely repeats the old complaint that Epicureanism is counterintuitive. And

Bianca's Brain, as stated, is incoherent: Bianca cannot "continue to live for several years" after the operation.

But this is unconvincing. Why think that Bianca ceases to exist? It can't be because she loses her capacity for pleasure and pain. Surely she can survive through that loss, especially if her other mental features remain largely intact. The Epicurean could instead argue that positive and negative well-being consists, at least in part, in something other than pleasure and pain—and more particularly in something that Bianca automatically has a capacity for (or even *has*) so long as she exists. One candidate might be *being alive*; another might be *being conscious*. Once she loses the relevant capacity, she ceases to exist. This is indeed a possible strategy. But any such view about well-being (and about personal identity over time) is bound to be highly contested. An argument for a wildly controversial claim, such as the claim that death is harmless, shouldn't depend on assumptions that are themselves wildly controversial.

It's worth reviewing Bianca's Brain's implications for the Timing Argument as well. Claims (a) and (b) would jointly refute its first premise, according to which there is no timeless harm. For given (a) and (b), the doctor's action harms Bianca, although there's no time at which it harms her (unless it somehow affects Bianca's *earlier* well-being). Furthermore, claims (a) and (c) would jointly undermine the Epicurean's support for the Timing Argument's second premise, according to which there's no time at which death is harmful. If it's possible for an event to harm you even when you have no capacity for positive or negative well-being, maybe death is such an event.

IX. Conclusion

The Epicurean's best option is probably to try to find some good reason for saying that while we occupy no well-being level after death, Bianca does occupy a well-being level after the doctor's operation. This would involve finding some plausible alternative to the view that if you occupy a well-being level at a time, then you have a capacity for positive or negative well-being at that time. That would be interesting to see. For the time being, however, I suggest we reject both the Timing Argument and the Future Well-Being Argument.[6]

Notes

1. Neil Feit rejects this argument in Feit (2016). For a response to Feit, see Carlson & Johansson (2018).
2. This is a version of "Broken Arm" in Rabenberg (2015: 10). See also Norcross (2005).
3. But see Bradley (2009), Feit (2015, 2016), and Luper (2009) for possible responses.
4. Contrast e.g. Luper (2009).
5. Thanks to Michael Cholbi and Travis Timmerman for discussion here.
6. I am grateful to Michael Cholbi and Travis Timmerman for their very helpful comments.

References

Bradley, Ben. 2009. *Well-Being and Death*. Oxford: Oxford University Press.

Carlson, Erik & Jens Johansson. 2018. "Well-Being without Being? A Reply to Feit." *Utilitas* 30: 198–208.

Epicurus. 1940. "Letter to Menoeceus." In *The Stoic and Epicurean Philosophers*, ed. W. J. Oates. New York: The Modern Library.

Feit, Neil. 2015. "Plural Harm." *Philosophy and Phenomenological Research* 90: 361–388.

Feit, Neil. 2016. "Comparative Harm, Creation, and Death." *Utilitas* 28: 136–163.

Feldman, F. 1991. "Some Puzzles about the Evil of Death." *Philosophical Review* 100: 205–227.

Johansson, J. 2013. "The Timing Problem." In *The Oxford Handbook of Philosophy of Death*, ed. B. Bradley, F. Feldman, and J. Johansson. New York: Oxford University Press.

Luper, S. 2009. *The Philosophy of Death*. Cambridge: Cambridge University Press.

Norcross, A. 2005. "Harming in Context." *Philosophical Studies* 123: 149–173.

Rabenberg, Michael. 2015. "Harm." *Journal of Ethics and Social Philosophy* 8, no. 3: 1–32.

10 Why Death is Not Bad for the One Who Dies

James Stacey Taylor

Why Death is Not Bad for the One Who Dies

Many people agree with Aristotle that "Death is the most terrible of all things."[1] It is thus not surprising that writing about death is often considered to be rather gloomy. But this doesn't have to be the case. Indeed, some writing about death can actually be comforting by showing that death is not a harm to the person who dies.

The view that death is not a harm to the person who died was famously proposed by Epicurus. Given that death is widely regarded as a terrible harm to the person who dies this Epicurean view strikes many people as "very odd" or even "freakish."[2] Before arguing that Epicurus was right, two clarifications are in order. First, to hold that death is not a harm to the person who dies does not mean that there is no reason to mourn the death of a loved one. It would still be perfectly reasonable for us to mourn the loss of someone we love on the grounds that we will no longer have the pleasure of their company or be able to share our achievements with them. An Epicurean would agree that these would be legitimate reasons to mourn a death. But she would remind us that they are not based on the view that our loved one's death was a harm *to him*, but that it harmed *us*, by depriving us of the pleasures of his company. Second, to hold that death is not a harm to the person who dies is not to deny that a person could be greatly harmed by the process of dying. This could be painful and frightening. If so, an Epicurean would agree that this would be a great harm to the person who is thereby hurt and frightened. But an Epicurean would remind us that a person could be harmed by the process that leads to her death does not imply that she is harmed by the state of being dead. This would still be "nothing" to her.

Two Epicurean Arguments

Epicurus believed that death is not a harm to the person who dies because he believed that "everything good or bad lies in sensation, and death is to be deprived of sensation." Since this is so, Epicurus continued, death "is nothing to us, since when we are, death is not present, and when death is present, then we are not."[3] Thus, since we are either alive (and so our death is "not present" to harm us) or dead (and so we are not present to be harmed) our own deaths cannot harm us.

Before moving to elaborate and defend Epicurus' argument one further clarification is in order. Epicurus' argument is based on the belief that death is the end of a human's existence (and so when our death is present "we are not"). This belief might be false—humans might continue to live on in some form after their "deaths," perhaps in some form of afterlife. The Epicurean argument would not, however, be wrong if this is the case. If humans did continue to live on after their "deaths" then such "deaths" would not be death as an Epicurean understands this; i.e., as the end of an individual's existence. If humans do live on in some afterlife, then the Epicurean argument would not apply, for "death" would not be "death" in the relevant sense of cessation of the existence of the person.

Although the Epicurean argument appears to be very straightforward it can be understood in two different ways. The first of these can be termed the "Hedonic Variant"; the second, the "Existence Variant."[4] The Hedonic Variant of the argument is based on the view that only events or states of affairs that affect a person's experiences can have any effect on his well-being. This is termed the "Hedonic" Variant because hedonism is the view that a person's well-being is constituted solely by the experiences that she has. Since a person who is dead cannot experience anything her death cannot be a harm to her after she dies. It also cannot be a harm to her before she dies, for a person cannot have any negative experiences as a result of her death before it occurs. The Existence Variant of the argument is based on the view that an event or a state of affairs can harm a person only if it occurs prior to his existence, or if he exists at the time of its occurrence. Since, on the Epicurean view, a person's death marks the first moment of his non-existence it will occur neither prior to his existence nor while he still exists. Thus, a person's death can never be a harm to him.

This chapter will focus on defending the Hedonic Variant of the Epicurean argument. This is because although these two variants appear to be independent of each other, when the Existence Variant is examined closely it becomes apparent that it relies on the central claim of the Hedonic Variant: that an event or a state of affairs is only harmful to a person if it adversely affects her experiences. Since the Hedonic Variant of the argument must thus be defended if the Existence variant is to be accepted, it is the more fundamental of the two arguments.

The Existence Variant

Before putting the Existence Variant of the Epicurean argument to one side and moving to defend the Hedonic Variant, we should establish that the Existence Variant is dependent on the central claim of the Hedonic Variant. Luckily, this can be done by defending the Existence Variant against the objection that it is not true that a person can only be harmed by an event or a state of affairs that occurs prior to, or at the time of, his existence.

This defense will thus achieve two things: It will show that the Existence Variant can be defended against this objection, and it will show that this variant of the Epicurean argument is dependent upon the truth of the central claim of the Hedonic Variant—and so the Hedonic Variant is the more fundamental of the two.

To see why someone might think that it is not true that a person could only be harmed by an event or a state of affairs that occurs prior to, or at the time of, his existence, consider two cases that have been developed by Joel Feinberg. In the first case a woman "devotes thirty years of her life to the furtherance of certain ideals and ambitions in the form of one vast undertaking."[5] Unfortunately, the "empire of her hopes" collapses and she is disgraced. However, she never learns of this as her friends keep this information from her and she dies soon after it occurs.[6] In the second of Feinberg's cases, everything is the same as in the first, except that the "empire of her hopes" collapses a month after her death and this leads to her disgrace. Feinberg states that it "would not be very controversial" to hold that the woman in the first case had been harmed through the thwarting of her interest in the success of her enterprise and the thwarting of her interest in having a good reputation.[7] Feinberg then claims that since these "very same interests" are thwarted in the second case there is no "relevant difference" between these cases. Thus, if we hold that the woman in the first case was harmed through the thwarting of her interests, we should also hold that she was harmed in the second case. But if this is so then an event that occurred after this woman ceased to exist would have harmed her. It would thus not be true that a person could only be harmed by an event or a state of affairs that occurs prior to, or at the time of, her existence. The Existence Variant of the Epicurean argument should thus be rejected.

It might be tempting to defend the Existence Variant by claiming that Feinberg has overlooked a distinction between his two cases that undermines his claim that the woman was just as harmed in the second case as in the first. In the first case the thwarting of the woman's interests occurred prior to her being (putatively) harmed by this. We could thus accept that the thwarting of her interests really did cause her to be harmed. But in the second case the woman's interests were thwarted after she was dead. Since we can only attribute harm to her while she exists, the thwarting of her interests in the second case would only cause her to be harmed if we accepted that causation flows backwards. But causation does not flow backwards. Thus, while we could accept that the woman as harmed in the first case, we should not accept that she was harmed in the second case. And if we should not accept that this woman was harmed in the second case, this case gives us no reason to think that a person could be harmed by an event or a state of affairs that occurred after her existence. Hence, the pair of cases that Feinberg has developed cannot be used to reject the Existence Variant of the Epicurean argument.

But this defense of the Existence Variant moves too quickly. This is because it is possible that the relationship between an event or a state of affairs and the attribution of harm to a person as a result of its occurrence is not *causal* but *conceptual*. On this view the occurrence of the event or the state of affairs does not *cause* harm to the person it harms. Instead, as George Pitcher argues, it would simply "make it true" that she was harmed.[8] To illustrate Pitcher's view, note that it must only be true that a person's children have children for it to be true that he is a grandfather. A person is not precluded from becoming a grandfather if he does not exist at the time when the first of his children's children is born. A person can thus become a grandfather after his death if his only daughter has her first child after he has died. The birth of his only daughter's first child does not *cause* him to become a grandfather, but it does *make it true* that the property of being a grandfather should be retroactively ascribed to him. A proper understanding of the concept of "grandfather" thus justifies ascribing this property to a person on the

basis of events that occurred after he was dead. And the property of being a "grandfather" is not the only property that can be retroactively ascribed to persons in this way. The property of being a "killer" could also be retroactively applied to someone after her death. For example, one person might shoot another, fatally wounding him, but the person she shot shoots back, killing her instantly. When the victim of the initial shooting later dies of his wounds this would make it true that the person who shot him was a killer.

Feinberg, then, is certainly correct that some properties (such as being a grandfather or a killer) can be ascribed to persons on the basis of events or states of affairs that transpire after they die. The defender of the Existence Variant of the Epicurean argument thus cannot claim that Feinberg is mistaken to claim that the woman in his second case was harmed on the grounds that if this were so he would have committed himself to endorsing backwards causation. This is because Feinberg could claim that the property of "harm" (like the properties of "grandfather" and "killer") can be ascribed to persons on the basis of a conceptual, rather than a causal, relationship between the persons to whom it was ascribed and the event or state of affairs that harmed them.

Yet while Feinberg can claim that the property of "harm" could be retroactively attributed to persons without needing to invoke the possibility of backwards causation he still needs to provide an argument as to why we should believe that harm is a property that can be retroactively attributed in this way. This is because many properties cannot be retroactively attributed. Consider, for example, the property of "weighing 200 lbs." This property can only be correctly ascribed to a person at the time at which he weighs 200 lbs. It cannot be retroactively ascribed to him at a time T1 on the basis of his weighing 200 lbs. at a future time T2. Feinberg, then, needs to show that the property of "harm" is in the same class of properties as "being a grandfather" and "being a killer" (i.e., those that can be retroactively applied to persons) and not in the same class of properties as "weighing a certain amount" (i.e. those that cannot be retroactively applied). If this can be done then it will not be true that a person could only be harmed by an event or a state of affairs that occurs prior to, or at the time of, his existence. And if this is so then the Existence Variant of the Epicurean argument will be false.

The truth or falsity of the central claim of the Existence Variant of the Epicurean argument thus turns on the conditions that must be met for the property of "harm" to be correctly attributed to a person. If a person would be harmed if one of her interests was thwarted (as Feinberg believes) then it would be possible for a person to be harmed by an event or a state of affairs that occurred after her death. If, however, a person could only be harmed by an event or a state of affairs that causes her to have adverse mental states (as claimed by the proponents of the Hedonic Variant of the Epicurean argument) then it would not be possible for a person to be harmed by an event of state of affairs that occurred after her death. Indeed, if this Hedonic account of harm is correct then the central claim of the Existence Variant would also be correct: A person could only be harmed by an event or a state of affairs that occurs prior to, or at the time of, his existence, for only these types of events or states of affairs could affect her mental states.

The Hedonic Variant

From the above discussion, it is clear that a defense of the Existence Variant of the Epicurean argument against the charge that it is not true that a person can only be harmed by an event or a state of affairs that occurs prior to, or at the time of, his existence rests on the truth of the central claim of the Hedonic Variant. Since this is so, the Hedonic Variant of the Epicurean argument is more fundamental than the Existence Variant. Why, then, should we accept the view that a person can only be harmed by an event or state of affairs that affects her experiences? The first point to make here is that that this hedonic account of

harm is intuitively plausible for it neatly identifies those events or states of affairs that are paradigmatic harms. A person who is upset by being insulted, a person who is physically hurt by an injury, and a person who has been disappointed by a bad grade on a test have all clearly been harmed.

A proponent of the interest-based account of harm that Feinberg endorses would say that all of these events or states of affairs would also be harmful on her view: A person would be harmed by having her interest in not being insulted thwarted, and would be harmed by having her interest in not experiencing pain thwarted, and so on. This response is to be expected. After all, these are all clear examples of harms and so any plausible account of harm must be able to identify them as such. However, as well as correctly identifying those events or states of affairs that are clearly harmful as such, the hedonic account of harm is also able to exclude events or states of affairs that are not harmful from being held to be so. Consider, for example, a version of the situation described in John Wyndham's short story "Pawley's Peepholes." In this story time travel is so commonplace in the future that it is used for entertainment purposes. Companies (such as "Pawley's Peepholes") offer day trips to the past so that their customers can watch how people lived – including how they behaved when they believed that they were in private. In Wyndham's story, the time travelers start off by being visible to those they are spying on; later, the future technology improves so they can visit the past without being seen. Now imagine a version of this story in which the time travelers are never detected by the people that they spy upon and their presence is never even suspected. If the people who were spied upon had an interest in privacy this would have been thwarted by the actions of Pawley's Peepholes. The interest-based account of harm would thus be committed to holding that they both would have been harmed by Pawley's Peepholes. By contrast, the hedonic account of harm would deny that Pawley's Peepholes harmed them as it did not affect them in any way. (Note that the hedonic account of harm does not hold that they are not harmed by Pawley's Peepholes because they are unaware that they are being spied upon. Instead, it holds that they are not harmed as this spying does not affect them in any way. It is possible on the hedonic account of harm for a person to be harmed by something that she has no knowledge of if this adversely affects her experiences. The hedonic view is thus not committed to the implausible claim "What you don't know can't hurt you"). Since it is implausible to hold that persons who were unwittingly watched by the customers of Pawley's Peepholes were thereby harmed the hedonic account of harm gives the right answer in this case while the interest-based account does not. Similarly, consider a person who has an interest in a pub that she frequented as an undergraduate remaining open. She never returns to the old grey town that houses her alma mater and so never learns that the pub closed shortly after she graduated. The hedonic account of harm correctly holds that she has not been harmed by the pub's closure, for this never affects her in any way. By contrast, the interest-based account of harm implausibly holds that the pub's closing harmed her and that this harm continued to blight her life until her death.

The hedonic account of harm thus correctly identifies situations in which an event or a state of affairs harms a person and situations in which it does not. By contrast, the interest-based account of harm is committed to holding that persons are harmed in cases when this is implausible. That the hedonic account of harm thus fits better with our intuitions concerning when a person is harmed and when she is not gives us a reason to endorse it.

Deprivation and Death's Badness

We thus have reason to believe that a person can only be harmed by an event or state of affairs that affects her experiences. But while the truth of this hedonic view would preclude the possibility of persons being harmed by events or states of affairs that occur after their deaths (for these could never affect their experiences) it does not automatically preclude the possibility that a person's death could be bad for her. This hedonic view of harm could allow that a person could be harmed by an event or a state of affairs whose occurrence would cause her experiences to be worse than they otherwise would have been. If, for example, a miserly uncle had embezzled the trust fund that had been established to pay for his niece's college education this would, on the hedonic view of harm, harm her if it made her experiences worse than they otherwise would have been (for example, by making it the case that she had to work her way through college performing unpleasant jobs). But this means that the hedonic view of harm can accept that a person could be harmed by an event if this deprived her of positive experiences that she otherwise would have had. Since this is so, it is possible that a proponent of the hedonic account of harm could hold that a person could be harmed by her own death if it deprived her of positive experiences that she would have had had she lived. It is thus possible, then, to endorse the hedonic account of harm and still reject the conclusion of the Hedonic Variant of the Epicurean argument that death is not a harm to the person who dies. To do so one would accept that the dead cannot experience anything but deny that this entails that a person's death could not be a harm to her: It could be a harm to her if it deprived her of positive experiences that she would have otherwise had.

The view that death could harm the person who dies by depriving her of the goods of life that she would otherwise have enjoyed is widespread. But it is not clear that we should accept it. To see this, consider two important arguments that have been offered in favor of the view that a person's death would harm her through depriving her of the goods of life. Thomas Nagel supports his view that death harms the person who dies through the example of an intelligent man who suffers a brain injury that reduces him to the status of a contented infant.[9] Nagel argues that we would hold that this man's brain injury was a great harm to him. However, since he would be looked after, the attribution of harm to him cannot be made on the basis of the view that this injury would cause him to have unpleasant experiences. Instead, argues Nagel, we would judge that this injury was a great harm to him as it would deprive him of positive experiences that he would have otherwise had.

A similar argument has been offered by Fred Feldman. Feldman asks us to imagine a woman who is born in a country where she is not taught to read and write, but, instead, is taught how to do laundry and raise children. She is reasonably satisfied with her lot—but she had a great talent for poetry that she never discovered as a result of her limited education. Feldman claims that "something very bad" happened to this woman as a result of her being deprived of the opportunity to nurture her talent, even though "she never suffered any pain as a result."[10] From this, Feldman concludes, "something is extrinsically bad for a person if and only if he or she would have been intrinsically better off if it had not taken place."[11] If Feldman is correct here then a person's death would be bad for her if and only if she would have been intrinsically better off had it not occurred.

Yet despite the plausibility of Nagel's and Feldman's arguments they do not show that death can be a harm to the person who dies. This is because in both of their examples the person who was putatively harmed by an event that deprived him or her of some future good experiences continued to exist after the harmful event had occurred. By contrast, a person who dies ceases to exist from the moment of her death. Thus, even if we agreed with Nagel and Feldman that the persons in their examples had been harmed through being deprived of good experiences that they would otherwise have enjoyed this gives us no reason to believe that a person's death would similarly harm her through depriving her of good experiences.[12] Having made this point the proponent of the Hedonic Variant of the Epicurean argument could make another. This is that while Nagel's and Feldman's examples both have a clear subject for the harm to befall

(the person who was affected by the events or states of affairs that putatively deprived him or her of positive experiences) and that it is clear when he or she was supposed to be harmed by these events or states of affairs (during the time when his or her existed after these events or states of affairs had transpired) such clarity is lacking in the case of a person who is supposed to have been harmed by her own death. While a person is still alive she cannot be harmed by being deprived of the goods of life that she would have enjoyed were it not for her death, for this has not yet occurred. And once a person is dead she cannot be harmed by her own death, for after her death there is no experiencing subject to whom the putative harm of deprivation could be attributed. Thus, since a person is either alive or dead – and since the harm of death cannot be attributed to her in either state – death cannot, concludes the proponent of the Hedonic Variant, harm the person who dies by depriving her of the positive experiences that she otherwise would have received.

Conclusion

The Epicurean view that death cannot be a harm to the person who dies thus has considerable merit, especially when it is understood as the Hedonic Variant. (This is not to say that the Existence Variant is not also meritorious, but the Hedonic Variant is the more fundamental of the two). To refute it its opponents must be able to provide an example in which a person is clearly harmed by an event or a state of affairs after whose occurrence he no longer exists to be a subject of harm. But until such an example is forthcoming we should agree with Epicurus: Death is nothing to us. And since we will all die, that should be a comforting claim.

Notes

1. Aristotle, "Nicomachean Ethics" 1115a27. In Richard McKeon, trans. and ed., *The Basic Works of Aristotle* (New York: Random House, 1941), 975.

2. Jack Li, *Can Death Be a Harm to the Person Who Dies?* (Dordrecht: Kluwer Academic Publishers, 2002), 19; Christopher Belshaw, *10 Good Questions about Life and Death* (Oxford: Blackwell, 2005), 43.

3. Epicurus, "Letter to Menoeceus"; this translation is in David Furley, "Nothing to Us?," in Malcom Schfield and Gisela Striker, eds, *The Norms of Nature: Studies in Hellenistic Ethics* (Cambridge: Cambridge University Press, 1986), 75.

4. These variants are more fully outlined in James Stacey Taylor, *Death, Posthumous Harm, and Bioethics* (New York: Routledge, 2012), Chapter 5.

5. Joel Feinberg, "Harm to Others," in John Martin Fischer, ed., *The Metaphysics of Death* (Stanford, CA: Stanford University Press, 1993), 181.

6. Ibid., 182.

7. Ibid., 182.

8. George Pitcher, "The Misfortunes of the Dead," in Fischer, ed., *The Metaphysics of Death*, 168.

9. Thomas Nagel, "Death," in Fischer, ed., *The Metaphysics of Death*, 65.

10. Fred Feldman, *Confrontations with the Reaper* (New York: Oxford University Press, 1992), 138.

11. Ibid., 138.

12. It could be argued that this is not the case in Nagel's example: That the shift from being an intelligent adult to being the mental equivalent of a contented infant was so great that the intelligent adult ceased to exist and was replaced by a different individual with differing mental abilities and interests. But while this understanding of this case would mean that it was analogous to the case where the intelligent man died it would then no longer support Nagel's contention that he was harmed by his ceasing to exist. We would no longer pity the contented infant for what he had lost, for he would have not lost anything as a result of the injury that brought him into existence. Instead, he would have gained something—his existence.

Death Is Bad for Us When We're Dead

Neil Feit

The ancient Greek philosopher Epicurus argued that death cannot be bad for the one who dies, and his argument relied on the claim that there is no *time* when death could be bad in this way. In this chapter, I am going to try to convince you that Epicurus was mistaken. I am going to argue that death can in fact be bad for the victim and that, when it is bad in this way, it is bad for the victim when she is already dead. The first of these claims, that death can be bad for the one who dies, is widely accepted and based on the *deprivation account* of the badness of death. This is the idea that death, among other things, is bad not in virtue of any positive evils that it brings about, but because of the good things in life of which it deprives the victim. The second claim, that in cases where death is in fact bad for the one who dies it is bad *after* the time of death, has its defenders but is less widely accepted. After I discuss Epicurus' perspective and the opposing deprivation account, I will defend the second claim.

I. Epicurus' Reasoning and the Deprivation Account

Think about a couple of things that would be bad for you, if they were to happen. Somebody might punch you in the stomach, causing you physical pain, or verbally abuse you, causing you emotional distress. In these cases, you come to be in a state that is *intrinsically bad* for you, which is to say that it is bad for you in and of itself. The punch and the verbal abuse are not themselves intrinsically bad for you. After all, you might have tightened your stomach muscles so that the punch did not hurt, and you might have been

so thick-skinned that you experienced no distress whatsoever as a result of the verbal abuse. When the intrinsically bad states do result, however, the punch and the abuse are bad for you. We may say that they are *extrinsically bad* for you, and this is because they lead to something that is intrinsically bad for you.

The punch and the verbal abuse, then, seem to be bad for you because they result in things that are intrinsically bad for you, namely physical pain or emotional distress. There is some good reason to think that Epicurus thought this is the *only* way that anything could be extrinsically bad for you. Epicurus wrote: "Become accustomed to the belief that death is nothing to us. For all good and evil consists in sensation, but death is deprivation of sensation" (Epicurus 1940, 31).

If the claim here is merely that death is not *intrinsically* bad for the one who dies, we may just agree with Epicurus. No pain or suffering, for example, is experienced at the very moment of death or afterwards. However, this does not prove that death is not bad for the one who dies since it does not rule out the possibility that death is *extrinsically* bad for the victim. It is tempting to interpret the quotation above so that Epicurus is claiming that something can be extrinsically bad for a person only if it results in sensations like pain or emotional distress for that person, that is, intrinsically bad states or *negative well-being*. Since death does not result in any such sensations, Epicurus would have his conclusion that death is not bad in any way—intrinsically or extrinsically—for the one who dies.[1]

Before we turn to a critical analysis of the reasoning attributed to Epicurus here, it might be helpful to set aside a couple of points that he was *not* trying to make. First, in arguing that *death* cannot be bad for the one who dies, Epicurus was not arguing that *the process of dying* cannot be bad for the one who is dying. It is a sad fact that dying, which occurs while one is still alive, is a process that often involves pain, suffering, and perhaps other intrinsically bad things for the one who is dying. I will understand the Epicurean thesis that death cannot be bad as a claim about the *event of death*, which is, roughly, the event of one's ceasing to be alive. This is an event, perhaps a momentary one, whereby one passes from the state of being alive to the state of being dead. (We might also understand the Epicurean thesis to concern the state of being dead. Much of what I have to say can be applied to this understanding as well.) Second, in arguing that *death* cannot be bad for the one who dies, Epicurus was not arguing that one person's death cannot be bad *for others*. The death of a love one causes grief and related bad states for those who are left behind. One person's death can clearly be bad for others, and the Epicurean thesis does not deny this.

Let's return, then, to Epicurus' argument. Earlier, I suggested that the important premise is this claim about extrinsic value: something can be extrinsically bad for a person only if it results in sensations like physical pain or emotional distress (intrinsically bad states) for that person. Given the additional premise that a person's death does not result in any sensations of this sort, the Epicurean conclusion follows: death cannot be bad for the one who dies. Remember that we have admitted that death is not intrinsically bad, or bad in itself, for the victim.[2]

Why did Epicurus think that a person's death cannot result in any unpleasant experiences for that person? The short answer is that on his account, we simply cease to exist when we die. And, of course, one cannot have experiences of any kind, pleasant or unpleasant, unless one exists. This is why he described death as "deprivation of sensation." On a morbid note, anybody who thinks that we continue to exist after death, but we do so as lifeless corpses, will also agree with Epicurus'

premise that death does not result in any bad sensations for the one who dies. If you think that upon death a person goes to Heaven or Hell, then you might question this premise. You might think that death is bad for those who go to Hell, because it results in suffering for them, and good for those who go to Heaven. I am going to discuss an objection to Epicurus' reasoning that *accepts* his premise about death being deprivation of sensation. But if you disagree with this premise, I will give you a couple of things to think about. First, it might be interesting to consider whether Epicurus *would* be right about the badness of death, *if* we did go out of existence (or conscious existence) upon death. Second, if the death of a good person will result in eternal bliss for that person in Heaven, then it might be challenging to account for the clear fact that it is morally wrong to kill good people. The discussion to follow might provide some help.

According to the deprivation account, something can be extrinsically bad for a person even if it does not result in pain, suffering, or anything intrinsically bad for that person. So, according to those who accept this account, what I described as the important premise in Epicurus' argument is false. The basic idea is simple. Events can be bad for us by causing us pain, suffering, and the like, but they can also be bad for us by *depriving* us of intrinsically good things that we would otherwise have had. Support for the deprivation account is widespread. With respect to death, the claim is that if a person's death deprives her of the good things associated with continued life—so that continued life would bring, on balance, positive well-being—then her death is bad for her, even though it does not result in pain, suffering, or the like.

Defenders of the deprivation account need not say that *every* death is bad for the one who dies. Consider an unfortunate man with painful, terminal cancer. Death might be a good thing for him. Suppose that he chooses death by physician-assisted suicide. Far from depriving him of the good things in life, his death might very well prevent further pain and suffering. If continued life *would have had*, on balance, more pain and suffering than pleasure and happiness (or, in general, more negative well-being than positive well-being) for him, then defenders of the deprivation account will say that his death was extrinsically good for him—it was a blessing.

If death is the *only* thing that can be bad for us by depriving us of good things, we might be suspicious of the deprivation account. However, there are other examples. Philosophers have described many cases where something seems clearly to be bad for a person by means of preventing benefits. Here are just a few. If a brain injury results in an intelligent man having the mental life of a happy infant (Nagel 1970, 77), then the injury seems to be bad for the man even though we may imagine that it does not result in pain, suffering, or any other intrinsically bad states for him. If a tree falls and prevents a surgeon from performing an operation that would restore a patient's sight (Hanser 2008, 427), then the falling of the tree might very well be bad for the patient (imagine that the operation must be performed today and no other doctor can do it). Finally, if a friend of yours leaves you tickets to a baseball game but then they are stolen from your mailbox (Bradley 2009, 71), then the theft of your tickets seems to be bad for you even though it results in no suffering, etc. (imagine that you love baseball and you would have been better off going to the game, but you never find out about the tickets).

So, the deprivation account is really a general theory that applies to events of any type. Here is one way in which we might formulate the general account:

Deprivation Account: An event is extrinsically bad for a person if and only if the person would have been intrinsically better off, on balance, if the event had not taken place.

Note that we could formulate a similar principle about when an event is extrinsically *good* for a person—it would be good provided that the person would have been intrinsically

worse off, on the whole, if it had not taken place. What do we mean by *intrinsically better off*? This is a matter of *well-being*, or what makes life worth living. I have been supposing that things like pleasure, or happiness, make a person intrinsically better off while things like pain and suffering make one intrinsically worse off. Recall that Epicurus said that "all good and evil consists in sensation." The most natural understanding of this is that pleasure is the *only* thing that is intrinsically good for a person and pain is the only thing that is intrinsically bad. This view is what philosophers call *hedonism*, and I will go along with Epicurus in supposing it. You are free to add whatever you like to the list of intrinsically good things (knowledge, virtue, etc.) and bad things. It won't make too much difference in what follows. It is interesting that Epicurus admitted that "death is deprivation of sensation" (Epicurus 1940, 31); it seems, however, that he failed to realize this could be a bad thing.

The deprivation account, as stated above, provides a sensible explanation of how death can be bad for the one who dies. A person's death is extrinsically bad for her if and only if she would have had more well-being on balance if she had not died. The same goes for our other examples. Let's consider just one, the tree's falling across the road on which the surgeon was driving. This is bad for the patient, who was to receive the operation, because the patient would have been better off if the tree had not fallen. It is important to note that the deprivation account handles cases of bad things that *do* result in pain, suffering, and the like. Think back to an example from the beginning of this section, where somebody punches you in the stomach. This is bad for you because (we may suppose) you would have been better off, on balance, if you had not been punched. So, the deprivation account is a fully general account of the relevant kind of badness. The pain you experience as a result of the punch is an important part of the reason why it is bad for you, but it is not the whole story. The deprivation account has us *compare* how well off you are, having been punched, with how well off you would have been if you had not been punched. Epicurus looked only at the result of the punch to find pain or similar unpleasant sensations.

II. The Deprivation Account and the Timing Problem

There is another element of the Epicurean argument that I have not yet considered. In the previous section, I quoted a short passage from Epicurus. That passage occurs just before another one in which he suggests that there is a special reason why death cannot be bad for the one who dies. He writes that

> death… is nothing to us, since so long as we exist death is not with us; but when death comes, then we do not exist. It does not then concern either the living or the dead, since for the former it is not, and the latter are no more.
> (Epicurus 1940, 31)

The idea here seems to be that death cannot be bad for the one who dies because after death, that person is no longer around to be the subject of the badness. So, philosophers who find the deprivation account plausible face a problem. This is *the timing problem*. It might be useful to take the timing problem to be a challenge, that is, the challenge of providing an adequate objection to an argument like the one below. Let's call it *the timing argument*.[3]

1. Nothing can be bad for a person before it happens.
2. Nothing can be bad for a person when that person does not exist.
3. From the time of a person's death onwards, that person no longer exists.
4. Anything that is bad for a person must be bad for that person at *some* time or other.
5. So, death cannot be bad for the one who dies.

The timing argument is *valid*, that is, the premises entail the conclusion. More precisely, it is impossible for all four of its premises to be true but its conclusion to be false. So, if we

are going to reject the conclusion, then, as a matter of logic, we need to deny one of its premises.

If the argument is *sound*, that is, if all of its premises are also true, then it seems there is something wrong with the deprivation account as it was given above. It might handle examples like the brain injury, the fallen tree, and the stolen baseball tickets—since the victim in each case still exists after the relevant event takes place—but it cannot handle death.

Each premise of the timing argument has a certain pull to it. You might think that the best objection to the argument is to deny premise 3 and maintain that we continue to exist after we die. You are welcome to do this, but I am going to take a different route. I am going to deny premise 2. My plan is to admit that when a person dies, she no longer exists from that point on. She is not *located* at any subsequent time. However, I will argue that this does not prevent a person's death from being bad for her at those subsequent times. In cases where death is in fact bad for us, it is bad for us when we're dead. In the recent philosophical literature on the timing problem, this position is called *subsequentism*. In the next sections, I will defend the view that death is bad for the victim after the victim has died (this is not to say that it is bad for the victim at *every time* after death) and compare it with some of its competitors.

III. The Timing Problem and Subsequentism

When is a punch bad for the one who gets punched? It seems that the answer is: after the punch (perhaps *very shortly* after the punch). The punch is bad for you when you are experiencing the pain and discomfort that results from it. After a while, most likely, the punch stops being bad for you. You start feeling better and perhaps at some point your life starts to go on just as it would have, had you not been punched. The badness stops at this time. The same is true for a bad thing that merely deprives you of happiness, for example the theft of your baseball tickets. Had the tickets not been stolen from your mailbox, you would have enjoyed the game. It seems that the theft is bad for you at this time, during the game when you are faring well at home but would have been even happier if the tickets had not been taken. So, the theft of the tickets is bad for you after it occurs, at those times when you are being deprived of things that would have made your life go even better than it actually goes.

Reflection on these ordinary cases of things that are bad for us suggests that subsequentism is true. These things are bad for us after they take place; not before, not at the precise instant when they occur, and not at no time at all. If we cease to exist at death, however, then death seems to be special in an important way. After your tickets were stolen, *you* missed out on the baseball game even though you never knew that the tickets were in your mailbox. Can *you* miss out on good things in life when you don't even exist? I think you can.

The timing problem challenges us to answer this question: *When* is death bad for the one who dies? (Note that this is not a question about when death occurs.) As we formulated it earlier, the deprivation account provides an answer to a similar question: *Under what circumstances* is something bad for someone? The answer was that an event is bad for someone provided that she would have been better off, that is, would have had more well-being, without it. The deprivation account can be expanded to provide an answer to the when-question, and the ordinary cases of bad things suggest that it should look like this:[4]

Time-Focused Deprivation Account: An event is bad for a person *at any given time* if and only if the person would have had a higher well-being level *at that time* if the event had not occurred.

Let's apply this to a couple of examples and then turn to the case of death. The punch to your stomach is bad for you when you feel the pain, since your well-being level would have been higher at that time (or those times) if you had not been punched. But we may suppose that the punch is not bad for you, say, three weeks later since you would not have been better off at *that* time if you had not been punched. Regarding the theft of the baseball tickets, you are well off at home during the game, but your well-being level would have been even higher if the tickets had not been stolen (you would have been at the ball park). So, the theft is bad for you at those times during the game. We might imagine that, had you gone to the game, you would have been bored or frustrated at certain times, and at these times you would have been better off at home. If so, then the account implies that the theft is not bad for you at *these* specific times though it is bad for you at those other times during the game. This seems plausible.

To tell when an event is bad for you, the time-focused deprivation account *compares* your actual well-being level—how well off you are as a result of the event—at a given time with the well-being level you *would have had* at that time if the event had not occurred. How does this apply to the case of a person's death? In *Confrontations with the Reaper*, Fred Feldman describes this example: "Suppose a boy is undergoing minor surgery, and as a result of some foul-up with the anesthesia, he dies while unconscious on the table" (Feldman 1992, 139). Feldman notes that even though the boy's death is painless it strikes us as a very bad thing for him. If the boy had not died, let us suppose, he would have recovered from the surgery and lived a long and happy life. Imagine some time when he would have had a high well-being level. We need to compare this with the boy's actual well-being level at that time, when he is dead (and perhaps when he no longer exists). I think that the boy's actual well-being level at the time is zero. Since he would have had a higher well-being level then, if he had not died, his death is bad for him at that time. Indeed, the time-focused deprivation account implies that his death is bad for him at all those times when his well-being level would otherwise have been greater than zero. Two things about this view are worth emphasizing: first, it does not imply that every death is bad for its subject, and second, it does not imply that a bad death is bad for the subject at all times when she is dead (after death, death might be bad at one time and good at another, depending on what would have occurred to the subject had she been alive).

Some people argue that it makes no sense to say that a person who no longer exists has a well-being level of zero. They think that in such a case there is no well-being level at all, and so the required comparison cannot be made. However, I think there is a perfectly good sense in which it is true to say that such a person has a well-being level of zero. To motivate this, I will use hedonism as an example. On this view, pleasure and pain are the only components of well-being. Your well-being level is above zero when you experience pleasure and no pain, or more pleasure than pain, and it is below zero when you experience pain and no pleasure, or more pain than pleasure. Otherwise—that is, when you experience equal amounts of pain and pleasure, or no pain or pleasure at all—it is zero. Does that poor boy, when he is dead, feel any pleasure or pain? No. So, at that time, his level of well-being is zero. This is not problematic since we can make reference to the boy after his death. We can also say many other true things about him when he is dead, for example that he is missed by his parents, remembered fondly by his friends, and so on. Likewise, even when a person no longer exists and has no *intrinsic* properties (like feeling pleasure or feeling pain), it is true to say that his level of well-being is zero.[5]

I just used hedonism as an example to motivate the idea that it is plausible to think that death is bad for the victim after the victim has died. Epicurus seems to have accepted a type of hedonism, and I myself am strongly inclined to accept it. But there are competing views about the components of well-being. I do not have the space here to argue for this point, but I think that any plausible view will also imply that the dead have zero well-being. For example, if the dead no longer exist, they have neither knowledge nor false beliefs, and they are neither virtuous nor vicious. If these

things are components of well-being, they too point to zero.

IV. Subsequentism and Other Solutions to the Timing Problem

It might be worthwhile to note that one could accept the time-focused deprivation account but say that death can be bad for a person *before* it happens. This requires denying hedonism and accepting a *desire satisfaction* view of well-being. The idea is that when you desire something to be true but it is not true, you have a negative well-being level. Suppose that before the young boy died in the hospital, he had some desires for his future: for example, he desired to go to college. Assuming that he would have done this if he had not died, his death ensures that his desire is not satisfied, unbeknownst to him. So, the boy has unsatisfied desires before his death that would otherwise have been satisfied, making his death bad for him before it occurs. This account of the time of death's badness, *priorism*, goes against premise 1 of the timing argument (Pitcher 1993).

On the bright side, this view makes the boy's death bad for him at a time when he exists, which avoids the challenge for subsequentism. However, this view has big problems. As we have seen, subsequentism seems true of ordinary, non-death-related, harms. It seems clearly wrong, for example, to say that stubbing my toe is bad for me *before* I stub it (even if I then desire not to stub it). Likewise, it seems clearly wrong to say that the poor boy's death makes his *childhood* go worse than it would otherwise have gone. There might be a way to fix the desire satisfaction view, but it would rule out priorism as a solution to the timing problem.

Among the views that agree that death can be bad for the one who dies, the main contender to subsequentism is *atemporalism*.[6] Those who hold this view will deny premise 4 of the timing argument. The idea is that death can be bad for us even if it is not bad at any time. This view is motivated by the thought that it makes no sense to say that someone who does not exist has any level of well-being at all, including zero. Atemporalists admit that death is an evil of deprivation and so it is bad for those who die because it prevents them from having more of the good things in life. However, they claim that the question about *when* death is bad for its victim is misguided. Death is an atemporal evil, they say, which is bad for its victim without being bad at any time.

If I were convinced that a dead person could not have a well-being level of zero, then I would accept atemporalism. However, I think that atemporalism makes death *too* special. Death seems to be bad for us in much the same way as other things—even things that cause us discomfort or pain, such as catching a cold—in that it prevents us from experiencing the good things in life. So, an account of the badness of death that treats death and these other things in a similar way is more attractive than an account that treats them differently. Since these other bad things are bad for us at times, we should take death to be bad for us at times.

To be fair, there is a good sense in which the atemporalist can treat death and other bad things uniformly. The atemporalist can use the deprivation account (along with hedonism or some other view of well-being) to handle them all. However, unless the atemporalist takes the extreme and very implausible position that *all* bad things are atemporally bad, some bad things are going to be bad for us at times while other bad things are not. I think that we should also want to say that how good or bad something is for you, on balance or all-things-considered, is determined by how good or bad it is for you at all of the times at which it *is* good or bad. So, I think that the time-focused deprivation account is a more basic principle than the deprivation account. Atemporalism, however, cannot allow this.

V. Conclusion

Along with many contemporary philosophers, I have used the deprivation account to resist the Epicurean argument that since death does not lead to pain or any other intrinsically bad states, it cannot be bad for the one who dies. I have also argued that subsequentism is the best solution to the timing problem. After death we do not feel pain or pleasure, or in general have the properties that would give us positive or negative well-being, and so our level of well-being is then zero. Death is bad for us at all and only those times at which we would have been faring better than this, had death not taken us.

Notes

1. Fred Feldman suggests and discusses the points made in this paragraph. See Feldman (1992, 127–142).
2. Not every philosopher admits even this Epicurean assumption. For example, David Benatar suggests that "annihilation can be bad in itself for the one who dies" (2017, 108), which may allow that death is intrinsically bad for the victim.
3. For some other versions of arguments along these lines and critical discussion, see Feit (2002) and Bradley (2009, 73–111).
4. For ease of exposition here, I am using "would have had a higher well-being level" instead of "would have been intrinsically better off." This is essentially the view defended by Ben Bradley, which I think is correct. See Bradley (2004, 2009). In Feit (2002), I defended a similar but distinct version of subsequentism.
5. For some recent defenses of the view that the well-being level of a dead person is zero, see Bradley (2009, 88–92) and Feit (2016). For some recent criticism, see Johansson (2012) as well as Carlson and Johansson (2018).
6. For a fairly recent defense of this position, see Johansson (2012).

References

Benatar, D. 2017. *The Human Predicament: A Candid Guide to Life's Biggest Questions.* New York: Oxford University Press.

Bradley, B. 2004. "When Is Death Bad for the One Who Dies?," *Noûs* 38, no. 1: 1–28.

Bradley, B. 2009. *Well-Being and Death.* New York: Oxford University Press.

Carlson, E., and J. Johansson. 2018. "Well-Being without Being? A Reply to Feit," *Utilitas* 30, no. 2: 198–208.

Epicurus. 1940. "Letter to Menoeceus," in *The Stoic and Epicurean Philosophers*, translated by C. Bailey, edited by W. Oates, 30–34. New York: The Modern Library.

Feit, N. 2002. "The Time of Death's Misfortune," *Noûs* 36, no. 3: 359–383.

Feit, N. 2016. "Comparative Harm, Creation and Death," *Utilitas* 28, no. 2: 136–163.

Feldman, F. 1992. *Confrontations with the Reaper*. New York: Oxford University Press.

Hanser, M. 2008. "The Metaphysics of Harm," *Philosophy and Phenomenological Research* 77, no. 2: 421–450.

Johansson, J. 2012. "The Time of Death's Badness," *Journal of Medicine and Philosophy* 37, no. 5: 464–479.

Nagel, T. 1970. "Death," *Noûs* 4, no. 1: 73–80.

Pitcher, G. 1993. "The Misfortunes of the Dead," in *The Metaphysics of Death*, edited by J.M. Fischer, 159–168. Stanford: Stanford University Press.

12 Making Death Not Quite as Bad for the One Who Dies

Kirsten Egerstrom

I. Introduction

In his "Letter to Menoeceus," Epicurus argues that death does not harm us while we are alive because the event of death has yet to occur. Moreover, it cannot harm us after our deaths because, once dead, there is no longer a subject who can be harmed. Epicurus's position is in tension with the widely held intuition that death is typically one of the worst things that happens to a person.

A theory that can account for this intuition is deprivationism. According to the *deprivationist view of the value of death*, death is usually bad for the one who dies if (and because) it deprives them of net good life. Deprivationism entails that the badness of our deaths can come in degrees and the degree of badness is determined by the net amount of good of which death prevents. For most people, an earlier death will be worse than a later one because an earlier death typically prevents one from living more good life than a later death. However, the deprivationist view also entails that some deaths may not be bad for the one who dies. In fact, they may even be good for the person who dies, such as those deaths that spare a person from substantial future evil, such as interminable suffering.

In this chapter, I address the following possibility: on deprivationist accounts of the value of death, events that take place after our deaths can affect the degree to which our deaths are bad for us. If this is true, it may be possible for loved ones to make conscious choices on our behalf to lessen the badness of our deaths. Jeff McMahan agrees that events that take place after our deaths can affect the degree of badness of those deaths (2002, 195–198). However,

he believes that *deliberate* attempts to diminish the badness of others' deaths would be "self-defeating," as they would not reduce the overall loss of goods occurring at the end of one's life (McMahan 2002, 130). I argue against McMahan's position that such attempts would be self-defeating. However, it remains an unanswered question whether or not we have good reason to act on behalf of deceased loved ones to diminish the badness of their deaths; this latter question will not be addressed here.

Before I discuss deprivationism further, it would be helpful to clarify the topic of this paper. First, I am concerned with what makes death bad *for the one who dies* and not with what makes death bad for other people (e.g., friends and family). I also distinguish between what makes death bad and what makes the *process* of dying bad. While the process of dying can certainly go better or worse for a person, I am only concerned with the final point in that process—i.e. the point at which a person ceases to exist. Finally, I will not consider the possibility that human beings continue to exist in some fashion (e.g., a spiritual afterlife) after their physical deaths.

II. Deprivationist Views of the Value of Death

To understand deprivationism, it will be helpful to understand the philosophical distinction between intrinsic and extrinsic value. We can understand things that possess intrinsic value or intrinsic goodness as things that possess inherent value. Intrinsic goods, when added to a person's life, *themselves* make a person's life go better for her (even if they result in other conditions that make a person's life worse overall). On the contrary, the presence of things that are intrinsically dis-valuable or intrinsically bad *themselves* make a person's life go worse for her.

While some goods are inherently valuable, other goods are valued extrinsically or instrumentally. For example, most people do not value money for its own sake; people value money as a means to acquire other goods thought to possess value (e.g., happiness, power). It is also the case that possessing money does not always make your life go better for you—i.e. money sometimes leads to happiness but other times to misery.

Philosophers have competing views on what sorts of goods add inherent value to a person's life. Epicurus held the hedonist position that pleasure states make our lives go better for us and pain states make our lives go worse; on this view, all other goods (e.g., friendship, money, knowledge) are extrinsically valuable if (and because) they result in pleasure. Other philosophers argue that there are *other* bearers of intrinsic value such as desire satisfaction, achievement, or knowledge. For the sake of simplicity, I will be adopting a hedonist interpretation of the good life in this chapter.

Epicurus thought his commitment to hedonism entailed that death could not harm the one who dies. On his view, only pain states can detract from the quality of a life and dead people no longer have experiences—positive or negative. However, on the deprivationist view, death (when bad) is *extrinsically* bad for us. Death is an evil of deprivation; it deprives us of intrinsic goods. The view's explanation of death's badness is like that of other misfortunes. Consider the following case of McMahan's.

> **The Accident Victim.** A young man of twenty suffers an accident that causes extensive brain damage, leaving him severely cognitively impaired in a way that blights his previous hopes for the future. A week later he is killed in the middle of the night by an earthquake that completely destroys the house in which he lives.
>
> (McMahan 2002, 128)

Let's assume that one effect of the brain damage is a loss of the capacity to experience pain or pleasure. If we examine the accident and the death separately *and* assume that the young man was victim to only one of these misfortunes, the accident seems nearly (if not equally) as bad for him as his death is a week later. Both events are also bad for him in the same way—they deprive him of more of a good life.

What also appears true in *The Accident Victim* is that the young man's death no longer seems bad for him, given the occurrence of the accident a week prior. Deprivationist views are (almost always) comparative. In order to evaluate how bad death is for the one who dies, we need to compare how things go for the person in the actual world, given their actual death, with how things would have gone had they not died when they did. The following is a simpler case to analyze.

> **Tyra's Early Death.** There are a limited number of things that Tyra finds enjoyable. She enjoys going for walks in her favorite park, she likes to eat Twinkies, and she enjoys reading Lee Child's "Jack Reacher" novel series (but never re-reads novels). Due to an undiagnosed heart condition, Tyra dies at the age of 40 from a heart attack during a strenuous walk.

In order to evaluate Tyra's death (according to deprivationism), we can utilize counterfactual conditionals. In evaluating *counterfactual* conditionals, we are interested in which states of affairs *would* have obtained had an event occurred (or not occurred). We can compare how things actually go for Tyra, given her death at time t_1, with how things *would* have gone had she not died at t_1. In evaluating counterfactuals, philosophers often utilize the concept of possible worlds. In evaluating what would have occurred had Tyra not died at t_1, we can ask what would have occurred at the nearest possible world to the actual world— i.e. the world most similar to the actual world except for the fact that Tyra does not die at t_1.

We can apply Ben Bradley's *Difference-Making Principle* (DMP) to determine how bad Tyra's death was for her (Bradley 2009, 50–51). I will stipulate that Tyra lives for an additional twenty years at the nearest possible world where she does not die at t_1. According to DMP, we calculate the overall hedonic value of Tyra's life, given her death at t_1 *and* the overall hedonic value of her life had she not died at t_1 (dying twenty years later).[1] The difference between values is the difference that her death makes to her overall well-being.

One question that I have not yet addressed is *when* death is bad for the one who dies. Unique problems arise in the case of death, as a subject of harm or benefit no longer exists *after* death. Based on this problem, some philosophers have argued that death makes a difference to well-being *before* a person's death—i.e. *priorism*.[2] For example, on a desire-satisfaction view of well-being, it could be that death is bad because it prevents the satisfaction of desires that one has while living.

In contrast, Bradley defends *subsequentism*—i.e. the view that death is bad during periods of time *after* one's death.[3] The primary benefit of subsequentism is that it is consistent with our evaluations of when other types of deprivations are bad for us. To illustrate, imagine that a woman breaks her leg one week before a ski trip. The question is: when is her broken leg bad for her? The pain of recovery will certainly be *intrinsically* bad for her. But her injury is also *extrinsically* bad for her *after* her injury during the period of time at which, had she not broken her leg, she would have enjoyed the ski trip. In the next section, I point to a unique implication of my thesis that arises when subsequentism is adopted. Thus, I'll say a bit more about Bradley's subsequentism now.

Returning to *Tyra's Early Death*, let's again stipulate that Tyra dies at t_1. On Bradley's view, in order to determine if Tyra's death is bad for her at a later time, t_2, we must compare the intrinsic value of t_2 for Tyra in the actual world with what would have been the intrinsic value of time t_2 for Tyra had she not died at t_1. Assuming hedonism, the intrinsic value for a time is based on the balance of pleasure over pain at that time.

Bradley refers to this view as the *Difference-Making Principle for Times* (DMPT) (2009, 90). Unlike DMP, DMPT requires us to assign a well-being level to Tyra at times she is dead. Bradley argues that dead people have well-being levels of zero. This is a controversial view. But, assuming its truth (and that of hedonism), Tyra's death would not be bad for her at t_2 if she would have experienced more pain than pleasure at t_2 in the nearest possible world in which she does not die at t_1.

III. Making Death Less Bad for the One Who Dies

There is one way to make one's death less bad while simultaneously maximizing the value of one's life—i.e. live a happy and healthy life for as long as possible. If a person dies at age 98, then the nearest possible world where they do not die at that time is probably one where they die relatively soon thereafter. As a result, their actual death will not deprive them of much good life. Living a healthy life in order to live as long and happy as possible is obviously good advice. However, not all of us will be so lucky. Is there anything that can be done to lessen the badness of our deaths for those of us destined to die well before we turn 98? I'll start to answer this question by considering a variation on *Tyra's Early Death*—i.e. *Tyra's Lucky Break*.

> ***Tyra's Lucky Break.*** Shortly after Tyra's death at age 40, her favorite park is destroyed by flooding, Hostess stops selling Twinkies, and Lee Child decides to retire from writing novels. Though Tyra is unaware of this fact (because she is dead), the series of random events makes it so that Tyra's death at age 40 is much less bad for her.

We can now ask: how good would things have gone for Tyra had she not died at age 40? Imagine that in *Tyra's Early Death*, Tyra's death at t_1 prevents +250 net pleasure (1000 pleasure units minus 750 pain units). However, the post-mortem events in *Tyra's Lucky Break* result in the loss of Tyra's primary sources of pleasure. Once these events occur, it could be that Tyra would only experience 200 units of pleasure during the twenty-year period after t_1 (had she not died at t_1). Assuming the total pain units remain the same at 750 units, then the post-mortem events in *Tyra's Lucky Break* make it so that Tyra's death is no longer bad for her (as it prevents more pain than pleasure).

If a random series of events unrelated to Tyra's death could make her death less bad for her (or even good for her), then we should question whether or not deliberate attempts to make Tyra's death less bad for her after her death could also be successful. We can compare *Tyra's Lucky Break* with the following case, proposed by Travis Timmerman:

> **Sick Suzy:** Suzy has a heart defect and is going to die within a month. She might think that the nearest possible world in which she does not die is one where she receives a heart transplant and lives a long happy life. However, Naïve Ned is Suzy's friend and he wants to minimize the badness of Suzy's death. Knowing that Suzy will die within a month, Ned hires a professional torturer to immediately torture Suzy iff [if and only if] she recovers from her heart defect. Now, the nearest possible world in which Suzy survives her illness is one where she is tortured for the remainder of her natural life.
>
> (Timmerman 2016, 19)

In *Sick Suzy*, we can assume Naïve Ned is 100 percent certain that Suzy will die within one month; as a result, Suzy will never be tortured. Timmerman argues that Naïve Ned *has* succeeded in making Suzy's death less bad for her, since her death prevents her from a future of suffering. Naïve Ned hires the torturer *before* Suzy's death, which makes this case slightly different from *Tyra's Lucky Break*. But the primary difference between *Tyra's Lucky Break* and *Sick Suzy* is that the events occurring after Tyra's death are *random* and unrelated to her death. Whereas, Naïve Ned *deliberately* hires the torturer to make Suzy's death less bad for her.

McMahan would agree that the random events occurring after Tyra's death make her death less bad for her. However, he argues that *deliberate* attempts to make another person's death less bad for her are "self-defeating," by which McMahan means they are futile. To explain why, he provides the following case. I will refer to his case as *Government Intervention* (McMahan 2002, 129–130).

> **Government Intervention.** Shortly after Jerry's death, the government considers raising the general standard of living. In raising the standard of living, the government's aim would be to make moderate improvements to each citizen's quality of life. And, if they adopt this policy change, they will be successful.

McMahan points out that *if* the government does implement this policy change, Jerry's death *would* become worse for him, as the death would now deprive Jerry of a higher quality of life. One could make the argument that the government should not make the policy change because they ought not to increase the losses attributable to Jerry's death. However, McMahan argues that once the government considers improving the standard of living, choosing not to do so on the basis that it would make Jerry's death worse for him would be futile; the total loss of intrinsic goods at the end of Jerry's life would remain the same. To illustrate why, here are a few ways in which *Government Intervention* could play out.

Scenario #1: the government raises the overall quality of life. Jerry's death is now worse for him because the government increased the losses attributable to his death.

Scenario #2: the government knows nothing of Jerry's death nor do they have any idea that raising the overall quality of life would impact the badness of Jerry's death. But, they choose *not* to raise the overall quality of life for citizens because it is too expensive.

Scenario #3: the government chooses not to raise the overall quality of life *to* make Jerry's death less bad for him.

Earlier, I presented McMahan's *Accident Victim* case. I suggested that the young man's death no longer seems bad for him, given the brain damage caused a week earlier. However, McMahan argues that while the losses attributable to the *death* are decreased, the man's overall losses remain the same. McMahan suggests that to properly understand the man's misfortunes (i.e. his loss of many goods), we must combine the misfortunes of the accident and the death. In doing so, we calculate the *overall loss in dying*— i.e. the overall deprivation caused by both the accident and the death. And McMahan states that we "do not conclude that his loss is less than we thought [given his accident]: rather, we should simply reassign responsibility for that loss" (2002, 129).

McMahan applies his concept of overall losses to *Scenario #2* and *#3* (of *Government Intervention*) in the following way. In *Scenario #2*, the event of Jerry's *death* does not deprive him of life at the higher level because he would not have benefited from the standard of living increase had he not died when he did (as the government chose not to implement it).

However, McMahan believes that Jerry's overall losses remain the same. In order to determine Jerry's overall losses, we need to combine the losses of his death with the losses attributable to the government's failure to raise the standard of living, and together they "deprive him of a future at a higher level" (McMahan 2002, 130). In *Scenario #3*, McMahan suggests that Jerry's overall losses also remain the same. In this case, choosing not to improve the standard of living *in an effort to* avoid making Jerry's death less bad for him entails that the overall losses will be attributable to the death alone.

If Jerry's overall losses remain the same regardless of whether or not the government implements the standard of living increase, then they may as well implement the standard of living increase. However, it seems bizarre to factor in the government's decision to *refrain* from raising the quality of life into an evaluation of Jerry's overall losses. For one, it is unclear what changed this option from a

mere possibility to a factor that contributes to Jerry's overall losses. Is it the fact that the government *discussed* raising the quality of life that made it so that Jerry now misses out on life at the higher quality? If so, could the government avoid making Jerry's death worse for him by not having a conversation about raising citizens' quality of life?

Similarly, let's imagine that shortly after Tom's death, McDonald's considers bringing back the McRib sandwich on a permanent year-round basis.[4] Tom loves the McRib sandwich and would have experienced considerable pleasure had he not died when he did (and had the opportunity to eat the sandwich daily). In making the McRib sandwich available year-round, McDonald's has just made Tom's death worse for him by depriving him of the ability to enjoy McRib sandwiches daily.[5]

Now imagine that the manager of Tom's local McDonald's ultimately decides *not* to sell the McRib year-round but **not** on the basis that doing so would make Tom's death worse for him. Is it correct to say that Tom's overall losses are equivalent to what his overall losses would have been if McDonald's had made the McRib available daily after his death? On McMahan's view, it seems they would be equivalent. But, is this really the sort of post-mortem event that could reasonably impact the badness of one's death? Relatedly, if McDonald's made the decision not to sell the McRib daily while Tom was still alive, we would not factor their choice into calculations of the hedonic value of Tom's life in the actual world.

It might be thought that combining McMahan's concept of overall losses with Bradley's DMP could metaphysically resolve these issues. In *Government Intervention*, McMahan could argue that the government's having a conversation about raising the standard of living affects which world counts as the nearest possible world to the actual world. In order to properly understand Jerry's misfortunes, we would then need to look to the nearest possible world where Jerry does not die (at the time of his actual death) *and* where the government raises the standard of living. In doing so, we will discover that Jerry's death deprives him of the future at the higher quality of living regardless of whether or not the government chooses to raise the standard of living.

In making this move, we are shifting the focus away from an evaluation of Jerry's death to that of Jerry's death *and* the government's decision not to raise the quality of living, thereby changing the subject. Moreover, to reach McMahan's outcome in *Government Intervention*, we must assume that the government's having the conversation fixes which possible world is nearest to the actual world. McMahan could, of course, stipulate this fact. But, surely this would not apply to every scenario. It may be, for example, that the nearest possible world to the actual world where Tom does not die at t_1 is one where McDonald's still chooses not to sell the McRib on a permanent basis, even if management discussed doing so before Tom's death. In this case, we would not have to factor McDonald's choice into Tom's overall losses.

If we want to continue evaluating a person's overall losses, we need a clearer way of sorting through which deprivational events occurring after a person's death ought to be factored into those losses. There may be a relevant difference between Scenario #2 and #3 of *Government Intervention*. In Scenario #2, a choice is made without consideration of Jerry's death. Whereas, in Scenario #3, a choice is made based on Jerry's death. The fact that, in Scenario #3, Jerry's death plays a role in deliberations about whether to raise citizens' quality of life may make one more inclined to think that their choice *not* to raise the quality of life ought to be factored into Jerry's overall losses. We can then say that if a choice is made for reasons unrelated to the value of Jerry's death, then the additional losses should not be added to Jerry's overall losses. If we go this route, we could at least say that (in the previous example) McDonald's choice not to sell the McRib for reasons unrelated to Tom's death would not count as one of Tom's misfortunes and thereby does not contribute to Tom's overall losses. I will

refer to this revised view of McMahan's as the *Revised Overall Losses in Dying* (ROLD) view.

ROLD places a restriction on which events, after death, affect the value of that death. In cases where one's death relevantly causes a future deprivation to occur, the overall loss will be based on a combination of the losses attributable to one's death and the losses attributable to the deprivation event after death. For example, if Tom's local McDonald's store chooses not to make the McRib a permanent item on the menu *because* they fear that it would affect the badness of Tom's death, then we would have to factor this into Tom's overall losses (otherwise, we would not). ROLD is consistent with McMahan's claim that deliberate attempts to lessen the badness of another's death (after their death) would be futile, as these attempts would be relevantly caused by the death, itself.

But the primary problem for ROLD is that it places far too much emphasis on the *reason why* events occur. If one's favorite restaurant closes shortly after one's death and this makes their death less bad for them, why should it matter *why* the restaurant is shut down? The restaurant could be shut down to make a death less bad for the one who dies. Or, the restaurant could be shut down because the owners cannot afford the rent. How could the reason why a restaurant shuts down plausibly affect the badness of one's death?

To illustrate further, imagine that Tyra's sister, Gwen, decides to destroy Tyra's favorite park after her death in an effort to make Tyra's death less bad for her. On ROLD, the loss of pleasure brought about by the destruction of the park would have to be included in Gwen's overall losses, as Tyra's death inspired Gwen to destroy the park. Thus, on ROLD, Gwen does not achieve her goal of diminishing the badness of Tyra's death.

In contrast to ROLD, DMP is not sensitive to the reason *why* a post-mortem event occurs. If Tyra's death can be made less bad for her by the destruction of her favorite park, it does not matter *why* the park is destroyed. What matters is if the park's destruction impacts the hedonic value of Tyra's life at the nearest possible world where she does not die at t_1. Yet, a related worry is that since Tyra's death is the catalyst for Gwen's choice to destroy the park, the nearest possible world where Tyra does not die, Gwen also does not destroy the park. It appears that Gwen has not made Tyra's death less bad for her by destroying the park.

It might be thought that one way around this problem is for Gwen to make arrangements to have the park destroyed *before* Tyra's death (once Tyra's death seems imminent). This is the approach Timmerman takes in *Sick Suzy*. In *Sick Suzy*, Naïve Ned plans before Suzy's death to have her tortured if she miraculously receives a heart transplant. However, it is Naïve Ned's *certainty* of Suzy's imminent death that causes him to hire the torturer. If Naïve Ned had any doubt that she would not die, he would not hire the torturer for fear of the very real possibility of signing his friend up for years of torture. As a result, at the nearest possible world where she does not die, her fate was not certain and therefore Naïve Ned would not have hired the torturer.

In order to properly respond, I will return to Bradley's DMPT. On DMPT, it seems we could also diminish the badness of another's death at *specific times* after their death.

It may be true that had Tyra not died at t_1, then Gwen would not have destroyed Tyra's favorite park shortly after t_1. As a result, at the nearest possible world where Tyra does not die at t_1, she still gets to enjoy her favorite park. Yet it is also true that once Gwen has destroyed Tyra's favorite park, the following counterfactual statement is true: "if Tyra was now alive, she would obtain less pleasure due to the park's destruction." This suggests that Gwen can make Tyra's death less bad for her for significant periods of time after her death. In fact, if Gwen times the destruction of the park to coincide with the timing of Tyra's death, the period of time during which Gwen successfully makes Tyra's death less bad for Tyra will coincide with the period of time that Tyra's death is bad for Tyra.

In this chapter, I have argued that we can take deliberate measures after a loved one's death to make their death less bad for them.

An important question remains: if we have the power to make another's death less bad for them, do we have good reason for doing so? I will not be addressing this question, here, other than to say that most often the reason a person has to make another's death less bad for them will be trumped by more important reasons. For example, in destroying Tyra's favorite park after Tyra's death, Gwen also deprives living people of the opportunity to enjoy the park. All things considered, Gwen should probably not destroy the park.

Yet it seems possible that there are cases where one has the power to make another person's death less bad for them in a way that does not frustrate the interests of other people who are still alive. If so, if one cares about the well-being of a loved one, and the degree of badness of their death matters, it seems perfectly reasonable to act on their behalf to make their death less bad for them

Notes

1. The hedonic value for a person at a world will be the balance of total pleasure over pain experienced during the person's life at that world.
2. For a defense of priorism, see Steven Luper in (2005) "Past Desires and the Dead" and in (2007) "Mortal Harm."
3. Priorism and subsequentism do not exhaust the possible views on when death is bad for the one who dies. For example, Luper (2007) has argued that dead people cannot be harmed while dead, as dead people are not *responsive* during this time. On a hedonist interpretation, something is not responsive at a time if it lacks the capacity to experience pain or pleasure at that time (Luper 2007, 244).
4. It now only becomes available for limited periods of times.
5. Note that if McDonald's has harmed Tom by making his death worse for him, this does not entail that McDonald's has morally wronged Tom.

Bibliography

Bradley, Ben. *Well-Being and Death.* New York: Oxford University Press, 2009.

Epicurus. "Letter to Menoeceus." Multiple sources.

Luper, Steven. "Past Desires and the Dead," *Philosophical Studies* 126, no. 3 (2005): 331–345.

Luper, Steven. "Mortal Harm," *The Philosophical Quarterly* 57, no. 227 (2007): 239–251.

McMahan, Jeff. *The Ethics of Killing: Problems at the Margins of Life*. New York: Oxford University Press, 2002.

Timmerman, Travis. "Your Death Might Be the Worst Thing Ever to Happen to You (But Maybe You Shouldn't Care)," *Canadian Journal of Philosophy* 46, no. 1 (2016): 18–37.

Part IV Can Lucretius' Asymmetry Problem Be Solved?

Death

Through some strange sense of sight or
   touch
I find what all have found before,
The presence I have feared so much,
The unknown's immaterial door.

I seek not and it comes to me:
I do not know the thing I find:
The fillet of fatality
Drops from my brows that made me blind.

Point forward now or backward, light!
The way I take I may not choose:
Out of the night into the night,
And in the night no certain clews.

But on the future, dim and vast,
And dark with dust and sacrifice,
Death's towering ruin from the past
Makes black the land that round me lies.

        —Madison Julius Cawein

Introduction to Part IV

As you know from the previous section, the ancient Greek philosopher Epicurus (341–270 B.C.E.) believed that death was not bad for us, and consequently believed that fearing death is irrational. Following in his footsteps, an Epicurean poet named Lucretius (unknown - mid to late 50s B.C.E.) wrote an epic poem titled *De Rerum Natura*, which translates to *On the Nature of Things*. In it, Lucretius gave an Epicurean argument against the badness of death.

Here is Lucretius' basic idea. Most people believe that it is bad for them to die at the time they do, instead preferring to die much later. Yet no one seems to believe that it was bad for them not to have been conceived much earlier than they were. Lucretius thought that the events of coming into, and going out of, existence are relevantly similar and so should be treated symmetrically. On his view, since it isn't bad for us not to have come into existence earlier than the time we came into existence, it likewise isn't bad for us not go out of existence later than the time we die.

Some people are persuaded by Lucretius' argument, but many people who work on the philosophy of death are not the least bit persuaded. In this section, you will get to read the central excerpts of Lucretius' epic poem, and two contemporary responses to Lucretius' famous argument.

Travis Timmerman will defend Lucretius in one respect. He agrees that, all else equal, coming into and going out of existence are relevantly similar. However, unlike Lucretius, Timmerman holds that death can be bad for the person who dies. He believes death is bad for people when, and because, it deprives them of additional, on the whole, good life. To maintain the symmetry between coming into and going out of existence, Timmerman argues for the surprising conclusion that it can also be bad for a person *not* to have come into existence earlier than they did. This may run contrary to commonsense, though Timmerman argues that his view can account for commonsense judgments by acknowledging the difference between how *salient* each potentially bad event is to us. His basic thought is that, while both events can be bad for us, people tend to reasonably think about, and be more emotionally affected by, prematurely going out of existence rather than belatedly coming into existence.

Frederik Kaufman will defend an alternative view to the ones mentioned above. Kaufman agrees with Lucretius that the event of coming into existence cannot be bad for a person. Yet he agrees with Timmerman that death is bad for the person who dies, at least when their death prevents them from living additional, on the whole, good life. In his chapter, Kaufman defends his seminal account of the supposedly relevant difference between coming into, and going out of, existence. In a sentence, Kaufman argues that death can be bad for us because it can deprive us of additional good life, but coming into existence can never be bad for us because it is simply not possible (in the relevant sense of possibility) for anyone to have come into existence earlier than they did. At least, according to Kaufman, it isn't possible in the relevant sense for us to have come into existence much earlier than we did, lived a longer, better, life as a result, and still maintained everything about our particular identity that we care about. So, he argues, our conceptions cannot have deprived us of anything! While defending their positive views, both Kaufman and Timmerman identify what they believe is wrong with the others' arguments.

If you're interested in reading more about the asymmetry problem, check out the following:

1. Frederik Kaufman's Death and Deprivation; or Why Lucretius' Symmetry Argument Fails (1996) *The Australasian Journal of Philosophy* 74 (2): 305–312.
2. Travis Timmerman's Avoiding the Asymmetry Problem (2018) *Ratio* 31 (1): 88–102.
3. Anthony Brueckner and John Martin Fischer's The Asymmetry of Early Death and Late Birth (1993) *Philosophical Studies* 71 (3): 327–331.
4. Elizabeth Harman's Fischer and Lamenting Nonexistence (2011) *Social Theory and Practice* 37 (1): 129–142.

13 On the Nature of Things (excerpts)

Lucretius

Lucretius, *De Rerum Natura* ('*On the Nature of Things*'), Book III, first century BCE, trans. R.C. Trevelyan, *Translations from Lucretius* (London: Allen & Unwin, 1920)

Death then is nothing to us, nor one jot
Does it concern us, since the nature of
    mind
Is thus proved mortal. And as in times
    long past
We felt no unhappiness when from every
    side
Gathering for conflict came the Punic
    hosts,
And all that was beneath the height of
    heaven,
Shaken by the tumult and dismay of war,
Shuddered and quaked, and mortals were
    in doubt
To whose empire all human things
    would fall
By land and sea, so when we are no more,
When body and soul, whereof we were
    composed
Into one being shall have been divorced,
'Tis plain nothing whatever shall have
    power
To trouble us, who then shall be no more,
Or stir our senses, no, not if earth with sea
In ruin shall be mingled, and sea with sky.

…

For if man be destined to endure
Misery and suffering, he must first exist
In his own person at that very time
When evil should befall him. But since
    death
Precludes this, and forbids him to exist
Who was to endure distress, we may be
    sure
That in death there is nothing we need
    dread,
That he who exists not cannot become
    miserable,
And that it makes no difference at all
Whether he shall already have been born
In some past time, when once he has
    been robbed
By death that dies not of his life that dies.

…

Consider likewise how eternal Time's
Bygone antiquity before our birth
Was nothing to us. In such wise does
    Nature
Show us the time to come after our
    death
As in a mirror. Is aught visible
Therein so appalling? aught that seems
    like gloom?
Is it not more secure than any sleep?

14 If You Want to Die Later, Then Why Don't You Want to Have Been Born Earlier?

Travis Timmerman

I. Introduction

Most people seem to think that death is bad for them. At least, they do if they believe their continued life would be, on the whole, good for them. We might wonder, though, whether this belief is rational. Could death be bad for a person and, if so, what makes it bad? Most philosophers who have thought about this question have said that death is usually bad for us and that what makes it bad is that it deprives the person who is dying of additional life worth living. This view is known as the *deprivation* view of the badness of death. According to deprivationists, the more good life death prevents a person from having, the worse death is for that person.

There is much to be said in favor of deprivationism. First, it nicely accounts for our intuitive judgements about standard cases of death. Consider, for instance, a case in which a healthy 10-year-old boy dies suddenly in a car crash. His death intuitively seems very bad for him and one good explanation of why we are disposed to make this judgment is because this child presumably would have lived a good life for many years to come had he not been in that car crash.

Compare this young boy's death with that of a 100-year-old man who dies suddenly in a car crash. The young child's death seems much worse for the child than the elderly man's death seems for the elderly man. If the elderly man were not in a car crash, he probably would have died relatively soon after. Again, the deprivation view gets the intuitively right result. Both deaths are bad for the persons who died, but the child's death is worse for the child than the elderly man's

death is for the elderly man. Why? According to the deprivation view, this is because the amount of good the child's death deprives the child of is much greater than the amount of good the elderly man is deprived of by his death. Simply put, the child's death prevents him from experiencing decades more good life, while the elderly man's death only prevents him from experiencing a few more years of good life.

Second, the explanatory power of the deprivation view also extends to common-sense judgments about when death is good for the dying. Quite generally, death is usually considered to be good for the dying in cases where the dying persons' quality of life, were they to continue living, would be worse than death. For instance, imagine a person who, in the final stages of amyotrophic lateral sclerosis (i.e. Lou Gehrig's disease), initiates physician-assisted suicide. Intuitively, this person's death is good for him because it prevents him from experiencing any more of the overwhelming agony caused by amyotrophic lateral sclerosis. It doesn't prevent him from experiencing any good life.

At this point, the deprivation view probably seems relatively straightforward and perhaps even clearly true. But, as with any substantive philosophical position, it can lead to surprising, and radically counterintuitive, conclusions. Here is one way the deprivation view does just that. Most people believe that it is bad for them to die at the time that they do, instead preferring to die much later. For instance, most would agree that it is bad for a healthy, happy, person to die at, say, 70 instead of 80 or 90. Yet, no one also believes that it was bad for them to not have been born earlier than the time they were actually born. No one believes that it was bad for them to have been born in, say, 1986 rather than 1976 or 1966.

This thought seems to have originated with the ancient Greek philosopher Lucretius, who was following in the footsteps of Epicurus. Lucretius argued that these asymmetrical beliefs were irrational. If my earlier-than-necessary death is bad for me because it prevents me from living additional good life, then why isn't my later-than-necessary birth[1] bad for me for the same reason? After all, holding one's birthdate fixed, if the 60 year old had died at 70 instead of 60, then she would have had an additional 10 years of good life. Similarly, holding one's death date fixed, if the 60 year old were born in 1947 instead of 1957, then she would have also had an additional 10 years of good life. If it is bad for this person to die at 60 instead of 70, then why isn't it also bad for her to have been born in 1957 instead of 1947? Lucretius thought that we have to treat these two cases symmetrically.

We can reconstruct a very simple version of Lucretius's Symmetry Argument in the following way.

The Symmetry Argument

1. It is not bad for one to miss out on an earlier birth.
2. If it is not bad for one to miss out on an earlier birth, then it is not bad for one to miss out on a later death.
3. Therefore, it is not bad for one to miss out on a later death.

This argument is valid, which means that if both premises are true, then the conclusion must be true as well. This poses a problem for deprivationism since, if this argument is sound (i.e. is valid and its premises are true), deprivationism must be false. Fortunately, for deprivationists such as myself, this argument is not sound.

Many deprivationists who have written on this question avoid the conclusion by rejecting premise (2).[2] They defend what I refer to as the *Impossibility Solution*, which holds that

it is impossible, in some important sense, for anyone to have been born substantially earlier than they actually were. It is, however, supposedly possible in the same important sense for one to die substantially later than they will. In the next section, I will review the Impossibility Solution in more detail and argue that it fails because, as I will demonstrate, it *is* possible to be born substantially earlier in time.[3] In the third section, I avoid the conclusion of the Symmetry Argument by rejecting premise (1) for reasons that have been largely overlooked in the literature. I realize that rejecting premise (1) seems implausible on its face. If our late birth was bad for us, shouldn't we be constantly thinking about, and fretting over, it in the same way we do about our death? The answer is "No." I will argue that even though both late birth and early death can be bad for us, there are good reasons for our potentially bad deaths to be on our minds much more than our potentially bad births. In a nutshell, I'll argue that while both later-than-necessary births and earlier-than-necessary deaths can be bad for us, we should primarily just be focused on our deaths.

II. Why the Impossibility Solution Fails

Again, one of the most popular responses to the Symmetry Argument rejects premise (2) on the grounds that it is supposedly impossible, in some important sense, to have been born earlier than you were, but not impossible, in that same important sense, to die later than you will. Why believe it is impossible to be born substantially earlier in time? Well, you might think this if you believe that your existence necessarily depends upon having the physical body you do with your exact genetic makeup. After all, your body and exact genetic makeup necessarily issued from your parents and theirs from each of their parents and so on back to the origin of parent-given life. So, you could not have been born in, say, 1820 because, at that time, it was impossible to create anyone with the same genetic material that you have. Your parents weren't alive in 1820 to create you, nor were their parents alive to create your parents, nor, likely, were your great-grandparents alive to create your grandparents. In order for you to be born, every one of your ancestors had to meet each other and reproduce in exactly the same way (creating exactly the same zygote from exactly the same sperm and egg combination) in order for you to be born at all. If just one of these events didn't happen, you would have never existed!

We will come back to this issue, but let us suppose for the moment that it *was* somehow possible for your body with the exact same genetic makeup to have been created substantially earlier in time. It seems as if there are at least some ways this could happen. Perhaps you find out that you were created through in vitro fertilization and that the two gametes used to create you were stored in a lab for 30 years before being turned into a zygote. Even in this case, you might still believe that it is impossible for you to have been born, say, 30 years earlier. Why? Well, consider the fact that people's personalities, values, interests, and goals are shaped by the environment in which they grow up. If I were born 30 years earlier, I might like doo-wop music, rather than punk. I might prefer *The Twilight Zone* and *The Flintstones* to *Black Mirror* and *The Simpsons*. I might prefer board games to video games, bell bottoms to straight-legged jeans, and so on. I would have different friends, family, goals, a different career and even some different values.

Here's the takeaway. If the zygote that became you were brought into existence 30 years earlier, then the person it would become might be so different than the person you are now that it simply wouldn't be *you*. Or, even if it would be you, it might not be a version of you that you prefer to exist, even if this version of you lives a longer, happier, life.[4] Would you want to have had an extra 10 years of good life if it meant you would have had a completely different set of friends and interests, with a completely different family and career and even different values? Most people would say "No." They prefer to live their actual life over a radically different one, even if that radically different one is longer and contains more good.

These are good points, ones to which I am sympathetic, albeit not entirely convinced.[5] Nevertheless, even if I grant these claims, they are not enough to show that premise (2) is false. Maybe it is not possible for you to have been born 30 years earlier *if everything else in the universe stayed the same*. But it *is* possible for you to have been born earlier if other parts of the universe changed too. If, for instance, the Milky Way galaxy formed 30 years earlier, then the Earth would have formed 30 years earlier, and everyone (including you) would have been born 30 years earlier.[6] You would then have the same physical body with the same genetic makeup. You would have the same friends, family, goals, career, values, aesthetic tastes, and so on. So, even if you think the issues Kaufman and Nagel raise are relevant to your personal identity, it is still possible, in some sense, for you to have been born earlier.

At this point, you might be saying to yourself that it is not physically possible for the Milky Way to have formed 30 years earlier. That *may* be right. But that won't help the person who wants to reject premise (2) of the Symmetry Argument, for it may not be physically possible for some (or all) people to die at a later time than they will. Yet the physical impossibility of living longer would not prevent death from being bad, just as the physical impossibility of avoiding certain pains does not prevent those pains from being bad. The type of possibility that matters, for the purposes of this argument, is a possibility that concerns different ways the world might have been, with different pasts and different physical laws. More precisely, my argument against the Impossibility Solution is as follows.

The Big Bang Argument

1. There was a very large amount of time that passed prior to every person's birth.
2. The Big Bang occurred at some point.

3. Once the Big Bang occurred, the world as we know it came about through a series of causes.
4. One of the effects in this series of causes was that the Milky Way came into existence at some point in time.
5. It is possible for the causal chain to have been altered so that our galaxy came into existence x years earlier in time than the actual time at which it did come into existence.
6. Holding the causal chain fixed after our galaxy comes into existence, the only difference between the possible world and the actual world would be the times at which things occur.
7. Therefore, there is a possible world where our galaxy came into existence at $t-x$ years, such that the people in that world are identical with the people in the actual world.
8. Therefore, it is possible for any actual person to have been born substantially earlier than they actually were.[7]

I take premises (1)–(5) to be independently plausible and do not see a good reason to reject any of them. I take premise (6) to be independently plausible as well, though Frederik Kaufman expresses some doubts about its truth in the next chapter. I will address his concerns shortly. Premise (7) should follow from premises (1)–(6). So, as a matter of logic, one cannot reject premise (7) without also rejecting one of the first six premises. Premises (1)–(7) entail the conclusion (8). So, as a matter of logic, one cannot reject (8) without rejecting at least one of the premises.

Now, the Big Bang Argument should establish that it is possible for everyone to have been born earlier. But if the Milky Way formed earlier, then wouldn't everyone die earlier too, thereby preventing anyone from benefitting from an earlier birth? Not necessarily. Suppose that a giant comet, originating from outside the Milky Way, is going to strike the Earth in 2051 and kill all life immediately upon impact.[8] In this case, anyone who is killed by the comet would have had a longer,

hopefully better, life had the Milky Way formed earlier in time. It seems to me that these persons' late births were bad for them.

III. Objections

III.1 Possibility and Deprivation

In his excellent chapter in this volume, Kaufman raises a few worries about my argument, particularly about what it means for the Milky Way to possibly have formed earlier. Kaufman is probably right to hold that it is also impossible, in some sense, for the Milky Way to have formed earlier in time. However, I maintain that it *is* possible for the Milky Way to have formed earlier in the sense(s) relevant for determining which events are good or bad for people. It's nomologically possible because there are different pasts that, when combined with the actual laws of nature, result in an earlier birth for every existing person. It's epistemically possible because we can't be *absolutely certain* that it is impossible in any sense for the Milky Way to have formed earlier. It's metaphysically possible because we can coherently imagine the Milky Way having formed substantially earlier in time and it's logically possible because there is no contradiction in asserting that the Milky Way could have formed earlier in time.

Perhaps Kaufman is worried that it's not physically possible for the Milky Way to have formed earlier than it did, and that might be right. But it may also not be physically possible for some people to die later than they will. Similarly, it may not be physically possible for some people to not feel certain intense pains they feel. Nevertheless, the physical impossibility of not feeling such pain or of living longer is not taken by anyone to show that those pains and deaths are not bad for people. So, physical possibility cannot be the relevant sense of possibility for determining the badness of events, be it the event of birth, death, or of feeling a painful state.

Kaufman raises another interesting worry in his chapter. He may grant that my Big Bang argument is sound, but nevertheless deny that later-than-necessary births *deprive* one of anything and so are not genuine bads. In his chapter in this book, Kaufman writes that deprivation "implies that I would have gotten or retained a good were it not for an occurrence that, as it were, cheated me out of it. That is what makes deprivations bad, and necessarily so; they are misfortunes." Kaufman's thought is that my death can deprive me of additional good life because, had I not died when I did, I likely would have had more good life. But my birth does not deprive me of any additional good life because, had I not been born when I was, I almost certainly wouldn't have had more good life. I wouldn't have existed at all! To make the point more intuitive, Kaufman adds "I do not think that I am deprived of Aladdin's lamp only because I do not have it even though having it would be better for me." Likewise, Kaufman does not think the Milky Way forming earlier deprives him of anything even though it's true that it forming earlier, in certain cases, would have been good for him. In a nutshell, Kaufman's objection is that cases in which one is born earlier and has a longer, better, life as a result are too far-fetched, too much like Aladdin's lamp to count as deprivations (and therefore are not genuine bads). On the other hand, cases in which one dies later and has a longer, better, life as a result are sufficiently realistic to count as deprivations (and therefore are genuine bads).

Kaufman's objection is a good one, and my response is somewhat conciliatory. I agree that every (or nearly every) person's birth doesn't deprive them of anything because, were their actual birth not to occur, they simply wouldn't exist. On the other hand, many people's deaths do deprive them of additional good life because, were their actual death not to occur, they would live a longer happier life.[9] That was the conciliatory point. Now here's where I want to push back against Kaufman's objection. I do not think that a possibility must be sufficiently "realistic" in order for it to be genuinely bad for us to miss out on it.[10] I defend this claim extensively elsewhere,[11] though in this chapter I only have space to provide a

brief defense of my position. First, consider the fact that many people long for immortality and regard it as bad for them that life is finite. It may well be impossible to live forever, yet it seems plausible to many that it's bad for us to have a finite life. Perhaps Kaufman is willing to bite the bullet on immortality. Perhaps he doesn't think it a genuine misfortune that we don't get eternal life. Notice, however, that it is also very improbable that certain people will get to live much longer than they will. Consider someone with Duchene's muscular dystrophy who dies at the age of 29. Most would regard this person's death as bad for him, even if it's not realistic for someone with that genetic disorder to live much longer. To me at least, it seems genuinely bad for someone with Duchene's muscular dystrophy to die so young.

In response to these examples, Kaufman may insist that it is much more realistic to radically extend the life of people with Duchene's muscular dystrophy than it is for our galaxy to have formed earlier in time. This may be right, though if it is, it still is insufficient to vindicate Kaufman's position. For one, I don't believe that achieving true immortality[12] is a more realistic possibility than the Milky Way having formed earlier in time, though I'll set that possibility aside for now. Second, and more importantly, this realism condition generates absurd verdicts when applied to other cases of harm, such as intrinsic harms, and so should be rejected. To illustrate, consider a world in which everyone, as a matter of physical necessity, lives until they're 100 and suffers in constant agony during the last 10 years of their life. Suppose that the laws of physics in this universe make it physically impossible (or simply highly unrealistic) for anyone to avoid suffering the 10 years of pure agony. Even under this assumption, it seems to me that it's genuinely bad for everyone to suffer this 10 years of agony. Moreover, they seem deprived of a life without suffering even though it's extremely unrealistic for them to avoid this suffering. I conclude, then, that bad events, whether they cause one to experience pain or miss out on pleasure, are genuinely bad (and genuine deprivations) no matter how unrealistic the better alternative happens to be.

III.2 What Does It Mean to Be Born Earlier?

In his ingenious (2018) paper, Lukas Meier offers another objection to my argument, suggesting that one is not born earlier in time *in the relevant sense* if everything in the galaxy happened earlier in time. He writes

> While it is technically true that this life would be earlier in relation to the Big Bang, the terms "earlier" and "later" in this context do not point just to an external anchor point at which the calculation of time starts; they refer to the states that the world is in during the periods in question. Timmerman writes that in his case "the only difference between the possible world and the actual world would be the times at which things occur." This is correct. However, what we really mean by "coming into existence earlier" (or by "dying later") is coming into existence (or dying) at a time when, in comparison with the actual world, different circumstances obtain. The question of whether one regrets not having come into existence earlier than one did is meaningful only if there exists an actual difference between these two options.[13]

The Symmetry Arguments dates back to Lucretius, and I do not know what he had in mind when he wrote of coming into existence earlier, nor am I sure whether every contemporary Epicurean meant to restrict this idea to cases in which "different circumstances obtain" apart from the different circumstances I stipulated in my example. But let's suppose they did. Even so, the case I provide is one where a person would genuinely come into existence earlier in time and would, as a result, live a longer, better, life. So, contrary to what Meier suggests, it seems to me that there is "an actual difference between these two options."

Nevertheless, Meier's point is instructive and, I take it, the cases he has in mind are the ones that are most salient to people when they imagine being born earlier. They may not regard missing out on an earlier birth in the sort of case he has in mind as genuinely bad for them, but may regard missing out on a delayed death as genuinely bad for them. On the other hand, in wishing that one was born earlier in the sort of case I have in mind, one seems to be wishing for additional life tacked on to the life they already led. Presumably, one would be indifferent between two introspectively indistinguishable lives even if one starts and ends earlier in time than the other. So, one lesson to draw from my cases is that, all else being equal, people really desire to live their actual life,[14] only with the addition of experientially posterior goods. They are indifferent to whether these experientially posterior goods are a result of an earlier birth or a later death. This should be a point of agreement between Kaufman, Meier, and myself.

IV. Asymmetrical Salience

Recall that proponents of the Impossibility Solution rejects premise (2) of the Symmetry Argument on the grounds that it is supposedly impossible to have been born substantially earlier in time. Now that I've argued that the Impossibility Solution fails, deprivationism may seem to be falsified by the Symmetry Argument. But it isn't, or so I argue. I will now defend my positive solution to the asymmetry problem. Instead of rejecting premise (2) of the Symmetry Argument, I reject premise (1), allowing that it *is* bad for us not to have been born earlier *if* being born earlier would have resulted in us living a longer, happier, life.[15] Like some early deaths, some late births are events that make us worse off, and any event that makes us worse off is bad for us. The fact that a late birth could be bad for us is a surprising conclusion, but it is only surprising because we tend not to think about how our life could have gone if we were born earlier. Rather than thinking about what our lives could have been like were we born earlier, we tend to focus on what our lives could be like if we were to continue living beyond the date of our death. I will now argue that this is perfectly rational. Our impending death should be *salient* to us (or, more colloquially, "on our mind") much more frequently than our birth. Once we recognize why this is so, rejecting premise (1) of the Symmetry Argument won't seem so implausible. At least, I hope it won't. Here are three considerations in favor of asymmetrical salience.

IV.1 Difference in Control

First, you can possibly avoid or delay your bad death, while you cannot change your bad birth (unless, of course, you can travel backwards in time). You can take measures to delay your death by being generally risk averse. You can, for instance, not smoke, maintain a healthy diet, exercise, not punch lions, and so on. The choices that you make on a daily basis affect the chances that you will die sooner rather than later, but they do not affect whether you will be born sooner rather than later. This provides reason for impending death to be on our mind (and factor into the decisions that we make) much more than our birth.

IV.2 Difference in the Times Each Event Is a Threat

Second, every moment you are alive, a bad death can still come for you. Birth, on the other hand, has already happened and a potentially bad birth is no longer a threat to your well-being. It seems plausible to me that the simple fact that death continues to threaten to shorten your life is a reason to think about it more than your birth *even if* there is nothing you can do to delay your death.

IV.3 Difference in Uncertainty

Third, unlike birth, the time that your death will occur is unknown, which creates uncertainty not only about the time this bad event will happen, but also about how it will affect your life. As with any harm, the ways in which death's harm will affect you depends, in part, on the time that it will occur. Knowing that a harmful event will definitely occur, but not knowing the time that it will occur or the

particular negative effects of the harm is sufficient to generate a non-trivial amount of anxiety in people. This uncertainty is a reasonable source of anxiety. This makes the potential badness of death salient in a way that the potential badness of birth is not.

V. Conclusion

I have done a few things in this short chapter. I first reviewed and motivated the Symmetry Argument. I then reviewed the Impossibility Solution to the Symmetry Argument and explained that proponents of this solution reject premise (2). After that, I argued that the Impossibility Solution fails by way of the Big Bang Argument, which demonstrates it is possible for people to be born substantially earlier in time. I then considered, and attempted to rebut, a few objections to my Big Bang Argument before, finally, arguing that there is good reason to reject premise (1) of the Symmetry Argument. Although it may at first seem counterintuitive to allow that later-than-necessary birth can be bad for you, it is not implausible once we recognize that we have reason to focus on our earlier-than-necessary deaths, while never (or almost never) focusing on our later-than-necessary births. These reasons include, but perhaps are not limited to, the typical differences in control, threat timing, and uncertainty between early deaths and late births.

Notes

1. For ease of exposition, I am using the term "birth" to refer to the moment one comes into existence even though everyone exists before they are born.
2. This move was originally defended in Thomas Nagel, "Death," *Noûs* 4, 1970, 73–80. However, Frederick Kaufman has done the most to develop and defend this view. See Frederick Kaufman, "An Answer to Lucretius' Symmetry Argument Against the Fear of Death," *Journal of Value Inquiry* 29, 1995, 57–64; Frederick Kaufman, "Death and Deprivation: Or, Why Lucretius' Symmetry Argument Fails," *Australasian Journal of Philosophy* 74, 1996,

305–312; Frederik Kaufman, "Pre-Vital and Post-Mortem Non-Existence," *Philosophical Quarterly* 36, 1999, 1–19; Frederick Kaufman, "Early Death, Late Birth, and the Problem of Lucretian Symmetry," *Social Theory and Practice* 37, 2011, section 4; Frederick Kaufman, "Lucretius and the Fear of Death," in *Immortality and the Philosophy of Death*, ed. Michael Cholbi (New York: Rowman and Littlefield, 2016), 53–66.

3. Others have suggested that one can be born substantially earlier in time too. See Dorothy Grover, "Death and Life," *Canadian Journal of Philosophy* 17, 1987, 711–732.

4. Jeff McMahan, *The Ethics of Killing* (New York: Oxford University Press, 2002), 77.

5. To understand why, see Ben Bradley, "The Worst Time to Die," *Ethics* 118, 2008, 291–314.

6. I make this line of argument in Travis Timmerman, "Avoiding the Asymmetry Problem," *Ratio* 31, 2018, 88–102.

7. Timmerman, "Avoiding the Asymmetry Problem," 93.

8. This is a variation of Belshaw's thought experiment in Christopher Belshaw, "Death, Pain and Time," *Philosophical Studies* 97, 2000, 74–78. A similar example is given in Kai Draper, "Epicurean Equanimity Towards Death," *Philosophy and Phenomenological Research* 69, 2004, 92–114.

9. Timmerman, "Avoiding the Asymmetry Problem," 93.

10. A "realism constraint" is also defended in McMahan, "The Ethics of Killing," 133.

11. See Travis Timmerman, "Your Death Might be the Worst Thing Ever to Happen to You (But Maybe You Shouldn't Care)," *Canadian Journal of Philosophy* 46, 2016, 18–37. See also Travis Timmerman, "Doomsday Needn't Be So Bad," *dialectica* 72, 2018, 275–296.

12. See John Martin Fischer and Benjamin Mitchell-Yellin, "Immortality and Boredom," *The Journal of Ethics* 18, 2014, 353–372. See also John Martin Fischer, *Death, Immortality, and Meaning in Life* (New York: Oxford University Press, 2019), 85–142.

13. Lukas Meier, "What Matters in the Mirror of Time: Why Lucretius' Symmetry Argument Fails," *Australasian Journal of Philosophy*, 2021, 658.

14. Or, perhaps, something close to their actual life. See John Martin Fischer, *Our Stories* (New York: Oxford University Press, 2011), 63–78.

15. Other philosophers, such as John Martin Fischer, have also rejected the first premise of the Symmetry Argument. Fischer argues that while both later-than-necessary birth and earlier-than-necessary death can be bad for us, we should have different *attitudes* toward each potentially bad event. We should lament our bad deaths, but be indifferent to our bad births. Humans do tend to be concerned about future harms, caring very little about past harms. If these attitudes are rational, then Fischer's solution may work as well. For more on Fischer's seminal solution, see his work cited in the previous two notes, as well as the following. Anthony Brueckner and John Martin Fischer, "Being Born Earlier," *Australasian Journal of Philosophy* 76, 1998, 110–114; John Martin Fischer and Anthony Brueckner, "The Evil of Death and the Lucretian Symmetry: A Reply to Feldman," *Philosophical Studies* 163, 2013, 783–789; John Martin Fischer and Anthony Brueckner, "Prenatal and Posthumous Non-Existence: A Reply to Johansson," *Journal of Ethics* 18, 2014, 1–9.

15 Coming Into and Going Out of Existence

Frederik Kaufman

Dying is at the top of my list of the bad things that might happen to me today. The ancient philosopher Epicurus would say that my belief is mistaken. Assuming that death is the permanent extinction of conscious biographical life, he reasons that it is not bad at all, "for while we exist death is not present, and when death is present we no longer exist."[1] Death, he so astonishingly pronounced, "is of no concern to us." If Epicurus is right, feeling anxiety about the prospect of dying is irrational.

I might reasonably fear dying painfully, but that is not what Epicurus is talking about, since I must exist in order to feel pain. Epicurus is saying that once I am dead (after the process of dying is over) and I no longer exist, that is no harm, and so the prospect of death should not be feared, since "that which gives no trouble when it comes, is but an empty pain in anticipation."[2]

Epicurus' argument has intrigued thoughtful people for millennia, since his assumption that death is annihilation is plausible, yet his conclusion that death should therefore be of no concern to us stands in sharp contrast to common sense. But what, exactly, is wrong with his reasoning? Thomas Nagel's reply is the touchstone for so many current discussions in this burgeoning area of philosophy, the philosophy of death.[3] Nagel argues, contrary to Epicurus, that death can be bad (and therefore of legitimate concern) if it deprives someone of life that she would have enjoyed by not dying when she did. Since death is nothingness it is not intrinsically bad (i.e. bad in itself), but it can shorten a good life and so can be extrinsically bad (i.e. lead to an intrinsic bad or prevent an intrinsic good). The thought that death can be bad if it deprives us of the good of life seems like an obvious rejoinder to Epicurus that might occur to anyone, but this answer is subject to a number of serious challenges, making rationally defending it more difficult than we ever would have imagined.

Among the most intractable is one discussed by Epicurus' disciple Lucretius in the first century BCE. Lucretius argued that if I think my death would be bad because it deprives me of life, then the same holds for when I came into existence (assuming that it would not affect when I will die). By coming into existence when I did, I also missed out on life that I could have enjoyed if I had come into existence earlier. The infinity before my existence is symmetrical to the infinity after my existence. Rationality requires treating likes alike, and since I am indifferent to the one, I should be indifferent to the other. Here is how Lucretius put it:

> Look back at the eternity that passed before we were born, and mark how utterly it counts to us as nothing. This is a mirror that Nature holds up to us, in which we may see that the times that shall be after we are dead. Is there anything terrifying in the sight—anything depressing—anything that is not more restful than the soundest sleep?[4]

Lucretius' Symmetry Argument is a serious threat to the claim that death can be bad because it deprives us of additional good life, because if Lucretius is right, then coming into existence when we did would similarly deprive us of additional good life and so be bad as well. Nagel recognized the threat and argued against Lucretius that while we can die later than we will, it is impossible for us to exist earlier than we do. This is because "any-one born substantially earlier than [this par-ticular person] was would be someone else."[5] Assuming my identity is fixed by the zygote from which I emerged, and that zygote could not exist earlier than it does, I could not have come into existence earlier than I did. According to Nagel, the Lucretian symmetry is thus broken. However, in an admirably frank footnote Nagel imagines a science fiction scenario in which the premature hatching of spores from which we develop *does* make earlier existence possible. He ruefully con-cludes that "Lucretius' argument still awaits an answer."[6] Answering Lucretius is important because if he is right, then we cannot say in response to Epicurus that death is bad because it deprives without thinking the same about when we came into existence, and that seems preposterous.

What can we say to Lucretius? Least help-ful, I think, is to agree that pre-natal and post-mortem non-existence can both deprive, so we should regard both as bad.[7] On this view, when I was born (or whenever it is that I began to exist) could be as bad as when I will die. Actually, it is worse than that, since a particular death might not deprive at all, whereas a late birth could deprive someone of a lot of good life. This suggests that I could go through life oblivious to the terrible dep-rivation that occurred to me by my late birth!

Other philosophers also seem to agree with Lucretius that late birth and early death can both deprive, but they argue that we just don't care about the deprivations of late birth, but do care about the deprivations of early death. John Martin Fischer and Anthony Brueckner proposed this solution to Lucretius' challenge.[8] Recall the dialectic: if we argue that death can be bad because it deprives, Lucretius responds that the same holds for when we came into existence. If one deprives, then so does the other. Fischer and Brueckner agree that both times can deprive (and so could be equally bad), but they argue that we are indifferent to the goods of life we missed by coming into existence when we did. We care only about the goods we will miss by going out of

existence when we will. In their view, we have different attitudes toward objectively equally bad things because we are biased toward the future.

Fischer and Brueckner appeal to a vari-ation on a famous thought experiment that purports to show our temporal bias. Here is their version of that thought experiment:

> Imagine that you are in some hospital to test a drug. The drug induces intense pleasure for an hour followed by amnesia. You awaken and ask the nurse about your situation. She says that either you tried the drug yesterday (and had an hour of pleasure) or you will try the drug tomorrow (and will have an hour of pleasure). While she checks on your status, it is clear that you prefer to have the pleasure tomorrow.[9]

This suggests that from our first-person inter-nal perspective we care more about future goods than past goods, perhaps because of evo-lution, since future-oriented creatures would obviously fare better than ones indifferent to the future. So because of our future-ori-entation we care more about the goods of a longer life than whatever life goods we missed by coming into existence late, even though both deprive. Thus, according to Brueckner and Fischer, "[d]eath deprives us of something we care about, whereas prenatal nonexistence deprives us of something to which we are indifferent."[10]

Is this a good answer to Lucretius? I don't think so. Even if people are temporally biased this does not answer the right question. The supposed fact that people are temporally biased may well *explain* why we care about missing goods by dying early, but it does not address Lucretius' fundamental claim that we are irrational to prefer goods we will miss by dying early over ones that we did miss by com-ing into existence late. It is easy to imagine Lucretius saying that we have here missed the point, since the dialectic goes like this: Lucretius challenges the deprivation response to Epicurus by arguing that if an early death is bad because it deprives, then coming into existence late deprives too (and is similarly bad). We should, he would insist, adopt the same attitude toward the goods we miss by coming into existence so late that we now have toward our early deaths. After all, those times are symmetrical and rationality requires us to regard them similarly. Responding to Lucretius by saying that we don't have to regard them similarly because we are temporally biased is no answer at all. Lucretius agrees that we are biased; that, he would say, is the problem. Were we rational, he would surely insist, we would see that both periods of non-existence deprive, so we have no good reason for our attitudinal asymmetry. If the one is bad because it deprives, then the other does too. Were Lucretius aware of evolution, he might point out that irrational preferences could have survival value, as perhaps shown by something like xenophobia as a precursor to racial prejudice. Therefore, an appeal to asymmetrical temporal attitudes toward equally bad periods of non-existence fails to address Lucretius' Symmetry Argument.

Jeff McMahan gives a better response to the Symmetry Argument. He agrees with Brueckner and Fischer that it is metaphysically possible for us to have existed earlier than we do, but the details of that earlier life would be so utterly different from our lives now that it would basically be the life of a stranger. The logic of identity implies that a person born earlier could still be me, but not in a way that has any emotional connection to the person that I currently am.

Here's how McMahan argues that I could have existed earlier:

[C]onsider someone who is the product of in vitro fertilization (IVF). Her parents wanted a child but not until they were older. But they worried that conceiving a child when they were older would carry a higher risk that their child would have a congenital defect. So they had IVF and had the resulting embryos frozen. They then waited 15 years before implanting the embryo that in fact developed into this person. This seems to be a case in which, if the parents had implanted this same embryo earlier, the same person would have had an earlier origin… If this is right, there are some people who could have come into existence earlier than they did.[11]

It is true that the earlier existing human being would be identical to the later existing one and so in that sense would be the same human being. But the term "human being" is ambiguous between human organism, which is a biological concept, and person, which is a metaphysical and moral concept. Brain dead individuals, for example, are obviously human organisms, but not persons in the sense in which you are a person, namely, as an ongoing biographical center of self-awareness. Conversely, Superman, were he to exist, would be a person in that sense too, though obviously not a member of the species *Homo sapiens*.

In McMahan's thought experiment, could the same *person* have existed earlier? It seems to me that questions about personal identity must deal with persons, not the colorless identity of human organisms that might exist at different times. John Locke (1632–1704) distinguished sharply between the "man" or the human organism and the "person," which Locke said is "a thinking intelligent being, that has reason and reflection, and can consider itself as itself, the same thinking thing, in different times and places."[12] So while the parents could have implanted the embryo earlier, which would have resulted in the same *human organism* as the one that was implanted later, I don't think that the earlier one would be the same *person*.

The distinguished Oxford philosopher Derek Parfit (1942–2017) argued that identity is not what should ultimately matter to us. What should ultimately matter to each of us is the continuity of our embedded biographical lives; that is, the rich details of our actual lives as we in fact live them: our concerns, our memories, our hopes, plans, desires, our continuous sense of ourselves, and all that makes our individual lives worth living. That, after all, is what death threatens; that is what an early death deprives us of, and that is what we can reasonably fear losing. I call this our "thick personhood," to distinguish it from "thin personhood" (read: the bare human organism shorn of all the particulars of one's biographical life). So even if an earlier existing human organism would be identical to a later existing one, that is not what should ultimately matter to each of us. It would not be me in the sense in which I conceive of myself to be the person who I am. I think that Nagel was on the right track when he said that it was impossible for me to exist earlier. But "me" is ambiguous between thick and thin personhood. Even if the thin me could have existed earlier, the thick me could not have, and the thick me is what I rationally care about.

Thought experiments that ask us to imagine different possible lives for a person associated with my organism are irrelevant to the question of whether my thick person could have existed earlier, even assuming my organism could have existed earlier. If, to use another of McMahan's examples, my parents had converted to Islam and emigrated to Pakistan when I was young, my life would be very different than it is now, since I grew up in America. It is tempting to argue that the Pakistani Muslim would nevertheless still be me because of the psychological continuity between that person and the child with whom I am in fact psychologically continuous. If I now am identical to that child and the Pakistani Muslim would also be identical to that child, then by the logic of identity, I would be identical to the Pakistani Muslim. (If A=B, and B=C, then A=C.)

"This shows," claims McMahan, "that I could have existed with a very different mental life." Perhaps, but does that show I could have existed earlier? That is the crucial question, not whether I could have had a different mental life. If we take some version of psychological continuity as constitutive of personhood, then because their organism would exist at different times, an earlier existing person would have to be different than a later existing one. The issue is not differing contents of their mental lives, but the fact that the biography of an earlier existing person would

begin before that of the later existing person; that is why their biographies will be different, making them distinct persons irrespective of whether the organism that supports them is the same. So, while the contents of my biography could be different, it seems that irrespective of its details my biography could not have started earlier than it did.

To see this more clearly, consider a statue and the metal from which it was formed. We could melt the statue down and make a different one from the same metal. But when a particular statue is formed is essential to its being *that* statue. Analogously then, even if the same human organism could exist earlier than it does, it does not follow that the thick person associated with that organism would be the same thick person as one supported by the later human organism. The contents of the mental lives of the earlier and later person will necessarily be different, but that is not what makes them different persons, as McMahan's example about the same person with a different biography shows. They will be different thick persons because of when their biographies began.

Still, maybe the thick me could exist earlier if *everything* could somehow exist earlier. In an ingenious thought experiment Travis Timmerman asks us to imagine that the entire Milky Way galaxy formed five years earlier than it actually did.[13] Assuming causal determinism, could everything that happens today on Earth (and throughout the entire Milky Way) have happened in lock step unison exactly as it did but tomorrow or yesterday instead? That is dizzying to contemplate and I don't know if it is even possible, but let's suppose with Timmerman that it is.

If the Milky Way could have formed five years earlier than it did, then it is true that I could have existed earlier, but only because everything could have existed earlier. How is this relevant to death? Recall the dialectic: on the deprivation account death is bad if it deprives, meaning that it robs us of time we don't get by dying when we do. Lucretius then points out that the same holds for when we came into existence, since if we had existed earlier we also could have had additional time. In response to Lucretius, I suggested a version of Nagel's view: we cannot possibly exist earlier and be the same thick persons that we are now, whereas it is easy to picture dying later than we will (while still being the same thick persons that we currently are). A later death would add more life experiences to one's already established thick personhood, whereas an earlier existence would result in a different thick person altogether. In response to *that* claim, Timmerman gives us his Milky Way thought experiment to show how thick me *could* have existed earlier. This puts us back to square one with Lucretius: if I could have gotten thicker by not dying so early, then I could also have gotten thicker had everything started sooner. This possibility preserves all that matters to me about my actual life— every aspect of my biographical existence and the entirety of my surroundings down to the minutest detail—but it all could have occurred earlier or later than it actually did.

Now, you may be wondering why the mere possibility that all galactic events could have occurred earlier demonstrates that our birth deprives our actual thick selves of good life. After all, if we were all born earlier, then wouldn't we all die earlier and have the same amount of good life either way? Here is how Timmerman develops his thought experiment to avoid that conclusion. Suppose that a giant comet from outside the galaxy will destroy the Earth tomorrow. But if the comet was not going to strike tomorrow, I would live five more years before dying in a car crash. So, if the Milky Way had formed five years earlier than it actually did, then right now I (and everyone else) would be as thick as I (we) will be after five more years of life given that the Milky Way formed when it actually did. In other words, the possible earlier Milky Way thick me right now will be same as the actual Milky Way thick me five years from now.

If the comet *is* going to destroy the Earth tomorrow, I would presumably lament the fact that the Milky Way formed when it did and not earlier, since had it formed earlier, I would have been able to have another five years of good life before I died. Had it formed five years earlier, right now I would be the thicker me that I would be in five years if the comet doesn't hit the Earth. (Nothing seems to hinge on a giant comet destroying the Earth; it could be just a small meteor or indeed anything else that will kill only me. Also, if my life takes a sudden nasty turn, I might wish that the Milky Way had formed later so that right now I would be younger, thus postponing having to deal with my unpleasant situation.)

This shows that I could have come into existence earlier (or later) than I actually did while retaining all that is important to me about my life. And the only way that can happen is if everything is shifted in unison forward or backward in time, since what matters to me about my life is bound to my existence relative to everything else. As Timmerman put it, "people really desire to live their actual life, only with the addition of experientially posterior goods. They are indifferent to whether those experientially posterior goods are a result of an earlier conception or a later death."[14]

In response to Timmerman, I think the crucial question is whether the possibility that the Milky Way could have formed earlier than it did can deprive me of time that I otherwise could have had. We must consider more closely what it means to be deprived, since that is the central idea in the view that death can be bad because it deprives.

To be deprived of something means more than just not having it. Deprivation implies that I would have gotten or retained a good were it not for an occurrence that, as it were, cheated me out of it. That is what makes deprivations bad, and necessarily so; they are misfortunes. I do not think that I am deprived of Aladdin's lamp only because I do not have it even though having it would be better for me. Merely not having the lamp is not a misfortune, even though I would be better with it than without it. Deprivations are a kind of comparative bad, but not all comparative bads count as deprivations. If we compare my winning the lottery to my not winning it, it is better for me to win the lottery, but not winning it doesn't mean that I have been deprived of that good.

Deprivation also presupposes possibility; I am not deprived of time travel. Moreover, among the possibilities, as Nagel noted, "we still have to set some limits on *how* possible a possibility must be for its nonrealization to be a misfortune."[15] So even if it is possible for the Milky Way to have formed earlier than it did, it's not clear that I am deprived of that additional possible time simply because it did not form earlier. In other words, is the non-realized possibility that the Milky Way could have formed earlier a misfortune for me (and everyone else)?

Unless we follow Nagel and set some limits on which non-realized possible goods count as misfortunes, I would be deprived of every possible good only because I do not have it, such as Aladdin's lamp, winning lottery tickets, or superhuman powers. I would be the *victim* (a normative term) of innumerable misfortunes just because I don't have every conceivable good. This does not seem correct to me. Dying in a car crash tomorrow intuitively seems like a misfortune that does deprive me of time I could have had, whereas not having additional time because the Milky Way formed when it did instead of earlier does not. It is true that in each case I do not get additional time, but that is not sufficient for both to count as deprivations even if I am comparatively worse off in each. If we insist that both are genuine misfortunes, they are of a vastly different order. It is a lot easier to see the car crash victim as unfortunate than someone who does not get additional good life because of when the Milky Way formed. Moreover, if the possibility of the Milky Way forming earlier deprives, then death necessarily deprives, since no matter when someone dies she could always have had additional time had the Milky Way formed earlier.

So we can agree that Timmerman's thought experiment shows how I could have existed earlier, but only in the strange sense of everything existing earlier (or later). This possibility confirms my intuition about the significance of the details of our lives relative to our surroundings. Thick me—the me I care about—cannot be plucked out from the world and moved forward or backward in time. That would be impossible. The only way thick me can move in time is if everything else moves in time. But then trying to use the possibility of the Milky Way forming earlier to show that I can be deprived of time if it had done so undercuts the idea of deprivation, since not every possible unrealized good counts as a deprivation.

We can now return to Lucretius' Symmetry Argument with a renewed understanding. If I am right, then the first part of Lucretius' Symmetry Argument is broken, since it assumes that the thick persons we currently are could exist earlier and so be deprived of that time. But can we die later than we will? Here we need only imagine our established biographies continuing past the time of death. There is nothing psychologically disruptive or incoherent in this. Let's suppose—contrary to fact, I fervently hope—that I die in a car crash tomorrow. It is easy to imagine what would happen had I not died: my life would continue on its established trajectory. I would work to fulfill my projects and carry my plans forward; I would continue to enjoy my family, friends, and familiar surroundings. In Locke's apt phrase, I would continue to see myself as myself, the "same thinking thing, in different times and places."

Imaginatively extending my established life past an untimely death raises none of the difficult issues we encountered in trying to understand what it would be like for thick me to exist earlier. Properly understood, I cannot exist earlier than I do, but I could exist later than I will. Whether this applies to time beyond a normal human lifespan is a separate issue that we do not have to settle to see that at least within the range of normality, I can only be *deprived* of time I could reasonably expect to live.

This is a real, objective, difference between pre-vital and post-mortem times. My death can be bad because it deprives me of time alive, whereas I cannot be deprived of time I could have had by existing earlier because that is not possible. Therefore, I don't have to have similar attitudes about my pre-vital and post-mortem non-existence; I can think my death would be bad without having to think the same about when I was born. If I am right, this answers Lucretius' Symmetry Argument. That death can be bad because it deprives is, I think, the correct response to Epicurus' denial that death can be bad, so answering Lucretius' Symmetry Argument is an important step in rationally defending what remains, at least to my mind, intuitively obvious.[16]

Notes

1. Epicurus, *Letter to Menoeceus*.
2. Ibid.
3. Thomas Nagel, "Death," *Noûs* 4 (1970), reprinted in *Mortal Questions* (Cambridge: Cambridge University Press, 1979), 1–10.
4. Lucretius, *On the Nature of Things*, trans. Cyril Bailey (Oxford: Oxford University Press, 1920), Bk III, 927.
5. Nagel, "Death," 8.
6. Ibid., footnote 3.
7. Fred Feldman, "Some Puzzles About the Evil of Death," *Philosophical Review* 100, no. 2, April (1991), 205–227 (reprinted in David Benatar, *Life, Death, and Meaning* (Lanham, MD: Rowman and Littlefield, 2004), 234), holds that we should try to view our births in the same way we view our deaths:

   There are, after all, two ways in which we can rectify the apparently irrational emotional asymmetry [between late birth and early death]. On the one hand, we can follow Lucretius and cease viewing early death as a bad thing for Claudette. On the other hand, we can at least try to start viewing late birth as a bad thing. My suggestion is that in the present case the latter course would be preferable. I think it must be granted that our emotional reactions toward pleasures lost by early death are quite different from our emotional reactions toward similar pleasures lost by late birth. If my proposal is right, this emotional asymmetry is irrational.

   That the lateness of our birth could be as tragic as our untimely death is even harder to accept than Lucretius' recommendation that we become indifferent to death.

8. Anthony Brueckner and John Martin Fischer, "Why Is Death Bad?," *Philosophical Studies* 50 (1986): 213–21.
9. Brueckner and Fischer, "The Asymmetry of Early Death and Late Birth," *Philosophical Studies* 71 (1993): 327–331, 328.
10. Brueckner and Fischer, "Why Death Is Bad," 219.
11. Jeff McMahan, "The Lucretian Argument," in *The Good, the Right, Life and Death: Essays in Honor of Fred Feldman*, ed. Kris McDaniel (Aldershot: Ashgate, 2006), 213–226.
12. John Locke, *An Essay Concerning Human Understanding*, Bk II, ch. XXVII, paragraph 9.
13. Travis Timmerman, "Avoiding the Asymmetry Problem," *Ratio* 31, no. 1, 2018, 88–102.
14. Ibid.
15. Nagel, "Death," 9.
16. Thanks to Travis Timmerman and Michael Cholbi for many helpful comments on earlier versions of this paper.

Part V Would Immortality Be Good for Us?

Immortality

Dreadest thou the aspect of death! Thou
   wishest to live on forever?
Live in the whole, and when long thou
   shalt have gone, 'twill remain!

—**Friedrich Schiller**

Because I Could Not Stop for Death

Because I could not stop for Death—
He kindly stopped for me—
The Carriage held but just Ourselves—
And Immortality.
We slowly drove—He knew no haste
And I had put away
My labor and my leisure too,
For His Civility—
We passed the School, where Children
   strove
At Recess—in the Ring—
We passed the Fields of Gazing Grain—
We passed the Setting Sun—
Or rather—He passed us—
The Dews drew quivering and chill—
For only Gossamer, my Gown—
My Tippet—only Tulle—
We paused before a House that seemed
A Swelling of the Ground—
The Roof was scarcely visible—
The Cornice—in the Ground—
Since then—'tis Centuries—and yet
Feels shorter than the Day
I first surmised the Horses' Heads
Were toward Eternity

—**Emily Dickinson**

Introduction to Part V

Do you want to live forever? The majority
of people in the world believe in an afterlife
and so believe they will, in some sense, live
forever. The majority of people, religious or
not, also believe that this outcome would be
good for them. Not everyone agrees, however,
that immortality would be good for creatures
like us. In this section, you will get to read
two works of fiction about immortality, ones
which highlight the potential drawbacks of at
least some kinds of immortal lives. You will
also get to read three contemporary takes on
the desirability of immortality. Ben Mitchell-
Yellin will argue that an immortal life could
be infinitely good for us. August Gorman and
David Beglin will grant the possibility that an
immortal life could be infinitely good, though
they draw more cautious conclusions about
whether we should choose to live forever if
granted the opportunity.

   You'll first get to read an excerpt from
The Epic of Gilgamesh (approximately 1800
B.C.E.), another epic poem. This one is from
ancient Mesopotamia and is one of the ear-
liest-surviving works of fiction. You'll read
tablets 9–11 that follow Gilgamesh's quest to
become immortal. Gilgamesh's futile efforts
can be contrasted with Utnapishtim's success
at achieving immortality, which he did with
the help of a god after a Noah's Ark-like flood
kills almost everyone else.

   This is followed by Yei Theodora Ozaki's
early twentieth-century retelling of the
Japanese fairy tale *The Story of the Man Who*

Did Not Wish To Die. The fairy tale centers around Sentaro seeking the elixir of life, first from hermits in a mountainous region of land, then seemingly achieving it on an island of immortals who, sick of life, strive to die in vain. Thanks to his spiritual guide Jofuku, Sentaro learns valuable lessons about life and death in his quest for immortality.

Much of the contemporary work on immortality spawns from Bernard Williams' famous (1973) argument that immortality would necessarily be bad for creatures like us. Williams offers a dilemma to those who desire immortality. He argues that an immortal human life would result in one either (a) satisfying all of their desires that give them reason to live, causing them to be interminably bored or (b) continually developing new desires that give them reason to live, eventually causing their character to change so much that it simply wouldn't be them, at least not in the relevant sense.

With John Martin Fischer, Ben Mitchell-Yellin has attacked the first horn of the dilemma, arguing that there are inexhaustible desires that give people reason to live, and which could be satisfied ad infinitum. In his chapter in this section, Mitchell-Yellin attacks the second horn of Williams' argument. He paints a picture of an immortal life where one's character undergoes radical changes, yet one's relevant sense of identity is maintained. His primary goal, however, is to allay concerns that an immortal life would "undermine individuality" because it would have no "ending" or because every immortal human might each eventually do everything there is to do, becoming indistinguishable from one another.

As you can tell, philosophers who have thought extensively about immortality still disagree about whether an immortal life could be desirable for humans. Most people probably don't know whether immortality would be good for them. This raises the question of whether, in light of our ignorance, we should choose immortality if given the option.

August Gorman and David Beglin tackle this sort of question in the last two chapters of this section.

Gorman begins by attacking Williams' first horn of the dilemma, arguing that it's at least possible for some people to desire to pursue infinitely many projects, consistent with their character, that give them reason to live. They then argue that doing so is only possible for a person if they have certain character traits that they can't *know* they have. As such, choosing an immortal life means one runs the risk of living an infinitely bad life, a risk which Gorman heavily cautions against taking.

Beglin also attacks Williams' first horn of the dilemma, though he too cautions against choosing immortality. According to Beglin, avoiding interminable boredom while maintaining one's character would require committing oneself to very abstract projects, such as intellectual inquiry or promoting justice. He argues that doing that for an eternity requires giving up a certain kind of meaning in life, one that derives from how mortality affects our values, projects, and relationships with others. Giving that up may not be desirable even if a certain type of immortal life would be infinitely good for us.

If you're interested in reading more about immortality, check out the following:

1. Chapter 6 of Bernard Williams' *Problems of the Self* (1973), Cambridge University Press.
2. Felipe Pereira's and Travis Timmerman's "The (Un)desirability of Immortality" (2020) *Philosophy Compass* 15 (2): 1–12.
3. [Sophie-Grace] Chappell's "Infinity Goes up on Trial: Must Immortality Be Meaningless?" (2009) *European Journal of Philosophy* 17 (1): 30–44.
4. John Martin Fischer and Benjamin Mitchell-Yellin's "Immortality and Boredom" (2014) *The Journal of Ethics* 18 (4): 353–372.

16 The Epic of Gilgamesh (excerpts)*

Trans. W. Muss Arnolt (1901)

TABLET X

… Gilgamesh drew nigh unto the shore, and he spoke unto Utnapishtim: "O, Utnapishtim, thou who surviveth the Deluge…" [The rest is lost.]

Utnapishtim said unto Gilgamesh: "Why art thou ashen and pale? Why art thy features sunken and hollow, thy countenance so sickly? Why is thine heart heavy with grief, and thy countenance like one who hath made a long journey? Why art thine features blasted by the weather, and why dost thou in lion's skin wander?"

Gilgamesh said unto Utnapishtim: "Wherefore should I not appear ashen and pale? Wherefore should not my features be sunken and hollow, my countenance so sickly? Wherefore should not my heart be heavy with grief, and my countenance like one who hath made a long journey? Wherefore should not my features be blasted by the weather, and I in lion's skin wander? My friend, Enkidu wert a swift wild ass, a donkey of the mountains, a panther of the wilderness. My friend, whom I loved more than any man, accompanied me through every peril until the fate of all mortals befell him. For six days and seven nights I mourned him, I left his body unburied until from his nostril a maggot came forth. I feared death for myself, and so on the distant road I wander the wilderness. My friend's fate was too grievous to bear, and so on the distant road I wander the wilderness. What happened to my beloved Enkidu was unbearable to me, and so on the distant road I wander the wilderness. Must I remain silent? The friend whom I loved has been turned to clay; Enkidu, my friend. And I will not, like unto him, lie down; not will I sink to where my friend is now."

And Gilgamesh said unto Utnapishtim: "Here I have come, and Utnapishtim, whom people call the 'distant,' I will see. To him I will turn. I have travelled through all the lands, I have crossed over the steep mountains, and I have traversed all the seas. I had little sleep and castigated myself by denying me rest. I have filled my very sinews with grief, and all in vain. Before I reached the tavern-keeper, my clothes had worn away. I killed wild beasts, the hyena, the panther, the cheetah, the stag, the jackal, the lion, the wild bull, the deer, and ibex. Their flesh I ate and their pelts I wore. But now close fast the gates of sorrow, seal them fast with tar and pitch! Sorrow shall never again interrupt my revelry and joy!"

Utnapishim said unto Gilgamesh: "Wherefore dost thou follow after sorrows? Thou art made of godly stuff, fashioned from flesh human and divine in the image of thine father and mother. Hast thou contrasted thy lot to that of the fool? For thee a throne was set up in the assembly on which thou wert commanded to sit. The fool eateth the yeast that remaineth, not fresh butter; he eateth bran and grist, not milled flour. He weareth rags, not fine robes; no belt but old rope. [Portions that follow are fragmentary and describe the actions of the gods.] Enkidu the gods have indeed brought down to his doom. But what hast thou gained from thy toil? As thou exhausteth thine energies and sap thy strength, thou only hasten the end of thy days. The life of a man may be snapped like a dry reed. The handsome youth and the comely maid, both may fall to Death all too soon. None might see Death or hear his voice, though Death reapeth us all.

"As long as houses are built, as long as tablets are sealed, as long as brothers are at enmity, as long as there exist strife and hatred in the land, as long as the river carries the waters to the sea, etc., so long is there no likeness of death drawn, never shall the dead great the living. The Anunnaki, the great gods, assemble and Mammitum, the goddess of fate, she who with them determines fate, will do so, for they determine death and life. But the days of death are unknown to mankind."

TABLET XI

Gilgamesh said to him, to Utnapishtim, the distant: "I gaze upon thee (in amazement), O Utnapishtim! Thy appearance has not changed, like unto me thou art also. And thy nature itself has not changed, like unto me thou art also, though thou hast departed this life. But my heart has still to struggle against all that no longer lies upon thee. Tell me, How didst thou come to dwell (here) and obtain eternal life among the gods?"

Utnapishtim then said unto Gilgamesh: "I will reveal unto thee, O Gilgamesh, the mysterious story, and the mystery of the gods I will tell thee. The city of Shuruppak, a city which, as thou knowest, is situated on the bank of the river Euphrates. That city was very old, as were the gods within it. Even the great gods, as many as there were, decided to bring about a deluge: their father, Anu; their counsellor, the warrior Enlil; their leader, Ninurta; their champion, the god Ennugi. But Ea, the lord of unfathomable wisdom, argued with them. Their plan he told to a reed-hut, (saying):

"'Reed-hut, reed-hut, clay-structure, clay-structure! Reed-hut, hear; clay-structure, pay attention! Thou man of Shuruppak, son of Ubara-Tutu, build a house, construct a ship; forsake thy possessions, take heed of the living! Abandon thy goods, save living things, and bring living seed of every kind into the ship. As for the ship, which thou shalt build, let its proportions be well measured: Its breadth and its length shall bear proportion each to each, and into the sea then launch it.'

"I took heed, and said to Ea, my lord:

"'I will do, my lord, as thou hast commanded; I will observe and will fulfil the command. But what shall I answer to (the inquiries of) the city, the people, and the elders?'

"Ea opened his mouth and spoke, and he said unto me, his servant:

"'Man, as an answer say thus unto them: "I know that Enlil hates me. No longer can I live in your city; nor on Enlil's territory can I live securely any longer; I will go down to the Apsu; I will live with Ea, my lord. Upon you he will pour down rich blessing. He will grant you fowl in plenty and fish in abundance, herds of cattle and an abundant harvest. In the morning he will pour down upon you bread, in the evening a rain of wheat."'

"As soon as early dawn appeared, the populace assembled 'round Atra-hasis's gate, the carpenter with his hatchet, the reed-worker with his flattening-stone, the […] men […]. The rich men brought pitch, and the poor men collected together all that was necessary.

"On the fifth day I set in place her exterior; it was an acre in area; its sides were ten *gar* high; ten *gar* also was the extent of its deck; I added a front-roof to it and closed it in. I built it in six stories, thus making seven floors in all; the interior of each I divided again into nine partitions. Beaks for water within I cut out. I selected a punting-pole and added all that was necessary. Three *šar* of pitch I smeared on its outside; three *šar* of asphalt I used for the inside (so as to make it water-tight). Three *šar* of oil the men carried, carrying it in vessels. One *šar* of oil I kept out and used it for sacrifices, while the other two *šar* the boatman stowed away. I slaughtered oxen; I killed lambs day by day. Jugs of beer, of oil, and of sweet wine, like river water (i.e., freely) I gave the workmen to make a feast like that of the New-Year's Day. To the god Shamash my hands brought oil. The ship was completed. Launching it was heavy work, and I added tackling above and below, and after all was finished, the ship sank in the water to two thirds of its height.

"With all that I possessed I filled it; with all the silver I had I filled it; with all the gold I had I filled it; with living creatures of every kind I filled it. Then I embarked also all my family and my relatives, cattle of the field, beasts of the field, and the uprighteous people—all them I embarked. A time had Shamash appointed, (namely): 'When the rulers of darkness send at eventide a destructive rain, then enter into the ship and shut its door.' This very sign came to pass, and the rulers of darkness sent a destructive rain at eventide. I saw the approach of the storm, and I was afraid to witness the storm; I entered the ship and shut the door.

"I entrusted the guidance of the ship to Puzur-Amurri, the boatman, and also the great house, and the contents thereof. As soon as early dawn appeared, there rose up from the horizon a black cloud, within which the weather god (Adad) thundered, and the heralds Shullat and Hanish went before across mountain and plain. The gods of the abyss arose. Nergal, the great, tore loose the dams of the deep. There went Ninurta and he caused the banks to overflow; the Anunnaki lifted on high (their) torches, and with the brightness thereof they illuminated the universe. The storm brought on by Adad swept even up to the heavens and all light was turned into darkness as Adad shattered the land like a pot.

"It blew with violence one whole day, submerging the mountains. Like an onslaught in battle it rushed in on the people. Nor could brother look after brother. Nor were recognised the people from heaven. The gods even were afraid of the storm; they retreated and took refuge in the heaven of Anu. There the gods crouched down like dogs; on the inclosure of heaven they sat cowering.

"Then Ishtar cried out like a woman in travail and the lady of the gods lamented with a loud voice, (saying): 'The world of old has been turned back into clay, because I assented to this evil in the assembly of the gods. Alas! that when I assented to this evil in the council of the gods, I was for the destruction of my own people. What I have created, where is it? Like the spawn of fish it fills the sea.' The gods wailed with her over the Anunnaki. The gods were bowed down, and sat there weeping. Their lips were pressed together (in fear and in terror).

"Six days and nights the wind blew, and storm and tempest overwhelmed the country. When the seventh day drew nigh the tempest, the storm, the battle which they had waged like a great host began to moderate. The sea quieted down; hurricane and storm ceased. I looked out upon the sea and raised loud my voice, but all mankind had turned back into clay. Likewise the surrounding sea became as flat as a roof-top.

"I opened the air-hole and light fell upon my cheek. Dumbfounded I sank backward and sat weeping, while over my cheek flowed the tears. I looked in every direction, and behold, all was sea. I looked in vain for land, but twelve leagues distant there rose (out of the water) a strip of land. To Mount Niṣir the ship drifted. On Mount Niṣir the boat stuck fast and it did not slip away. The first day, the second day, Mount Niṣir held the ship fast, and did not let it slip away. The third day, the fourth day, Mount Niṣir held the ship fast, and did not let it slip away. The fifth day, the sixth day, Mount Niṣir held the ship, fast, and did not let it slip away. When the seventh day drew nigh I sent out a dove, and let her go. The dove flew hither and thither, but as there was no resting-place for her, she returned. Then I sent out a swallow, and let her go. The swallow flew hither and thither, but as there was no resting-place for her she also returned. Then I sent out a raven, and let her go. The raven flew away and saw the abatement of the waters. She settled down to feed, went away, and returned no more.

"Then I let everything go out unto the four winds, and I offered a sacrifice. I poured out a libation upon the peak of the mountain. I placed the censers seven and seven, and poured into them calamus, cedar-wood, and sweet incense. The gods smelt the savour; yea, the gods smelt the sweet savour; the gods gathered like flies around the sacrificer. But when now the lady of the gods (Ishtar) drew nigh, she lifted up the necklace with precious jewels which Anu had made according to her wish (and said):

"'Ye gods here! by my lapis lazuli necklace, not will I forget. These days will I remember, never will I forget (them). Let the gods come to the offering; but Enlil shall not come to the offering, since rashly he caused the flood-storm, and handed over my people unto destruction.'

"Now, when Enlil drew nigh, and saw the ship, the god was wroth, and anger against the gods, the Igigi, filled his heart, (and he said): 'Who then has escaped here (with his life)? No man was to survive the universal destruction.'

"Then Ninurta opened his mouth and spoke, saying unto Enlil, the warrior: 'Who but Ea could have planned this! For does not Ea know all arts?'

Then Ea opened his mouth and spoke, saying unto Enlil, the warrior:

"'Ay, thou wise one among the gods, thou warrior, how rash of thee to bring about a flood-storm! On the sinner visit his sin, and on the wicked his wickedness; but be merciful, forbear, let not all be destroyed! Be considerate, let not mankind perish! Instead of sending a flood-storm, let lions come and diminish mankind; instead of sending a flood-storm, let tigers come and diminish mankind; instead of sending a flood-storm, let famine come and smite the land; instead of sending a flood-storm, let pestilence come and kill off the people. I did not reveal the mystery of the great gods. I only caused Atra-hasis to see it in a dream, and so he heard the mystery of the gods.'

"Thereupon Enlil arrived at a decision. Enlil went up into the ship, took me by the hand and led me out. He led out also my wife and made her kneel beside me; He turned us face to face, and standing between us, blessed us, (saying) 'Ere this Utnapishtim was only human; But now Utnapishtim and his wife shall be lofty like unto the gods; let Utnapishtim live far away (from men) at the mouth of the rivers.'

"Then they took me and let us dwell far away at the mouth of the rivers."

After Utnapishtim had finished this account, he turned to Gilgamesh and said: "Now as for thee, which one of the gods shall give thee strength, that the life thou desirest thou shalt obtain? Now sleep!" And for six days and seven nights Gilgamesh resembled one lying lame. Sleep came over him like a storm wind. Then Utnapishtim said to his wife: "Behold, here is the hero whose desire is everlasting life! Sleep came upon him like a storm wind." And the wife replied to Utnapishtim, the distant: "Touch him that he may waken and return to his land. Let him, restored in health, return on the road on which he came. Let him pass out through the great door unto his own country." And Utnapishtim said to his wife: "All men deceive, and this one will deceive you. Therefore, cook now for him loaves and place one at his head each day, and mark on the wall the days he has slept."

And while Gilgamesh slept, she cooked the loaves to place it at his head and marked the wall. And while he slept, the first loaf became hard; the second became leathery; the third became soggy; the fourth became white; the fifth became gray with mold; the sixth, it was fresh; the seventh—of a sudden the man awoke upon being touched.

Then spoke Gilgamesh, and said unto Utnapishtim, the distant: "I had sunk down, and sleep had befallen me. Of a sudden thou didst touch me, and I awoke!" And Utnapishtim said unto Gilgamesh: "Gilgamesh, look over yonder and count the loaves, heed the marks on the wall. The first loaf is hard; the second is leathery; the thirdly is soggy; the fourth is white; the fifth is gray with mold; the sixth, it is fresh; the seventh, while still warm I touched you and you awoke."

And Gilgamesh said unto Utnapishtim, the distant: "What shall I do, Utnapishtim? Whither shall I go? The demon has seized my flesh. Upon my couch death now sits. And where my foot treads, there is death."

And Utnapishtim said to Urshanabi, the ferryman: "Urshanabi, thou have become loathsome to this harbor; let the boat carry thee away; you are forever excluded from this place. The man, before whom thou goest, has his body covered with foulness, and the wild skins he wears have hidden the beauty of his body. Take him, Urshanabi, and bring him to the place of purification, where he can wash his hair in water that it may become clean as snow; let him cast off his skins and the sea will carry them away; his body shall then appear beautiful. Let the fillet also be replaced on his head, and the garment that covers his nakedness. Until he returns to his city, until he arrives at his road, the garment shall not wear with age; it shall remain entirely new."

And Urshanabi took him and brought him to the place of purification, where he washed his hair in water so that it became clean as snow; he cast off his skins and the sea carried them away; his body appeared beautiful. He replaced also the fillet on his head and the garment that covered his nakedness until he should return to his city, until he should arrive at his road; the garment would not wear with age; it remained entirely new.

Then Gilgamesh and Urshanabi embarked again, and during their journey the ship tossed to and fro. The wife of Utnapishtim spoke unto her husband, the distant, (saying): "Gilgamesh did come here weary and exhausted. What now wilt thou give him, that he may return to his country?"

And Gilgamesh lifted up the pole, and drew the boat nearer to the shore.

Then Utnapishtim spoke unto Gilgamesh (and said): "Gilgamesh, thou didst come here weary; thou didst labour and row. What now shall I give thee, that thou mayest return to thy country? I will reveal unto thee, Gilgamesh, a mystery of the gods I will announce unto thee. There is a plant resembling buckthorn; its thorn stings like that of a bramble. When thy hands can reach that plant, then thy hands will hold that which gives life everlasting."

When Gilgamesh had heard this he opened the sluices that the sweet water might carry him into the deep; he bound heavy stones to his feet, which dragged him down to the sea floor, and thus he found the plant. Then he grasped the prickly plant. He removed from his feet the heavy stones, and the sea carried him and threw him down on to the shore.

And Gilgamesh said unto Urshanabi, the ferryman: "Urshanabi, this plant is a plant of great marvel; and by it a man may attain renewed vigour. I will take it to Uruk the strong-walled, I will give it to the old men to eat. Its name shall be 'Even an old man will be rejuvenated!' I will eat of this and return (again) to the vigour of my youth."

At twenty double-leagues they then took a meal: and at thirty double-leagues they took a rest. And Gilgamesh saw a well wherein was cool water; he stepped into it and bathed in the water. A serpent smelled the sweetness of the plant and darted out; he took the plant away, and as he turned back to the well, he sloughed his skin. And after this Gilgamesh sat down and wept. Tears flowed down his cheeks, and he said unto Urshanabi, the ferryman:

"Why, Urshanabi, did my hands tremble? Why did the blood of my heart stand still? Not on myself did I bestow any benefit. On the 'ground-lion' this benefit has been bestowed. Already twenty double-leagues the waters have taken the plant away. I opened the sluices and lowered my equipment into it. I saw the sign; it has become an omen to me. I am to return, leaving the ship on the shore."

Then they continued on and took a meal after twenty double-leagues, and after thirty double-leagues they took a rest. When they arrived at Uruk the strong-walled, Gilgamesh then spoke to Urshanabi, the ferryman, (and said):

"Urshanabi, ascend and walk about on the wall of Uruk, inspect the corner-stone, and examine its brick-work, whether its wall is not made of burned brick, and its foundation laid by the Seven Sages. One third for city, one third for garden, one third for field, and a precinct for the temple of Ishtar. These parts and the precinct comprise Uruk."

Note

★ Editors' note: *The Epic of Gilgamesh* (c. eighteenth century BCE) is an ancient epic poem from Mesopotamia. In its first half, Gilgamesh, the king of Uruk, befriends Enkidu, a wild man that the gods create to stop Gilgamesh from oppressing Uruk's population. Though Gilgamesh bests Enkidu in a contest of strength, they become friends and embark on a journey to the Cedar Forest. En route, the pair kill the

Bull of Heaven, sent by the goddess Ishtar, whose advances Gilgamesh had earlier spurned. The gods nevertheless sentence Enkidu to death and kill him. A distressed and bereaved Gilgamesh then resolves to find the secret to eternal life. The excerpts below begins with Gilgamesh approaching Utnapishtim, the sole immortal human. Utnapishtim admonishes Gilgamesh that death is humanity's fate. He relates how he alone survived a flood that killed all other people and tells Gilgamesh of an undersea plant believed to confer immortality.

17 The Story of the Man Who Did Not Wish to Die

Yei Theodora Ozaki

Japanese Fairy Tales (New York: A.L. Burt Company, 1908)

Long, long ago there lived a man called Sentaro. His surname meant "Millionaire," but although he was not so rich as all that, he was still very far removed from being poor. He had inherited a small fortune from his father and lived on this, spending his time carelessly, without any serious thoughts of work, till he was about thirty-two years of age.

One day, without any reason whatsoever, the thought of death and sickness came to him. The idea of falling ill or dying made him very wretched.

"I should like to live," he said to himself, "till I am five or six hundred years old at least, free from all sickness. The ordinary span of a man's life is very short."

He wondered whether it were possible, by living simply and frugally henceforth, to prolong his life as long as he wished.

He knew there were many stories in ancient history of emperors who had lived a thousand years, and there was a Princess of Yamato, who, it was said, lived to the age of five hundred. This was the latest story of a very long life record.

Sentaro had often heard the tale of the Chinese King named Shin-no-Shiko. He was one of the most able and powerful rulers in Chinese history. He built all the large palaces, and also the famous great wall of China. He had everything in the world he could wish for, but in spite of all his happiness and the luxury and the splendor of his Court, the wisdom of his councilors and the glory of his reign, he was miserable because he knew that one day he must die and leave it all.

When Shin-no-Shiko went to bed at night, when he rose in the morning, as he went through his day, the thought of death was always with him. He could not get away from it. Ah—if only he could find the "Elixir of Life," he would be happy.

The Emperor at last called a meeting of his courtiers and asked them all if they could not find for him the "Elixir of Life" of which he had so often read and heard.

One old courtier, Jofuku by name, said that far away across the seas there was a country called Horaizan, and that certain hermits lived there who possessed the secret of the "Elixir of Life." Whoever drank of this wonderful draught lived forever.

The Emperor ordered Jofuku to set out for the land of Horaizan, to find the hermits, and to bring him back a phial of the magic elixir. He gave Jofuku one of his best junks, fitted it out for him, and loaded it with great quantities of treasures and precious stones for Jofuku to take as presents to the hermits.

Jofuku sailed for the land of Horaizan, but he never returned to the waiting Emperor; but ever since that time Mount Fuji has been said to be the fabled Horaizan and the home of hermits who had the secret of the elixir, and Jofuku has been worshiped as their patron god.

Now Sentaro determined to set out to find the hermits, and if he could, to become one, so that he might obtain the water of perpetual life. He remembered that as a child he had been told that not only did these hermits live on Mount Fuji, but that they were said to inhabit all the very high peaks.

So he left his old home to the care of his relatives, and started out on his quest. He traveled through all the mountainous regions of the land, climbing to the tops of the highest peaks, but never a hermit did he find.

At last, after wandering in a region for many days, he met a hunter.

"Can you tell me," asked Sentaro, "where the hermits live who have the Elixir of Life?"

"No," said the hunter; "I can't tell you where such hermits live, but there is a notorious robber living in these parts. It is said that he is chief of a band of two hundred followers."

This odd answer irritated Sentaro very much, and he thought how foolish it was to waste more time in looking for the hermits in this way, so he decided to go at once to the shrine of Jofuku, who is worshiped as the patron god of the hermits in the south of Japan.

Sentaro reached the shrine and prayed for seven days, entreating Jofuku to show him the way to a hermit who could give him what he wanted so much to find.

At midnight of the seventh day, as Sentaro knelt in the temple, the door of the innermost shrine flew open, and Jofuku appeared in a luminous cloud, and calling to Sentaro to come nearer, spoke thus:

"Your desire is a very selfish one and cannot be easily granted. You think that you would like to become a hermit so as to find the Elixir of Life. Do you know how hard a hermit's life is? A hermit is only allowed to eat fruit and berries and the bark of pine trees; a hermit must cut himself off from the world so that his heart may become as pure as gold and free from every earthly desire. Gradually after following these strict rules, the hermit ceases to feel hunger or cold or heat, and his body becomes so light that he can ride on a crane or a carp, and can walk on water without getting his feet wet."

"You, Sentaro, are fond of good living and of every comfort. You are not even like an ordinary man, for you are exceptionally idle, and more sensitive to heat and cold than most people. You would never be able to go barefoot or to wear only one thin dress in the winter time! Do you think that you would ever have the patience or the endurance to live a hermit's life?"

"In answer to your prayer, however, I will help you in another way. I will send you to the country of Perpetual Life, where death never comes—where the people live forever!"

Saying this, Jofuku put into Sentaro's hand a little crane made of paper, telling him to sit on its back and it would carry him there.

Sentaro obeyed wonderingly. The crane grew large enough for him to ride on it with comfort. It then spread its wings, rose high in the air, and flew away over the mountains right out to sea.

Sentaro was at first quite frightened; but by degrees he grew accustomed to the swift flight through the air. On and on they went for thousands of miles. The bird never stopped for rest or food, but as it was a paper bird it doubtless did not require any nourishment, and strange to say, neither did Sentaro.

After several days they reached an island. The crane flew some distance inland and then alighted.

As soon as Sentaro got down from the bird's back, the crane folded up of its own accord and flew into his pocket.

Now Sentaro began to look about him wonderingly, curious to see what the country of Perpetual Life was like. He walked first round about the country and then through the town. Everything was, of course, quite strange, and different from his own land. But both the land and the people seemed prosperous, so he decided that it would be good for him to stay there and took up lodgings at one of the hotels.

The proprietor was a kind man, and when Sentaro told him that he was a stranger and had come to live there, he promised to arrange everything that was necessary with the governor of the city concerning Sentaro's sojourn there. He even found a house for his guest, and in this way Sentaro obtained his great wish and became a resident in the country of Perpetual Life.

Within the memory of all the islanders no man had ever died there, and sickness was a thing unknown. Priests had come over from India and China and told them of a beautiful country called Paradise, where happiness and bliss and contentment fill all men's hearts, but its gates could only be reached by dying. This tradition was handed down for ages from generation to generation—but none knew exactly what death was except that it led to Paradise.

Quite unlike Sentaro and other ordinary people, instead of having a great dread of death, they all, both rich and poor, longed for it as something good and desirable. They were all tired of their long, long lives, and longed to go to the happy land of contentment called Paradise of which the priests had told them centuries ago.

All this Sentaro soon found out by talking to the islanders. He found himself, according to his ideas, in the land of Topsyturvydom. Everything was upside down. He had wished to escape from dying. He had come to the land of Perpetual Life with great relief and joy, only to find that the inhabitants themselves, doomed never to die, would consider it bliss to find death.

What he had hitherto considered poison these people ate as good food, and all the things to which he had been accustomed as food they rejected. Whenever any merchants from other countries arrived, the rich people rushed to them eager to buy poisons. These they swallowed eagerly, hoping for death to come so that they might go to Paradise.

But what were deadly poisons in other lands were without effect in this strange place, and people who swallowed them with the hope of dying, only found that in a short time they felt better in health instead of worse.

Vainly they tried to imagine what death could be like. The wealthy would have given all their money and all their goods if they could but shorten their lives to two or three hundred years even. Without any change to live on forever seemed to this people wearisome and sad.

In the chemist shops there was a drug which was in constant demand, because after using it for a hundred years, it was supposed to turn the hair slightly gray and to bring about disorders of the stomach.

Sentaro was astonished to find that the poisonous globe-fish was served up in restaurants as a delectable dish, and hawkers in the streets went about selling sauces made of Spanish flies. He never saw any one ill after eating these horrible things, nor did he ever see any one with as much as a cold.

Sentaro was delighted. He said to himself that he would never grow tired of living, and that he considered it profane to wish for death. He was the only happy man on the island. For his part he wished to live thousands of years and to enjoy life. He set himself up in business, and for the present never even dreamed of going back to his native land.

As years went by, however, things did not go as smoothly as at first. He had heavy losses in business, and several times some affairs went wrong with his neighbors. This caused him great annoyance.

Time passed like the flight of an arrow for him, for he was busy from morning till night. Three hundred years went by in this monotonous way, and then at last he began to grow tired of life in this country, and he longed to see his own land and his old home. However long he lived here, life would always be the game, so was it not foolish and wearisome to stay on here forever?

Sentaro, in his wish to escape from the country of Perpetual Life, recollected Jofuku, who had helped him before when he was wishing to escape from death—and he prayed to the saint to bring him back to his own land again.

No sooner did he pray than the paper crane popped out of his pocket. Sentaro was amazed to see that it had remained undamaged after all these years. Once more the bird grew and grew till it was large enough for him to mount it. As he did so, the bird spread its wings and flew, swiftly out across the sea in the direction of Japan.

Such was the willfulness of the man's nature that he looked back and regretted all he had left behind. He tried to stop the bird in vain. The crane held on its way for thousands of miles across the ocean.

Then a storm came on, and the wonderful paper crane got damp, crumpled up, and fell into the sea. Sentaro fell with it. Very much frightened at the thought of being drowned, he cried out loudly to Jofuku to save him. He looked round, but there was no ship in sight. He swallowed a quantity of sea-water, which only increased his miserable plight. While he was thus struggling to keep himself afloat, he saw a monstrous shark swimming towards him. As it came nearer it opened its huge mouth ready to devour him. Sentaro was all but paralyzed with fear now that he felt his end so near, and screamed out as loudly as ever he could to Jofuku to come and rescue him.

Lo, and behold, Sentaro was awakened by his own screams, to find that during his long prayer he had fallen asleep before the shrine, and that all his extraordinary and frightful adventures had been only a wild dream. He was in a cold perspiration with fright, and utterly bewildered.

Suddenly a bright light came towards him, and in the light stood a messenger. The messenger held a book in his hand, and spoke to Sentaro:

"I am sent to you by Jofuku, who in answer to your prayer, has permitted you in a dream to see the land of Perpetual Life. But you grew weary of living there, and begged to be allowed to return to your native land so that you might die. Jofuku, so that he might try you, allowed you to drop into the sea, and then sent a shark to swallow you up. Your desire for death was not real, for even at that moment you cried out loudly and shouted for help."

"It is also vain for you to wish to become a hermit, or to find the Elixir of Life. These things are not for such as you—your life is not austere enough. It is best for you to go back to your paternal home, and to live a good and industrious life. Never neglect to keep the anniversaries of your ancestors, and make it your duty to provide for your children's future. Thus will you live to a good old age and be happy, but give up the vain desire to escape death, for no man can do that, and by this time you have surely found out that even when selfish desires are granted they do not bring happiness."

"In this book I give you there are many precepts good for you to know—if you study them, you will be guided in the way I have pointed out to you."

The angel disappeared as soon as he had finished speaking, and Sentaro took the lesson to heart. With the book in his hand he returned to his old home, and giving up all his old vain wishes, tried to live a good and useful life and to observe the lessons taught him in the book, and he and his house prospered henceforth.

18 How to Live a Never-Ending Novela

(Or, Why Immortality Needn't Undermine Identity)

Benjamin Mitchell-Yellin[1]

The award-winning short film *The Fantastic Flying Books of Mr. Morris Lessmore* (2011) enjoys a second life as a children's book (Joyce 2012). This is something like a proof of concept. For this tale is unabashed in its embrace of the oft-repeated truism that a human life is like a book. After a storm upends his home in the New Orleans' French Quarter, our titular silent protagonist finds himself all in a jumble, his story reduced to scattered letters strewn across wind-swept pages. A flying book, gifted by an airborne young woman in a letter-patterned poodle skirt, eventually leads him to a library of sorts. He spends the rest of his days there, caring for a collection of books containing the stories of protagonists passed. He repairs frayed edges and loose bindings, while writing "of his joys and sorrows, of all that he knew and everything that he hoped for" in a volume of his own (Joyce 2012). Upon filling the final page, he himself takes flight, lifted to the heavens by a coterie of flying books. His own winged volume returns to the library in the clutches of a young girl, who sits down to read it. "And our story ends as it began, with the opening of a book" (Joyce 2012).

This tale more or less aligns with a prominent view about personal identity. According to the narrative view, people are books too; more precisely, we're autobiographies (Dennett 1988; Schechtman 2011). The basic idea is that it's profitable to conceive of the self, who you are across time, as the central character in your own book of life. But there's a catch. Life can cut your story short, and, unlike Morris Lessmore, you may not be able to pick up the pieces. You may no longer be able to add to the narrative arc. And if you're no longer able to pen more pages in the book of your life, then you're no longer living it. Someone may still be alive and kicking, but they're no longer *you*. A break in narrative is a disruption in being.

It appears to follow that to know thyself is to grasp thy narrative. This seems benign enough. But it quickly runs aground on the shores of human desire. For if there's one thing many people want—and have wanted for ages—it's to live forever. Human literature, so far as we know, begins with an accounting of the exploits of Gilgamesh, who recoils at the recognition of his own mortality and sets off on a quest for immortality (Anonymous 2018). He's not alone. Tales of people seeking longer life litter the literary landscape. And it's not just the stuff of fiction. The history of modern science and medicine is aptly conceived of as a series of salvos in the war against death (Weiner 2010). The quest for immortality is with us even now in the age of tech and big data, as Silicon Valley fortunes are being thrown at the problem of aging. Senescence, some say, is like a disease, one that plagues us all and must be defeated (Bostrom 2005). The question whether immortality is desirable is as urgent as ever.

There are, of course, the haters. Some like to point out that humanity has been at this for a long time now and we've yet to succeed. Sure, we can expect to live much longer than our stone-age ancestors, but we'll never live forever (Dong et al. 2016). And yet, if you squint just right, our track record on longevity can look like reason for optimism—we'll get there eventually! Some warn against playing God (Glannon 2002). Who knows what horrors may be unleashed by tinkering with our makeup? But this can come to seem alarmist in the face of all the welcome advancements our ingenuity has yielded. We're healthier these days because we learned to inject ourselves with pathogens. There was a time when people wouldn't have thought that wise; many people think it's unwise even now. We're not always the best judges of things. Some naysayers turn to doom and gloom. They argue that immortality would exacerbate inequality and further tax already scarce resources (Varghese 2017). But these aren't objections to immortality, so much as to distributive injustice. These problems are with us already in some form or another, and it's at least conceivable that immortal human beings would be more equitable and steadfast in their ecological stewardship than we mortals.

The criticism that has sucked up the most philosophical air has been the claim that no one could live forever without succumbing to an irreversible existential boredom (Williams 1973). But it's just not clear that there is a good argument for this one (Fischer and Mitchell-Yellin 2014). At bottom, it relies on something of a "one-size-fits-all" conception of human character. Can it really be that anyone, no matter what they're like, would become bored if they lived long enough? Anyway, there may be no need to answer the question. After all, it's only a problem if you'd remain *you* forever. The boredom objection is really a dilemma: you'll either live so long that you become bored or you'll change so much you'll cease to be you. And this brings us back to personal identity, back on narrative.

The idea that your life is an autobiography sits uneasily with the desire to keep it going indefinitely. As David Velleman nicely puts it, immortality would deprive you of "life's most persistently anticipated consummation" (Velleman 2015, 196). You expect to die, just like an author expects to finish her novel and a reader expects to turn the final page. Frustrating this expectation would seem to have grave consequences. Not knowing how your story ends would entail not knowing what story it is in particular. How can you be sure until it's all said and done? To lack knowledge of one's death is to lack knowledge of

one's life is to lack knowledge of one's self. An immortal David Velleman would be no one in particular, a never-ending story that might go anywhere and become any tale.

And it's not just Velleman. According to Martin Heidegger, your death is a horizon—the only horizon, really— that individuates you (Heidegger 1962). Your death is the impossibility of any future possibilities for you. And this is what, ultimately, demarcates you from all others. A related idea features in Jorge Luis Borges' short story "The Immortal" (Borges 1962). Borges' narrator seeks and drinks from the river of immortality. But he soon realizes that never-ending life is not all it's cracked up to be. It commits one to an interminable cycle of actualizing all possible human lives, one's life story merging with all others. So he sets out to find the river of mortality. Eventually having drunk from these waters, he celebrates his release. No longer faced with the prospect of being no one—in the sense of having no unique identity—he joyously anticipates the prospect of becoming no one—in the sense of being dead.

And so it seems that the all-too-human desire to keep on living rubs up against an inconvenient truth. Both your identity and your grasp of it depend on your story coming to an end. Immortality would entail self-erasure.

★★★

But things aren't always what they seem. There are good reasons to resist this conclusion. Let's begin by thinking about a cast of characters as ancient as the human literary canon. The gods have long been conceived of as immortal. And yet we don't think that they lack particular identities, nor do we find ourselves incapable of grasping who each one is. We speak confidently about Zeus in comparison with Hades—the one a wily deity throwing lightning bolts from the sky, the other a sullen shepherd of departed souls in the underworld. And we don't expect our confidence in grasping these deities' identities to wane over time. It's not as if nowadays we are less sure that Zeus and Hades are different individuals, simply because they've been around (figuratively, if not literally) for ages. We're certain about who they'll be in an indefinitely far-off future. If immortality doesn't undermine divine identity and our ability to grasp it, why should it undermine human identity and our ability to grasp it?

Perhaps human immortality would be fundamentally different from divine immortality, with the difference coming down to expectations. The gods have always known they're immortal and so they haven't anticipated death. But we mortals have. Our anticipation that our stories will end shapes how we think of ourselves and immortality would frustrate this. But while it may be true that immortality would foil your plan to die, this doesn't yet show that it would undermine your ability to grasp yourself as an individual. Expectations change. An immortal human being may have started off with a death wish, only to find himself faced with a different reality. Instead of bemoaning a frustrated sense of what he has to look forward to, our immortal may instead change his mind. He may embrace the charge of penning his never-ending tale.

But maybe you don't believe in gods. In that case, the fact that many others have found immortal gods comprehensible may fail to impress you. No problem. There are even better reasons for thinking that immortality wouldn't undermine identity. As a first step, consider that this discussion has so far focused only on the future. It's been about your anticipating the end, and how this may interact with the possibility of its never arriving. The argument has been that you can't tell what story you're writing until you complete it. Or, to paraphrase Joni Mitchell, you don't know who you are till you're gone.

There's a counterargument to be made here. But before making it, we should consider an interestingly different argument for the claim that immorality would undermine identity. This second argument focuses, not on your grasp of who you are, but on your having a particular identity to grasp in the first place. Borges' narrator lays it out as only a Borges narrator can.

Homer composed the *Odyssey*; if we postulate an infinite period of time, with infinite circumstances and changes, the impossible thing is not to compose the *Odyssey*, at least once. No one is anyone, one single immortal man is all men. Like Cornelius of Agrippa, I am god, I am hero, I am philosopher, I am demon and I am world, which is a tedious way of saying that I do not exist (Borges 1962, 114–115).

The claim here is that immortality would undermine individuality because an existence stretching indefinitely far into the future would become indistinguishable from all others. But would it, really?

One reason to think not is that this second line of argument ignores the role of history. Suppose it's true that if you live long enough you will eventually write the *Odyssey*. This doesn't make you identical to Homer. He will always be the one who wrote it first (and if he didn't, then congratulations! You did). This point generalizes. Even if it's true that every immortal individual will eventually actualize each and every possible human circumstance and change, it doesn't follow that they will actualize them at the same time or in the same sequence. There will be differences between these life stories. Being the first person to write the *Odyssey* is something that sets Homer apart from the rest of us, even if we each end up writing it one day.

Still, there may seem to be something to the claim that immortality undermines individuality. One possibility is that there are two life stories that include the same exact events in the same exact order. And following Borges' logic, given immortality, it would seem only a matter of time before this possibility is actualized and there are identical life stories both in content and sequence. Still, this doesn't show that they are identical in all respects. It doesn't seem to be a coherent possibility that these two lives could be lived out at exactly the same time. Thus, we might end up with two life stories that contain the same events set in the same narrative structure, but one of them would have occurred first and the other second. There would still be a distinction between them.

Moreover, it seems safe to assume that each of us has, up until now, lived a unique life. So even if we go on to live never-ending lives that contain all possible events that may befall a human being, we would not thereby have lived identical stories. Each of our stories would have a unique beginning. And if there were ever to be another story that began in the same way as yours, this would only mean that you were the first in a line of similar individuals. Your story would remain unique because it's anchored in a unique past. This suggests a response to the first line of argument, which focused on the role of an ending in your ability to grasp your life story. The suspicion that you can't grasp who you are until your story's all told ignores the fact that you've been telling it all along.

The lesson here is that history matters. To focus only on the future and what difference it can make to one's particular life story is to lose sight of the past and how it can serve to individuate narrative arcs. The force of this point remains even if we suppose that the shape of one's story depends on the future. The significance of a past event may not be determinable independently of future events—a break-up comes to mean something very different if the couple eventually gets back together (Velleman 1991). But the point cuts both ways. The significance of a future event is, in part, a function of what's come before—two people falling for each other means one thing if the romance is new, and another if it's a rekindled flame.

★★★

Immortality doesn't undermine individuality because our stories have beginnings, whether or not they have endings. And they are embedded in the context of human history, which allows us to distinguish between repeat storylines in terms of which came first. Thinking of your life as an autobiography isn't an impediment to accepting the possibility that you—the very same person you are now—could live forever. It doesn't even get

in the way of the possibility that you might know who you are all along. But thinking of your life as an autobiography can constrain your ability to imagine the form your story will take. And this may get at the root issue.

A mortal life is aptly conceived of as a bound volume, like the books Morris Lessmore cared for. It can be completed and shelved. Each story, with its first and last page, is easily separable from the others. Conceived of in this way, humanity is like a vast library of stories, some in the midst of being written, others waiting to be rediscovered, all of us with beginnings and endings, edges and bindings to mend. But this is an impoverished view of what a story might be, of what stories are. Human beings have crafted narratives of various shapes and styles. Sure, we've written novels, but we've also recited epic poems, penned serials, and recorded soap operas. In this last example, we see that human narratives need not be structured towards an anticipated consummation. Soap operas weave various storylines together, each episode ending with the promise that there's more to come. Their timeline is indefinite, and they're no less gripping for that. They're also no less intelligible as distinct narratives. People love their soaps, and they have no problem telling them apart. Fans of one show are not automatically fans of another. And though there may be thematic overlap and shared storylines, there's certain to be one show that did it first.

Our lives are not just like soaps—though they may at times feel that way. Soaps don't typically focus on the story of one person's life. Rather, they knit together several storylines, united by location or family ties. But this doesn't set them apart from stories generally. Not every story has a single protagonist and some are told from multiple points of view. We recognize them as intelligible stories nonetheless. The same goes for soap operas. They contain the necessary elements for narrative understanding (Velleman 2003). They're chock full of highs and lows; we can track them emotionally. A cliffhanger may not be an ending, but it holds out promise that the conflict, whatever it happens to be, will be resolved next time—or eventually. And there's no reason to think that the basic format of a soap opera couldn't apply to a single person's life. Of course, all soaps have, in fact, come to an end. But there's no reason one couldn't, in principle, continue on forever, with cliffhangers strung out for decades and centuries. And though it may be true that the immensely popular subgenre, telenovelas, typically focus on a discrete storyline with a limited timeframe, this doesn't seem to be necessitated by narrative form. They could continue on indefinitely, so long as they kept our attention. Come to think of it, perhaps soaps are like lives, after all.

This observation helps to deflect one final worry. Even if you agree that immortality need not undermine identity, you might not see why that matters. So what if you could remain the same person over an indefinite lifetime? It's cold comfort to find out that immortality is compatible with metaphysical identity, if it's not also compatible with preserving what matters to you about remaining who you are. Here's where the appeal to narrative proves to be a real advantage. There's a sense in which what matters just is what you care about, what you track emotionally. If you can remain emotionally invested in a never-ending story, then it can continue to matter, even—perhaps, especially—if that story is your own.

★★★

The view that a human life is a story, written by the one living it, may readily bring to mind the image of a person scribbling on pages between two covers. We know Morris Lessmore is finished when he reaches "The End." This manifests a specific conception of what it is to tell a story, one that fits a mortal existence well. But we shouldn't let its familiarity inhibit our powers of imagination. An immortal life may yet be an intelligible story, even if it doesn't submit to a definite binding and fit neatly on a shelf. We can appreciate it as a unique story, so long as its narrative arc is grasped in the proper historical context. Immortality needn't undermine your identity or ability to grasp it. But it may force you to reconsider the form your story will take.

We've looked at two arguments for the claim that immortality would undermine personal identity. The first focused on the thought that you can't know who you are until your story is finished; the second focused on the thought that if you live long enough there'll be no unique you to know about. Both arguments failed to properly account for the role of history. Stories have beginnings, as well as endings. And even if two stories contain the same events in the same sequence, they remain distinct so long as one occurred before the other. Free from the confines of a conception of stories as bound books, we're able to recognize that immortal lives may continue to matter to us because we can continue to care about them.

Note

1. I would like to thank Bob Fischer and the editors of this volume, Michael Cholbi and Travis Timmerman, for helpful comments on an earlier version of this chapter.

References

Anonymous. *The Epic of Gilgamesh*. Translated by Kevin H. Dixon. New York: Seven Stories Press, 2018.

Borges, J. L. "The Immortal." In *Labyrinths*, edited by D. A. Yates and J. E. Irby, 105–118. New York: New Directions, 1962.

Bostrom, Nick. "The Fable of the Dragon Tyrant." *Journal of Medical Ethics* 31, no. 5 (2005): 273–277.

Dennett, Daniel. "Why Everyone Is a Novelist." *The Times Literary Supplement*, September 16–22, 1988.

Dong, Xiao, Brandon Milholland, and Jan Vijg. "Evidence for a Limit to Human Lifespan." *Nature* 538 (October 2016): 257–259.

Fischer, John M. and Mitchell-Yellin, Benjamin. "Immortality and Boredom." *The Journal of Ethics* 18 (December 2014): 353–372.

Glannon, Walter. "Extending the Human Life Span." *Journal of Medicine and Philosophy* 27, no. 3 (2002): 339–354.

Heidegger, M. *Being and Time*. Translated by John Macquarrie and Edward Robinson. New York: Harper & Row, 1962.

Joyce, William. *The Fantastic Flying Books of Mr. Morris Lessmore*. Directed by William Joyce and Brandon Oldenburg. Shreveport, LA: Moonbot Studios, 2011.

Joyce, William. *The Fantastic Flying Books of Mr. Morris Lessmore*. New York: Atheneum, 2012.

Schechtman, Marya. "The Narrative Self." In *The Oxford Handbook of the Self*, edited by Shaun Gallagher, 394–415. New York: Oxford University Press, 2011.

Varghese, Sanjana. "The First Men to Conquer Death Will Create a New Social Order—A Terrifying One." *New Statesmen America*, August 25, 2017. www.newstatesman.com/science-tech/future-proof/2017/08/first-men-conquer-death-will-create-new-social-order-terrifying.

Velleman, J. David. "Dying." In *Beyond Price: Essays on Birth and Death*, edited by J. David Velleman, 195–198. Cambridge: Open Book Publishers, 2015.

Velleman, J. David. "Narrative Explanation." *The Philosophical Review* 112 (January 2003): 1–25.

Velleman, J. David. "Well-Being and Time." *Pacific Philosophical Quarterly* 72 (1991): 48–77.

Weiner, Jonathan. *Long for This World: The Strange Science of Immortality*. New York: Harper Collins, 2010.

Williams, Bernard. "The Makropulos Case: Reflections on the Tedium of Immortality." In *Problems of the Self*, edited by Bernard Williams, 82–100. Cambridge: Cambridge University Press, 1973.

19 Taking Stock of the Risks of Life without Death

August Gorman

I. Introduction

We usually take it to be a bad thing when someone dies. But is the general fact that humans die a bad thing? Some have argued that our own mortality is for the best; if we lived long enough each one of us would become fatally bored and, as a result, find nothing meaningful in the prospect of continuing to live.[1]

Others claim that they would very gladly take an elixir that promised them eternal life on Earth, and accuse those who think immortality would be a bad thing of being merely curmudgeonly. If we enjoy our lives right now even though we sometimes get bored, they reason, what difference should it make how many days, months, years, or centuries we extend them by?[2] Call this the Anti-Curmudgeon position.[3]

In this chapter I defend a middle position between the Curmudgeon and Anti-Curmudgeon positions: I believe that there *is* a special worry about boredom for immortal lives, but there are several ways that a person might be able to avoid it, in theory. However, none of us are in a very good position to determine whether or not we are one of the lucky few that would be able to avoid it via any of these ways. Because of the structure of this decision, I argue that it would be irrational to approach the choice to take (or pass on) an immortality elixir with anything approaching confidence.

II. Boredom and the Threat of Running Out of Life's Pages

In order to assess whether or not we would fall into an intolerable state of boredom if we lived forever, we'll need to get a clearer understanding of just what boredom is, exactly, and what sorts of things it is sensitive to. Although boredom is a near-ubiquitous experience, it is surprisingly puzzling. Think about watching your favorite movie five times in a row. Your favorite movie is something you presumably care about, so why on the fifth watching in a row does it appear to you as something you don't care about? It's not as if something has changed about the movie itself or about your ability to appreciate it, in theory. If you wait a few months and watch it again you might find that it's not boring at all. You come to care about it all over again.

The same can be true of boredom with life in general. One day you might feel like there is nothing in the world that could possibly hold your interest, but the next day the world opens itself up to you again and everything feels full of possibility. It temporarily *appears* to you as though you have run out of ways to take an interest in your favorite movie, or run out of things in life to participate in that you could take an interest in. But as we all know, perceptions can be deceiving. We might perceive there to be water by the horizon on the street in front of us, but it is only the reflection of sunlight on the pavement.[4]

What causes the illusion in everyday sorts of boredom? One conjecture is that we acquire a sort of evaluative tunnel vision when we engage with something in the same manner over and over again. In doing so, we temporarily close ourselves off to engaging our other capacities for interacting in a way that will hold our interest.[5] Maybe we can't possibly listen to the lilting in Judy Garland's voice as Dorothy when she says "there's no place like home" any more after the fifth watching and this temporarily overshadows how much there is left to discover about the symbolism of the Wizard, or the cinematography of the Yellow Brick Road scenes. Getting too accustomed to a narrow set of life activities might also produce a sort of tunnel vision towards the value of life itself.

What, then, is the particular worry about boredom in a life without death? Curmudgeons sometimes talk as though we would need to find some sort of life project that could stave off boredom at every moment. Here I think Anti-Curmudgeons are right to point out that there is no more reason to worry about the ordinary fleeting sorts of boredom in an immortal life than there is in a moral one.

But sometimes boredom isn't fleeting; the perception that there's nothing about a particular pursuit left that one cares about is accurate. *The Wizard of Oz* on not the fifth, but the hundredth watching might be an example. You might have actually exhausted all of the things about the film that you would find worthwhile to engage with. Call this "insurmountable boredom." The real concern with boredom in immortal life, as I see it, is that a person might come to find herself insurmountably bored with life itself. Such a person would believe that she has run out of pursuits that she would find worthwhile to engage in, and she would actually be right about this.

Anti-Curmudgeons John Martin Fischer and Ben Mitchell-Yellin describe those who are worried about this kind of boredom as being almost as if they were "caught in the grips of a problematic metaphor." According to Fischer and Mitchell-Yellin, Curmudgeons

> sometimes seem to think of the relevant projects as though they were books in a library that contains a large but finite number of books. The idea is that, given an infinite amount of time, a human being could read all the books in the library.
>
> (Fischer and Mitchell-Yellin 2014, 358)

What, exactly, is meant to be problematic about this metaphor? Well, for one, you might question why you need *projects* to have an enjoyable infinite life in the first place. Some Anti-Curmudgeons allege that they would be very happy to live an infinite life consisting of just enjoying the pleasures of nice meals and kissing their spouses, no projects required. And these sorts of pleasures are not the sorts of things we need to worry about running out of.

However, I think our inquiry into the nature of boredom helps illuminate why we might think we would need projects of some sort to live a worthwhile life. While it might be that if we're going to be alive we prefer to have a life filled with these sorts of pleasures, I doubt that if it were to really come down to it, they could give us a *reason* to want to continue living for billions of years. In our mortal lives, the kinds of pleasure we get from these sorts of things can be temporarily interrupted when we feel an overwhelming sense of boredom. And boredom, it seems, is not sensitive to the availability of pleasant activities, but the availability of activities that we see as interesting and worthwhile. So having something novel to give you a reason to go on does seem to be crucial, since insurmountable boredom could permanently impinge on our ability to enjoy life.

This is why I think the idea of a library of pursuits is somewhat apt, after all. In the remainder of this chapter I will explore the different ways a person might nevertheless avoid running out of pages to read.

III. Is There Really a Finite Number of Books in the Library?

Even if we concede that we need life projects in order to stave off the threat of boredom, we may legitimately wonder whether or not there is really any risk of running out of possibilities. Aren't there an infinite number of pursuits any one person could take on? And even if there aren't now, with an increasing number of inventions and the progress of technology, won't there constantly be new activities to pursue? In 1950 no one could have anticipated that becoming a skilled hacker could be a life project someone could choose and our current imaginations may be severely limited in terms of predicting what may become possible over the stretch of eternity.

But even if in one sense anyone is free to take up poker, or linguistic anthropology, or competitive dog grooming at any time, only certain pursuits will be ones that a particular person will be able to get herself to actually come to take a genuine interest in. I am not sure whether our personalities constrain our interests to the point in which the field of possibility for potential interesting pursuits it includes only a finite number of things in the first place. But I think there is a real risk here that they do. In other words, it's not a library of all the pursuits a person could take on in theory that we have to worry about being finite, but our personal libraries of possible pursuits.

You might think that being faced with the necessity of finding new pursuits is a special sort of case that would enable new paths forward. Perhaps we could build our personal libraries to be larger out of necessity. I think these circumstances might encourage us to look beyond the obvious candidates for projects towards other things that we would realize we do have genuine interest in if we were to try them. That said, a long list of things you can do on a rainy day does not stave off a severe case of everyday boredom, a case in which you merely perceive yourself to have run out of things that would actually engage you. Similarly, the mere availability of things you can, in theory, do with your life won't magically make you genuinely interested in any of them. No matter how much I may want to become interested in opera in order to share in my grandmother's passion, I can still fail to take an interest in it. This may be the case even if I have willingly repeatedly exposed myself to the art form; it might, for me, just never "take."[6] Similarly, the sheer necessity of taking up new pursuits to stave off boredom would not enable us to jerry-rig new interests. Our personalities, it seems, sometimes set narrower bounds on what we can come to take a genuine interest in than the circumstances we find ourselves in.

IV. Do All of the Books Really Have a Finite Number of Pages?

Another way we might circumvent insurmountable boredom is by having at least one book in our personal library that is infinitely long. Some Anti-Curmudgeons claim that it would be very easy to acquire one, or even to write more pages ourselves. They draw on the idea that new opportunities for fulfilling desires related to old projects can refresh old desires. For example, Jeremy Wisnewski imagines a case in which a musician has the goal to "be the best musician ever by mastering every instrument" (Wisnewski 2005, 33–34). Even after this goal is completed, in a few hundred years, he reasons, a new instrument could be invented and it could revive the old project. Furthermore, the musician could actually invent her own instruments for this purpose, and could do so infinitely.

I think this is a bit too fast, though. Not every new instrument that could be invented would provide a musician with an interestingly different challenge. And in order to successfully stave off boredom, a person needs a project to have available ways of engaging with it that haven't already been exhausted. Now, there is surely a large number of variations on musical instruments that would be interestingly different to try to master, but I'm not sure how we could come to know that it would actually be an infinite number. The risk here is that what sustained the initial interest in the pursuit may not persist and that the musician would be left with the desire to pursue mastery of each new instrument *only because* it provides her with a life project that in theory could keep her busy throughout eternity. But it's not as though just having the desire "I want to master every instrument" sustains one's genuine interest indefinitely independent of the conditions that made it seem like a worthwhile pursuit in the first place.

This raises an interesting question, though. Could there be a pursuit that a person could both pursue infinitely and also find infinitely interesting? If there are any such pursuits, they would need to involve repetition in the sense that in your 5000th year doing it, what you're doing is still describable under the same description as when you started doing it. That is, if your pursuit is to become an experienced bird-watcher, you can't have avoided boredom just by moving on to watching squirrels instead; "becoming an experienced bird-watcher" still has to be the goal you're aiming at. But somehow, the repetition of this pursuit has to be such that it wouldn't cause boredom. What bores though, as we've discovered, is not just repetition of any sort, but rather, running out of ways to engage with something. So the things a person would do in order to satisfy her desire to engage in this pursuit would have to be topically linked while producing an infinite number of ways to engage.

Perhaps there are such pursuits. Consider certain kinds of desires of self-improvement. For example, maybe a person could spend a lifetime attempting to satisfy a desire to paint the best painting she has ever painted. As long as you would never reach a point that you paint a painting that you know is the best you could ever paint, this would be guaranteed to be an infinitely pursuable goal for you. This stands in contrast to the leap of faith you would have to make to bank on being able to infinitely artificially extend a pursuit like mastering every instrument. While it seems *likely* that there are an infinite number of instruments we could invent, we already know that once you've painted the best painting you've ever painted you can still aim to do better.

What's more, it doesn't seem outside of the realm of possibility that this pursuit could be not only endlessly pursuable but also endlessly interesting. While each painting you would paint would be motivated by the same desire—the desire to paint the best painting you have ever painted—the things that you might do to go about fulfilling that desire might drastically differ over time. The varieties of technique and style, subject matter and color scheme that that you might employ to create an infinite array of compositions seems like a good candidate for the kind of thing that could stave off boredom of the worrisome sort.

That said, we can only speculate about a human's ability to genuinely take an interest in one of these sorts of pursuits for eternity. I doubt that our intuitions about whether or not there are people who could take an interest in these sorts of projects will be reliable when we scale up to think about eternity. Even less reliable, I imagine, are our intuitions about whether any of us *as an individual* is in fact a person who could come to genuinely take an interest in such a pursuit and sustain it indefinitely.

V. Couldn't We Just Re-read the Books Once We've Forgotten Them?

Why though, do we need infinitely long books, when we could just read old books where we've forgotten the story or perhaps even forgotten that we read them in the first place? In practice, after a long enough time wouldn't we forget all about what we've pursued in the past, allowing us to resurrect an interest in our old pursuits, even those not infinitely pursuable or infinitely interesting, by coming to them afresh?[7]

There seems to be something to this thought. After all, our memories are certainly finite, whereas our lives would be infinite. Why couldn't I take up playing chess again one thousand years later after having previously mastered it to the point where I exhausted everything I found interesting about it?

Are you bound to forget everything that was interesting about learning to play chess, though? It would be a massive oversimplification to think of memory loss in mortal lives like a disk drive that just erases the earliest years to make room for the new ones once it's full up. Instead, we find that memory retention is often selective. You likely remember the day you graduated from high school, whereas it's much less likely you remember what you did ten days later. The risk here is that the sorts of pursuits we would come to genuinely take the most interest in, or at least the aspects of them that most command our attention, are not the sorts of things that are easily forgotten. It's hard to say what memory loss would look like over the span of thousands of years. Perhaps we might even develop increased capacities for retaining what's most valuable to us with practice over thousands of years! This should give us pause.

But say we are able to forget what it was like to master chess playing after enough years. Would there be something futile about living only to become good at chess when you know that you've already gotten everything there was to get out of it way back when?

Consider a brief thought experiment. Imagine you're feeling like there is no way for you to enjoy life and you go to a therapist. The therapist tells you that there is only one way that she can help you. She can offer you a pill that will erase part of your memory so that you can have the opportunity to re-enjoy what you once did before you felt like there was nothing left to enjoy about living. If this idea bothers you, then you should worry that in the scenario in which you want to live forever only to pursue things you've forgotten you'll similarly start to find these pursuits to be futile.[8] This is a problem because this feeling of futility can potentially interfere with your ability to genuinely take an interest in your activities.

Now, intuitions may vary quite a bit here due to different natural propensities: some people re-read *Harry Potter* any time it starts to fade from memory, and some people don't see the point.[9] But it's not just this difference in personality as it manifests in mortal life that comes into play. It is, I think, quite difficult to know how one would react when running up against the enormity of facing a justified inability to find anything in life meaningful for the rest of eternity.

What if we could take a pill that would make us forget not only what it was like to become a chess master whether or not we ever pursued learning to play chess, but also forget the fact that we ever erased our memory in the first place? While this cordons off the futility worry, it introduces a new worry. On this view, the only way that immortality would not be intolerably boring would be to take a pill that interrupts the psychological continuity of our selves to a rather large degree. This sort of break in psychological continuity threatens to sever our very identities. We might then wonder what interest we really should have in these futures if it may not even really be *us* who survive.

VI. How Do These Contingencies Bear on What We Should Choose for Ourselves?

I have argued that there are more contingencies to whether or not someone would enjoy immortal life than either Curmudgeons or Anti-Curmudgeons have generally conceived of. And the sorts of things that make a difference to whether or not you are the kind of person who could enjoy a meaningful life without death are very difficult to assess without already having lived for a very long time. I have focused on the contingencies related to whether or not you would face intolerable boredom, but there are other possible contingencies (just to name one: are you the kind of person who needs a due date to get motivated to do anything? If so, you might spend a lot of time procrastinating with the entire expanse of forever stretched out before you to fulfill your dreams).

This leads to an interesting question: what, then, should you do if faced with the opportunity to take an elixir that would make you live forever? This question is particularly vexed because the structure of the decision runs into two somewhat notorious problems for decision theory.

First, there is the fact that, as I have argued, there are various features that affect what it's like to live forever that you wouldn't be privy to without having actually lived for a very long time and/or lived with the understanding that you'd continue doing it forever. This is potentially an example of what L.A. Paul calls a "transformative decision" (Paul 2015).[10] According to Paul,

> in cases of transformative choice, the rationality of an approach to life where we think of ourselves as authoritatively controlling our choices by imaginatively projecting ourselves forward and considering possible subjective

futures is undermined by our cognitive and epistemic limitations. If we attempt to fix the problem by adjusting our decision-theoretic models and eliminating the role for imagination and first personal assessment, the authenticity of our decision-making is undermined.

(Paul 2015)

Even if you *were* able to imaginatively project yourself into the future in order to ascertain exact probabilities for the chances that you would be able to pursue interesting projects indefinitely, assuming the probabilities are somewhere in between 0% and 100% the decision would still not be straightforward. This is because decision theory runs into a number of paradoxes with infinite values and so seems unable to give us straightforward answers in these sorts of cases. Notice, for example, that the value of a choice that leads to a 3% chance of an infinitely bad outcome is still $-\infty$ and the value of a choice that leads to a 97% chance of an infinitely good outcome is still ∞. Given these problems, unless you are willing to bet all your chips on some form of transfinite decision theory, it strikes me that it would be somewhat irrational to be confident about how to proceed.[11]

VII. Conclusion

To summarize, while I have agreed with Anti-Curmudgeons that it might be misleading to think that the library of potential pursuits that exist in general has a finite number of books, each of which has a finite number of pages, there are still several reasons to worry about running out of pages to read that will genuinely sustain your interest. Whether or not any one individual would run out of pages is contingent on the contents of their personal library, which contains only the pursuits she would be able to genuinely take an interest in that would, for her, effectively stave off insurmountable boredom. While it is theoretically possible that a person might have an infinite number of books, books that are infinitely long, or books that are infinitely re-readable, it would be a real gamble to bet on any one of those things being the case. Given the presence

of these sorts of contingencies, I have left open the possibility that it may be theoretically possible for a person to live an infinitely long life on earth free of insurmountable boredom. However, I believe that you should proceed very cautiously, as you have no reason to be confident that that person is you.

Notes

1. For one of the most famous versions of this argument, see Williams (1973). For a similar take on the argument I provide in this chapter that builds off of an interpretation of Williams' argument, see Gorman (2016).
2. Nagel (1986) writes that, "given the simple choice between living for another week and dying in five minutes I would always choose to live for another week.... I conclude that I would be glad to live for ever" (224). Coren (2018) provides a criticism of this argument.
3. Curmudgeons (of both stronger and weaker varieties) include Williams (1973), Moore (2006), Temkin (2008), Burley (2009a), Altshuler (2015), Cholbi (2015), and Beglin (2017). Anti-Curmudgeons include Wisnewski (2005), Chappell (2007), Smuts (2009), Fischer (2009), Bortolotti and Nagasawa (2009), Bruckner (2012), Galloway (2012), Tanyi and Karlander (2013), Fischer and Mitchell-Yellin (2014), and Lauinger (2014).
4. Without arguing for it here, I assume something like a perceptual theory of emotion. For more on perceptual theories of emotions, see Helm (2001), Roberts (2003), Prinz (2006), and Tappolet (2012).
5. My account of fleeting boredom here is greatly influenced by Calhoun (2011).
6. I owe this example to Michael Cholbi.
7. For more on the role of forgetting, see Bruckner (2012), Belshaw (2015), and Felder (2018).
8. See Blumenfeld (2009) for additional motivation for the futility worry. Blumenfeld gives several cases that aim to elicit this intuition via illustrating the way in which many of us seem to value new genuine achievement rather than merely having the experience of having achieved something. He also notes and diagnoses the diversity of responses to the futility worry.
9. Temkin (2008) points to the extreme variation as a factor in the stratification of views in the literature about the desirability of living forever.

10. Beglin (2016) also makes this connection.
11. See Cholbi (2015) for an argument that, given the probabilities, mortality is the better bet.

Bibliography

Altshuler, R. (2015), "Immortality, Identity, and Desirability," in M. Cholbi (ed.), *Immortality and the Philosophy of Death*. London: Rowman & Littlefield, pp. 191–203.

Beglin, D. (2016), "Should I Choose to Never Die? Williams, Boredom, and the Significance of Mortality," *Philosophical Studies*, 174 (8): 2009–2028.

Belshaw, C. (2015), "Immortality, Memory and Imagination," *The Journal of Ethics*, 19 (3-4): 323–348.

Blumenfeld, D. (2009), "Living Life over Again," *Philosophy and Phenomenological Research*, 79 (2): 357–386.

Bortolotti, L. and Nagasawa, Y. (2009), "Immortality without Boredom," *Ratio*, 22 (3): 261–277.

Bruckner, D. (2012), "Against the Tedium of Immortality," *International Journal of Philosophical Studies*, 20 (5): 623–644.

Burley, M. (2009a), "Immortality and Boredom: A Response to Wisnewski," *International Journal for Philosophy of Religion*, 65 (2): 77–85.

Burley, M. (2009b), "Immortality and Meaning: Reflections on the Makropulos Debate," *Philosophy*, 84 (4): 529–547.

Burley, M. (2015), "'The End of Immortality!' Eternal Life and the Makropulos Debate," *Journal of Ethics*, 19 (3-4): 305–321.

Calhoun, C. (2011), "Living with Boredom," *Sophia*, 50: 269–279.

Chappell, S. G. (2007), "Infinity Goes Up On Trial: Must Immortality Be Meaningless?," *European Journal of Philosophy*, 17: 30–44.

Cholbi, M. (2015), "Immortality and the Exhaustibility of Value," in *Immortality and the Philosophy of Death*. London: Rowman & Littlefield, pp. 221–236.

Coren, D. (2018), "Always Choose to Live or Choose to Always Live?," *Southwest Philosophy Review*, 34 (2): 89–104.

Felder, R. M. (2018), "Forgetting in Immortality," *Journal of Applied Philosophy*, 35 (4): 844–853.

Fischer, J. M. (2009), "Why Immortality Is Not So Bad," in *Our Stories: Essays on Life, Death, and Free Will*. Oxford: Oxford University Press.

Fischer, J. M. and Mitchell-Yellin, B. (2014), "Immortality and Boredom," *Journal of Ethics*, 18: 353–372.

Galloway, D. (2012), "Bernard Williams on Living Long and Living Well," *Journal of Evaluation in Clinical Practice*, 18 (5): 1087–1090.

Gorman, A. G. (2016), "Williams and the Desirability of Body-Bound Immortality Revisited," *European Journal of Philosophy*, 24 (3): 1062–1083.

Helm, B. W. (2001), "Emotions and Practical Reason: Rethinking Evaluation and Motivation," *Noûs*, 35 (2): 190–213.

Lauinger, W. (2014), "Eternity, Boredom, and One"s Part-Whole-Reality Conception," *American Catholic Philosophical Quarterly*, 88 (1): 1–28.

Moore, A. W. (2006), "Williams, Nietzsche, and the Meaninglessness of Immortality," *Mind*, 115 (458): 311–330.

Nagel, T. (1986), *The View from Nowhere*. Oxford: Oxford University Press.

Nagel, T. (2014), *Transformative Experience*. Oxford: Oxford University Press.

Paul, L. A. (2015), "Précis of Transformative Experience," *Philosophy and Phenomenological Research*, 91 (3): 760–765.

Prinz, J. J. (2006), "Is Emotion a Form of Perception?," *Canadian Journal of Philosophy*, 36 (sup1): 137–160.

Roberts, R. C. (2003), *Emotions: An Essay in Aid of Moral Psychology*. New York: Cambridge University Press.

Rosati, C. (2013), "The Makropulos Case Revisited: Reflections on Immortality and Agency," in B. Bradley F. Feldman, and J. Johansson (eds), *The Oxford Handbook of Philosophy of Death*. Oxford: Oxford University Press.

Smuts, A. (2009), "Wings of Desire: Reflections on the Tedium of Immortality," *Film and Philosophy*, 13: 137–150.

Tanyi, A. and Karlander, K. (2013), "Immortal Curiosity," *Philosophical Forum*, 44 (3): 255–273.

Tappolet, C. (2012), "Emotions, Perceptions, and Emotional Illusions," in C. Clotilde (ed.), *Perceptual Illusions. Philosophical and Psychological Essays*. New York: Palgrave Macmillan, pp. 207–224.

Temkin, L. S. (2008), "Is Living Longer Living Better?" *Journal of Applied Philosophy*, 25 (3): 193–210.

Williams, B. (1973), "The Makropoulos Case: Reflections on the Tedium of Immortality," in *Problems of the Self: Philosophical Papers 1956–1972*. Cambridge: Cambridge University Press.

Wisnewski, J. (2005), "Is the Immortal Life Worth Living?," *International Journal for Philosophy of Religion*, 58: 27–36.

20 Immortality, Boredom, and Standing for Something

David Beglin

I. Introduction

Death is generally regarded as a bad thing. We fear it, we lament it, we go to great lengths to avoid it—and so far as it goes this all seems reasonable. But if death is bad, does that mean never dying would be good? Not according to Bernard Williams. In a well-known essay, Williams argues that if we lived forever, we'd necessarily become alienated from our environment and existence, "bored" in his words.[1] As Williams sees it, we are in a kind of bind; there is a predicament at the center of our existence. Life is generally worth living and so it is regrettable that it ends. But, according to Williams, mortality—the fact that we die—underpins the ability to meaningfully engage with the people, projects, and values around us in the first place. In this respect, he argues, life is worth living, in part, precisely because it ends, because we die.

Williams' discussion of immortality raises important questions about the role that death plays in making life meaningful for us. In what ways does death underpin meaningfulness in life? Is it really necessary for meaningfulness? Could we live fulfilling lives without it? Much ink has been spilled over these questions. Here, I'll defend a modest version of Williams' answer to them. I agree with many of Williams' critics, who argue that he overstates the necessity of death for meaningfulness in life. Still, I believe that Williams is right to be pessimistic about the prospects of an immortal existence being fulfilling for us.

II. The Necessary Boredom Thesis

Williams begins his discussion of immortality by reflecting on Karel Capek's play, *The Makropulos Case*. The play is about a woman who goes by a number of names, all with the initials "EM." EM is 342 years old.[2] Her life has been extended by an elixir of life, which her father, a physician to a sixteenth-century emperor, tested on her. The elixir extends one's life by 300 years and so to continue living EM has to take it again. When the time comes, though, she refuses opting instead to die and to end an existence that has come to be completely miserable. Indeed, EM's life has come to a state of "indifference" and "coldness." Nothing excites her or makes her happy anymore; she has become completely alienated from her environment and existence. "In the end it is the same," she says, "singing and silence."[3]

What happened to EM? As Williams sees it, she was simply "at it for too long." He characterizes her state of alienation as a kind of boredom: "a boredom connected with the fact that everything that could happen and make sense to one particular human being of 42 had already happened to her."[4] And Williams believes that boredom like this, alienation and indifference, would overcome anyone who continued to live forever. He thus argues that EM's story reveals something true of everyone: "that the supposed contingencies are not really contingencies, that an endless life would be a meaningless life, and that we could have no reason for living eternally a human life."[5] Immortality, according to Williams, would, at least for humans, *necessarily* lead to the sort of boredom that EM experienced. Call this claim Williams' *Necessary Boredom Thesis*.[6] It suggests that death is necessary for our living fulfilling, meaningful lives. Without death, in other words, we would necessarily become alienated from our existence and environment; we would necessarily become bored, like EM.

A central debate about immortality has concerned this thesis. Many theorists argue that immortality would necessarily be boring; many others argue that it wouldn't.[7] For my part, I'm sympathetic with those who criticize the Necessary Boredom Thesis. I doubt, though, that this thesis is as important as theorists have taken it to be. As I'll explain below, even if we grant that immortality wouldn't *necessarily* be boring, this doesn't entirely resolve our predicament.

III. The Value-Filled World Argument

Before turning to my own view of things, however, it's worth stopping to consider and set aside one way in which the Necessary Boredom Thesis is often criticized. We can call this criticism the *Value-Filled World Argument*. This argument, I believe, misconstrues what Williams was worried about. As a result, it also misses what is interesting about his discussion. Pinpointing where the Value-Filled World Argument goes wrong, then, is illuminating. Particularly, it promises to give us a better sense of what Williams has in mind when he talks about boredom and, consequently, what's potentially at stake when it comes to giving up our mortality.

The Value-Filled World Argument begins with an observation: the world is full of value. It's full, that is, of meaningful ways to spend one's time. Moreover, this value seems inexhaustible; the world seems to offer endless opportunities for meaningful engagement. And this, proponents of the argument say, flies in the face of what Williams is suggesting. After all, consider, once more, what Williams says about EM. He says that her boredom was connected to the fact that "everything that could happen and make sense to one particular human being of 42 had already happened to her." This makes it sound as though EM simply ran out of new experiences to have. But why think that *everyone* would run out of new experiences to have? And, moreover, why think that experiences have to be new to be meaningful or fulfilling?

Consider, for example, pursuits like art and intellectual inquiry. Such pursuits seem to offer endless occupation: there is always more art to appreciate and create, just as there are always more theoretical questions to puzzle over and investigate. Likewise, many experiences can be enjoyed again and again. Think of the satisfaction one can achieve from exercise or sport, or consider the comfort of sitting in a park on a sunny day or drinking coffee on a chilly morning. These sorts of experiences always seem to be there for our enjoyment. Given all the world has to offer, then, why think that everyone would be like EM? Why think we'd all run out of fulfilling experiences?

To be clear, the Value-Filled World Argument doesn't claim that the world must necessarily be full of value. Nor does it claim that everyone necessarily has the opportunity to engage with that value. Some people, for example, might be socially situated in such a way that they are blocked from getting to pursue the meaningful activities that the world has to offer. The Value-Filled World Argument can grant all of this because it simply aims to show that boredom isn't a *necessary* consequence of immortality. So long as it is possible for someone to meaningfully engage with the world forever, in other words, the Necessary Boredom Thesis is false. And given how much value there is in the world, some have argued, it certainly seems possible that *someone* could live forever without boredom.[8]

As I suggested above, though, the Value-Filled World Argument misconstrues Williams' point and, in doing so, it misses what is interesting about the questions posed by his discussion. Williams doesn't deny that the world contains enough value to, in theory, sustain a meaningful immortal existence. He doesn't think, in other words, that we'd necessarily become bored because we'd necessarily run out of valuable things with which to engage. His worry, rather, concerns our ability to continually engage with those valuable things in the first place. His worry isn't about the world or our environment; his worry is about us and our agency.

Consider how Williams describes the sort of boredom that he sees in EM. He describes this kind of boredom as a "reaction almost perceptual in nature to the poverty of one's relation to the environment."[9] He contrasts this with boredom of a more familiar sort. Think, for example, of the boredom you might experience while waiting for an appointment or when tasked with some unnecessary project. If it helps, imagine that your phone has died and that you don't have a friend with you. The sort of boredom that you might feel on such occasions is the consequence of your surroundings being dull or uninteresting. You have nothing to do; you've been betrayed by the world. But this isn't the sort of boredom that Williams has in mind when he worries that immortality would necessarily be boring. Williams' sense of boredom isn't a response to any poverty of value in the world. It is, rather, a response to the poverty of one's *relation* to the world. Something about living forever, Williams thinks, would impoverish our ability to meaningfully engage with what the world has to offer, and so, Williams argues, we'd become bored, alienated from our environment and existence.[10]

This makes it clearer why it won't do for a critic of the Necessary Boredom Thesis to point to all of the valuable things that there are to do in the world. One might be unable to meaningfully relate to the world despite its containing an endless number of valuable activities and experiences. As Cheshire Calhoun points out, one might even be aware of all of these valuable activities and experiences and yet, tragically, find oneself unable to find them engaging.[11]

The Value-Filled World Argument's shortcoming, then, is that it is driven by a particular way of thinking about boredom, one that takes boredom to be the consequence of our environment. Williams, though, isn't worried about this kind of boredom. The boredom that worries him is boredom as a reaction to one's impoverished relation to the world. Its source, then, isn't in the world; it's in us. A proponent of the Necessary Boredom Thesis, then, needs to show that there is something about how we relate to the world that is necessary for living a meaningful and fulfilling life, and they need to show that this would necessarily be undermined by immortality.

IV. Skepticism about the Necessary Boredom Thesis

Earlier, I said that I have doubts about the Necessary Boredom Thesis. Let me now explain them. To defend the Necessary Boredom Thesis, we've just seen, one has to show two things. First, one has to show that there is something about how we currently relate to the world that is necessary for living a meaningful, fulfilling life, and, second, one has to show that this would necessarily be undermined by immortality. My doubts stem especially from skepticism about establishing the first claim.

Consider just how strong that claim is. Our mortality surely informs how we currently engage with and find meaning in the world. But why think that the way we currently relate to the world is the only possible way of relating to it that could be meaningful? Or, to put the point positively, why think that there aren't other ways of relating to the world, other ways of being, which, perhaps, aren't on our radar but could still be meaningful? Perhaps immortality would undermine certain of our distinctive, mortal ways of relating to the world. But why think we couldn't adjust? Why think we couldn't develop new ways of relating to the world, new ways of being? It seems difficult to show that we necessarily couldn't.[12]

I thus think there is good reason to doubt the Necessary Boredom Thesis. It simply seems too strong. Still, I don't think denying the Necessary Boredom Thesis settles things.

V. A More Modest Predicament

Even if we deny the Necessary Boredom Thesis, it is far from obvious that we should choose to give up our mortality, given the option. Indeed, even if we grant that we wouldn't *necessarily* become bored, that our existence wouldn't *necessarily* become meaningless, that we wouldn't *necessarily* lose the ability to engage with the world in a fulfilling way, this is at best cold comfort. It seems that we'd reasonably want assurance that we *wouldn't* become bored, that we wouldn't find immortal existence alienating. And I doubt that much assurance is to be had on this front.

Of course, one might wonder about this claim. Maybe not much assurance is to be had that we wouldn't become bored, alienated in the way that Williams describes, but surely there also isn't strong reason to think that we would become bored. We don't really know what immortal life would be like. Isn't it a wash?

Not quite. After all, we do know at least one thing about immortal existence: it requires giving up mortality.[13] And if we reflect on the ways that our mortality undergirds our current lived experience, the current ways that we find meaning and fulfillment in our particular relationships, activities, and environments, I think we find good reason to worry about choosing to give it up. This, I think, is the best way to understand Williams' driving idea.

In particular, as I'll explain below, I believe that giving up mortality would likely mean giving up one particularly important sort of meaning. Without mortality, we have good reason to think that our lives couldn't stand for something, at least in one familiar sense of that phrase. Choosing to give up our mortality would thus, I suspect, change the significance that the things in our lives can have for us. And this would likely be alienating.

If this is right, then a more modest version of Williams' predicament emerges. Death, after all, still seems to be a bad thing, something reasonably lamented, feared, and avoided. But if our mortality makes possible a particularly important way in which we can commit ourselves to things, and thus a particularly important way in which specific people, projects, and values can be meaningful to us, then it is far from clear that never dying would be good. Again, we find ourselves between a rock and a hard place. We might avoid death by giving up our mortality; but there's reason to think that doing so would mean abandoning our

distinctive ways of relating to the world, which currently make our lives feel worthwhile. And it is far from clear that this is desirable.

The basic thought here, then, is this. It isn't clear that mortality is necessary for meaningfulness in life; it isn't clear that we couldn't possibly live a fulfilling, immortal existence. But to do so would seem to require becoming a very different kind of creature. And given that we are already living in a certain way, with certain commitments, with particular things in our lives that carry a distinctive kind of significance for us, it isn't clear how well we could withstand such a radical transformation. From our particular mortal perspectives, that is, I doubt immortality would be, or should be, especially enticing.

VI. Immortality and the Source of Boredom

I'm suggesting, then, that there is a distinctive way in which we commit ourselves to things, one that is central to most of our lives. And moreover, I'm suggesting that immortality would undermine this form of commitment and would thus likely be alienating for us. Let's explore these suggestions in more detail.

Williams claims that EM's boredom was "connected with the fact that everything that could happen and make sense to one particular human being of 42 had already happened to her." I'd like to try to make sense of this suggestion. And to do so, I'd like to begin by considering a surprising claim that Williams makes.[14] He writes:

> Just as being bored can be a sign of not noticing, understanding, or appreciating enough, so equally not being bored can be a sign of not noticing, or not reflecting, enough. One might make the immortal man content at every moment, by just stripping off from him consciousness that would have brought discontent by reminding him of other times, other interests, and other possibilities.[15]

Williams' idea here is counterintuitive. On the face of it, it would seem that being reminded "of other times, other interests, and other possibilities" would promise to keep one from becoming bored. Indeed, Connie Rosati, in a rich discussion of Williams' paper, argues that our ability to reevaluate and reimagine our lives should lead us to doubt Williams' certainty that we'd become bored during an immortal existence. Rosati believes that our capacity to imaginatively engage with possibility is precisely a solution to boredom.[16] Why, then, does Williams claim the opposite? Why does Williams think our capacity to imagine other times and possibilities gives us *reason* to worry about becoming bored, alienated?

Williams doesn't explain his claim; however, I believe we can make sense of it. The worry, I think, has to do with the significance of our commitments becoming diluted. When one commits oneself to different people, projects, or values, that is, one gives them a distinctive place in one's life. And as one continues to commit oneself to things, one continues to mark those things as significant in this way. After enough time, though, after marking enough people, projects, and values as significant like this, one risks diluting the significance of the people, projects, and values to which one has already committed oneself. It seems, in other words, that one can only place so many things at the center of one's life and history. Just as I might feel less confident that I'm really your close friend when I find out that you have 600 other "close" friends, one might feel one's past commitments lose their significance as one continues to commit to more and more things.

To better see the worry, it might help to reflect more on the significance of our substantive commitments. Samuel Scheffler observes that temporal scarcity is a condition under which "the attitude of valuing comes to play an important role in human life." Scheffler's idea is that our morality, along with the temporal scarcity it creates, forces us to "establish priorities, to guide our lives under a conception of which things are worth doing and caring about and choosing."[17] Scheffler's thought, then, is that when one commits oneself to some person, project, or value, one does so against a background of finitude, against a background of the people, projects, and values that one isn't and won't be committing oneself to. This helps us see what it is to mark some person, project, or value as especially significant for one's life: the person, project, or value to which one commits oneself is especially significant relative to the other people, projects, and values that one won't be committing oneself to, that one won't be making central to one's life. In a sense, then, when we commit ourselves to something, our life comes to stand for it. And the worry—about the dilution of significance—is that if one gives up one's mortality, if one thus gives up temporal scarcity, one gives up the finitude that makes sense of this kind of significance. Consequently, it seems that one also gives up one particular purpose one's life can have: making one's life stand for something.

The significance of commitment, along with its attending sense of purpose, seems to be of great importance to us. Think, for example, of the kinds of attitudes we take toward our own and others' lives. When some writer or artist or businessperson dies, we might marvel at and admire the way they "dedicated their life" to their pursuit. When our friend continues to float from one thing to the next, with no commitments, working a dead-end job, getting drunk all the time, we might worry our friend is "wasting their life." And from time to time, we might worry about how we are "living our lives" and about whether we've "made our lives" about the right stuff. Likewise, consider the following common piece of advice: "live each day like it's your last." This advice tells us to put our energy only into those people, projects, and values that merit our limited time. Or consider the common hypothetical question: "What would you do if you only had 5 more years to live?" Our answer to this question is supposed to reveal our most important commitments, those most central to our lives.

The idea, then, is that our mortality, and particularly the finitude that it brings with it, is the condition for the possibility of a familiar and important way in which we commit ourselves to the people, projects, and values in our lives. Because we're mortal, our commitments accrue a symbolic significance—our lives can stand for things. If we were to give up our mortality, then, we would seemingly lose this way of committing ourselves to things, and our particular commitments would eventually lose this significance.

This helps us to see how immortality threatens us with boredom, with a kind of alienation from our own existence. When considering whether to become immortal, we have already lived a finite life, characterized by commitments to certain people, projects, and values. And the significance of these commitments is threatened by a life that never ends. If we relinquish our mortality, that is, we also give up on this significance. Of course, this may not occur to us immediately. But, as Williams points out, it seems that as long as we remain conscious of other times, interests, and possibilities, the loss will eventually become salient. And this, I think, constitutes the realization that one's relation to one's environment has become impoverished. One will come to realize, in other words, that the significance of one's commitments have been diluted, that the things one took one's life to stand for have stopped being central to one's life. Moreover, one will realize that one can no longer commit to things in the way in which one once could. So, I believe, one will become alienated from one's environment and existence—one will become bored.

We can apply this line of thought to EM. Williams, we've seen, explains her boredom by suggesting that it is "connected to the fact that everything that could happen and make sense to one particular woman of 42 had already happened to her." His point, though, shouldn't be understood in terms of EM running out of new experiences to have. In a sense, I suspect, her problem was the opposite. The world marched on, and she, as a particular person, with a particular history, had to keep pace. She had to continue to engage with new people, projects, and values. And after enough time, it might have simply become unclear what the point of it all was. Committing herself to this

person or that project began to lose its meaning. Singing and silence began to look the same. She could no longer live a recognizably human life. She was simply at it for too long.

VII. A Lingering Hope

Still, there is a lingering hope for the proponent of immortality. And it is worth considering this hope, in part, because I think it makes clearer what we might lose if we were to give up our mortality. The hope is this: it doesn't seem like life-standing commitments would *necessarily* be undermined by immortality. After all, it seems possible that one might make one's life about something like intellectual inquiry or promoting justice. And it seems like if one did, then this would provide a stable commitment. One wouldn't, in other words, have to commit oneself to anything new, and so the significance of one's commitment wouldn't necessarily become diluted or undermined.

What should we make of this possibility? It certainly provides further reason to doubt the Necessary Boredom Thesis. But should we find this possibility reassuring? That is, does it give us much reason to choose to live forever, to think that we wouldn't find an immortal life alienating? I don't think that it does, or, at least, I don't think it provides as much assurance as one might hope.

First, even if we dedicate ourselves to such abstract, inexhaustible ends, we'd have to mediate those commitments through particular people, projects, and activities. For example, one cannot promote justice in the abstract. One would have to take up particular causes, or come to the aid of particular people in particular situations. An interesting feature of a life dedicated only to abstract, inexhaustible ends, then, is that it would change the way in which one relates to the particular people and projects in one's life. Those people and projects would become something more like means to some grander activity that one will never finish. And this way of relating to the particular people and projects around one isn't clearly desirable.

Moreover, as Williams points out, our commitments to activities like intellectual inquiry or promoting justice are reflective of more about us than some pure appreciation of the value of the activity itself.[18] We commit to the things that we do because of our character and interests and because of other commitments we have. And there is a good chance that these other aspects of us might be affected by immortality. Indeed, this point is strengthened when considered in light of the foregoing idea, about the way in which we must pursue abstract, inexhaustible ends through the particular, concrete people, projects, and environments around us. Dedicating one's life to intellectual inquiry or promoting justice might lose its appeal without particular colleagues or once one finishes some particular project, which might have spurred one to those larger pursuits in the first place.

I doubt, then, that there is much consolation to be had in our lingering hope, the hope of dedicating our lives to abstract, inexhaustible ends. While it is certainly possible that one could find a life dedicated to such ends meaningful and fulfilling; it would still mean abandoning certain more immediate ways of relating to the people, projects, and values around one. And it isn't clear that abandoning those more immediate ways of relating to the world is desirable. It would still mean abandoning, in a sense, our commitments to the particular people, projects, and values in our life.

VIII. Conclusion

What, then, is the take-away from the foregoing discussion? I haven't meant to argue that boredom—alienation—would be a necessary consequence of immortality. Indeed, I don't even mean to suggest that boredom would necessarily afflict any human who chose to give up their mortality. Perhaps one could find a different way of relating to the world. One might become more present-oriented, with things only being important to one *now*, with no claim to mattering for one's life as a whole. My point is only that immortality seems to threaten one particularly important way in

which many of us live our lives, one particularly important way that many of us relate to our worlds. And it is far from obvious that we would be fulfilled after having lost this way of committing ourselves to things. Boredom, I think—alienation in the way Williams described—is far from unthinkable for most of us. And this gives us good reason to worry about choosing to give up our mortality.

We're left, then, with a version of Williams' predicament. It's worth noting, though, that there is a silver lining here. After all, implicit in the foregoing point is something else: there is something to celebrate about our mortality. Our mortality, through the finitude that it brings, makes possible a particular way of committing to things, a particular way of engaging with the world, of creating a life. As mortals with a reflective awareness of our mortality, we're capable of living our lives for certain people, projects, and values. It isn't all bad, then.

Notes

1. Bernard Williams, "The Makropulos Case: Reflections on the Tedium of Immortality," reprinted in *The Metaphysics of Death*, ed. John Martin Fischer (Stanford: Stanford University Press, 1993), 71–92.
2. This is the age Williams reports. In the play, EM is 347.
3. Williams, "Makropulos Case," 74.
4. Ibid., 82.
5. Ibid., 81.
6. I borrow this term from John Martin Fischer and Benjamin Mitchell-Yellin, "Immortality and Boredom," *Journal of Ethics* 18 (2014), 354.
7. For defenses of the Necessary Boredom Thesis, see, e.g., Martha Nussbaum, *The Therapy of Desire* (Princeton: Princeton University Press, 1994); Shelly Kagan, *Death* (New Haven: Yale University Press, 2012). For criticisms, see, e.g., John Martin Fischer, "Why Immortality Is Not So Bad," reprinted in *Our Stories: Essays on Life, Death, and Free Will* (Oxford: Oxford University Press, 2009), and Martha Nussbaum, "The Damage of Death: Incomplete Arguments and False Consolations," in *The Metaphysics and Ethics of Death*, ed. J.S. Taylor (Oxford: Oxford University Press 2013), 25–43.

8. Fischer and Mitchell-Yellin, in "Immortality and Boredom," make this kind of argument. They worry proponents of the Necessary Boredom Thesis sometimes conceive of the world as though it has only a finite amount of valuable experiences.

9. Williams, "Makropulos Case," 87.

10. There is another aspect of Williams' argument that I won't emphasize here. He worries that not becoming bored would require becoming a different person. Becoming a different person, though, would undermine the value of immortal existence, since, presumably, we want *ourselves* to be the person who persists. See Williams, "Makropulos Case," 83–84.

11. Cheshire Calhoun, "Living with Boredom," *Sophia* 50 (2011), 275.

12. See, e.g., Nick Bostrom and Rebecca Roache, "Ethical Issues in Human Enhancement," in *New Waves in Applied Ethics*, ed. J. Ryberg, T. Petersen, and C. Wolf (Palgrave Macmillan, 2008), 120–152.

13. Here, I have in mind what is sometimes called *true* immortality, as opposed to *medical* or *contingent* immortality. The latter are forms of immortality wherein one can still ultimately die; one's vulnerability to death is just radically circumscribed or temporarily suspended.

14. What follows draws heavily from David Beglin, "Should I Choose to Never Die? Williams, Boredom, and the Significance of Mortality," *Philosophical Studies* 174 (2017), 2009–2028. There, I provide a more detailed discussion of Williams and of how we should understand the boredom that would likely result from immortal existence.

15. Williams, "Makropulos Case," 87.

16. Connie Rosati, "The Makropulos Case Revisited: Reflections on Immortality and Agency," in *The Oxford Handbook of Philosophy of Death*, ed. B. Bradley, F. Feldman, and J. Johansson (Oxford: Oxford University Press, 2013), 373.

17. Samuel Scheffler, *Death and the Afterlife* (Oxford: Oxford University Press, 2013), 99.

18. Williams, "Makropulos Case," 88–89.

Part VI What Is the Best Attitude to Take Toward Our Mortality?

O Living Always, Always Dying

O LIVING always, always dying!
O the burials of me past and present,
O me while I stride ahead, material, vis-
    ible, imperious as ever;
O me, what I was for years, now dead,
    (I lament not, I am content;)
O to disengage myself from those corpses
    of me, which I turn and look at where
    I cast them,
To pass on, (O living! always living!) and
    leave the corpses behind.

—Walt Whitman

Introduction to Part VI

In this section, you'll get to read two contemporary philosophers' take on the questions raised by Lucretius' epic poem *De Rerum
Natura* (discussed in Part IV) about how we
should feel about death. This will be followed
by Epictetus's sanguine answer to the question, contained in his *Enchidrion*. After that,
you'll get to read two quite distinct works.
The first is Buddha's earliest sermon on the
Four Noble Truths, and the second is a poetic
excerpt from Friedrich Nietzsche's magnum
opus *Thus Spake Zarathustra*.

How should you feel about your death?
Following Epicurus (341–270 B.C.E.),
Lucretius (unknown–mid to late 50s B.C.E.)
seemed to think that you shouldn't feel bad
about it at all. If you read Part IV, then you're
already familiar with Lucretius' epic poem *De
Rerum Natura*. In it, he wrote

Death… is nothing to us and does not affect
us in the least… when we are no more, when

body and soul, upon whose union our being
depends, are divorced, you may be sure that
nothing at all will have the power to affect us
or awaken sensation in us.
(Lucretius: Book III, Lines 829–840)

Lucretius' thought seems to be that we
shouldn't feel bad about our death since once
we're dead, we no longer exist, and once we no
longer exist, nothing bad could happen to us.

Perhaps, however, Lucretius wasn't saying
that we shouldn't have *any* negative attitudes
toward death. Perhaps his view is consistent
with holding that we should have a negative attitude toward death when it prevents
us from missing out on additional good life.
After all, in *De Rerum Natura*, he also wrote
that "Anyone who has been born must wish
to remain in life so long as the caresses of
pleasure hold him there" (Lucretius: Book
V, Lines 177–178). It might be the case that
Lucretius was just trying to convince his readers that death is nothing to fear *in itself*, even if
we should have a negative attitude towards it
for extrinsic reasons.

In the first chapter of this section, Todd
May argues that, on the one hand, we should
be grateful for death since the meaningfulness of our lives depends on us dying. May
argues that death provides a framework of
meaningfulness in our lives since, without
it, we would supposedly lose interest in the
projects that give our life meaning, and our
lives would become "shapeless." On the other
hand, though, May argues that death is lam-
entable because it simultaneously threatens
(and often thwarts) the very projects that give
our lives meaning. On May's view, then, death
at once provides a necessary condition for a

meaningful life, but often occurs in such a way that it prevents us from achieving a maximally meaningful life. It is a mixed blessing.

Ben Bradley defends a different view in the second chapter of this section. He is interested in the question of what attitudes are fitting to have toward death itself. Bradley believes that death is only (extrinsically) bad in virtue of it preventing us from missing out on good life. He argues that, because of this fact, we should not have a negative attitude toward death itself. Our attitudes should be directed at things that are intrinsically good (such as pleasure) and intrinsically bad (such a pain). Since death is neither intrinsically good nor bad, we shouldn't feel good or bad about death *itself*. Though, you should prefer more good life to less, and can have a positive attitude towards receiving intrinsic goods and a negative attitude towards receiving intrinsic bads.

These contemporary takes on the question will be followed by Epictetus' Stoic take on the question. The third chapter of the section contains selections from Epictetus' classic *The Enchiridion*, which was written around 135 A.D. Epictetus was a Greek Stoic philosopher from the first and (early) second century. In this work, he nicely articulates a number of Stoic commitments, which not only aim at truth, but are also meant to serve as a practical guide about how to live well.

At the core of the Stoic philosophy is the idea that there is an important difference between things which are under your control and those which are not. The basic thought is that you should concern yourself with your *actions*, which are under your control and not with anything else which is outside of your control. If you only desire what is under your control, then you can satisfy those desires and live well. On the other hand, if you desire that the world is different in a way that you cannot control, then you are bound to be frustrated and worse off.

This is no easy feat, but Epictetus offers various suggestions about how to make this happen. For example, he writes that if "you are fond of a specific ceramic cup, remind

yourself that it is only ceramic cups in general of which you are fond. Then, if it breaks, you will not be disturbed." When it comes to death itself, Epictetus suggests, that death itself is not terrible, but is only viewed that way given our "principles." Were we to change our desires to want what actually happens (rather than what doesn't and won't happen), we could see that death isn't really bad after all. Following this reasoning, Epictetus suggests that we should not wish for immortality, as that would again be wanting something we won't get and that is outside of our control.

In the fourth chapter of this section, you will get to read an excerpt of the *Dhammacakkappavattana Sutta* (translated in English as *Setting the Wheel of Dhamma in Motion*). The exact date is unknown, but it is thought to be a record of the first sermon given by Gautama Buddha and, in it, Buddha discusses the Four Noble Truths. These are the foundational teachings of the Buddha, which are intended to help others on the path to enlightenment, with the ultimate spiritual goal of nirvana, or freedom from being reborn into suffering.

Put in the simplest terms, the Four Noble Truths state that (1) there is suffering, (2) there are origins for suffering, (3) there is a way to end suffering, and (4) there are means to achieve that end. Suffering is an inherent characteristic of unenlightened life. Rather than having a negative connotation, though, suffering is meant to be seen as a pragmatic approach to understanding the physical and mental ailments that motivate and characterize life. Acknowledging the First Noble Truth, the truth of suffering, allows individuals to address the causes and means to end suffering. The Second Noble truth is the truth of the cause of suffering. Suffering occurs when individuals form attachment to impermanent things and states of being, as rebirth is a tenet of unenlightened life. Ignorance of the impermanence of being can generate strong desires and attachments, resulting in vices (e.g. lust, greed, gluttony, envy, and so on) that perpetuate suffering. The truth of the end of suffering, or the Third Noble Truth, acknowledges nirvana as the means of ending the cycle of rebirth into suffering by becoming enlightened and eliminating all cravings, desires, and attachments.

To achieve that end goal, the Fourth Noble Truth (not discussed in the excerpt) introduces the Noble Eightfold Path that cultivates enlightenment through practices related to morality, meditation, and insight. The eight practices include: right view, right resolve, right speech, right conduct, right livelihood, right effort, right mindfulness, and right concentration (*samadi*). Guidance on how to walk the Noble Eightfold Path differs across Buddhist traditions and between mundane and monastic practitioners. Our text is only able to provide a small window into the rich Buddhist literature on the Four Noble Truths.

To quote John Cleese, "and now for something completely different." In the final chapter of this section, you will get to read an excerpt from Nietzsche's philosophical novel *Thus Spake Zarathustra* (1883–1885), which follows the spiritual development of the character Zarathustra as he gives influential poetic monologues that espouse his (and, by extension, Nietzsche's) philosophical views. In the excerpt you will read, Zarathustra is concerned with the general question of how one should want to die. He first notes the apparent irony in people regarding their deaths as events of great importance, but not treating it like a "festival." The best death, he argues, would do this. It wouldn't be a celebratory occasion, but it would be a consummating one, where the soon-to-be deceased are surrounded by those near and dear to them who hope, exchange promises, and "consecrate the oaths of the living."

That was *how* one should die. Now, *when* should one die? Nietzsche's view, as simultaneously tautological and odd as it may sound, is that one should die at the right time. When is that? Well, Zarathustra claims that everyone should have a "goal and an heir," which is to say everyone should want to see the world become a certain way and have followers who will help realize that vision. One should seek death, then, at the optimal time for one's goal and heir(s). That is, they should want to die at the time that will most help one's heir(s) thrive and realize their vision. In Zarathustra's case, this was the time that would be optimal to create a pathway for the proper conditions that would give rise to the Übermensch. The Übermensch refers to the so-called ideal human that would buck "Christian morality" in favor of imposing their own values.

According to Zarathustra, however, people typically don't die at the right time. Rather, they tend to hold onto life until they're old and bitter because of their "cowardly" fear of death. In doing so, they ensure they won't be remembered fondly as a result. Just as people can hold on to life too long, so too can they end their life too early when they are still "immature" and haven't accomplished what they're supposed to have accomplished. This is meant to be illustrated by reference to Jesus' crucifixion. Had Jesus not sacrificed himself, Zarathustra provocatively claims, he might have lived long enough to have come to love life, and disavowed his own teachings.

If you're interested in more readings on the issue of how to feel about death, check out the following:

1. Ben Bradley's "Existential Terror" (2015) *The Journal of Ethics* 19 (3–4): 409–418.
2. Todd May's book *Death* (2014) Routledge.
3. Kai Draiper's "Epicurean Equanimity Towards Death" (2004) *Philosophy and Phenomenological Research* 69 (1): 92–114.
4. Martha Nussbaum's "The Damage of Death: Incomplete Arguments and False Consolations" in *The Metaphysics and Ethics of Death: New Essays* (2013) edited by James Stacey Taylor, Oxford University Press.

21 Death, Mortality, and Meaning

Todd May

Death at once provides a framework of meaningfulness for our lives and leaches that meaningfulness from us.[1] How can this be?

To begin, let's look first at the second half of this seeming paradox: that death leaches the meaningfulness of our lives. As the philosopher Martin Heidegger points out, death—the ending of our existence—is a source of anxiety. For him, "death, as the end of Dasein, is Dasein's ownmost possibility non-relational, certain and as such indefinite, not to be outstripped."[2]

What does this mean? First, death is not a goal or a telos. It is simply the stoppage of our lives. It does not bring our lives to a narrative conclusion, one that would wrap up its themes in the way many novels do. Our lives just end, and that ending has no intrinsic relationship to the life that precedes it; it doesn't bring it to a conclusion, it just ends it. Second, our deaths are inevitable and yet uncertain. They are inevitable because, of course, we are mortal creatures. But that inevitability does not have a date attached to it. We might die of cancer later in our lives or be hit by a car tomorrow. While a few of us, in our old age, are aware of our dying, the moment of our deaths is largely elusive to us. This, however, means that at every moment of our lives we could die, and that recognition is integrated into our lives. We are mortal creatures not simply at the end of our trajectories, but during every instant of them. If I could put it this way, our eventual nothingness is a constant companion to our lives. Finally, death is our own possibility—nobody can substitute for us in death.

Most of the time, as Heidegger notes, we live this companionship in the mode of denying it. We don't actually deny that we are mortal. Of course, we recognize that we all die. Rather, we refuse to look at our own death. It is an absence rather than a presence in our lives—or, perhaps more accurately, it is an absence that is constantly present. We see death around us. Our parents die, some of our friends die, we read about the death of famous people in the newspapers. But these deaths, even when tragic, are the deaths of others. They have died, not us.

However, when we come to consider our own death—seriously to be gripped by it—this is another matter entirely. The ending of my life is the ending of my relationships: with my spouse, my children, and my friends. It is the ending of all of my other projects as well. I will no longer be a philosopher or a political organizer or even an avid reader of books. I will no longer be any of these things, not because they have come to some sort of completion or final consummation, but instead because they have just stopped for me. I will have been cut off. Even that is saying too much, however. There will no longer be an "I" to be cut off, because I will be gone.

It is a difficult thought to wrap one's mind around—that one will no longer exist. When I do this, I am tempted to bring myself back into existence imaginatively to see the world without me, to think of people thinking of me or mourning me or carrying on without me. But my death isn't like that. I won't, in contrast to the plot of some contemporary novels, be there to see what happens after I die. I will just be gone.

This absence is what threatens to sap the meaningfulness from my life. As Heidegger argues, we live our lives toward the future.[3]

We live prospectively, engaged in our projects in the context of assuming their continuing existence. This does not mean that no project ever comes to an end. We complete certain jobs, adventures that we have planned come to an end, hobbies we've taken up become fulfilled. Moreover, while we're engaged with many of these activities we are caught up in the moment, not necessarily thinking about the future. However, even when we are caught up in the moment of our activity, the activity itself is oriented toward the future, toward wherever it is headed and when this or that activity ends, we take up others. We do not just become passive, but instead move toward the future with other projects.

When we die, when our lives stop or are cut off, all of this comes to an end. Our future is gone, and with it the projects we were engaged in, which include our closest relationships. Moreover, since our deaths are not only inevitable but uncertain, every moment is the moment in which that future could be gone. Death, in that sense, is always with us. It accompanies us throughout our lives. We are beings that are characterized by the way our deaths are woven into the fabric of our existence.

For some philosophers, this accompaniment of our lives by death is not a source of concern. Perhaps most famous among these is Epicurus, who argued that we should not fear death because "death, the most frightening of bad things, is nothing to us; since when we exist, death is not yet present, and when death is present, then we do not exist."[4] That is to say, if we are alive there is no death, and when we are dead, since we are no longer there, there is nothing to be afraid of. However, to the extent to which we are forward-living beings—beings of projects that look toward the future—and inasmuch as those projects can be terminated by our death, our projects are perpetually threatened by the fact that we die.

To the extent, then, that our projects—those engagements that give our life meaning—are threatened by death, death it seems would leach away meaningfulness from our lives. This might happen in any number of ways. We might become less attached to our own projects, knowing that we can be lost to them at any moment. After all, why invest your emotional energy into something that could end at any moment? The problem, of course, is that our lives are largely our projects, and so to become distant from our projects is to become distant from one of the most important component of our lives.

The term "largely" in the above paragraph is important. In a famous essay on death, Thomas Nagel observes that,

> There are elements which, if added to one's experience, make life better... But what remains when these are set aside is not merely neutral: it is emphatically positive... The additional positive weight is supplied by experience itself, rather than by any of its contents.[5]

To be alive is, in Nagel's eyes, a positive experience, above and beyond our projects.

In addition to the concern that we will be cut off from our projects, death can sap meaningfulness from life in other ways. Someone might, for instance, wonder what the point of engaging in projects is in the first place if they are perpetually threatened with coming to an end without conclusion through our deaths? Or one might ask generally, since we are all fated to die and then ourselves be forgotten (at least most of us), what is the point of living in the first place? In these ways, death can threaten the sense of our lives as having meaning and of the projects of those lives as being meaningful for us to engage in.

All of this might tempt us to conclude that death is a flaw in our design. We should not be mortal creatures; instead, we should be immortal. Immortality, it might seem, would eliminate the problem of death and by doing so restore the fullness of meaningfulness to our lives. After all, if we knew that we would never be cut off from our projects but instead would be able to see them through, then there would be no need to feel distant or tenuous in relation to those projects. To be sure, our projects might fail on their own: a creative effort might ultimately be fruitless, a relationship can turn sour, a child might not love us as we would wish. It's not that immortality would guarantee that everything would be wonderful. There is, after all, no guarantee that our projects would succeed or maintain their worthiness. However, if we were truly immortal, we could at least immerse ourselves in them without fear that our death would intervene (and could at any moment) to separate us from them.

However, things are not quite so clear-cut as that. While immortality might remove certain obstacles to meaningfulness on the one hand, it would throw up other obstacles—maybe more difficult ones—on the other. In order to see this, we need to imagine what immortality would be like and how it would affect our relationship to our lives.

Imagine here the things you like to do most. They can be athletic, musical, literary, or something else. The list may include hiking, eating good food, enjoying the company of friends, immersion in a hobby, or anything that is a project that lends your life meaning. Now imagine doing this for a thousand years. That's probably not a real hurdle to clear. Imagine doing this for ten thousand then, or a hundred thousand, or even a million years.

Here's an image that might begin to capture the idea. Imagine a desert as large as the Sahara. A bird comes along and picks up a grain of that sand and then flies away. Ten thousand years later, another bird flies over and picks up another grain of sand and flies away. In the time it would take all of these birds to clear the entire Sahara of sand, not a flicker of an instant of your immortality would have taken place. It would be as though no significant amount of time had passed. Immortality, we must recognize, is not a short affair. Even if one imagines oneself healthy during all this time and not like Jonathan Swift's Struldbugs, who are immortal creatures that just continue to get older, it still seems a long time to continue to do or to enjoy whatever it is that is meaningful now, or would be in a thousand or ten thousand years.

Martha Nussbaum argues that an immortal life would be shapeless. It is mortality that gives us a framework within which our projects take up meaning. Without such a framework, the things that move us would have less urgency or passion. She writes,

> the intensity and dedication with which very many human activities are pursued cannot be explained without reference to the awareness that our opportunities are finite, that we cannot choose these activities indefinitely many times. In raising a child, in cherishing a lover, in performing a demanding task of work or thought or artistic creation, we are aware, at some level, of the thought that each of these efforts is structured and constrained by finite time.[6]

This idea is reinforced through a short story by Jorge Luis Borges, "The Immortal." In the story the protagonist is seeking a river in Egypt that promises immortality. Unintentionally, he discovers it as well as the territory of the immortals that inhabit the area. But to his disappointment he finds that these immortals are entirely unconcerned with their lives. Their buildings are in ruins and they rarely help one another out of difficult situations. There is, for these creatures, time for everything, and where there is time for everything, nothing is urgent to accomplish. As the protagonist's interlocutor in this story, Homer, tells him,

> Death (or its allusion) makes men precious and pathetic... every act may be their last; there is not a face that is not on the verge of dissolving like a face in a dream. Everything among the mortals has the value of the irretrievable and the perilous.[7]

Aside from the accusation of being "pathetic" (a term that Borges clearly uses ironically), Nussbaum would certainly agree.

One might object here, though, that this mischaracterizes the situation. After all, history keeps changing and evolving, new practices arise while old ones drop away. Wouldn't it be possible for one to let certain projects go, say after a millennia or two, and then take up others? That way life would continue to be fresh, or at least fresh enough? And if that's the case, shouldn't immortality—or at least indefinite life extension—be a goal of ours? Or, more to the current point, would immortality really be something that necessarily saps the meaningfulness of our lives? Quite the opposite, wouldn't immortality add to the meaningfulness of our lives by circumventing the problems we have seen associated with mortality?

To take this view misses something important about our existence, something that has been underlined by Bernard Williams. To assume that we are capable of moving from new project to new project assumes that we are infinitely plastic in our interests and commitments, that our lives can assume just any shape. It assumes that we are fundamentally formless in the way that Nussbaum worried our lives would become if we were immortal, that we can become interested in anything whatsoever. In fact, the situation with us is very different. Although most of us grow and change to some extent, there are a limited number of things that can hold a person's interest. For different people, those things are, of course, different. In my own case, for instance, I am enthralled by philosophy, political organizing, and my friends and family (I was enthralled for years by running, but then my knees had their say). On the other hand, for me to imagine a life that consisted largely in needlepoint, accounting, watching golf, and (with apologies to Jeff Bridges) bowling, would be hell itself. I might be able to soldier through such a life, but it would not be a meaningful one for me.

In "The Makropulos Case: Reflections on the Tedium of Immortality," Williams insists on the idea that for us to be involved in projects they must be meaningful, not only in themselves, but to us. Regarding the person who is interested, for instance, in activities of pure intellectual inquiry, he writes, "If they are genuinely fulfilling… then the ground and shape of the satisfactions that the intellectual enquiry offers him, will relate to *him*,

not just to the enquiry."[8] It is who a person is, what their interests and passions and normative commitments are, that is the ground of what they can and cannot find meaningful. Elsewhere Williams refers to ground projects, projects "which are closely related to his existence and which to a significant degree give meaning in his life."[9] Absent those projects, our lives become something other than ours. They become lives that must be inhabited or undergone, but not lives with which we identify.

If we cannot be just anybody, that is just take up any projects to confer meaningfulness on our lives, then immortality would not, even as a speculative matter, confer meaningfulness upon them. And so we find ourselves in this situation: on the one hand, death seems to threaten the meaningfulness of our lives by continuously accompanying them with the prospect of cutting off the future of our projects; on the other hand, an open-ended existence would not so much fulfill those projects as render the lives in which they arise shapeless. Death is bad for us, but so is immortality.

How shall we cope with this dilemma? I can only suggest a path here. There may be others. Some have argued that immortality would not be bad for us,[10] but for the reasons I have given here I think that view underestimates how long immortality lasts and misunderstands what kinds of creatures we are. In any event, we aren't immortal creatures, and so perhaps it would be best to ask how to live with our own impending death and how to think about the meaningfulness of our lives within it.

A hint has already been given us by Borges in his story of the Immortals. "Everything among the mortals has the value of the irretrievable and the perilous," Homer tells us. He means it dismissively but, as often with Borges, there is irony involved. If we are to die, then what we have now, the lives that we are living, are the only ones we get. And they don't last forever (a good thing, as I have argued). This lends a certain urgency, a certain imperativeness, to our lives. The moments that we are allotted are limited and irreplaceable; we ought not to take them for granted. In this sense, we ought to attend to the present, recognizing the precious character of the moments we do have rather than losing ourselves in future prospects.

At the same time, however, we have seen that we are also beings oriented toward the future. To live solely in the present would be to abandon our projects *as projects*, to neglect their temporally unfolding character, their opening out on to a future that we envision as we participate in them. We cannot, then, forsake the future and the threat of death that always lies in wait there. While recognizing the precious and fleeting character of the present moment we must at the same time engage ourselves in the fragility of our future through the projects we participate in. We must become beings that abandon neither the present for the future nor vice versa.

Is this a paradox? Can it be done? To one extent or another, I do not see why it cannot be done. While fully inhabiting both present and future may be a bit of an ideal, and while that ideal character might entail that we never achieve as fully meaningful lives as we might like, cultivating the ability to lodge ourselves as firmly as possible in both present and future is not an impossible task. Moreover, it is an enriching one, a task that can allow us to cultivate our mortal lives in a way that offers meaningfulness even if not complete fulfillment.

Death, then, is not only that which leaches meaning from our lives. It is, at the same time and in the same gesture, that which allows them to be meaningful at all. Perhaps our calling—or at least one of our callings—as human beings is to come to terms in our thought and in our lives with the painful and yet promising gift that our mortality offers us.

Notes

1. For the purposes of his essay I will leave the idea of meaning and meaningfulness undefined. There are many different views of this. My own view is articulated in *A Significant Life: Human Meaning in a Silent Universe* (Chicago: University of Chicago Press, 2015). However, nothing hinges on adopting my view of meaningfulness. Many different views can be accommodated in what follows.
2. Martin Heidegger, *Being and Time*, tr. John Macquarrie and Edward Robinson (New York: Harper Collins, 2008), p. 303.
3. For a contemporary view of this, see *Homo Prospectus*, by Martin Seligman, Peter Railton, Roy Baumeister, and Chandra Sripada (Oxford: Oxford University Press, 2016).
4. Epicurus, "Letter to Menoeceus," in *The Epicurus Reader: Selected Writings and Testimonia*, tr. and ed., Brad Inwood and L.P. Gerson (Indianapolis: Hackett Publishing Co., 1994), p. 29.
5. Thomas Nagel, "Death," in *Mortal Questions* (Cambridge: Cambridge University Press, 1991), p. 2.
6. Martha Nussbaum, *The Therapy of Desire* (Princeton: Princeton University Press, 1994), p. 229.
7. Jorge Luis Borges, "The Immortal," in *Labyrinths* (New York: New Directions Press, 1962).
8. Bernard Williams, "The Makropulos Case: Reflections on the Tedium of Immortality," in *Problems of the Self* (Cambridge: Cambridge University Press, 1976), p. 100.
9. Bernard Williams, "Persons, Character, and Morality," in *Moral Luck: Philosophical Papers 1973–1980* (Cambridge: Cambridge University Press, 1981), p. 12.
10. See, for example, John Martin Fischer's "Why Immortality Is Not So Bad," in *Our Stories: Essays on Life, Death, and Free Will* (Oxford: Oxford University Press, 2011).

22 Fitting Attitudes Towards Deprivations

Ben Bradley

There is a simple Epicurean argument that we should not worry about death. Death marks the end of existence. If you don't exist, you can't experience any pain. So it is not bad to be dead, and your death won't bring about anything else bad for you. If something isn't bad for you in itself, and it doesn't bring about anything else bad for you, then it is not bad for you in any way. If something is not bad for you in any way, you shouldn't worry about it. So you shouldn't worry about death.

A standard reply to Epicurus is to adopt a *deprivation account* of the badness of death. According to this account, death is bad in virtue of depriving its victim of a good future life; the better the future that is deprived, the worse the death. Thus death can be bad for us without being bad in itself and without causing them pain. bringing about anything bad for us.

This reply blocks the Epicurean argument, but it does not show that any negative attitude is appropriate to feel towards death. If the deprivation account is true, as I believe it is, what attitude should we have towards death? I will defend the view that we should prefer a good life to an early death, but that no further negative attitudes towards death are warranted.

The chapter will proceed as follows. First I will clarify the question I am attempting to answer. Then I will present the argument for my view. Finally I will discuss some possible objections.

Clarifying the Question

I am asking what response to death is fitting— not what response would make someone feel better, or would make someone mentally healthier, or would be good in some other way. Compare with belief: there are beliefs that might make you feel better despite being false, like believing that you are above average in some respect even though you are not. These beliefs are not fitting, though they might be advantageous. I am asking, with respect to death, which responses fit the facts about death. That attitudes or emotions can be fitting in such a way might be denied. Some might think that there is nothing wrong with having whatever kind of feelings you want. But that would be a surprising view. When Donald Trump falsely claimed that thousands of Muslims in the US were cheering the September 11 attacks, the emotional response he ascribed to those Muslims was unfitting – that was the whole point of his false claim. While we may accept some latitude in emotional responses to events, there are some responses that are morally beyond the pale, such as taking pleasure in the pain and suffering of others. As long as we think it is possible to be wrong about anything at all, we should accept that it is possible to be wrong in our attitudes and emotions.

I am concerned in this chapter with the question of how to respond to death *for the sake of the one who dies*. I am not concerned here with the question of how concerned to be about death for the sake of *other* people. It is natural to be concerned about one's own death because of the effects it will have on one's friends and family. That sort of concern is less interesting philosophically, because some of the effects of death on other people are bad intrinsically, such as the pain one's death causes others to feel. It seems clear that some negative reaction is warranted towards intrinsically bad things like pain. It is less clear what reaction is warranted towards a mere deprivation of good things.

Relatedly, I am granting the Epicurean assumption that death marks the end of an individual's existence. If there is an afterlife in which dead people continue to have conscious experiences, then our attitude towards a person's death for that person's sake should track the nature of that conscious experience. If they are enjoying the afterlife then we should not feel bad for them; if they are being jabbed with pitchforks then we should.[2] Again, the question becomes philosophically less interesting. The interesting question arises on the supposition that there is no afterlife. If a person goes out of existence upon death, then death cannot cause that person any bad experiences. This puts important limits on the ways in which death can harm its victim, and makes the question of what attitude to have towards death more challenging to answer.

I am assuming that death is often bad for its victim. If the Epicureans are right that death is never bad for anyone, it is hard to see how it could make sense to be troubled by death.[3] I am assuming that the Epicurean arguments about death's badness can be answered by deprivation theorists; I won't try to respond to those arguments here.

An important thing to emphasize is that according to the deprivation account, death is *instrumentally* bad, not intrinsically bad, for its victim. To say that something is intrinsically bad is to say it is bad in itself; it is bad in a way that does not depend on what else it brings about. To say that something is instrumentally bad is to say that it is bad in virtue of its effects. Many, including Epicurus, have thought that pleasure is intrinsically good and pain is intrinsically bad. Pleasure seems good, and pain bad, even if they don't lead to any further valuable effects. Most things that are good are good merely in virtue of what they bring about. For example, eating healthy food seems pointless unless it leads to some good effects in the future. Death row inmates having their last meal do not eat kale. Being dead cannot be intrinsically bad for you, since (as I

am assuming) you don't exist when you are dead. Nor is it plausible to say that the event of your death—the thing that happens at the moment you stop living—is intrinsically bad for you. That event is bad for you, according to the deprivation account, solely in virtue of the good things it prevents you from getting. Thus it is instrumentally bad, supposing that it deprives you of more good than bad.

Summing up these clarifications, the question is: given that death is bad for me solely in virtue of the fact that it deprives me of some goods in life, what is a fitting attitude to have about my death, for my own sake?

Fitting Attitudes

According to a much-discussed view about value, what it is for something to be good or bad is for it to be the fitting object of a "pro-" or "con-" attitude such as love or hate (Brentano 1969; Ewing 1948; Jacobson 2011). This has been called the "fitting attitude" analysis of value. The fitting attitude analysis provides a reduction of other value concepts to the concept of fittingness. Thus, if someone were to ask, "Why should I care about goodness?", the defender of the fitting attitude analysis can say: "because *what it is* to be good is to be a thing that is fittingly cared about. If you acknowledge that this thing is good, you are thereby acknowledging that loving it is fitting."[4]

Whether the fitting attitude analysis of value is true is a controversial matter.[5] But it does seem true that there is, at least, an important connection between value and our attitudes. Someone who takes pleasure in an innocent's suffering is wicked because their attitude towards disvalue is incorrect; likewise the person who becomes angry at others enjoying deserved happiness. For our purposes it is sufficient to say that other things being equal, it is fitting to love what is good and to hate what is bad, and unfitting to hate what is good and love what is bad; it is fitting to have a neutral attitude to what is neither good nor bad.

One important feature of the fitting attitude analysis is that it concerns *intrinsic* value.

For something to be intrinsically good is for it to be the fitting object of a pro-attitude *for itself*, or considered in itself. Nonexistence is, intrinsically, neither good nor bad. So the fitting attitude analysis requires us to have a neutral attitude towards our future nonexistence for itself. What is a fitting attitude to have towards something, not for itself, but for what it precludes or prevents or deprives us of? That is the question that concerns us here, and fitting attitude theorists have said little about this.

My suggestion is that we should not have a negative attitude towards something in virtue of the good things it prevents. Our attitudes should be directed only towards the intrinsic goods and evils. If our attitudes towards things depended on what those things prevent us from getting or deprive us from having, we would have inappropriate attitudes. I will give two examples to show why this is the case.

The first is an example adapted from one given by Kai Draper (2013, 78). Suppose for the sake of argument that your attitude towards something should be a function of both its intrinsic value and its non-intrinsic value, such as what it prevents from happening. Suppose you go to Bjorn and Sven's house of massage and get a pleasant massage from Bjorn. You get 10 units of pleasure from this massage. But if you hadn't got the massage from Bjorn, you would have got one from Sven. That one would have also given you 10 units of pleasure. How should you feel about your massage? Well, you should have a pro-attitude corresponding to the 10 units of pleasure you got from the Bjorn massage. But given our supposition, you should also have a negative attitude based on what the Bjorn massage prevents: an equally pleasant Sven massage. So you should have a negative attitude corresponding to the 10 units of pleasure the Bjorn massage deprives you from getting from Sven. In sum, your attitude towards the Bjorn massage should be neutral, since it does not make you any better off than you would have been otherwise. But that cannot be correct. You should have a pro-attitude towards the Bjorn massage. It should make no

difference to your attitudes that you would have received a valuable Sven massage if you hadn't got the Bjorn massage.

Here is the second example.[6] Suppose you know your nemesis will murder you today. He is a skilled assassin who never fails. If he were not to kill you, you would have years of happiness to look forward to. You are dismayed at this fact. You decide to hire a backup assassin to kill you tomorrow. The backup won't be needed due to the certainty that your nemesis will succeed. But his presence changes what your death deprives you of. Instead of being deprived of years of happiness, you will be deprived of just one day. Supposing your attitude towards your death should depend on what you are deprived of, you should feel much less upset about your death now. But that seems wrong. Your attitude towards your death should not change as a result of hiring this backup assassin.

These examples lead me to think that our attitudes should be confined to the intrinsic goods and evils. Suppose someone has all the appropriate attitudes, of the correct magnitudes, towards intrinsic goods and evils. Suppose they have all the relevant associated preferences – they prefer the better to the worse, and they are indifferent between equally good things. And suppose they have no attitudes at all towards things that are merely instrumentally valuable. What would they be missing? I suggest the answer is: nothing. To the extent that their behavior is guided by their attitudes, they will make all the correct choices, prudentially speaking (though see Objection 1 below). That is some evidence that their attitudes are correct. But this means they would have no negative attitude towards death, or to their future nonexistence. They would prefer a continued good existence to going out of existence, but they would regard future nonexistence as neutral, and they would have no negative attitude towards death. If this is the case, then it is possible to have a perfectly fitting set of attitudes that is, in an important respect, Epicurean.[7]

Here is one more, slightly more complicated example to show why it cannot be fitting to have attitudes corresponding to instrumental values. There is a tendency to focus on cases that have only two outcomes, but this can lead us to overlook some potential difficulties.

Suppose S is applying for a grant to attend summer camp. There are three events that could happen, each with an associated outcome:

Event A (max funding): S gets the maximum funding, leading to outcome A: S goes to the super-fun sports camp where she gets 50 units of sports pleasure.

Event B (good funding): S gets funded at a lesser rate, leading to outcome B: S goes to the pretty-fun music camp where she gets 40 units of music pleasure.

Event C (no funding): S gets no funding, leading to outcome C: S does not go to any camp, and gets no pleasure at all.

Let us also add the following details. Supposing that S actually gets the lower funding rate, this would be because a large number of people applied, making it more difficult to get the higher rate. Thus, if S had not received the lower funding rate, she would have received no funding. On the other hand, supposing S actually gets the higher funding rate, that would be because a relatively small number of people applied, and thus her application would have been one of the strongest submitted. If she hadn't received the maximum funding, due to the lack of competition, she would still have received the lesser funding rate and gone to the pretty-fun music camp.[8] In other words: if B obtains, then if B hadn't obtained, C would have; if A obtains, then if A hadn't obtained, B would have.

We know what attitudes S should have towards these outcomes for themselves. S should have a pro-attitude towards A of magnitude +50 in virtue of the intrinsic goodness S gets in A; etc. What attitudes should S have towards events A, B, and C in virtue of their instrumental values? In three-outcome cases, it will be useful to distinguish between what an event *prevents* and what it *precludes*. Let us

say that an event E prevents an outcome O if and only if O *would* have happened if E had not happened. Let us say that an event E precludes an outcome O if and only if, given that E happens, O does not occur (whether or not it would have occurred had the event not happened). So, in this example, each event precludes both of the other outcomes. An event can preclude an outcome without preventing it. For example, my death tomorrow would *preclude* my becoming the first person to walk on Mars, but it would not *prevent* that from happening, since I was not going to be the first person to walk on Mars anyway. Getting a flu shot *precludes* me from getting the flu no matter where I happen to be, but it only *prevents* me from getting the flu if I am in an area where the flu exists.

Now let us apply this distinction to our example. Suppose S's attitude towards an event should be a function of its value and the values of all the things it causes and *precludes*. On a simple way of developing this thought, we could just add the values of all the outcomes precluded by an outcome, and say that one should have an attitude that is equal in magnitude but opposite in valence to the sum. In this case, event A precludes outcomes B and C; the sum of the values of B and C is +40; so in virtue of what A precludes, S's attitude towards A should be a negative attitude of strength 40. Event A also causes outcome A, which has positive value of +50; so, all things considered, S should have a slightly positive attitude towards getting the maximum funding. Applying the same procedure tells us that S should have a slightly negative attitude towards event B if it obtains, and a strong negative attitude towards event C.

However, this cannot be right. Any actual outcome will preclude infinitely many other outcomes of positive and negative magnitudes. For example, my writing this chapter right now precludes my being emperor of the world right now, and also precludes my being tortured to death right now. Any outcome inconsistent with what I am currently doing is precluded by what I am currently doing. Thus, in any actual situation, we would be required to have the same neutral attitude towards every event that occurs. Since that is absurd, what an event precludes cannot be relevant to our attitudes towards it. It is simply too easy for an event to preclude an outcome.

The deprivation theorist thinks that death is bad in virtue of what it *prevents*, not what it precludes. Death precludes many outcomes without preventing them all; most of the things it precludes would not have happened anyway. Recall that in our example, on the supposition that S receives the maximum funding, if S had not received the maximum funding, she would have received the moderate funding; and on the supposition that S received the moderate funding, if that hadn't happened, she would have received no funding. Given these details, event A (max funding) prevents an outcome with value +40, while event B (good funding) prevents an outcome with value zero. So B is better than A with respect to what they prevent. So, on the view under consideration, S should have a much stronger pro-attitude towards receiving the moderate funding than towards receiving the maximum funding. Such attitudes cannot be fitting. S should have a stronger pro-attitude towards receiving the maximum funding than towards receiving moderate funding. In S's deliberations about which outcome to choose, attitudes towards each outcome in virtue of what would be prevented by bringing about that outcome should be inert if they are held at all – otherwise, S may incorrectly choose the moderate funding on the grounds that it would be fitting for him to be happiest if he were to choose the moderate funding.[9]

To sum up, the roughly Epicurean attitude that I recommend can be characterized as follows. You prefer more of a good life;[10] you have pro-attitudes towards future intrinsic goods; you have no negative attitude towards future nonexistence (that's the Epicurean part). So consider the deaths of Kris and Joshua. Joshua has a lot of goods to look forward to at the time of his death, while Kris has only a modest amount. Joshua should have a strong pro-attitude towards his future goods, while Kris should have only a modest pro-attitude

towards his future goods. Both Joshua and Kris should be neutral towards future nonexistence for itself. The strength of a preference should track a difference in strength of more basic pro-attitudes. Thus, Joshua's preference for continued life should be stronger than Kris's, given his fittingly greater pro-attitude towards the goods in his future. But neither Joshua nor Kris should have a negative attitude towards death.

Objections

Objection 1: instrumental rationality

One might object as follows. It's irrational to have pro- and con-attitudes towards the intrinsic goods and evils, but no attitude towards things that bring them about. You'd violate a principle of instrumental rationality by desiring an end but not desiring the means to it.[11] The person wants to be free but doesn't want to use the hacksaw to saw through the bars on his cell, so he remains in jail; the person wants to get in shape but doesn't want to go to the gym so she remains on the couch. Something is going wrong with these people. If someone has a pro-attitude towards their future goods, but no desire to avoid death, they will end up failing to do what is necessary to avoid death, and thereby act irrationally. So a negative attitude towards death must be required.

There is something to this objection, but it only goes so far. Let us make a distinction between two ways of thinking about desire. There is a behavioral sort of desire according to which we desire something just in case we are disposed to behave in certain ways towards it. There is also a warm and fuzzy sort of desire that we have towards something when we feel a certain way (imagine your favorite food being put in front of you when you are hungry, and think about how you feel). You can desire something in the behavioral sense without having any good feelings about it. If you hear that one of your cars was stolen, you may desire that it was your Yaris rather than your Lexus, but you don't have warm fuzzy feelings about your Yaris being stolen. It may be possible to have desires in the behavioral sense without being able to feel anything at all, as when I say that my computer doesn't want to shut down.

The principle of instrumental rationality might hold for desire and aversion in the behavioral sense. Maybe you can't do an action without having some relevant desire, in which case you will need to have desires for non-intrinsically good things in order for it to be possible to bring about the intrinsic goods. If to be averse to something is just to be disposed to choose to avoid it, then if you have correct preferences you will be averse to death when continued life would be good, and that is a kind of attitude.

But it can't be required to have warm fuzzy feelings about the instrumentally good things. Consider two people, George and Sandra, who are locked up against their will. Both want to be free, and freedom would be intrinsically good for them. Both have a positive attitude towards freedom. George finds a hacksaw and saws his way to freedom. Sandra gains her freedom via an elaborate plot involving several accomplices and a number of lucky events. If we are required to be happy about instrumentally valuable things, Sandra should be a lot happier than George. Many more instrumentally valuable events happened to Sandra than to George. But it seems to me they should be equally happy, because both got only one thing they *really* care about: freedom.[12]

Objection 2: Draper's challenge

I am saying that both of the following are true: death is bad for you, but you have no reason to feel bad about death. How can that be? As Kai Draper has said, isn't it odd to call something bad for you and at the same time tell you not to worry about it?

> It may be a conceptual truth… that all misfortunes merit emotional distress on the part of their victims. "I know you've suffered a misfortune here, but there's no reason to be troubled by it' certainly invites the reply, 'I'm not sure you know what a misfortune is".
>
> (Draper 2012, 301)

It would indeed be strange to say that something was harmful for you but you should be indifferent towards it. But indifference involves having no preference as to whether it obtains or not. That would be a more radical view than mine. I have not argued that you should have no preference concerning whether you live or die—in fact, I have argued that it would be irrational. Correct attitudes towards the intrinsically good and intrinsically bad things require having a preference for what is better. What I have argued is incorrect is having a negative attitude towards death. Death's badness is merely instrumental, and I have argued that we should ignore that value in our attitudes.

It is also possible that having some negative attitudes towards death could be correct, provided they are merely ways of expressing a correct preference. Here I have in mind a distinction between attitudes that are directed at a single object and attitudes that are relational. For example, I might say that I fear I will die *rather than live to old age*. This is a way of expressing a relational fear of death. In saying this, I might just be expressing a strong *preference* to live to old age. That is a correct preference. What would be incorrect would be a fear of death that is not relational or contrastive in this way.

Concluding Remarks

The view I am defending here does not depend on the claim that death is not bad. I am saying that even though death is bad, it is incorrect to fear it. Thus, my view is unlike many other views that defend the unfittingness of fearing death. The Epicurean argument at the start of this chapter is one example of such a view. Another view is that it is unfitting for one to have a negative attitude towards death when one has already enjoyed a long and happy life.[13] For such a person to lament death would be unfitting in something like the way it would be unfitting for someone to lament the end of a long and enjoyable banquet, when one is already full and tired. I think this view is mistaken. Related claims would be rejected. If someone has got a lot of good stuff in the past, we don't think that they shouldn't be too concerned about being punched in the face. Maybe the objection involves a justice-based thought: it's more unfair for someone to die when they have not received many goods in life, so we should lament those deaths more. Or there could be a related virtue-based thought: complaining about not getting even more goods, when you've already received plenty, shows a character defect to which we should have a negative attitude. Those considerations are supposed to be bracketed here, because we are interested in attitudes towards death that we have for the sake of the welfare of the person who dies, not for the sake of justice or virtue.

Finally, there is an important caveat to what I have argued here. I have argued that it is inappropriate to have negative attitudes towards death in virtue of what it deprives us from having. But my arguments would not establish that a negative attitude towards death could be warranted by some other feature of death. One particular feeling that people sometimes have about death is existential terror or angst. This feeling has nothing in particular to do with deprivation. It is the feeling some people get when thinking about the fact that in the future they will not be around; or, in the more distant future, nobody will be around. It is not that they could be getting some good things in life but they wouldn't be; it's just their permanent extinction that is terrifying. Nothing I've said in this chapter is relevant to the rationality of this feeling. Elsewhere I've argued that the feeling is likely tied to the belief that future nonexistence robs our lives of meaning.[14] Whether I am right about that or not, there remains the question of whether existential terror can be rationally justified. There are two reasons I suspect it cannot. First, it is difficult to provide a defense of the rationality of the feeling (Bradley 2015b). Second, similar feelings can evidently be produced in people in experiments by, for example, changing the color/symbol combination on a deck of cards (Bruner and Postman 1949; Proulx and Heine 2006; Behrendt 2019, 23). Apparently,

showing someone a black diamond makes them angsty. This doesn't prove anything, of course, but if we assume that there is obviously no good reason to feel bad in any way when seeing a black diamond, and yet people do anyway, we may wonder whether such feelings are more like reflexes that are not susceptible to reason.[15]

Notes

1. Here I depart from the views I defend in Bradley (2009) and Bradley (2015a).
2. See Cyr (2016) for a defense of the view that death can be bad for someone who is paradise-bound.
3. However, see Ekendahl and Johansson (2016) and Timmerman (2016).
4. The fitting attitude analysis can be applied to different sorts of value, but we are here interested in value for an individual, or welfare value.
5. See Jacobson (2011) for an overview.
6. For more examples like this, see Bradley (2009, 156) and Timmerman (2016).
7. There might be room for an intermediate position according to which some, but not all, instrumentally bad things are worthy of negative attitudes. For example, you might think that it makes sense to direct negative attitudes towards the causes of bad things, such as the traffic jam that makes you late for work, but not towards the preventers of good things. This raises complicated issues that I will not take up here.
8. The example is, of course, simplified; in any real case, we would speak of probabilities – "she probably would have received the lower funding rate."
9. Things get even more complicated when we realize that according to popular ways of thinking about causation (and hence deprivation), the truth of assertions of causality depend on conversational context, in particular what we are treating as the default state of a system (see e.g. Hall (2007, 126–127)). I bracket those considerations here.
10. Epicurus might seem to be denying this when he says: "Unlimited time and limited time afford an equal amount of pleasure, if we measure the limits of that pleasure by reason" (Principal Doctrines, 19).

11. See Kolodny and Brunero (2019) for discussion of various principles of instrumental rationality and their drawbacks. Those principles concern the rationality of actions rather than emotions.
12. Thanks to Richard Galvin for pressing me on my reply to this objection.
13. McMahan (2002) argues that death is less bad when the person who died lived a long and happy life. One might think that whether or not death is less bad in such cases, feeling bad about death is unwarranted.
14. Bradley (2015b). See Behrendt (2019) for an argument that I am wrong.
15. Versions of this chapter were presented at the 2019 Texas Ethics Workshop and at SUNY Upstate Medical University's Department of Psychiatry. Thanks to all those present, especially Alyse Spiehler and Richard Galvin, for their helpful comments. Also thanks to Michael Cholbi and Travis Timmerman for very helpful comments on a previous draft.

References

Behrendt, Kathy. 2019. "Unmoored: Mortal Harm and Mortal Fear." *Philosophical Papers* 48 (2): 179–209. doi: 10.1080/05568641.2018.1462668.

Bradley, Ben. 2009. *Well-Being and Death*. Oxford: Clarendon Press.

Bradley, Ben. 2015a. "How Should We Feel About Death?" *Philosophical Papers* 44: 1–14.

Bradley, Ben. 2015b. "Existential Terror." *The Journal of Ethics* 19: 409–418.

Brentano, Franz. 1969 [1889]. *The Origin of our Knowledge of Right and Wrong*. Oskar Kraus and Roderick Chisholm (eds), Roderick Chisholm and Elizabeth Schneewind (trans.). London: Routledge & Kegan Paul.

Bruner, Jerome and Postman, Leo. 1949. "On the Perception of Incongruity: A Paradigm." *Journal of Personality* 18: 206–223.

Cyr, Taylor. 2016. "A Puzzle About Death's Badness: Can Death Be Bad for the Paradise-Bound?" *International Journal for Philosophy of Religion* 80: 145–162.

Draper, Kai. 2012. "Death and Rational Emotion." In Bradley, Feldman and Johansson (eds), *The Oxford Handbook of Philosophy of Death*. New York: Oxford University Press, pp. 297–316.

Draper, Kai. 2013. "Epicurus on the Value of Death." In James Stacey Taylor (ed.), *The Metaphysics and Ethics of Death*. New York: Oxford University Press, pp. 71–79.

Ekendahl, Karl and Johansson, Jens. 2016. "Epicureanism, Extrinsic Badness, and Prudence." In Michael Cholbi (ed.), *Immortality and the Philosophy of Death*. Lanham, MD: Rowman & Littlefield, pp. 39–52.

Ewing, A. C. (1948). *The Definition of Good*. London: Routledge & Kegan Paul

Epicurus. Principal Doctrines. Robert Drew Hicks (trans.). In *The Internet Classics Archive*, http://classics.mit.edu/Epicurus/princdoc.html.

Hall, Ned. 2007. "Structural Equations and Causation." *Philosophical Studies* 132: 109–136.

Jacobson, Daniel. 2011. "Fitting Attitude Theories of Value." In Edward N. Zalta (ed.), *The Stanford Encyclopedia of Philosophy*. Spring, https://plato.stanford.edu/archives/spr2011/entries/fitting-attitude-theories/.

Kolodny, Niko and Brunero, John. 2018. "Instrumental Rationality." In Edward N. Zalta (ed.), *The Stanford Encyclopedia of Philosophy* (Winter 2018 Edition), https://plato.stanford.edu/archives/win2018/entries/rationality-instrumental/.

McMahan, Jeff. 2002. *The Ethics of Killing*. New York: Oxford University Press.

Proulx, Travis and Heine, Steven. 2006. "Death and Black Diamonds: Meaning, Mortality, and the Meaning Maintenance Model." *Psychological Inquiry* 17: 309–318.

Timmerman, Travis. 2016. "Your Death Might Be the Worst Thing Ever to Happen to You (But Maybe You Shouldn't Care)." *Canadian Journal of Philosophy* 46: 18–37.

23 The Enchiridion (excerpts)

Epictetus

The Enchiridion, c. 135 AD, trans. Elizabeth Carter (1758)

1. Some things are in our control and others not. Things in our control are opinion, pursuit, desire, aversion, and, in a word, whatever are our own actions. Things not in our control are body, property, reputation, command, and, in one word, whatever are not our own actions.

The things in our control are by nature free, unrestrained, unhindered; but those not in our control are weak, slavish, restrained, belonging to others. Remember, then, that if you suppose that things which are slavish by nature are also free, and that what belongs to others is your own, then you will be hindered. You will lament, you will be disturbed, and you will find fault both with gods and men. But if you suppose that only to be your own which is your own, and what belongs to others such as it really is, then no one will ever compel you or restrain you. Further, you will find fault with no one or accuse no one. You will do nothing against your will. No one will hurt you, you will have no enemies, and you not be harmed.

Aiming therefore at such great things, remember that you must not allow yourself to be carried, even with a slight tendency, towards the attainment of lesser things. Instead, you must entirely quit some things and for the present postpone the rest. But if you would both have these great things, along with power and riches, then you will not gain even the latter, because you aim at the former too: but you will absolutely fail of the former, by which alone happiness and freedom are achieved.

Work, therefore to be able to say to every harsh appearance, "You are but an appearance, and not absolutely the thing you appear to be." And then examine it by those rules which you have, and first, and chiefly, by this: whether it concerns the things which are in our own control, or those which are not; and, if it concerns anything not in our control, be prepared to say that it is nothing to you.

2. Remember that following desire promises the attainment of that of which you are desirous; and aversion promises the avoiding that to which you are averse. However, he who fails to obtain the object of his desire is disappointed, and he who incurs the object of his aversion wretched. If, then, you confine your aversion to those objects only which are contrary to the natural use of your faculties, which you have in your own control, you will never incur anything to which you are averse. But if you are averse to sickness, or death, or poverty, you will be wretched. Remove aversion, then, from all things that are not in our control, and transfer it to things contrary to the nature of what is in our control. But, for the present, totally suppress desire: for, if you desire any of the things which are not in your own control, you must necessarily be disappointed; and of those which are, and which it would be laudable to desire, nothing is yet in your possession. Use only the appropriate actions of pursuit and avoidance; and even these lightly, and with gentleness and reservation.

3. With regard to whatever objects give you delight, are useful, or are deeply loved, remember to tell yourself of what general nature they are, beginning from the most insignificant things. If, for example, you are fond of a specific ceramic cup, remind yourself that it is only ceramic cups in general of which you are fond. Then, if it breaks, you will not be disturbed. If you kiss your child, or your wife, say that you only kiss things which are human, and thus you will not be disturbed if either of them dies.

4. When you are going about any action, remind yourself what nature the action is. If you are going to bathe, picture to yourself the things which usually happen in the bath: some people splash the water, some push, some use abusive language, and others steal. Thus you will more safely go about this action if you say to yourself, "I will now go bathe, and keep my own mind in a state conformable to nature." And in the same manner with regard to every other action. For thus, if any hindrance arises in bathing, you will have it ready to say, "It was not only to bathe that I desired, but to keep my mind in a state conformable to nature; and I will not keep it if I am bothered at things that happen."

5. Men are disturbed, not by things, but by the principles and notions which they form concerning things. Death, for instance, is not terrible, else it would have appeared so to Socrates. But the terror consists in our notion of death that it is terrible. When therefore we are hindered, or disturbed, or grieved, let us never attribute it to others, but to ourselves; that is, to our own principles. An uninstructed person will lay the fault of his own bad condition upon others. Someone just starting instruction will lay the fault on himself. Some who is perfectly instructed will place blame neither on others nor on himself.

6. Don't be prideful with any excellence that is not your own. If a horse should be prideful and say, "I am handsome," it would be supportable. But when you are prideful, and say, "I have a handsome horse," know that you are proud of what is, in fact, only the good of the horse. What, then, is your own? Only your reaction to the appearances of things. Thus, when you behave conformably to nature in reaction to how things appear, you will be proud with reason; for you will take pride in some good of your own.

★★★

8. Don't demand that things happen as you wish, but wish that they happen as they do happen, and you will go on well.

9. Sickness is a hindrance to the body, but not to your ability to choose, unless that is your choice. Lameness is a hindrance to the leg, but not to your ability to choose. Say this to yourself with regard to everything that happens, then you will see such obstacles as hindrances to something else, but not to yourself.

★★★

11. Never say of anything, "I have lost it"; but, "I have returned it." Is your child dead? It is returned. Is your wife dead? She is returned. Is your estate taken away? Well, and is not that likewise returned? "But he who took it away is a bad man." What difference is it to you who the giver assigns to take it back? While he gives it to you to possess, take care of it; but don't view it as your own, just as travelers view a hotel.

12. If you want to improve, reject such reasonings as these: "If I neglect my affairs, I'll have no income; if I don't correct my servant, he will be bad." For it is better to die with hunger, exempt from grief and fear, than to live in affluence with perturbation; and it is better your servant should be bad, than you unhappy.

Begin therefore from little things. Is a little oil spilt? A little wine stolen? Say to yourself, "This is the price paid for equanimity, for tranquillity, and nothing is to be had for nothing." When you call your servant, it is possible that he may not come; or, if he does, he may not do what you want. But he is by no means of such importance that it should be in his power to give you any disturbance

13. If you want to improve, be content to be thought foolish and stupid with regard to external things. Don't wish to be thought to know anything; and even if you appear to be somebody important to others, distrust yourself. For, it is difficult to both keep your faculty of choice in a state conformable to nature, and at the same time acquire external things. But while you are careful about the one, you must of necessity neglect the other.

14. If you wish your children, and your wife, and your friends to live forever, you are stupid; for you wish to be in control of things which

you cannot, you wish for things that belong to others to be your own. So likewise, if you wish your servant to be without fault, you are a fool; for you wish vice not to be vice, but something else. But, if you wish to have your desires undisappointed, this is in your own control. Exercise, therefore, what is in your control. He is the master of every other person who is able to confer or remove whatever that person wishes either to have or to avoid. Whoever, then, would be free, let him wish nothing, let him decline nothing, which depends on others else he must necessarily be a slave.

15. Remember that you must behave in life as at a dinner party. Is anything brought around to you? Put out your hand and take your share with moderation. Does it pass by you? Don't stop it. Is it not yet come? Don't stretch your desire towards it, but wait till it reaches you. Do this with regard to children, to a wife, to public posts, to riches, and you will eventually be a worthy partner of the feasts of the gods. And if you don't even take the things which are set before you, but are able even to reject them, then you will not only be a partner at the feasts of the gods, but also of their empire. For, by doing this, Diogenes, Heraclitus and others like them, deservedly became, and were called, divine.

16. When you see anyone weeping in grief because his son has gone abroad, or is dead, or because he has suffered in his affairs, be careful that the appearance may not misdirect you. Instead, distinguish within your own mind, and be prepared to say, "It's not the accident that distresses this person, because it doesn't distress another person; it is the judgment which he makes about it." As far as words go, however, don't reduce yourself to his level, and certainly do not moan with him. Do not moan inwardly either.

17. Remember that you are an actor in a drama, of such a kind as the author pleases to make it. If short, of a short one; if long, of a long one. If it is his pleasure you should act a poor man, a cripple, a governor, or a private person, see that you act it naturally. For this is your business, to act well the character assigned you; to choose it is another's.

18. When a raven happens to croak unluckily, don't allow the appearance hurry you away with it, but immediately make the distinction to yourself, and say, "None of these things are foretold to me; but either to my paltry body, or property, or reputation, or children, or wife. But to me all omens are lucky, if I will. For whichever of these things happens, it is in my control to derive advantage from it."

★★★

21. Let death and exile, and all other things which appear terrible be daily before your eyes, but chiefly death, and you win never entertain any abject thought, nor too eagerly covet anything.

★★★

48. The condition and characteristic of a vulgar person, is, that he never expects either benefit or hurt from himself, but from externals. The condition and characteristic of a philosopher is, that he expects all hurt and benefit from himself. The marks of a proficient are, that he censures no one, praises no one, blames no one, accuses no one, says nothing concerning himself as being anybody, or knowing anything: when he is, in any instance, hindered or restrained, he accuses himself; and, if he is praised, he secretly laughs at the person who praises him; and, if he is censured, he makes no defense. But he goes about with the caution of sick or injured people, dreading to move anything that is set right, before it is perfectly fixed. He suppresses all desire in himself; he transfers his aversion to those things only which thwart the proper use of our own faculty of choice; the exertion of his active powers towards anything is very gentle; if he appears stupid or ignorant, he does not care, and, in a word, he watches himself as an enemy, and one in ambush.

★★★

52. Upon all occasions we ought to have these maxims ready at hand:

"Conduct me, Jove, and you, O Destiny, Wherever your decrees have fixed my station."

Cleanthes

"I follow cheerfully; and, did I not,
Wicked and wretched, I must follow still
Whoever yields properly to Fate, is deemed
Wise among men, and knows the laws of heaven."
—**Euripides, Frag. 965**

And this third:

"O Crito, if it thus pleases the gods, thus let it be. Anytus and Melitus may kill me indeed, but hurt me they cannot."
—**Plato's *Crito* and *Apology***

24 Setting the Wheel of Dhamma in Motion (excerpts)

Buddha

Dhammacakkappavattana Sutta, "Setting the Wheel of Dhamma in Motion" (From Venerable Narada Mahathera, *The Buddha and His Teachings*. Taipei: Buddha Educational Foundation, 1998)

Thus have I heard:

On one occasion the Exalted One was residing at the Deer Park, in Isipatana, near Benares. Thereupon the Exalted One addressed the group of five Bhikkhus[1] as follows:

> "There are these two extremes, O Bhikkhus, which should be avoided by one who has renounced:
>
> i) Indulgence in sensual pleasures – this is base, vulgar, worldly, ignoble and profitless; and,
> ii) Addiction to self-mortification – this is painful, ignoble and profitless.

Abandoning both these extremes the Tathāgata[2] has comprehended the Middle Path which promotes sight and knowledge, and which tends to peace higher wisdom, enlightenment and Nibbāna.

What, O Bhikkhus, is that Middle Path the Tathāgata has comprehended which promotes sight and knowledge, and which tends to peace, higher wisdom, enlightenment, and Nibbāna?

The very Noble Eightfold Path – namely, Right Understanding, Right Thoughts, Right Speech, Right Action, Right Livelihood, Right Effort, Right Mindfulness, and Right Concentration – This, O Bhikkhus is the Middle Path which the Tathāgata has comprehended."

(The Buddha continued):

"Now, this, O Bhikkhus, is the Noble Truth of Suffering!

Birth is suffering, decay is suffering, disease is suffering, death is suffering, to be united with the unpleasant is suffering, to be separated from the pleasant is suffering, not to get what one desires is suffering. In brief the five aggregates of attachment are suffering.

Now, this, O Bhikkhus, is the Noble Truth of the Cause of Suffering: It is this craving which produces rebirth, accompanied by passionate clinging, welcoming this and that (life). It is the craving for sensual pleasures, craving for existence and craving for non-existence.

Now, this, O Bhikkhus, is the Noble Truth of the Cessation of Suffering. It is the complete separation from, and destruction of, this very craving, its forsaking, renunciation, the liberation there-from, and non-attachment thereto.

Now, this, O Bhikkhus, is the Noble Truth of the Path leading to the Cessation of Suffering. It is this Noble Eightfold Path, namely: Right Understanding, Right Thoughts, Right Speech, Right Action, Right Livelihood, Right Effort, Right Mindfulness and Right Concentration.

i) "This is the Noble Truth of Suffering."
ii) "This Noble Truth of Suffering should be perceived." Thus, O Bhikkhus, with respect to things unheard before, there arose in me the eye, the knowledge, the wisdom, the insight, and the light.

iii) "This Noble Truth of Suffering has been perceived." Thus, O Bhikkhus, with respect to things unheard before, there arose in me the eye, the knowledge, the wisdom, the insight, and the light.

★★★

(Concluding His Discourse, the Buddha said): As long, O bhikkhus, as the absolute true intuitive knowledge regarding these Four Noble Truths... was not perfectly clear to me, so long I did not acknowledge in this world inclusive of gods, Māras and Brahmas and amongst the hosts of ascetics and priests, gods and men, that I had gained the Incomparable Supreme Enlightenment.

When, O Bhikkhus, the absolute true intuitive knowledge regarding these Four Noble Truths..., became perfectly clear to me, then only did I acknowledge in this world inclusive of gods, Māras, Brahmas, amongst the hosts of ascetics and priests, gods and men, that I had gained the Incomparable Supreme Enlightenment.

And there arose in me the knowledge and insight – "Unshakable is the deliverance of my mind. This is my last birth, and now there is no existence again."

Thus the Exalted One discoursed, and the delighted Bhikkhus applauded the words of the Exalted One.

Notes

1. Monks, learners.
2. One who has travelled, learned, or transcended (an honorific term for the historical Buddha, Siddhartha Gautama).

25 Voluntary Death (excerpts)

Friedrich Nietzsche

Thus Spake Zarathustra (1883–1885), trans. Thomas Common (2008). Licensed by Project Gutenberg.

XXI. Voluntary Death

Many die too late, and some die too early. Yet strange soundeth the precept: "Die at the right time!"

Die at the right time: so teacheth Zarathustra.

To be sure, he who never liveth at the right time, how could he ever die at the right time? Would that he might never be born!—Thus do I advise the superfluous ones.

But even the superfluous ones make much ado about their death, and even the hollowest nut wanteth to be cracked.

"Everyone regardeth dying as a great matter: but as yet death is not a festival. Not yet have people learned to inaugurate the finest festivals.

The consummating death I show unto you, which becometh a stimulus and promise to the living.

His death, dieth the consummating one triumphantly, surrounded by hoping and promising ones.

Thus should one learn to die; and there should be no festival at which such a dying one doth not consecrate the oaths of the living!

Thus to die is best; the next best, however, is to die in battle, and sacrifice a great soul.

But to the fighter equally hateful as to the victor, is your grinning death which stealeth nigh like a thief,—and yet cometh as master.

My death, praise I unto you, the voluntary death, which cometh unto me because *I* want it.

And when shall I want it?—He that hath a goal and an heir, wanteth death at the right time for the goal and the heir.

And out of reverence for the goal and the heir, he will hang up no more withered wreaths in the sanctuary of life.

Verily, not the rope-makers will I resemble: they lengthen out their cord, and thereby go ever backward.

Many a one, also, waxeth too old for his truths and triumphs; a toothless mouth hath no longer the right to every truth.

And whoever wanteth to have fame, must take leave of honour betimes, and practise the difficult art of—going at the right time.

One must discontinue being feasted upon when one tasteth best: that is known by those who want to be long loved.

Sour apples are there, no doubt, whose lot is to wait until the last day of autumn: and at the same time they become ripe, yellow, and shrivelled.

In some ageth the heart first, and in others the spirit. And some are hoary in youth, but the late young keep long young.

To many men life is a failure; a poison-worm gnaweth at their heart. Then let them see to it that their dying is all the more a success.

Many never become sweet; they rot even in the summer. It is cowardice that holdeth them fast to their branches.

Far too many live, and far too long hang they on their branches. Would that a storm came and shook all this rottenness and worm-eatenness from the tree!

Would that there came preachers of SPEEDY death! Those would be the appropriate storms and agitators of the trees of life!

But I hear only slow death preached, and patience with all that is "earthly."

Ah! ye preach patience with what is earthly? This earthly is it that hath too much patience with you, ye blasphemers!

Verily, too early died that Hebrew whom the preachers of slow death honour: and to many hath it proved a calamity that he died too early.

As yet had he known only tears, and the melancholy of the Hebrews, together with the hatred of the good and just—the Hebrew Jesus: then was he seized with the longing for death.

Had he but remained in the wilderness, and far from the good and just! Then, perhaps, would he have learned to live, and love the earth—and laughter also!

Believe it, my brethren! He died too early; he himself would have disavowed his doctrine had he attained to my age! Noble enough was he to disavow!

But he was still immature. Immaturely loveth the youth, and immaturely also hateth he man and earth. Confined and awkward are still his soul and the wings of his spirit.

But in man there is more of the child than in the youth, and less of melancholy: better understandeth he about life and death.

Free for death, and free in death; a holy Naysayer, when there is no longer time for Yea: thus understandeth he about death and life.

That your dying may not be a reproach to man and the earth, my friends: that do I solicit from the honey of your soul.

In your dying shall your spirit and your virtue still shine like an evening after-glow around the earth: otherwise your dying hath been unsatisfactory.

Thus will I die myself, that ye friends may love the earth more for my sake; and earth will I again become, to have rest in her that bore me.

Verily, a goal had Zarathustra; he threw his ball. Now be ye friends the heirs of my goal; to you throw I the golden ball.

Best of all, do I see you, my friends, throw the golden ball! And so tarry I still a little while on the earth—pardon me for it!

Thus spake Zarathustra.

Part VII How Should We React to the Deaths of Others?

When Chuang Tzu's wife died, Hui Tzu came to the house to join in the rites of mourning. To his surprise he found Chuang Tzu sitting with an inverted bowl on his knees, drumming upon it and singing a song.

> "After all," said Hui Tzu "she lived with you, brought up your children, grew old with you. That you should not mourn for her is bad enough, but to let your friends find you drumming and singing – that is going too far!"
>
> "You misjudge me," said Chang Tzu. "When she died, I was in despair, as any man well might be. But soon, pondering on what had happened, I told myself that in death no strange new fate befalls us. In the beginning, we lack not life only, but form. Not form only, but spirit. We are blended in one great featureless indistinguishable mass. Then a time came when the mass evolved spirit, spirit evolved form, form evolved life. And now life in its turn has evolved death. For not nature only but man's being has its seasons, its sequence of spring and autumn, summer and winter. If someone is tired and has gone to lie down, we do not pursue him with shouting and bawling. She whom I have lost has lain down to sleep for a while in the Great Inner Room. To break in upon her rest with the noise of lamentation would but show that I knew nothing of nature's Sovereign Law. That is why I ceased to mourn."

**—Chuang Tzu (third century BCE),
trans. Arthur Waley**

Introduction to Part VII

After the last section, it should be clear why questions about how we should feel about *our own* death can be rather puzzling. Nevertheless, questions of how we should feel about the death *of others* may seem so straightforward as to be undeserving of philosophical inquiry. But that is not so, as this section will make clear. You'll get to read one ancient letter addressing this issue through the discussion of the death of a friend and three contemporary philosophers' take on distinct issues that fall within the scope of this section's broad question.

You'll first get to a letter Seneca wrote to Lucillus (in 65 A.D.) about the death of Lucillus' friend Flaccus. In that letter, Seneca suggests that the ideal is not to mourn the death of a friend at all. But recognizing that is not a feasible option for humans, he urges Flaccus to merely temper his grief. "We may weep, but we must not wail," writes Seneca. Public displays of sorrow are suggested to be self-serving, in that they aim to prove "our bereavement." Seneca suggests an alternative. Instead of wailing, we should look back fondly on our lost friends, grateful for our gift from Fortune. Rather than dwelling on our loss, we should relish the friends we still have and make more friends, and when they too are gone, we should be grateful for the time we had with them.

The Seneca letter will be followed by Michael Cholbi's account of grief. Drawing from C. S. Lewis' life, Cholbi first raises the paradox of grief. Grief is something we at once have good reason to avoid, yet is also valuable and worthwhile. How could this be? According to Cholbi, we (ought to) grieve the loss of people in whom our "practical identities" were invested and, while grief is painful, it is also valuable because it provides us with a certain kind of self-knowledge. More precisely, it provides us with knowledge both of who we were before our practical identity was disrupted, and who we will be now that it's been permanently changed by our loss.

Cholbi's chapter is followed by Roman Altshuler's discussion of so-called Doomsday Scenarios. Imagine that you learn that an asteroid is going to strike the Earth shortly after your natural death, ending all life on the planet. Would this affect the meaningfulness of *your* life? Immediately, you might think "No" since the asteroid didn't shorten your life at all. Yet, Sam Scheffler has used this thought experiment to argue that the meaningfulness of our lives largely depends upon the existence of future generations. Without future generations, our current activities (e.g. cancer research) would benefit much fewer people, our histories would be forgotten, and our traditions would cease to be carried on. Altshuler carefully articulates Scheffler's central arguments before showing that somewhat parallel concerns were raised by Hans Morgenthau and Simone de Beauvoir. Altshuler argues that Scheffler's concerns apply not just to the eradication of human life, but also more narrowly to the eradication of one's culture(s). This should not worry us, he argues, since we have the opportunity to create things that various future cultures can use, thereby bridging a connection between them and us. In doing so, we will be engaging in meaningful projects.

In the last chapter of this section, Patrick Stokes will discuss a philosophical problem that has arisen as a result of social media. How, if at all, should the existence of one's posthumous digital footprint affect our view of the deceased? After a brief overview of different views of personal identity, Stokes draws from science fiction to argue that (in the near future) we may come to view AI versions of deceased persons as being *identical* to those deceased persons. While we may in fact come to view them in this way, Stokes ends the chapter with a discussion of whether we actually have a right to view them as such.

If you're interested in more readings on these various issues, check out the following:

1. Samuel Scheffler's book *Death and the Afterlife* (2013) Oxford University Press. This includes chapter contributions from Susan Wolf, Harry G. Frankfurt, Seana Valentine Shiffrin, and Niko Kolodny.
2. Michael Cholbi's book *Grief: A Philosophical Guide* (2021) Princeton University Press.
3. Jens Johansson's "The Importance of a Good Ending: Some Reflections on Samuel Scheffler's Death and the Afterlife" (2015) *The Journal of Ethics* 19 (2): 185–195.
4. Dan Moller's "Love and Death" (2007) *Journal of Philosophy* 104 (6): 301–316.

26 Letter to Lucilius

Lucius Annaeus Seneca

Moral Letters to Lucilius, Lucius Annaeus Seneca, 65AD, trans. R.M. Grummere (1920)

Letter LXIII. On Grief for Lost Friends

1. I am grieved to hear that your friend Flaccus is dead, but I would not have you sorrow more than is fitting. That you should not mourn at all I shall hardly dare to insist; and yet I know that it is the better way. But what man will ever be so blessed with that ideal steadfastness of soul, unless he has already risen far above the reach of Fortune? Even such a man will be stung by an event like this, but it will be only a sting. We, however, may be forgiven for bursting into tears, if only our tears have not flowed to excess, and if we have checked them by our own efforts. Let not the eyes be dry when we have lost a friend, nor let them overflow. We may weep, but we must not wail.

2. Do you think that the law which I lay down for you is harsh, when the greatest of Greek poets has extended the privilege of weeping to one day only, in the lines where he tells us that even Niobe took thought of food?[1] Do you wish to know the reason for lamentations and excessive weeping? It is because we seek the proofs of our bereavement in our tears, and do not give way to sorrow, but merely parade it. No man goes into mourning for his own sake. Shame on our ill-timed folly! There is an element of self-seeking even in our sorrow.

3. "What," you say, "am I to forget my friend?" It is surely a short-lived memory that you vouchsafe to him, if it is to endure only as long as your grief; presently that brow of yours will be smoothed out in laughter by some circumstance, however casual. It is to a time no more distant than this that I put off the soothing of every regret, the quieting of even the bitterest grief. As soon as you cease to observe yourself, the picture of sorrow which you have contemplated will fade away; at present you are keeping watch over your own suffering. But even while you keep watch it slips away from you, and the sharper it is, the more speedily it comes to an end.

4. Let us see to it that the recollection of those whom we have lost becomes a pleasant memory to us. No man reverts with pleasure to any subject which he will not be able to reflect upon without pain. So too it cannot but be that the names of those whom we have loved and lost come back to us with a sort of sting; but there is a pleasure even in this sting.

5. For, as my friend Attalus[2] used to say: "The remembrance of lost friends is pleasant in the same way that certain fruits have an agreeably acid taste, or as in extremely old wines it is their very bitterness that pleases us. Indeed, after a certain lapse of time, every thought that gave pain is quenched, and the pleasure comes to us unalloyed."

6. If we take the word of Attalus for it, "to think of friends who are alive and well is like enjoying a meal of cakes and honey; the recollection of friends who have

passed away gives a pleasure that is not without a touch of bitterness. Yet who will deny that even these things, which are bitter and contain an element of sourness, do serve to arouse the stomach?"

7. For my part, I do not agree with him. To me, the thought of my dead friends is sweet and appealing. For I have had them as if I should one day lose them; I have lost them as if I have them still. Therefore, Lucilius, act as befits your own serenity of mind, and cease to put a wrong interpretation on the gifts of Fortune. Fortune has taken away, but Fortune has given.

8. Let us greedily enjoy our friends, because we do not know how long this privilege will be ours. Let us think how often we shall leave them when we go upon distant journeys, and how often we shall fail to see them when we tarry together in the same place; we shall thus understand that we have lost too much of their time while they were alive.

9. But will you tolerate men who are most careless of their friends, and then mourn them most abjectly, and do not love anyone unless they have lost him? The reason why they lament too unrestrainedly at such times is that they are afraid lest men doubt whether they really have loved; all too late they seek for proofs of their emotions.

10. If we have other friends, we surely deserve ill at their hands and think ill of them, if they are of so little account that they fail to console us for the loss of one. If, on the other hand, we have no other friends, we have injured ourselves more than Fortune has injured us; since Fortune has robbed us of one friend, but we have robbed ourselves of every friend whom we have failed to make.

11. Again, he who has been unable to love more than one, has had none too much love even for that one. If a man who has lost his one and only tunic through robbery chooses to bewail his plight rather than look about him for some way to escape the cold, or for something with which to cover his shoulders, would you not think him an utter fool? You have buried one whom you loved; look about for someone to love. It is better to replace your friend than to weep for him.

12. What I am about to add is, I know, a very hackneyed remark, but I shall not omit it simply because it is a common phrase: a man ends his grief by the mere passing of time, even if he has not ended it of his own accord. But the most shameful cure for sorrow, in the case of a sensible man, is to grow weary of sorrowing. I should prefer you to abandon grief, rather than have grief abandon you; and you should stop grieving as soon as possible, since, even if you wish to do so, it is impossible to keep it up for a long time.

13. Our forefathers have enacted that, in the case of women, a year should be the limit for mourning; not that they needed to mourn for so long, but that they should mourn no longer. In the case of men, no rules are laid down, because to mourn at all is not regarded as honorable. For all that, what woman can you show me, of all the pathetic females that could scarcely be dragged away from the funeral-pile or torn from the corpse, whose tears have lasted a whole month? Nothing becomes offensive so quickly as grief; when fresh, it finds someone to console it and attracts one or another to itself; but after becoming chronic, it is ridiculed, and rightly. For it is either assumed or foolish.

14. He who writes these words to you is no other than I, who wept so excessively for my dear friend Annaeus Serenus[3] that, in spite of my wishes, I must be included among the examples of men who have been overcome by grief. Today, however, I condemn this act of mine, and I understand that the reason why I lamented so greatly was chiefly that I had never imagined it possible for his death to precede mine. The only thought which occurred to my mind was that he was the younger, and much younger, too, —as if the Fates kept to the order of our ages!

15. Therefore let us continually think as much about our own mortality as about that of all those we love. In former days I ought to have said: "My friend Serenus is younger than I; but what does that matter? He would naturally die after me, but he may precede me." It was just because I did not do this that I was unprepared when Fortune dealt me the sudden blow. Now is the time for you to reflect, not only that all things are mortal, but also that their mortality is subject to no fixed law. Whatever can happen at any time can happen to-day.

16. Let us therefore reflect, my beloved Lucilius, that we shall soon come to the goal which this friend, to our own sorrow, has reached. And perhaps, if only the tale told by wise men is true and there is a bourne to welcome us, then he whom we think we have lost has only been sent on ahead. Farewell.

Notes

1. Homer, *Odyssey*.
2. Seneca's teacher.
3. An intimate friend of Seneca, probably a relative, who died in 64 AD from eating poisoned mushrooms (Pliny, *N. H.* xxii. 96).

27 Why Grieve?

Michael Cholbi

In the summer of 1960, 45-year-old Joy Davidman—an American poet and the wife of well-known writer and Christian theologian C.S. Lewis—died of cancer. As he grieved, Lewis recorded his thoughts in a set of journals, published a year later under the title *A Grief Observed*. But the book was initially published not under Lewis' name but under the pseudonym N.W. Clerk.[1]

Biographies of Lewis shed little light on why he was reluctant to publish *A Grief Observed* under his own name. One suggests his goal was to spare his friends embarrassment.[2] A more plausible hypothesis is that Lewis published it pseudonymously in order to spare *himself* embarrassment. For even a cursory reading of this memoir suggests that Lewis was not only profoundly embarrassed by his own grief, but that Joy's death nearly drove him to delirium.

Lewis' grief is an emotional cavalcade; no single feeling or reaction dominates. But the overwhelming impression is that Lewis was caught unprepared for the variety and intensity of forms grief can take. He is surprised to learn that grief involves such a tangle of emotions: agony and "maudlin tears" he expected, but Lewis is by turns afraid, bewildered, and lethargic (he finds it difficult to muster the energy to shave, much the less to write). Lewis is also mentally unfocused. He feels almost drunk or "concussed," easily driven to distraction by thoughts of Joy when others speak to him. At first reluctant to visit places where he and Joy had happy times, Lewis returns to those settings in the hope of finding peace. He instead finds that they make "no difference," for "her absence is no more emphatic in those places than anywhere

else." Her absence is "like the sky, spread over everything." When Lewis goes looking for Joy, she is elusive. And yet grief registers in one place Lewis "can't avoid": his own body, which he describes as an "empty house." For Lewis, a staunch Christian, the entire experience of grief even induces a crisis of faith. "Meanwhile," he asks in the midst of all this anguish, "where is God?"

Reading his first-hand account of his grief, it is hard not to worry that Lewis—Oxford don, world-renowned author, and archetype of masculine reason—is cracking up, being driven mad by grief. His mind is fractured and disoriented. And as Lewis depicts it, grief haunts us, alienates us from our surroundings and from our selves, and impedes our ability to pursue good things in life. Admittedly, most grief experiences are probably not as emotionally harrowing as Lewis' was. Still, his experience captures something essential about grief: It is often arduous, occasionally terrible.

At the same time, though, there is something recognizably human about Lewis' grief. He suffers, yes, but in a way that many people suffer in grief. A compassionate reader, observing Lewis' suffering, would still not wish *for Lewis' sake* that he not grieve at all. He loved and appeared to be in love with Joy, whom he described as his "trusty comrade, friend, shipmate, fellow-soldier." We expect people to grieve in such situations, and, indeed, it would be unwise and even pathological for them not to. Admittedly, we might wish that Lewis were *less* pained by his grief. But to expunge grief altogether—to render Lewis blithely indifferent to the fact of Joy's death—is not the solution to his plight. That would amount to a "cure" worse than Lewis' "disease". For while grief is painful it is also essential and, in some elusive way, *good*.

Grief thus presents us a paradox: It involves emotional states we ordinarily have good reason to avoid, but grief itself seems valuable or worthwhile nevertheless. The aim of this article is to understand why we ought to grieve despite its involving painful or difficult emotions. In order to answer this question about grief's value, we must first address two questions about the nature of grief. First, for which individuals do we grieve? Second, for what exactly do we grieve?

Before we begin, a few clarifications are in order: Grief, as I shall understand it, is the specific and personal emotional reaction individuals have to others' deaths. It should therefore be distinguished from *mourning*, the behaviors that we engage in so as to publicly acknowledge others' deaths. Many mourning individuals are also grieving, but it is possible to mourn without grieving. We will have a great deal more to say about the nature of grief. But for now, let it suffice that grief arises because others' deaths register as *losses* to the grieving person. Thus, in asking "Why grieve?", we are not asking about the social or moral value of grief (or of mourning). We are instead seeking after the reasons we have for wanting to grieve—why, in other words, Lewis' grief might have been good for him, or why your grieving could be good *for you*.

Grief is a *selective* reaction to the deaths of others. Well over 100,000 people die every day on Earth, and most of these deaths escape our particular notice. We grieve when others die—but only *some* others. To grieve every death would not only be impossible; it would require us to have the kind of relationship with each of those individuals for which grief would be appropriate, and we do not (and probably cannot) have the requisite relationship with everyone. But that raises the question of what *kind* of relationship with another person we must have in order for grief to be appropriate.

Our paradigm cases of grief are reactions like Lewis', grief felt in response to the death of someone with whom we are emotionally intimate, such as a parent or spouse. But we do not grieve only for persons we love or share our lives with. We sometimes grieve the deaths of prominent artists, political leaders, or scientists we admire, for example, despite having no intimate ties with them. We need not even *like* those we grieve for. The Kennedy administration hatched 42 schemes to kill Cuban leader Fidel Castro, but Castro was rueful upon hearing of Kennedy's assassination, and Barack Obama eulogized John McCain, his 2008 election opponent. So enemies or rivals can grieve each other. We might think that we grieve only those whose deaths *harm* us. But sometimes others' deaths can be beneficial to us, and we grieve all the same. An overburdened caregiver may grieve when her patient dies, despite the fact that being relieved of those burdens is (arguably) good for her. We can even grieve those whose identity we hardly have an opportunity to know. Parents are known to grieve miscarried fetuses, and adopted individuals sometimes grieve birth parents they never met.

We thus grieve those who *matter* to us. But as the preceding paragraph indicates, others can matter to us in a variety of ways. They may be life partners, friends, dependents, role models, antagonists, co-workers, professional collaborators, and the like. What unites all those for whom we grieve is what I call *identity investment*.

Each of us has a set of concerns, commitments, values, and goals. Let us call this set a person's *practical identity*. Other people play different roles in our practical identities. Role models, even those we do not know intimately, may shape our practical identities by helping us figure out what we care about. Others—for example, our spouses or romantic partners—play a role in our practical identities by being objects of concern, by sharing values or goals with us, and by caring for us. Some of our commitments or goals only make sense if there are rivals or enemies who stand in the way of their realization. Thus, our practical identities are, in a diversity of ways, invested in the existence of others. We grieve a person's death—and it is *appropriate* that we grieve a person's death—to the extent that our practical identities are invested in their existence. The more central another person is to our practical identity, the greater cause we have for grieving them upon their deaths.

That we grieve for those who are central to our practical identities explains a number of facts about grief. First, it explains how episodes of grief can differ from one another and yet still be instances of the same general emotional phenomenon. Despite the fact that your husband matters to you in a way that differs from how your college roommate matters to you, you might nevertheless grieve their deaths. Your practical identity is more richly invested in your husband than in your college roommate. Second, this thesis helps explain why episodes of grief will vary in their emotional contents. We stand in different kinds of relationships with those we grieve, and the quantity and quality of our grief will tend to reflect these different kinds of relationships. For example, it would be surprising if someone grieved for a business colleague with the intensity that Lewis grieved Joy Davidman. Everyone whose death we grieve plays some role in our practical identity, but how an episode of grief unfolds will depend on the precise role that the deceased has played in our practical identities.

Still, knowing what conditions must be met in order for us to grieve someone's death does not inform us about exactly what we grieve *about*. We often say to grieving people, "I'm sorry for your loss." But what exactly has a grieving person lost? There is a tendency, in my observation, to leave this question unaddressed.

On its face, others' deaths result in several different sorts of losses. When friends die, we lose their companionship. When parents die, we lose their love and support. When national heroes die, we lose their ability to immediately inspire us.

Once again, though, the philosophical challenge is finding the common thread, if any, in all of these losses. Fortunately, our earlier discussion of who we grieve for helps tease out this common thread.

As I argued, we grieve for those in whom our practical identity is invested. In investing our practical identity in another person, we come to have a relationship to them. Such relationships need not be symmetrical (parents do not have the relationship to their children that children have to their parents) or even reciprocal (you may relate to a famous artist but the artist may not even know you). But all such relationships are such that our choices and actions are shaped by them. These relationships are sources of guidance, obligations, and purpose. This is the sense in which these individuals are sources of *practical* identity for us: We choose and act in ways that make reference to them and that we recognize as influenced by them. Lewis, for example, has clearly crafted many of his aspirations and habits around Joy and on the assumption that she would continue to exist.

In short, we build our lives around those in whom our practical identities are invested. We form expectations about our lives and our futures on the assumption that these individuals and the relationships we have with them will continue in some guise.

The deaths of those in whom our practical identities are invested, I suggest, thus represents a kind of relationship crisis for us. Their deaths entail that they cannot play the same role in our lives we presumed they would. The concerns, commitments, values, and goals we pursued while they were alive either no longer make any sense (those of Lewis' future goals that rested on Joy's continued existence can no longer be pursued) or have to be cast in a new light (Lewis can visit his and Joy's favorite pub but not because *they* will enjoy doing so). When someone who matters to us dies, we cannot 'go on' just as we were. We must adapt our practical identities—our understandings of ourselves and of what matters to us—to a new set of realities. The loss we suffer in grief, then, need not be the complete loss of the relationship in question. Indeed, the relationship often continues inasmuch as we hold the deceased in memory, etc. But we do lose the relationship *as it was* or as we assumed it to be, and we cannot be invested in it exactly as we were before.

That we grieve for the loss of a relationship in which we have invested our practical identities makes sense of how grief, while nearly always sad or sorrowful, is often suffused with confusion and bewilderment. This is evident in Lewis' case. He is anguished, yes, but above all else, Joy's death throws him for a loop. The familiar—pedestrian places and activities, even his own body—has become unfamiliar to him. Beset by grief, Lewis is not at home in his own world. Grief, it is sometimes said, is a 'questioning' emotion, and we see in Lewis someone searching for something whose nature he cannot quite pin down. He is restless, lacking his usual sense of direction or habit. He is trying to discover how best to continue his life given that one of the cornerstones of his practical identity— Joy Davidman—can no longer serve as one of those cornerstones. Grief is not only a loss *to* the self. It often feels like a loss *of* the self.

Note that in arguing that the loss that defines grief is the loss of the relationship insofar as that relationship is central to a person's practical identity, I am not denying that we grieve for other more specific losses as well. When friends die, we suffer the loss of their companionship; when siblings, we suffer the loss of their support, their knowledge of our histories and personalities, and the shared sense of the past; etc. Again, we have a wide variety of relationships with those whose deaths we grieve, relationships we value in different ways. In grieving the loss of the relationship as it was, we are simultaneously attempting to come to terms with the losses of the various goods associated with that relationship. I only claim that what we grieve for cannot be reduced to a list of goods the deceased person provided. This is why a remark made by the Roman philosopher Seneca, in a letter to his grieving friend Lucilius, seems insensitive, even chilling:

> If a man who has lost his one and only tunic through robbery chooses to bewail his plight rather than look about him for some way to escape the cold, or for something with which to cover his shoulders, would you not think him an utter fool? You have buried one whom you loved; look about for someone to love. It is better to replace your friend than to weep for him.[3]

Seneca's analogy between a friend lost to death and a cloak lost to robbery is inapt because he seems to view the friend's value in purely instrumental terms, as if the value of a friend (like the value of a cloak) could be reduced to whatever goods the friend provided. Certainly Lucilius ought, at some point, seek out new friends. But not in the expectation that he could *replace* his deceased friend in the way he might replace a stolen cloak. Having invested his practical identity in his deceased friend, Lucilius has integrated his friend into his self-understanding or self-conception. And in so doing, he made his friend *irreplaceable*. This loss of self is significant part of why grief is painful and disorienting. C.S. Lewis cannot replace Joy, even if he could (say) find another romantic partner who provided him whatever goods he found in his relationship with Joy.

With a richer understanding of who we grieve for and of what sort of loss prompts grief, let us now turn to our central question, how grief can be good or desirable for us.

One tempting answer is that grief, owing to the painful or arduous emotions it involves, is not good or desirable in its own right. Rather, experiencing these emotions is a necessary counterpart to the kinds of relationships human beings have, relationships characterized by love, attachment, or affection. If those sorts of relationships are valuable, then the pain we endure when they conclude is simply a price we bear for having those relationships in the first place. In the movie dramatizing Lewis' grief over Joy Davidman's death, Lewis expresses the core of this answer: "Why love if losing hurts so much?... The pain now is part of the happiness then. That's the deal."[4] Let us call this proposal—that grief is simply the cost of having the kinds of relationships where another's death leads to the sufferings associated with grief—the *necessary cost* view of grief's value.

The necessary cost view should be rejected, though, for two reasons. First, it would seem to imply that grief, insofar as it is painful or distressing, is *purely* a cost: We cannot enjoy certain kinds of valuable relationships without grieving once the other participant in the relationship dies, so we must simply tolerate or put up with grief. The problem here is that the pain or distress associated with grief is not experienced as purely a cost. For many bereaved persons seem to embrace the more painful or distressing aspects of grief. Recall that Lewis does not avoid the locations he and Joy enjoyed together. He instead seeks them out, knowing that he will feel haunted or distraught whilst there. For Lewis, these negative emotions, which would otherwise be unwelcome in ordinary life, do not feel like costs. They seem rather to be indispensable to his grieving Joy—they seem to be appropriate or fitting reactions to his loss. Were they purely costs, the rational response for Lewis (and other grieving individuals) would be to try to *minimize* the costs, in the way that we seek out the lowest prices for the goods we buy. But Lewis does not try to minimize his painful emotions, nor does he seem irrational for not doing so. And the best episodes of grief—the ones that seem most important or valuable—are not necessarily those with the least amount of negative feelings. Insofar as the negative cost view denies this, it misunderstands the place of these feelings in grieving.

Second, the necessary cost view cordons off grief, seeing it merely as residue of the grieving person's now-defunct relationship with the deceased. But as the case of Lewis indicates, grief does not mark the end of our relationship with the deceased. It instead tends to mark a turning point *within* our relationship with the deceased, a turning point necessitated by the fact that the deceased can no longer play exactly the same role in our practical identity as she did previously. As Lewis recognized, grief "follows marriage as normally as marriage follows courtship or autumn follows summer. It is not a truncation of the process but one of its phases; not the interruption of the dance but the next figure." Yet if grief is part of our relationship with the deceased, then how we grieve will shape the relationship itself and what it means to us. The necessary cost view depicts grief as a static cost to be weighed against the value of certain relationships, when in fact grief dynamically contributes to the value of those relationships.

Any account of grief's goodness cannot ignore the sufferings associated with it. However, the necessary cost view, I contend, overemphasizes the role of suffering within grief, and, in so doing, overlooks other crucial facts about grief. First, grief is emotionally complex, in that involves many other emotions *besides* suffering. As Lewis' grieving illustrates, episodes of grief commonly involve other emotions, including anger, guilt, fear, confusion, and joyfulness. Moreover, focusing on the sufferings of grief can mislead us into thinking that grief is a passive experience, something we undergo or that happens to us. But grief—or better yet, *grieving*—is a process in which we are active participants. In the course of his grief, Lewis undergoes various emotions, but he also reacts and acts in light of those emotions. Grieving is therefore something we do, not merely something we feel.

But if grieving is an emotionally complex activity, then we may well ask: What is the point of this activity? What valuable end can be pursued by grieving?

My own view is that grief is a particularly distinctive opportunity for a good that we might call *self-knowledge* or *self-understanding*. As noted earlier, the deaths of those in whom are practical identities are invested induce in us something of a relationship crisis: We cannot continue in the relationship as before, but it is often not evident how, if at all, to continue that relationship. But this crisis also represents a crucial opportunity to examine our values and commitments and identify which of these we hope will carry us into the future. When Joy dies, Lewis struggles to figure out what his life might be like in her absence but under her influence. This struggle is an attempt to integrate the past and the future, a struggle to understand the place of Joy in his practical identity. But such a struggle is simultaneously Lewis' struggle to figure himself out and craft a new practical identity. Even if Lewis (or other grieving people) do not recognize this at the time, the tacit point of grieving is to understand, articulate, and endorse, in ways that are rationally responsive to the fact of the other's death, the values and commitments that will constitute the grieving person's prospective practical identity. Having lost an element of identity, we grieve so as to find our way again. In this respect, grief represents a poignant opportunity to engage the question at the heart of the philosophical enterprise: How shall I live?

Grief makes possible this self-knowledge because the deaths of others upset the contingencies around which our practical identities are built. Many of our central values and commitments depend on others' continuing to exist. We know this, but it is easy in the blur of everyday life to forget this and take their existences for granted. We thereby fail to live in light of other people's mortality. And once others die, the fragility of our practical identities is exposed—we see that much of what we have cared about has depended on persons whose existence was finite and contingent. We grieve in the hope that we can move forward in life under a different set of contingencies and with a revised practical identity. If this hope is realized, we have gained a richer knowledge of who we have been and who we seek to be.

To evade grief, or to grief halfheartedly or in bad faith, is therefore bad for us because it deprives us of one of our greatest opportunities for self-knowledge. Only in rare cases, I suggest, would it be sensible to forego this opportunity in order to avoid the emotional tumult of grief.

My answer, then, to 'why grieve?' is that the activity of grieving offers us an especially fruitful chance of attaining the good of self-knowledge. One might wonder, though, why self-knowledge is good.

Unfortunately, I cannot defend that claim fully here. But let me say a few words about the value of self-knowledge in the context of grief in particular.

First, self-knowledge of the sort grief can yield enables us to avoid the unfortunate conditions of *inauthenticity* and *alienation*. Imagine, for example, that Lewis, who was evidently embarrassed by grief, had managed to suppress altogether his grief for Joy. We would, I expect, think that Lewis was trying to proceed forward in life as someone other than himself—as if Joy had not been such a central figure in his life. The self-knowledge that grieving can provide thus seems intrinsically worthwhile, a mark of a life lived honestly and with integrity.

Second, the self-knowledge grief enables also has good consequences for us. Grief, I have suggested, reflects a central feature of the human condition, namely that our identities are invested in others. We should hence be apprehensive about attempts to pathologize or medicalize grief, to see it as an illness rather than an entirely understandable reaction to the fracture that occurs when those in whom we have invested our identities die. But grief can clearly become detrimental to us (to my eyes, Lewis' grief becomes perilously close to being harmful to him). The therapeutic community speaks of how grief can be prolonged, complicated, delayed, or unresolved. In such cases, the grieving individual has not ascertained how to live after the loss of her prior relationship with the deceased. She lacks, in other words, the self-knowledge that I have proposed is the culmination of beneficial episodes of grief. The sufferings of these forms of grief reflect the frustration of the grieving individual's hope to incorporate the deceased individual, and her relationship with the deceased, into a stable and satisfactory practical identity.

Grief presents us a philosophical puzzle because it involves emotional states that we ordinarily suppose are bad and should therefore be avoided: sadness most crucially, but also anguish, confusion, distress, and the like (of course, it can also involve good states too, such as joyfulness or gratitude). At the same time, we should welcome our capacity to grieve inasmuch it nourishes self-knowledge. This fact does not lessen the emotional burdens associated with grief by eliminating them. Rather, it helps us appreciate why those burdens can be worth bearing.

Notes

1. Faber and Faber, 1961. The executors of Lewis' estate permitted to appear under Lewis' name after his death in 1963.
2. Alister McGrath, *C.S. Lewis—A Life: Eccentric Genius, Reluctant Prophet* (Colorado Springs: Tyndale House, 2013), p. 342. McGrath notes that Lewis took other measures to conceal his authorial identity, including not using his usual publisher and using "H." to designate Davidman, whose rarely used middle name was Helen.
3. *Moral Letters to Lucilius* [65 AD] trans. R.M. Grummere (1920) (Letter LXIII, "On Grief for Lost Friends," para. 11).
4. Richard Attenborough, dir., *Shadowlands* (1993, Price Entertainment/Spelling Films International).

28 The Significance of Future Generations

Roman Altshuler

"Why should I care about future generations," asks an old joke. "What have they ever done for me?" Quite a lot, according to a series of arguments. If nothing else, future generations give our lives value and meaning. Most of us value a great number of things, relationships, and activities, and sometimes we find engaging with them meaningful. In our darkest moments we might doubt that there is any meaning to life and suppose our limited life spans mean that nothing we do matters. But most of us do not spend our days in permanent gloom, because even if we don't know what the meaning of life might be and even doubt that such a thing is coherent, we manage to find meaning in life anyway.[1] We do so, by and large, by engaging in what philosophers often call projects: we involve ourselves with art or business, aim at higher degrees that will allow us to research environmental preservation or deadly illnesses, and cultivate relationships with our friends and family. When we engage in these projects, we treat them as something valuable, and we think engaging in them matters. But the value of these projects and their mattering to us doesn't depend merely on what the projects are about. In many cases, it depends also on the future generations that will replace us, or so the argument goes.

I. Doomsday

Recently, the argument has been developed in detail by Samuel Scheffler in his 2013 *Death and the Afterlife*. After presenting the key argument, I will dash back in time to look at some important twentieth-century precursors—Hans Morgenthau and Simone de Beauvoir—to see how the core ideas of Scheffler's argument have been developed in parallel ways. I will then return to Scheffler to look at some implications of his view and what avenues it, together with these precursors, can lead us toward.

Scheffler begins by asking us to imagine two, hopefully fictional, scenarios:

> *The Doomsday Scenario*: You discover that you will live out the rest of your natural life, but thirty days after your death, the Earth will be destroyed by a collision with a giant asteroid, killing all life.[2]

In asking us to imagine this gloomy scenario, Scheffler urges us to reflect on *why* it is gloomy. How does the thought that humanity will disappear shortly after our deaths affect us? Our first thoughts might turn to people we love and the concern that, although they may outlive us, it will not be for long. But Scheffler asks us to overlook this feature of the thought experiment, and proposes that we may consider another in its place:

> *The Infertility Scenario*: Human beings have become infertile. While you, along with everyone you know, have a chance to live out a normal life, there will be no future generations of human beings.[3]

It does not matter for the purposes of this discussion whether we focus on the first scenario, provided we don't focus our attention on the people we care about, or on the second, which is inspired by P. D. James's novel *The Children of Men*, and the 2006 movie directed by Alfonso Cuarón based on it. Here, I will focus on the Doomsday Scenario.

Scheffler uses the term "the afterlife" to refer to the existence of future generations, rather than the traditional meaning of that term as personal survival after death. And, in fact, he explicitly aims his remarks at people who do not believe in the afterlife in the traditional sense. He is asking us to imagine both that we will die—permanently—and that after our own deaths, there will be no future generations of humans. How would we react to such scenarios?

For the most part, he believes we would react with dismay. This in itself is interesting, because it shows that we do care what happens after our deaths. But Scheffler thinks we are likely to discover something more significant, which he summarizes in what he calls the "Afterlife Conjecture": "people would lose confidence in the value of many sorts of activities, would cease to see reason to engage in many familiar sorts of pursuits, and would become emotionally detached from many of those activities and pursuits" (Scheffler 2013, 44). According to this thesis, many of the projects that we currently value would become less significant to us, or lose their significance altogether, in the Doomsday scenario. In fact, Scheffler wants to go even further: not only would the projects lose their significance *to us*, but they would lose it objectively. This might seem improbable at first: just how many of the projects people commonly engage with would be affected in this way and why?

Consider Scheffler's most prominent example: cancer research. Cancer research has two features that would make it especially susceptible to a loss of value under the conditions of the Doomsday Scenario: it is likely to benefit large numbers of people upon its completion, but that completion is unlikely to occur in the lifetimes of those now working on it. A cancer researcher, then, would have little reason to continue engaging in such research if she knew there would be no future generations of human beings, since there would be no one to benefit from the research. This is a strong example, since it's clear that insofar as the value of cancer research rests on its outcome, that value would be annulled altogether if the

outcome were never to occur. However, this example may also seem like an outlier, since most of us are not engaged in cancer research.[4]

The same sort of reasoning, however, translates widely to other projects. A good deal of medical and scientific research in general has a similar structure. That's true of research on other diseases, reliable methods of predicting earthquakes, and effective methods of teaching math, among many other examples. Outside of science, something similar holds for engagement in politics and social justice, from the international to the community level. Why bother with large-scale efforts to fight racial discrimination, for example, if no one will be around to enjoy their benefits? Of course, many such projects aim at incremental change, so people now living might benefit from them. But insofar as the most significant benefits of these efforts are assumed to occur long after our deaths, the value of participating in such projects would shrink dramatically.

A different kind of example concerns the various activities we engage in when we aim at preserving and promoting various traditions such as rabbinical study, collecting stamps, or Cajun cooking. We may pursue some of these alone and some in groups, but the aim is to ensure that the things we care about continue to be valued after we are gone.[5] Just as most people care about the well-being of their children after their deaths, so Scheffler thinks we care about the continuation of the things we value, because to value something is typically to care about its continuing existence. We can easily imagine someone delving into beer brewing for the sheer joy of experimentation and deliciousness, but it is harder to picture someone growing passionate about the craft without any desire that future beer brewers continue to practice and enjoy it; there is a reason hobbyists of all stripes tend to join groups online and in person, not only to learn from others but also to educate them, and to preserve ongoing interest in younger members. Thus, even if we join in traditions or begin new hobbies simply to keep ourselves occupied, if we stick with them for any length of time we tend to find ourselves caring about their continuation, not merely in our lives but among future others. As the initial joy we took in these activities as initiates grows into a deeper commitment, it thus also becomes more vulnerable to devaluation at the thought of humanity's demise.

We also join such groups in order to gain a sense of comfort. There is something depressing in the thought that the world will simply continue without us one day, and engaging with traditions, religious groups, or national cultures allows us the sense that so long as these enterprises continue to exist, we will somehow belong to them, even long after our deaths. This kind of participation "personalizes one's relation to [the] future. Rather than looming simply as a blank eternity of nonexistence, the future can be conceptualized with reference to an ongoing social world in which one retains a social identity" (Scheffler 2013, 29). To contemplate a world in which all of this has been destroyed is to imagine an especially bleak future.

Many of our activities have other features that concern future generations. Many, for example, aim not only to preserve a sense of belonging for ourselves, but also a set of resources, cultural or practical, for future generations. This need perhaps better explains our interest in perfecting recipes or brewing techniques to share with others. Sometimes the very same projects display yet another feature: our concern with activities instrumental in "helping us to make sense of our social world and its future possibilities" (Scheffler 2018, 51). This might include interest in history or art, and may partly explain not only why we devote ourselves to producing such things, but also why we consume them. Listening to a song can fill us with a sense of potential for the future, and appreciation of art often derives much of its value from that feeling. Even participating in such ordinary cultural activities as athletics or student journalism gains value from confidence in the afterlife via some of these channels. However minuscule our contributions in these areas might be, those contributions have value not simply because we devote our efforts to them,

but because they belong to ongoing human endeavors with a past and a future, and simply participating in them allows people to feel like they are "part of something larger than themselves" (Scheffler 2018, 50). Even playing baseball on weekends or volunteering to help at the local library matters to us, at least partly, against the background of our confidence that these practices will continue beyond us, and we can play some small role in ongoing human endeavors.

Some of our projects seem safe from the threat posed by Doomsday. Producing art, for example, is typically an intrinsically fulfilling activity, and would be worthwhile even in the absence of future human beings. Friendship, too, would seem to fall into this category (Frankfurt 2013). Our interpersonal relationships might become *more* important, not less, in the Doomsday Scenario (Wolf 2013). This may be true to some extent, of course, but, as we've already seen, activities such as artistic production do have some reference to future generations, all the more so because when we engage in working out the perfect drum solo, or a critique of yet another book about human mortality, even if we never plan to share the results with others, we tend to have an audience in mind. The collapse of confidence in the possibility of any future audience might make even such intrinsically fulfilling activities somewhat less motivating.[6] As for our relationships, Scheffler suggests that our valuation of them often rests on a sense of how they fit into a good life, and he notes that our sense of a good life may be altered dramatically were our confidence in the afterlife to vanish. He even suggests that there may be something to P. D. James's portrayal, in *Children of Men*, of a future in which people seem to become far more indifferent even to the pursuit of personal pleasure as extinction approaches. In any case, though, Scheffler grants that plenty of our projects might retain their value even against the backdrop of imminent human extinction; the disagreement with his critics is often primarily about how many of our projects might retain that value and how much of it they might keep.

The core of Scheffler's argument, then, is the thought that our confidence in the afterlife is the background of much of our valuing. It's easy to make slight tweaks to this thesis, holding that confidence in the afterlife doesn't so much prop up our valuing, as it does our sense of meaning in life, by making the meaning of our projects largely depend on their place in ongoing human enterprises; confidence in the afterlife also helps to overcome fear of our own deaths, through the reassurance that the things we value will continue without us (Blumenthal-Barby 2016). All of these elements, in fact, seem to be at work to various degrees in many of our projects, and it is clear that they reinforce each other.

Scheffler draws several conclusions from this point. First, he notes that the sort of demoralization that occurs when we consider the Doomsday Scenario is far more extreme than anything that happens when we contemplate our own deaths, and thus he concludes that the survival of future strangers matters more to us than our own survival (Scheffler 2013, 45). Second, he argues that what reflection on the Doomsday Scenario shows is that the survival and flourishing of future generations matters more to us than we might otherwise think. When inquiring into why we should care about future generations, moral philosophers often propose that we have a duty of benevolence to care about the well-being of future humans, just as we have a duty to care about the well-being of people now living. Scheffler, however, thinks he can show that we have other reasons to care. Because we need the afterlife to preserve the things we now value, we have reason to ensure future generations can do so (Scheffler 2018, 70). Because we depend on the afterlife for much of what is valuable in our lives, we have reason to contribute something of value to theirs, both out of reciprocity and in order to maintain the value they grant us (Scheffler 2018, 77). Finally, the very fact that so many of our projects are, in one way or another, aimed at leaving something for future generations demonstrates that we have a love of humanity (Scheffler 2018, 62). Before examining some

implications of these conclusions, I want to turn to two older arguments for perspective.

II. Lessons from the Past

In considering the importance of the afterlife to our lives, Scheffler—despite drawing on fictional scenarios—has in mind the threat climate change poses to human survival. But in the 1960s, a different threat loomed: that of nuclear war. In 1962 the Cold War came to a head with the Cuban Missile Crisis, which threatened to make the doctrine of Mutually Assured Destruction a reality. In the run-up, American attitudes toward nuclear war were surprisingly blasé. A report on American attitudes commissioned by the Eisenhower Administration suggested that nuclear war could provide a chance for Americans to display heroism, and in 1961 magazines *Life* and *Time* ran stories optimistically imagining Americans emerging from their nuclear bunkers days after an attack to rebuild (McQueen 2018, 160–161). Worried that such attitudes toward nuclear war might actually hasten it, the political thinker Hans J. Morgenthau, who had emigrated to the US from Germany in 1937, hoped to counter nuclear optimism with his 1961 editorial, "Death in the Nuclear Age."

Morgenthau argues that the possibility of nuclear war transforms the meaning of death, and thus of life. Within our finite lifespans, human beings seek to overcome the limitation of death in a number of ways. Traditionally, the desire for immortality is satisfied through religious impulses, but as society grows more secular we seek to replace "the belief in the immortality of the human person with the attempt to assure the immortality of the world he leaves behind" (Morgenthau 1961). Collective immortality thus provides a replacement for personal immortality, and we strive to transcend our deaths by leaving behind something for others to remember.

> All of us, from the peasant and handicraft man to the founders of churches, the architects of empires, the builders of cities, the tamers of

the forces of nature, seek to leave behind the works of our wills… At best, he as a person will live on in his works; at worst, he has the satisfaction of living on anonymously in what he has created.

(Morgenthau 1961)

In his vivid description of how we give meaning to our lives by seeking to overcome death in these ways, Morgenthau draws on language that brings him close to Scheffler's thinking:

[T]he man endowed with a creative mind knows himself to be a member in an unbroken chain emerging from the past and reaching into the future, which is made of the same stuff his mind is made of and, hence, is capable of participating in, and perpetuating, his mind's creation. He may be mortal, but humanity is not, and so he will be immortal in his works.

(Morgenthau 1961)

Nuclear war would break this "unbroken chain." Insofar as "[o]ur life… receives one of its meanings from the meaning we give to death," nuclear war "destroys the meaning of life by throwing life back upon itself" (Morgenthau 1961). It would not only kill the individuals who make up societies, but also destroy all their works along with any civilization within which those works would normally be embedded. But since we give meaning to our lives partially through our efforts to attain immortality within the chain of human history, nuclear war makes that meaning impossible; it reduces our lives to their biological limits and blocks our efforts to transcend those limits. Even heroism would be impossible under such conditions. On one hand, the meaning of individual acts of heroism is lost amid death at such a scale. On the other hand, "[t]he very concept of fame would disappear, and the historians, the professional immortalizers, would have nothing to report" (Morgenthau 1961). No individual projects can survive such destruction, and therefore our individuality vanishes in it forever. For Morgenthau, as for Scheffler,

generational continuity provides meaning for our lives; without continuity, little of that meaning remains.

While Morgenthau focuses on the idea of seeking immortality through a collective afterlife, we find another sort of argument in the early work of Simone de Beauvoir, French existentialist philosopher and author of the feminist classic *The Second Sex*. Beauvoir, in seeking to find a foundation for ethics while writing under the Nazi occupation, begins with the following problem: why should we bother acting, given that every action must come to an end? On one hand, action is unavoidable. It is simply a fact about human beings that we necessarily commit ourselves to something, and sitting still is as much a project as scaling Mount Everest. But on the other hand, every action seems pointless. As long as we act, our projects are important to us; but as soon as they are completed, we have to begin anew.

In Beauvoir's existentialism, the world can only provide a context within which we make decisions, but it cannot *force* decisions on us. We have to decide how to act within that context, and we do so necessarily by going beyond, or transcending, what the world gives us. We are essentially free. Our past, including past actions, is a part of the context in which we act. The fact that I'm used to brushing my teeth every morning does not determine that I will brush my teeth tomorrow; I must choose that. My transcendence thus implies both that I necessarily must commit myself to projects and that those projects, as soon as they are completed, must be transcended. What, then, was the point of my earlier projects? Beauvoir is asking whether any particular kind of commitment can make our projects meaningful. The alternative would be to accept that, although none of my projects are worth carrying out, I am nevertheless condemned to them, making life absurd (Webber, 2018).

Beauvoir rejects that alternative. It might seem like solving the problem requires finding some goal capable of justifying any project whatsoever. But after considering a number of such goals, Beauvoir denies that any of them will work. Some people think serving God is the goal proper to human beings. But different people will interpret the will of God in different ways, so in the end it is always our own interpretations that determine what we do. A grand project like serving humanity fares no better, because humanity is a collection of people with different goals, some starkly opposed to each other, so that "[o]ne will always work for certain men against others" (de Beauvoir 2004, 108). But if no aim can justify all of our projects, perhaps what *can* justify them is other people.

Every end that we aim at in our projects, Beauvoir argues, is only a "point of departure": it is something in the world that human beings can build on or ignore. I write articles hoping that others will be stimulated enough by them to develop my ideas. Engineers build bridges hoping that others will use them. Rabbis study and teach the Talmud hoping that others will continue to do so. Beauvoir's point isn't just that we *want* others to take up our projects, but that taking on projects in anticipation of others taking them up is built into the decision to engage in them in the first place. "The movement of my transcendence appears futile to me as soon as I have transcended it, but if, through other men, my transcendence is always prolonged further than the project I am now forming, I could never surpass it" (de Beauvoir 2004, 135). The upshot of the view is this: to act is necessarily to commit oneself to a project, and to do so is to commit oneself to that project's being meaningful. For it to remain meaningful, however, it must be possible for others to take it up. Our freedom is such that it "is only by prolonging itself through the freedom of others that it manages to surpass death itself and to realize itself as an indefinite unity" (de Beauvoir 1948, 32). Beauvoir denies that this need is an egoistic one. It isn't that it is in my self-interest for others to take up my project—in fact, it is only my projects that determine what matters to me and thus what is in my self-interest—but that engagement with projects itself seeks other freedoms to take it up.

Others cannot freely take up my projects and allow them to escape my transcendence unless those others are free, and unless they have their basic needs met so that they can devote themselves to other things. My projects thus involve a commitment to the freedom and flourishing of others, especially the future others who can allow my project to "surpass death itself." However, this picture invites the sort of objection raised by Thomas Nagel (1979): if my projects aren't meaningful simply by virtue of my taking them up, why would others' taking them up make them meaningful? This problem seems especially pressing given that Beauvoir insists that the possibility of failure is built into meaning: because human beings are free, some will refuse to take up my projects, while others will take them up in ways inimical to my own understanding of those projects. But such criticism would miss the force of Beauvoir's argument. Her claim is not that my projects become meaningful only if others take them up; it is that my projects *are* meaningful only by virtue of being potential points of departure for others. It is in the nature of commitment to seek to be taken up by free and flourishing others.

III. Back to the Future

If we follow Morgenthau, the appeal of future generations is a direct appeal to our interest in personal immortality. It isn't the afterlife we care about as such, on this view, but our own survival. If we take the idea metaphorically, as Morgenthau does, this would mean that we would live on, in a sense, as long as our individuality is remembered through our works or somehow felt in other ways. But we can also take the idea of immortality through the afterlife literally. According to an important argument articulated by Derek Parfit (1984), what matters to us in continuing to exist through time is that there be continuous connections among some of our mental states. Typically, this means that we care that we in the future will still remember some of our current experiences, or still want to carry out our current plans. Thus, for example, if my body is destroyed but a robotic body is built that somehow is given many of my old memories, that's good enough to count as my having survived. But we can tweak this picture: if I die but others remember some of the things I once thought, this creates enough continuity that I literally continue to exist, though in a reduced form (Altshuler 2017). I don't even need future generations to remember me; it's enough if they merely care about some of the things I care about. Merely participating in widely shared projects allows for immortality.[7]

Scheffler would reject the implication that we care about future generations *only* because we care about personal immortality. And he would be right to reject it. In his view, we care about our contributions to future generations *because* we care about those future generations. One could thus argue that we care about immortality precisely because we care about future generations: the desire to overcome our mortality is in part a desire to exist among future people enough to be one of them, much in the same way that a commitment to a project, taken seriously, is a commitment to that project's surpassing of our freedom through other people. What Scheffler's argument is meant to show is that we care about future generations, not that we don't care about our own survival, and he grants that the two concerns are deeply intertwined. Whether we care *more* about future generations than our own survival or, rather, care about both via such intertwined concerns is a less significant question.

All three thinkers, however, point to another problem for Scheffler's claim about our love for humanity. All of Scheffler's examples involve future generations that are continuous with us. We care that they value some of the things we do, make use of our innovations, and preserve a "social identity" for us, personalizing our relationship with the future. We know, of course, that in the distant future, should humanity survive long enough, our descendants may be fundamentally different

from us. Still, we can find comfort in the knowledge that continuity will be preserved: our social world will transition gradually into another one, in ways that allow most of our concerns to be preserved. However, were our culture to die out altogether, to be replaced by another, this would look very much like the Doomsday Scenario. Notice, for example, that Morgenthau reasonably does not consider how much better it would be if, following a nuclear apocalypse, the US were eventually fully resettled. While Scheffler does not address this issue, in a response Mark Johnston (2014) asks whether people would be willing to sacrifice their "tribe" in exchange for the guarantee that humanity will survive for a few more generations. The answer is not obvious, but it seems to me that humanity as such, disconnected from continuity with *our* culture, would not be able to personalize our relationship with the future, would not contribute meaning to anything we now do, would not be able to impart immortality on us, and—if it had no interest in or need for our projects—would render our lives meaningless. This, of course, is precisely the concern many nationalists raise around the world today, when they worry not about climate change, but about being "swamped" by immigrants. Do we have the resources to respond to such worries?

I think we do. No wave of immigration is likely to *replace* us. More likely is a continuous process in which cultures merge. But such a process is exactly one in which our lives can continue to be meaningfully lived. If we make our lives meaningful, in part, through contributions to future generations, then we have every opportunity to contribute to the lives of those who come to join us. We can gain immortality by creating things that *they* can use. And we can engage in meaningful projects by providing points of departure for them. Scheffler's work, then, can tie meaning and value in our lives to the existence of future generations. It can show us why those generations matter. But it can also give us hope for immortality and a blueprint for embracing a changing future.

Notes

1. On some views, of course, what we find isn't meaning, but only something that we *think* is meaning. This is a more complex issue than I can address here, but most contemporary views have abandoned the idea that there is some "one-size-fits-all" meaning of life like serving God or benefiting humanity. Rather than searching for the meaning *of* life, most recent approaches are more invested in finding conditions for meaning *in* life, which is to be located – perhaps with some restrictions – in our commitments and projects. For one such prominent view, see Susan Wolf (2012).
2. This is a paraphrase of the scenario described by Scheffler (2013, 18).
3. This is a paraphrase of the scenario described by Scheffler (2013, 38).
4. This point is made in Timmerman (2018, 291–292); Scheffler responds in his (2018, 58–59) by noting that people who have the means to engage in these sorts of activities often do seem to do so.
5. Someone might object that we only care about these things insofar as we think they will continue to *benefit* future generations. I'm not at all certain that people are any more likely to preserve a practice or tradition in the hope that it will benefit future others than in the hope that the practice itself will continue, but in any case it's important that for Scheffler these motivations are mutually reinforcing. That we care about preserving beneficial practices for future generations shows that we already care about those future generations, and we care about them, on the other hand, in part because we hope they will continue to preserve the things we value. Thanks to Travis Timmerman for raising this objection.
6. Of course, some may object that the loss of such motivation might be less likely than Scheffler thinks and even if it occurred it would be misguided (Timmerman 2018, 282). On the latter issue, I disagree for reasons I provide later in this chapter: the loss of future audiences removes even the possibility of immortality. Of course, someone could object that all sorts of artistic activities are valuable in themselves, and thus do not require any audience. I see no good reason to believe that artistic creation without an audience has any value, but that is a far wider issue. On the former issue, it is perhaps true that many people would still find artistic expression intrinsically rewarding. But an important point here is that artistic expression isn't a matter of a magic flash of inspiration followed by the appearance of a complete work of art. It is, rather, a matter of lengthy and effortful work, which requires a good deal of motivation to sustain it. It is this motivation – not the sense of fulfillment – that I think would be undermined (Altshuler 2017, 203, fn. 3).
7. Of course, it is possible that at some future point all life will cease, so that this immortality will not be *true* immortality, but only longevity. That may well be the case. But, first of all, we cannot *know* that this is the case; only that the current state of our physics necessitates it. Second, although we may *believe* that all life will eventually end, this abstract belief tends to pale in comparison with our typical confidence in the afterlife. Finally, even if we expect that human life will eventually – perhaps very soon – come to an end, these considerations give us reason to want to prevent such an outcome.

References

Altshuler, Roman. 2017. "Bootstrapping the After-life." *Journal of Moral Philosophy* 14 (2): 201–216.

Beauvoir, Simone de. 1948. *The Ethics of Ambiguity*. New York: Philosophical Library.

Beauvoir, Simone de. 2004. "Pyrrhus and Cineas." In *Simone de Beauvoir: Philosophical Writings*, edited by Margaret A. Simons, Mary Beth Mader, and Marybeth Timmermann, 89–149. Champaign, IL: University of Illinois Press.

Blumenthal-Barby, J.S. 2016. "What Sort of Collective Afterlife Matters and How." *Philosophia* 44 (1): 87–100.

Frankfurt, Harry G. 2013. "How the Afterlife Matters." In *Death and the Afterlife*, by Samuel Scheffler, edited by Niko Kolodny, 131–142. Oxford: Oxford University Press.

Johnston, Mark. 2014. "Is Life a Ponzi Scheme?" *Boston Review*, January 2, 2014. http://bostonreview.net/books-ideas/mark-johnston-samuel-scheffler-death-afterlife-humanity-ponzi-scheme.

McQueen, Alison. 2018. *Political Realism in Apocalyptic Times*. Cambridge: Cambridge University Press.

Morgenthau, Hans J. 1961. "*Death in the Nuclear Age*." Commentary, September 1961.

Nagel, Thomas. 1979. "The Absurd." In *Mortal Questions*, 11–23. Cambridge: Cambridge University Press.

Parfit, Derek. 1984. *Reasons and Persons*. Oxford: Oxford University Press.

Scheffler, Samuel. 2013. *Death and the Afterlife*. Edited by Niko Kolodny. Oxford: Oxford University Press.

Scheffler, Samuel. 2018. *Why Worry About Future Generations?* Oxford: Oxford University Press.

Timmerman, Travis. 2018. "Doomsday Needn't Be So Bad." *dialectica* 72 (2): 275–296.

Webber, Jonathan. 2018. "Beauvoir and the Meaning of Life." In *The Meaning of Life and the Great Philosophers*. edited by, Stephen Leach and James Tartaglia: 224-231. London: Routledge.

Wolf, Susan. 2012. *Meaning in Life and Why It Matters*. Princeton, NJ: Princeton University Press.

Wolf, Susan. 2013. "The Significance of Doomsday." In *Death and the Afterlife, by Samuel Scheffler*, edited by Niko Kolodny, 113–129. Oxford: Oxford University Press.

29 Death and Survival Online

Patrick Stokes

Introduction

In a remarkably short span of time the internet has impacted almost every aspect of human life: how we talk, eat, shop, travel, work, study, have sex, form relationships, engage in politics, and a variety of other facets of human existence and interaction. But what about human *death*? Has the digital era changed how we understand the nature of death, and how we view the dead?

At first blush, we might well assume the answer is "no." While there have been many attempts to define death, death is universally understood as either a biological event, or, at least, as an event whose criteria are biological. It's true that some technologies have caused us to question and perhaps even revise some of our understandings of death as a biological event. For instance, the issue of whether "brain death" does or does not count as death was raised by the development of new life support technologies, while the cryogenic preservation of corpses poses similar questions about the role irreversibility plays in our judgments of who is, and is not, dead (see e.g. Luper 2009: 48–59; Belshaw 2009). The question "if your brain has stopped functioning but a machine is keeping your body oxygenated, are you alive or dead?" is one that in theory people could have come up with at any time through sheer imagination; but it wasn't until such a feat became medically possible that the question came to be seriously pondered. But the internet, we might think, doesn't raise biological questions of that sort. No matter how major a role it plays in our lives, it doesn't change basic facts about whether our bodies are functioning or not. Nor, we might think, would it change our relationship to the dead.

Yet in fact, the internet *does* appear to be raising interesting questions about where human lives begin and end, and how we should respond to the death of others accordingly. As with new medical technologies, however, what the internet is doing is helping us to see questions about the nature of death that were there all along. In this chapter, we'll look at two such technologies—one existing, one emerging—and the questions they pose about surviving death and respecting the dead.

1. Memorialized Digital Remains

Social media is still a relatively young phenomenon, yet it has already become one of the main ways in which we communicate with each other and are present in each other's lives. Indeed, some philosophers and social scientists argue that internet-mediated communication is now so pervasive that the distinction between online and offline existence has collapsed. Where once we had to physically sit in front of a desktop computer to use the internet, and so the metaphor of a self-contained realm known as "cyberspace" made some sense, now internet communication is simply part of how we move through our physical world: say, sharing a photo of your surroundings on social media then sharing the responses with the person standing next to you. The philosopher Luciano Floridi, for instance, has been at the center of a movement to reconceptualize how we live now as "onlife," a state in which digital communication blends seamlessly into our embodied lives with each other (Floridi 2015). Floridi has also made a startling claim about the nature of some kinds of data, based on how we think about information privacy. Some forms of data, he argues, are "detached"—that is, they're not *essentially* related to who we are. I still remember my student number from when I was an undergraduate, but those *particular* numbers don't have any special meaning for me. Life would have been much the same if I'd had a different set of digits attached randomly to my record. But other data is what Floridi calls *constitutive* data: "data *that make you yourself*, such as your intimate beliefs, or your unique emotional involvement" (Floridi 2014: 125).

The idea that certain pieces of information are constitutive of our identities (in at least one important sense of "identity")[1] finds support in the way in which we present ourselves online. On social networks, we are constantly producing and narrating our identities, and achieving varying degrees of electronically mediated presence in each other's lives. With the collapse of the online/offline distinction, our "online presence" is just, well, our presence. The way in which someone is present to you in a social network is perhaps less compelling and immediate than the way they are present to you when standing face-to-face. But it's presence nonetheless.[2] This way of thinking about our online lives also fits in with important trends in philosophy of mind, which have moved away from the idea that thinking is something that takes place entirely within our skulls. According to "extended" or "enactivist" views of cognition, thinking is something that organisms do in concert with their environment, and, for humans, this means "our cognitive capacities depend on and are (sometimes) constituted by a complex web of social and artifactual structures," from notebooks and pocket calculators to peers, libraries, and of course the internet (Heersmink 2017: 3136). Instead of being in our heads, our minds are distributed across these features of our world. And if our mental lives are distributed in that way, and we *are* our mental lives—as one dominant mode of thinking about personal identity since John Locke has argued—then *we* are increasingly distributed across online networks in this way.

What are the implications of such distribution for how we understand death? For

one thing, it changes how we view the online traces we leave behind us. When social media users die, their profiles are not automatically deleted, but may either persist in the form in which the user left them, or may be placed into a "memorialized" state. Either way, some of their online presence, both visual and textual, persists long after the biological death of the user. They are dead, but remain within social space, so to speak, and other users can and do "interact" with these profiles. As such they are, in at least some sense, less completely lost to us than previously. This may seem like a mere quirk of the online era, but it is an increasingly visible one: no one knows for sure how many dead people there are on Facebook, for instance, but with nearly a billion active users at any one time, we can safely assume that there are many millions of accounts belonging to the dead.

How to deal with these "digital remains" has become an increasingly pressing problem for governments, tech companies, communities, and individuals struggling to respond to the death of other people. This is not, however, a solely practical or commercial question, but an ethical one as well. As Richard Heersmink puts it in a discussion of distributed selfhood, "If cognition and self are indeed distributed, the constitutive parts of those distributed systems obtain a particular moral status" (Heersmink 2017: 3148). Consider the moral status we accord to our bodies: one of the reasons why we think it wrong to violate, damage, or destroy people's bodies is precisely that our bodies are (partly or wholly, depending on your view) constitutive of what we *are*. To damage them in these ways may be wrong for a number of reasons, but one of these is simply the widespread intuition that what is done to our bodies is done *to us*. Hence, argues Floridi, the *violation* that comes with breaches of our privacy with respect to constitutive data (Floridi 2013).

Hence, as I've argued elsewhere (Stokes 2015, 2019b), we arguably have a duty not to delete the dead, as doing so would amount to removing, to a lesser or greater extent, people—legitimate objects of moral regard—from our shared life-world. When you delete a profile, you're erasing a person. Such a duty not to delete is not absolute, however. There may sometimes be good reasons to delete someone's digital remains, for instance if their ongoing presence online is deeply distressing to the living (indeed, such distress was one of the reasons Facebook introduced its "memorialisation" function in 2009: people were upset at receiving friend or contact suggestions for dead users). It may be that there is no principled way to determine ahead of time when we should preserve such artefacts and when we should delete them. But then, that's true of many, perhaps most, complex moral decisions we face. In asking "should we delete the dead?" we may have to grapple with several competing considerations, but we can see that the interests of the dead themselves here are one of the things we need to take into account.

Notice, however, that this is not so much a *new* question as a question that has always existed, just in a form that made it less visible to us. Consider the way we sometimes agonize over whether to throw out physical objects that the dead have left behind, particularly things such as jewelry, photos, and letters. Such objects have always been a crucial, and sometimes fraught, part of how we deal with the fact of death and the bonds between the dead and the living (Gibson 2008). Even corpses themselves seem to have something of this special status: we need to dispose of them (because they decompose), but we can't simply treat them like rubbish either. We treat them with a certain reverence because of the way in which they once constituted a living person and continue, for some time, to present that person's likeness, their "face," to the world (Stokes 2019a). The rise of social media and the increased importance of "constitutive data" suggests that what we do to these artefacts is, in some nontrivial sense, what we thereby do to the dead. This brings into focus, though, something that was true all along: the dead continue to persist with us as objects of our loving regard, embodied in the traces they leave behind. Online persistence is a change in degree, perhaps, but not a change in kind.

This way of putting things is likely to ring very false to many people. For one thing, the idea that when we delete the digital traces of a dead person we are somehow "deleting" *the person themselves* violates a very widespread assumption that the dead simply *do not exist*. You can't delete something that doesn't exist! In philosophy of death, this belief is known as the "Termination Thesis," a name coined by Fred Feldman (1992). The Termination Thesis says, in its simplest form, that "people go out of existence when they die" (Feldman 2000).[3] But if, as Feldman and others have argued, we *do* continue to exist for a time (as corpses) then it's not outrageous to think we also continue to exist as digital remains as well.

2. Digital Reanimation

When social media users die, the "digital remains" they leave behind are quite inert. Other users may continue to interact with the profiles; for instance, many people come back to Facebook profiles of dead people to post messages to them for years after the user's deaths (Brubaker et al. 2013; Kasket 2012). But just like corpses, our "digital remains" don't answer back. To that extent, we can view things like memorialized social media profiles as just another memorial practice, perhaps something similar to embalming the dead and putting them on display.

Yet the dead needn't remain so quiet. There are a number of technological scenarios that would allow the dead to continue to interact with the living. Some of these remain purely speculative, the stuff of inventive science fiction—such as "Be Right Back," an episode of the TV series *Black Mirror* that imagines a replica of a dead man constructed from his voicemails, texts, and social media posts. Yet in fact the technology is gradually catching up to the fiction, so we'd do well to explore these issues before it becomes a reality.

Consider the following scenarios:

a) Before I die, I write messages to my friends and family and arrange for these to be emailed to them on specific occasions, such as their birthdays.

b) Before I die, I set up a program that will make my social media account respond to certain events—for instance, on my friends' birthdays, my profile will send a birthday message to them, generated by selecting randomly from a set of greeting phrases; or if someone uses the words "engaged" or "graduated" my profile will congratulate them.

c) Before I die, I sign up for a service that will analyze my existing social media profile and use the data contained in it to generate and send new messages and posts that sound like me.

d) Before I die, I sign up for a service that will analyze my existing social media profile and use the data contained in it to create an AI-driven chat bot with which other people can interact.

e) After I die, and without my prior involvement, someone analyses my existing social media profile and use the data contained in it to create an AI-driven chat bot with which other people can interact.

Of these scenarios, a) is very much a reality. Some terminally ill parents, for example, write letters to their children for them to open on birthdays and anniversaries in the distant future. There are also services available that will send out prepared messages on your behalf once the service is told (or guesses!) that you've died. We can view this as a sort of extended agency, in much the same way as making a will, for instance, extends our agency beyond our death. In this case, the relevant communicative acts are already made before the person dies: the letters are written and are just waiting to be sent and opened. In scenario b), the communicative acts are generated by an algorithm after death, but the user has set up the algorithm before death.

Scenario c) has also been attempted, but the results so far have not been compelling. There have also been attempts at d) and e) which have mostly been very unconvincing. But as Artificial Intelligence (AI) gets better and the ability to tell humans from bots in online environments gets harder, it's likely that both d) and e) will become increasingly common and increasingly impressive. As one

example of e), the tech entrepreneur Roman Mazurenko "lives" on as a chat bot created from the text messages he sent his friend Eugenia Kuyda before his sudden death in a traffic accident. Anyone can now download Roman Mazurenko as an app (Newton 2016). The more online traces that are fed into such a bot—photos, audio recordings, text messages, social media posts, diaries and so on—the more convincing it might become.

These scenarios raise several questions, particularly ontological and ethical questions. Can we genuinely keep the dead with us through apps and avatars? Should we? First, let's consider the ontological ones.

3. Ontological Questions

Nobody, as far as I am aware, claims that because we make wills or write letters for our survivors, this means we do not die. Nor, as far as I am aware, does anyone think a will or a preplanned email amount to surviving our death. There is, we might think, nothing about scenario a) that amounts to continuing to exist *as a person* after we die. In the case of b), the only real difference is that the content of the communication is created *after* the "communicator" has died (I put "communicator" in scare quotes here so as not to beg the question whether the dead person or the program is the actual communicator in this case), though following their broad instructions. This still doesn't seem very much like survival.

What about c) and d)? In these cases, we might also think that this is nothing like surviving death. A key reason for this is that when we think about surviving death, we tend to think about what we *care about* in surviving death, even though this may not be the same thing as survival as such (Parfit 1984 Part 3, Section 4). And a big part of what we care about in survival is that there are experiences in the future that *we can anticipate having* (Martin 1997). This is why few people would prefer surviving in a permanent vegetative state to simply being dead: there would be no experience in either case (assuming there's no afterlife at least!) and so both states would be equally bad for us. Likewise, a social media profile or a computer program has no subjective experience of its own. There is nothing it is like to be your Facebook profile, and so the idea that you'll "live on" in that form offers no real comfort in the face of death (Stokes 2012). Nor is there anything it's like to be an AI chatbot. So while I may be comforted at the thought that my AI chatbot will continue to say things I think should be said—for instance, imagine if the bot analyses my Twitter feed, identifies my politics, and continues to speak out about injustices I cared about while I was alive—I can't *look forward to being* that chatbot. I can only look forward to having experiences, and the chatbot has no experience at all. That also means there is no relevant difference here between scenarios c) and d).

But let's not be too hasty. We may not survive *for ourselves* in the form of a chatbot as in c) and d), for the reasons just given. But might we survive *for others*? Might we take at least some comfort in the ongoing online existence of other people even if we can take no comfort in our *own* online survival?

Many philosophers would reject the idea that the existence of persons depends on perspective in that way. After all, the other sorts of beings we're familiar with aren't like that. Cows, doorknobs, and football teams do not exist for some people and not for others. They either exist, or they don't. The *way* they exist might differ: the football team's existence might depend on convention in a way the cow doesn't. But it's still assumed there's *some* fact about whether or not they exist. Most metaphysicians who think about personal identity try to identify what persons or selves *are*, usually by identifying them with one class of entity or another. Neo-Lockeans, for example, take it that we *are* our minds. Animalists, on the other hand, think each of us essentially *is* a human animal. Most of the time this disagreement presents no problem, as human minds and human animals tend to go together and usually die at the same moment. But to see what sort of difference this metaphysical commitment makes, ask yourself

what would happen if you could somehow upload your consciousness into a computer at the exact moment you died. Would you survive in that case, or not? "Transhumanists" have often envisaged this sort of mind-upload as a kind of digital immortality, and philosophers like Kevin O'Neill have argued that only such a scenario would count as *genuine* internet immortality (O'Neill 2016). For a neo-Lockean, insofar as you are your mind, you would indeed survive your death. Your body would die, but *you* would be safely ensconced in a computer. For an animalist, on the other hand, *you* would not survive the mind transfer process—all that would survive would be a computer containing a mind that once belonged to you, a dead animal.

Yet it may be that selves or persons aren't unitary in this way. What we are for ourselves and what we are for others might be quite different. "Person" may not pick out one thing or type of thing, but rather apply to a cluster of things that tend to go together. I can't give a full argument for this view here, but one crucial piece of evidence would be this: if we were confronted by an AI bot that continues to operate our deceased friend's social media profile in such a way that the profile was indistinguishable from how it was before our friend died, what would happen? Would we perhaps come to care about that AI in the way we had once cared about our friend? Would we be insulted on our friend's behalf if someone else insulted the chatbot, for instance? Persons, as Marya Schechtman (2014) has put it, exist in "person space," a sort of conceptual space in which psychological, physical, and social facts about persons are brought to bear. If we got used to AI chatbots of the dead, would we treat those dead people as persisting in "person space"? Would we, quite rationally in that case, come to grieve less for those who have died?

This is, I think, an open question (it's precisely the question that "Be Right Back" asks, and I won't spoil the ending for you by telling you the answer it gives). Like many questions around personal identity, it comes down to how flexible our practical ideas about identity might be, something that might not be easy to tell just through imagination alone. Philosophers of personal identity often use examples such as teleportation as problem cases: if a teleporter disintegrates us on Earth and rebuilds us instantly on Mars, is this a form of transport or an elaborate form of suicide? Is that us on Mars, or an imposter? Just running this "thought experiment" may not tell us very clearly, but if, as Mark Johnston (2010) argues, we actually lived in a world where people regularly teleport, we may simply come to identify with the future replica as if it was us. We would look forward to "our" experiences on Mars, and on Mars, "we" might feel guilt for things we'd done on Earth. For practical purposes, the replica *would be* us. Likewise, if we lived in a world where our dead friends (particularly those physically remote from us who we only interact with via the internet) were replaced by AI bots when they died, would we come to see those bots *as being* the person?[4] We already have fictional examples of coming to relate to an AI bot as a person, such as Spike Jonze's movie *Her* (2013) about a man who forms a relationship with a virtual assistant. It's not hard to imagine such scenarios playing out in real life as we become more and more familiar with AI agents. That makes it possible that we might indeed come to view bots as being the same person as the dead users whose personalities they are based on, whatever metaphysicians might tell us. The question that then arises is: *should* we?

4. Ethical Questions

If digitally reanimating the dead via AI becomes possible, do we have a right to use the dead in this way or not, and if so under what conditions? Some ethical views, for instance some forms of hedonic utilitarianism, will insist that, on the assumption the dead cannot have negative experiences because of anything we do after they die, we do not harm the dead by reusing their online traces to animate a bot. What the dead don't know can't hurt them. Alternatively, in a more Epicurean vein, we might insist that the dead

do not exist as bearers of rights at the relevant times, and so we cannot violate their rights. The problem of posthumous harms is a heavily discussed one, which you'll find covered elsewhere in this volume. For the moment, let's simply assume for the sake of argument that *some* form of posthumous harm is possible. Does digital reanimation constitute such a harm, and if so, what sort of harm is it?

One consideration here is whether the dead would want their image to be used in this way. We take it that people do have some right to control how their image is used, at least in some contexts. In this case, such a right is even more pressing if the bot presents itself *as being* the deceased, rather than, say, a tribute (or parody!). Reanimating images of the dead has been done for various purposes for some decades now; most recently, the Star Wars movie *Rogue One* used CGI versions of actors Carrie Fisher and Peter Cushing to revive characters they had played in the original 1977 film (Cushing was long deceased at the time; Fisher was alive, but sadly had died by the time the movie hit cinemas). But a bot that would operate in the same social media environments as the deceased did when alive, in a way designed to be as indistinguishable as possible from the dead person, is something else. It's not contained in the way that using a dead actor's image and voice for a film or advertisement is. Rather it's pretty close to being a *replacement*: the bot is meant to do a range of things the person themselves did, and continue to do so indefinitely.

Adam Buben (2015) has drawn just this distinction between remembrance of the dead and replacement, and has argued that AI chatbots of the dead would be a way of replacing the dead rather than simply a tool for remembrance. While in remembrance we remember the dead as the distinctive, valuable people they were, in replacement we use their online traces as a resource to fill the gap left by their passing. In effect, says Buben, this reduces the dead to what Heidegger called "standing reserve," a resource with purely instrumental value that we can exploit, instead of something worthy of regard in its own right. Treated like this, "the dead, if not forgotten outright, exist only insofar as they can play pre-ordered roles in our lives" (Buben 2015: 28). If that's right, then it seems such AI bots might do a sort of ontological disrespect to the dead *and the living*, by treating our loved ones as if they could be replaced by a bot without any huge loss. The problem is not so much replacement itself as treating people *as replaceable*.

Other problems are raised by this technology too: what happens if these chat bots start learning and their personalities gradually evolve away from their "source"? What if these bots start interacting solely with other bots? Would they start to inherit the rights, responsibilities, and liabilities of the dead humans they are based upon? (cf. O'Neill 2016: 102; Arnold et al. 2018: 134–137). Again, some of these apparently novel technologies are likely just bringing into focus deep questions about personhood, death, and ethics that were there all along. The question is, are we ready to face them? Or will these technologies get here faster than we can understand what they mean for us?

Notes

1. There is an important distinction drawn in the literature on personal identity between "numerical" and "practical" identity. Very roughly, the former is what we might be asking about if we want to know if the person the police have arrested is the same person as the person who committed the crime, while the latter is the sense in which we might say things like "I'm not that person anymore!" However, there have been some attempts to push back against such a distinction; see for instance Schechtman (2014) and Rudd (2012).
2. For an influential argument against the adequacy of "telepresence," see Dreyfus (2008).
3. The Termination Thesis is widely accepted, but not universally; for arguments against it, see Feldman (2000, 1992), Francescotti (2018), Stokes (2019b).
4. If, as Robert Nozick (1981) argues, a person is the same person just if the latter person is the closest continuer of the former, then the bot may well have a good case to be the dead person, though much will depend here on whether a bot is the same sort of thing as the original

person (if the Rolling Stones split up and Mick Jagger immediately forms another band with the same name but no other original members, that band arguably *is* the Rolling Stones if there's no other band with a claim to be an as close or closer continuer. If he forms a bird-watching club, however, we might decide that *that* can't be the Rolling Stones simply because it is the wrong sort of thing to be a continuer of a band). Again, a bot may not be the same sort of thing I am *for myself*, but may well be good enough *for others*.

References

Arnold, Michael, et al. (2018), *Death and Digital Media* (Abingdon: Routledge).
Belshaw, Christopher (2009), *Annihilation: The Sense and Significance of Death* (Montreal and Kingston: McGill University Press).
Brubaker, Jed R., Hayes, Gillian R., and Dourish, Paul (2013), "Beyond the Grave: Facebook as a Site for the Expansion of Death and Mourning", *The Information Society*, 29 (3), 152–163.
Buben, Adam (2015), "Technology of the Dead: Objects of Loving Remembrance or Replaceable Resources?", *Philosophical Papers*, 44 (1), 15–37.
Dreyfus, Hubert (2008), *On the Internet* (2nd edn, Thinking in Action; New York: Routledge).
Feldman, Fred (1992), *Confrontations with the Reaper: A Philosophical Study of the Nature and Value of Death* (Oxford: Oxford University Press).
Feldman, Fred (2000), "The Termination Thesis", *Midwest Studies in Philosophy*, 24 (1), 98–115.
Floridi, Luciano (2013), *The Ethics of Information* (Oxford: Oxford University Press).
Floridi, Luciano (2014), *The Fourth Revolution. How the Infosphere is Reshaping Human Reality* (Oxford: Oxford University Press).
Floridi, Luciano (ed.) (2015), *The Onlife Manifesto: Being Human in a Hyperconnected Era* (Dordrecht: Springer).
Francescotti, Robert (2018), "Surviving Death: How to Refute Termination Theses", *Inquiry: An Interdisciplinary Journal of Philosophy*, 61 (2), 178–197.
Gibson, Margaret (2008), *Objects of the Dead: Mourning and Memory in Everyday Life* (Melbourne: Melbourne University Press).
Heersmink, Richard (2017), "Distributed Selves: Personal Identity and Extended Memory Systems", *Synthese*, 194 (8), 3135–3151.
Johnston, Mark (2010), *Surviving Death* (Princeton, NJ: Princeton University Press).

Kasket, Elaine (2012), "Being-Towards-Death In The Digital Age", *Existential Analysis*, 23 (2), 249–261.

Luper, Steven (2009), *The Philosophy of Death* (Cambridge: Cambridge University Press).

Martin, Raymond (1997), *Self-Concern: An Experiential Approach to What Matters in Survival* (Cambridge: Cambridge University Press).

Newton, Casey (2016), "Speak, Memory", *The Verge*. Available at: www.theverge.com/a/luka-artificial-intelligence-memorial-roman-mazurenko-bot

Nozick, Robert (1981), *Philosophical Explanations* (Oxford: Clarendon Press).

O'Neill, Kevin (2016), *Internet Afterlife: Virtual Salvation in the 21st Century* (Santa Barbara, CA: Praeger).

Parfit, Derek (1984), *Reasons and Persons* (Oxford: Oxford University Press).

Rudd, Anthony (2012), *Self, Value, and Narrative: A Kierkegaardian Approach* (Oxford: Oxford University Press).

Schechtman, Marya (2014), *Staying Alive: Personal Identity, Practical Concerns, and the Unity of a Life* (Oxford: Oxford: Oxford University Press).

Stokes, Patrick (2012), "Ghosts in the Machine: Do the Dead Live on in Facebook?", *Philosophy and Technology*, 25 (3), 363–379.

Stokes, Patrick (2015), "Deletion as Second Death: The Moral Status of Digital Remains", *Ethics and Information Technology*, 17 (4), 237–248.

Stokes, Patrick (2019a), "The Decay of Digital Personhood: Towards New Norms of Disposal and Preservation," in Tamara Kohn, et al. (eds), *Residues of Death: Disposal Refigured* (Houndmills: Palgrave).

Stokes, Patrick (2019b), "Are there Dead Persons?", *Canadian Journal of Philosophy*, 49 (6), 755–775.

Part VIII Is Suicide Rationally or Morally Defensible?

The Suicide's Argument

Ere the birth of my life, if I wished it or no
    No question was asked me, it could not
      be so!
    If the life was the question, a thing sent
      to try
    And to live on be YES; what can NO
      be? to die.

NATURE'S ANSWER

Is't returned, as 'twas sent? Is't no worse
    for the wear?
Think first, what you ARE! Call to mind
    what you WERE!
I gave you innocence, I gave you hope,
Gave health, and genius, and an ample
    scope,
Return you me guilt, lethargy, despair?
Make out the invent'ry; inspect, compare!
Then die, if die you dare!

            —Samuel Taylor Coleridge

Introduction to Part VIII

In the world's most famous soliloquy, Shakespeare writes the character Hamlet to passionately assert "To be, or not to be: that is the question." While it's certainly not *the* question, philosophical questions surrounding suicide are no doubt very important. In this section, you will get to read the most historically relevant philosophical arguments for, and against, the permissibility of suicide. This will be followed by three contemporary philosophers' take on the issue.

You will first get to read excerpts from Thomas Aquinas' (1273) *Summa Theologica*, where he considers, and responds to, a number of objections in favor of the permissibility of suicide. He also mounts three related arguments against the permissibility of suicide. Most notably, Aquinas argues that life is God's gift to man and that this gift is part of God's established order for the world. Suicide supposedly violates that order and is therefore wrong. Aquinas also argues that it's in our nature to (and thus we ought to) love ourselves, which is inconsistent with committing suicide. Finally, Aquinas appeals to the fact that individuals are part of communities and since suicide would, he believes, injure the community, as well as the individual, Aquinas claims it would thus be wrong.

The Aquinas chapter is followed by an excerpt of David Hume's posthumously published (1783) work "Of Suicide." In it, Hume directly responds to Aquinas. Hume offers a trilemma, asserting that if suicide is impermissible, then it must be so because it violates a duty to God, our neighbor, or ourselves. Contrary to Aquinas, Hume argues that suicide cannot violate God's order since God allows us to "disturb nature" by responding to disease and other calamities. Suicide, he argues, is not relevantly different. Nor could suicide violate a duty to our neighbor since, if one wants to commit suicide, Hume claims that their prospective life would be so terrible that it would be a great burden to them to continue living and, as such, they could at best provide a "frivolous advantage" to the community were they to continue living. Finally, Hume argues that suicide cannot violate a duty to ourselves supposedly because, for those who desire to end their life, their continued existence would be worse than death. Having taken himself to have demonstrated that suicide does not violate a duty to God, our neighbor, or ourselves, Hume concludes that suicide is permissible.

Hume's chapter is followed by David Benatar's contemporary defense of suicide. While Benatar's arguments are roughly in the same vein as Hume's, his conclusions are much more nuanced. Early on in the chapter, Benatar considers, and rebuts, four arguments against the permissibility of suicide. He then advances his positive arguments. Rather than arguing that suicide is *always* permissible or *always* impermissible, Benatar argues that suicide is *sometimes* rationally permissible, *sometimes* morally permissible, and *sometimes* both. According to Benatar, it will be (prudentially) rationally permissible when one's continued life would be so bad as to be worse than death. Prudentially rationally permissible suicides will nevertheless be immoral when the person committing suicide hasn't given sufficient weight to the interests of the people who will be affected by their death. Suicide is both rationally and morally permissible when one's continued life would be worse than death and when that fate is bad enough to outweigh the other-regarding considerations of whoever would suffer as a result of the suicide in question.

Just as the Hume chapter is largely a direct response to Aquinas, Philip Reed's chapter is largely a direct response to Hume. In the response portion of his chapter, Reed first aims to show how suicide can indeed harm one's "neighbor," which most notably includes immediate family and friends. Reed then argues that it makes perfect sense to hold that suicide is a violation of a duty to God, assuming God can will that people act other than they do. Turning to ourselves, Reed argues that changing social norms in Western cultures has resulted in humans being seen as "discrete, autonomous individuals who act in order to realize whatever contingent preferences they happen to have," rather than as communal beings working towards some common good. These changing social norms, Reed suggests, underlie Western societies' change in attitudes

toward suicide, where it's now (generally) regarded as rationally and morally permissible. Reed believes this is a mistake, and arrives at the conclusion that suicide is morally impermissible because it prevents people from realizing their species-specific good.

This section ends with Jukka Varelius' discussion, and somewhat limited defense, of suicide. Varelius starts off by considering a paradigmatic case of suicide that would be done from a not terribly uncommon kind of motivation. This sets up the central question of the chapter. Would it be irrational for this person to commit suicide? Varelius proceeds to consider three broad sorts of answers meant to show that the answer to this question is "Yes." Suicide may be though to be "unfathomable," "insane" (i.e. either impulsive or a product of mental illness) or "unreasonable" for a variety of reasons, such as its being supposedly unnatural, depriving one of, on the whole, good life, harmful to others, and contrary to one's true desires. Varelius carefully considers cases of suicide where these objections wouldn't apply, thereby identifying the conditions under which a suicide is rationally permissible. But when it comes to the example he considers at the outset of the chapter, these conditions are not met, and so Varelius concludes that *that* particular suicide would be irrational.

If you're interested in reading more about suicide, check out the following:

1. Chapter 7 of David Benatar's book *The Human Predicament: A Candid Guide to Life's Biggest Questions* (2017) Oxford University Press.
2. Michael Cholbi's "Suicide" (2017) *The Stanford Encyclopedia of Philosophy* (https://plato.stanford.edu/entries/suicide/).
3. Margaret Battin's "Manipulated Suicide" (1980) *Journal of Medical Humanities* 2 (2): 123–134.
4. Jukka Varelius' "Ending Life, Morality, and Meaning" (2013) *Ethical Theory and Moral Practice* 16 (3): 559–574.

30 Whether One is Allowed to Kill Oneself (excerpts)

St Thomas Aquinas

Summa Theologiae, 2A 2AE, Question 64, Article 5 [1264–1275] (Second and Revised Edition, 1920, trans. Fathers of the English Dominican Province)

1. It would seem lawful for a man to kill himself. For murder is a sin in so far as it is contrary to justice. But no man can do an injustice to himself, as is proved in *Ethics* v, 11. Therefore no man sins by killing himself.
2. Further, it is lawful, for one who exercises public authority, to kill evil-doers. Now he who exercises public authority is sometimes an evil-doer. Therefore he may lawfully kill himself.
3. Further, it is lawful for a man to suffer spontaneously a lesser danger that he may avoid a greater: thus it is lawful for a man to cut off a decayed limb even from himself, that he may save his whole body. Now sometimes a man, by killing himself, avoids a greater evil, for example an unhappy life, or the shame of sin. Therefore a man may kill himself.
4. Further, Samson killed himself, as related in Judges 16, and yet he is numbered among the saints (Hebrews 11). Therefore it is lawful for a man to kill himself.
5. Further, it is related (2 Maccabees 14:42) that a certain Razias killed himself, "choosing to die nobly rather than to fall into the hands of the wicked, and to suffer abuses unbecoming his noble birth." Now nothing that is done nobly and bravely is unlawful. Therefore suicide is not unlawful.

On the contrary, *Augustine* says (*City of God*, i, 20): "Hence it follows that the words 'Thou shalt not kill' refer to the killing of a man—not another man; therefore, not even thyself. For he who kills himself, kills nothing else than a man."

I answer that, It is altogether unlawful to kill oneself, for three reasons. First, because everything naturally loves itself, the result being that everything naturally keeps itself in being, and resists corruptions so far as it can. Wherefore suicide is contrary to the inclination of nature, and to charity whereby every man should love himself. Hence suicide is always a mortal sin, as being contrary to the natural law and to charity. Secondly, because every part, as such, belongs to the whole. Now every man is part of the community, and so, as such, he belongs to the community. Hence by killing himself he injures the community, as the Philosopher[1] declares (Ethics v, 11). Thirdly, because life is God's gift to man, and is subject to His power, who kills and makes to live. Hence whoever takes his own life, sins against God, even as he who kills another's slave, sins against that slave's master, and as he who usurps to himself judgment of a matter not entrusted to him. For it belongs to God alone to pronounce sentence of death and life, according to Deuteronomy 32:39, "I will kill and I will make to live."

1. Murder is a sin, not only because it is contrary to justice, but also because it is opposed to charity which a man should have towards himself: in this respect suicide is a sin in relation to oneself. On relation to the community and to God, it is sinful, by reason also of its opposition to justice.
2. One who exercises public authority may lawfully put to death an evil-doer, since

he can pass judgment on him. But no man is judge of himself. Wherefore it is not lawful for one who exercises public authority to put himself to death for any sin whatever: although he may lawfully commit himself to the judgment of others.

3. Man is made master of himself through his free-will: wherefore he can lawfully dispose of himself as to those matters which pertain to this life which is ruled by man's free-will. But the passage from this life to another and happier one is subject not to man's free-will but to the power of God. Hence it is not lawful for man to take his own life that he may pass to a happier life, nor that he may escape any unhappiness whatsoever of the present life, because the ultimate and most fearsome evil of this life is death, as the Philosopher states (Ethics iii, 6). Therefore to bring death upon oneself in order to escape the other afflictions of this life, is to adopt a greater evil in order to avoid a lesser. On like manner it is unlawful to take one's own life on account of one's having committed a sin, both because by so doing one does oneself a very great injury, by depriving oneself of the time needful for repentance, and because it is not lawful to slay an evildoer except by the sentence of the public authority. Again it is unlawful for a woman to kill herself lest she be violated, because she ought not to commit on herself the very great sin of suicide, to avoid the lesser sin of another. For she commits no sin in being violated by force, provided she does not consent, since "without consent of the mind there is no stain on the body," as the Blessed Lucy declared. Now it is evident that fornication and adultery are less grievous sins than taking a man's, especially one's own, life: since the latter is most grievous, because one injures oneself, to whom one owes the greatest love. Moreover it is most dangerous since no time is left wherein to expiate it by repentance. Again it is not lawful for anyone to take his own life for fear he should consent to sin, because "evil must not be done that good may come" (Romans 3:8) or that evil may be avoided especially if the evil be of small account and an uncertain event, for it is uncertain whether one will at some future time consent to a sin, since God is able to deliver man from sin under any temptation whatever.

4. As Augustine says (*City of God* i, 21), "not even Samson is to be excused that he crushed himself together with his enemies under the ruins of the house, except the Holy Ghost, who had wrought many wonders through him, had secretly commanded him to do this." He assigns the same reason in the case of certain holy women, who at the time of persecution took their own lives, and who are commemorated by the Church.

5. It belongs to fortitude that a man does not shrink from being slain by another, for the sake of the good of virtue, and that he may avoid sin. But that a man take his own life in order to avoid penal evils has indeed an appearance of fortitude (for which reason some, among whom was Razias, have killed themselves thinking to act from fortitude), yet it is not true fortitude, but rather a weakness of soul unable to bear penal evils, as the Philosopher (Ethic. iii, 7) and Augustine (*City of God*, 22,23) declare.

Note

1. Aristotle. The references to "Ethics" here are to book and chapter in Aristotle's *Nicomachean Ethics*.

31 Of Suicide (excerpts)

David Hume

Essays on Suicide and the Immortality of the Soul (1783)

One considerable advantage, that arises from philosophy, consists in the sovereign antidote which it affords to superstition and false religion. All other remedies against that pestilent distemper are vain, or, at least, uncertain. Plain good-sense, and the practice of the world, which alone serve most purposes of life, are here found ineffectual… But when sound philosophy has once gained possession of the mind, superstition is effectually excluded;

It will here be superfluous to magnify the merits of philosophy, by displaying the pernicious tendency of that vice, of which it cures the human mind. The superstitious man… is miserable in every scene, in every incident of life. Even sleep itself, which banishes all other cares of unhappy mortals, affords to him matter of new terror; while he examines his dreams, and finds in those visions of the night, prognostications of future calamities. I may add, that, tho' death alone can put a full period to his misery, he dares not fly to this refuge, but still prolongs a miserable existence, from a vain fear, lest he offend his maker, by using the power, with which that beneficent being has endowed him. The presents of God and Nature are ravished from us by this cruel enemy; and notwithstanding that one step would remove us from the regions of pain and sorrow, her menaces still chain us down to a hated being, which she herself chiefly contributes to render miserable.

It is observed of such as have been reduced by the calamities of life to the necessity of employing this fatal remedy, that, if the unseasonable care of their friends deprive them of that species of death, which they proposed to themselves, they seldom venture upon any other, or can summon up so much resolution, a second time, as to execute their purpose. So great is our horror of death, that when it presents itself under any form, besides that to which a man has endeavored to reconcile his imagination, it acquires new terrors, and overcomes his feeble courage. But when the menaces of superstition are joined to this natural timidity, no wonder it quite deprives men of all power over their lives; since even many pleasures and enjoyments, to which we are carried by a strong propensity, are torn from us by this inhuman tyrant. Let us here endeavor to restore men to their native liberty, by examining all the common arguments against Suicide, and shewing, that That action may be free from every imputation of guilt or blame; according to the sentiments of all the ancient philosophers.

If Suicide be criminal, it must be a transgression of our duty, either to God, our neighbor, or ourselves.

To prove that Suicide is no transgression of our duty to God, the following considerations may perhaps suffice. In order to govern the material world, the Almighty creator has established general and immutable laws, by which all bodies, from the greatest planet to the smallest particle of matter, are maintained in their proper sphere and function. To govern the animal world, he has endowed all living creatures with bodily and mental powers; with senses, passions, appetites, memory, and judgment; by which they are impelled or regulated in that course of life, to which they are destined. These two distinct principles of the material and animal world continually encroach upon each other, and mutually retard or forward each other's operation. The powers of men and of all other animals are restrained and directed by the nature and qualities of the surrounding bodies; and the modifications and actions of these bodies are incessantly altered by the operation of all animals. Man is stopped by rivers in his passage over the surface of the earth; and rivers, when properly directed, lend their force to the motion of machines, which serve to the use of man. But tho' the provinces of the material and animal powers are not kept entirely separate, there result from thence no discord or disorder in the creation: On the contrary, from the mixture, union, and contrast of all the various powers of inanimate bodies and living creatures, arises that surprising harmony and proportion, which affords the surest argument of supreme wisdom.

The providence of the deity appears not immediately in any operation, but governs everything by those general and immutable laws, which have been established from the beginning of time. All events, in one sense, may be pronounced the action of the almighty: They all proceed from those powers, with which he has endowed his creatures. A house, which falls by its own weight, is not brought to ruin by his providence more than one destroyed by the hands of men; nor are the human faculties less his workmanship than the laws of motion and gravitation. When the passions play, when the judgment dictates, when the limbs obey; this is all the operation of God; and upon these animate principles, as well as upon the inanimate, has he established the government of the universe.

… the elements and other inanimate parts of the creation carry on their action without regard to the particular interest and situation of men; so men are entrusted to their own judgment and discretion in the various shocks of matter, and may employ every faculty, with which they are endowed, in order to provide for their ease, happiness, or preservation.

What is the meaning, then, of that principle, that a man, who, tired of life, and hunted by pain and misery, bravely overcomes all the natural terrors of death, and makes his escape from this cruel scene; that such a man, I say, has incurred the indignation of his creator, by encroaching on the office of divine providence, and disturbing the order of the universe? Shall we assert, that the Almighty has reserved to himself, in any peculiar manner, the disposal of the lives of men, and has not submitted that event, in common with others, to the general laws, by which the universe is governed? This is plainly false. The lives of men depend upon the same laws as the lives of all other animals; and these are subjected to the general laws of matter and motion. The fall of a tower or the infusion of a poison will destroy a man equally with the meanest creature: An inundation sweeps away everything, without distinction, that comes within the reach of its fury. Since therefore the lives of men are forever dependent on the general laws of matter and motion; is a man's disposing of his life criminal, because, in every case, it is criminal to encroach upon these laws, or disturb their operation? But this seems absurd. All animals are entrusted to their own prudence and skill for their conduct in the world, and have full authority, as far as their power extends, to alter all the operations of nature. Without the exercise of this authority, they could not subsist a moment. Every action, every motion of a man innovates in the order of some parts of matter, and diverts, from their ordinary course, the general laws of motion. Putting together, therefore, these conclusions, we find, *that* human life depends upon the general laws of matter and motion, and *that* 'tis no encroachment on the office of providence to disturb or alter these general laws. Has not everyone, of consequence, the free disposal of his own life? And may he not lawfully employ that power with which nature has endowed him?

In order to destroy the evidence of this conclusion, we must shew a reason, why this particular case is excepted. Is it because human life is of so great importance, that it is a presumption for human prudence to dispose of it? But the life of man is of no greater importance to the universe than that of an oyster. And were it of ever so great importance, the order of nature has actually submitted it to human prudence, and reduced us to a necessity, in every incident, of determining concerning it.

Were the disposal of human life so much reserved as the peculiar province of the almighty that it were an encroachment on his right for men to dispose of their own lives; it would be equally criminal to act for the preservation of life as for its destruction. If I turn aside a stone, which is falling upon my head, I disturb the course of nature, and I invade the peculiar province of the almighty, by lengthening out my life, beyond the period, which, by the general laws of matter and motion, he had assigned to it.

A hair, a fly, an insect is able to destroy this mighty being, whose life is of such importance. Is it an absurdity to suppose, that human prudence may lawfully dispose of what depends on such insignificant causes?

It would be no crime in me to divert the *Nile* or *Danube* from its course, were I able to effect such purposes. Where then is the crime of turning a few ounces of blood from their natural channels!

… human life may be unhappy, and that my existence, if farther prolonged, would become uneligible. But I thank providence, both for the good, which I have already enjoyed, and for the power, with which I am endowed, of escaping the ill that threatens me. To you it belongs to repine at providence, who foolishly imagine that you have no such power, and who must still prolong a hated being, tho' loaded with pain and sickness, with shame and poverty.

Do you not teach, that when any ill befalls me, tho' by the malice of my enemies, I ought to be resigned to providence; and that the actions of men are the operations of the almighty as much as the actions of inanimate beings? When I fall upon my own sword, therefore, I receive my death equally from the hands of the deity, as if it had proceeded from a lion, a precipice, or a fever.

The submission, which you require to providence, in every calamity, that befalls me,

excludes not human skill and industry; if possibly, by their means, I can avoid or escape the calamity. And why may I not employ one remedy as well as another?

…

There is no being, which possesses any power or faculty, that it receives not from its creator; nor is there any one, which, by ever so irregular an action, can encroach upon the plan of his providence, or disorder the universe. Its operations are his work equally with that chain of events, which it invades; and whichever principle prevails, we may, for that very reason, conclude it to be most favored by him. … Divine providence is still inviolate, and placed far beyond the reach of human injuries.

It is impious, says the old *Roman* superstition, to divert rivers from their course, or invade the prerogatives of nature. 'Tis impious, says the *French* superstition, to inoculate for the small-pox, or usurp the business of providence, by voluntarily producing distempers and maladies. 'Tis impious, says the modern *European* superstition, to put a period to our own life, and thereby rebel against our creator. And why not impious, say I, to build houses, cultivate the ground, and sail upon the ocean? In all these actions, we employ our powers of mind and body to produce some innovation in the course of nature; and in none of them do we any more. They are all of them, therefore, equally innocent or equally criminal.

But you are placed by providence, like a sentinel, in a particular station; and when you desert it, without being recalled, you are guilty of rebellion against your almighty sovereign, and have incurred his displeasure. I ask, why do you conclude, that Providence has placed me in this station? For my part, I find, that I owe my birth to a long chain of causes, of which many and even the principal, depended upon voluntary actions of men. *But Providence guided all these causes, and nothing happens in the universe without its consent and co-operation.* If so, then neither does my death, however voluntary, happen without its consent; and whenever pain and sorrow so far overcome my patience as to make me tired of life, I may conclude, that I am recalled from my station, in the clearest and most express terms.

...

It is a kind of blasphemy to imagine, that any created being can disturb the order of the world, or invade the business of providence. It supposes, that that being possesses powers and faculties, which it received not from its creator, and which are not subordinate to his government and authority. A man may disturb society, no doubt; and thereby incur the displeasure of the almighty: But the government of the world is placed far beyond his reach and violence.

... Let us now examine, according to the method proposed, whether Suicide be of this kind of actions, and be a breach of our duty to our *neighbor* and to society.

A man, who retires from life, does no harm to society. He only ceases to do good; which, if it be an injury, is of the lowest kind.

All our obligations to do good to society seem to imply something reciprocal. I receive the benefits of society, and therefore ought to promote its interest. But when I withdraw myself altogether from society, can I be bound any longer?

But allowing, that our obligations to do good were perpetual, they have certainly some bounds. I am not obliged to do a small good to society, at the expense of a great harm to myself. Why then should I prolong a miserable existence, because of some frivolous advantage, which the public may, perhaps, receive from me? If upon account of age and infirmities, I may lawfully resign any office, and employ my time altogether in fencing against these calamities, and alleviating, as much as possible, the miseries of my future life: Why may I not cut short these miseries at once by an action, which is no more prejudicial to society?

But suppose, that it is no longer in my power to promote the interest of the public: Suppose, that I am a burthen to it: Suppose, that my life hinders some person from being much more useful to the public. In such cases my resignation of life must not only be innocent but laudable. And most people, who lie under any temptation to abandon existence, are in some such situation.

... suppose a malefactor justly condemned to a shameful death; can any reason be imagined, why he may not anticipate his punishment, and save himself all the anguish of thinking on its dreadful approaches? He invades the business of providence no more than the magistrate did, who ordered his execution; and his voluntary death is equally advantageous to society, by ridding it of a pernicious member.

That Suicide may often be consistent with interest and with our duty to *ourselves,* no one can question, who allows, that age, sickness, or misfortune may render life a burthen, and make it worse even than annihilation. I believe that no man ever threw away life, while it was worth keeping. For such is our natural horror of death, that small motives will never be able to reconcile us to it. And tho' perhaps the situation of a man's health or fortune did not seem to require this remedy, we may at least be assured, that any one, who, without apparent reason, has had recourse to it, was cursed with such an incurable depravity or gloominess of temper, as must poison all enjoyment, and render him equally miserable as if he had been loaded with the most grievous misfortunes.

If Suicide be supposed a crime, 'tis only cowardice can impel us to it. If it be no crime, both prudence and courage should engage us to rid ourselves at once of existence, when it becomes a burthen. 'Tis the only way, that we can then be useful to society, by setting an example, which, if imitated, would preserve to everyone his chance for happiness in life, and would effectually free him from all danger of misery.

32 Suicide Is *Sometimes* Rational and Morally Defensible

David Benatar

The ethical debate about suicide is misdirected. Most of it concerns whether suicide is *ever* rational or morally permissible. Some deny that it ever is. They say that taking one's own life is always either irrational or morally wrong, or both. Their opponents do not typically take the opposite view, namely that suicide is *always* rational and morally permissible. Instead, they make the more modest claim that it *sometimes* is. "Sometimes" is a very vague word, one that ranges across the spectrum from "almost never" to "almost always." The debates and discussions about suicide should be about *when* it is rational and permissible and *when* it is not.

However, because there is so much categorical opposition to suicide, ethical evaluations of self-killing must still begin with the more foundational questions (and where there are space constraints, as in this essay, also provisionally end there).

Fates Worse than Death: The Rationality of Suicide

The case for suicide sometimes being both prudentially rational and morally permissible begins, although it does not end, with the premise that there are fates worse than death. When we consider all the horrific fates that can and often do befall people, this premise seems reasonable. However, some people will object that because we do not know, at least for certain, what happens after death, we cannot know whether other fates are worse than death. Perhaps the torments of an afterlife are even worse, with the implication that we should cling on with and to dear life.

This suggestion is so speculative that the opposite argument could be made as easily: Perhaps the delights of the afterlife are so immense that we should all take our lives as soon as possible. Mere possibilities such as these are insufficient to justify either unfailing commitment to life, or our hasty abandonment of it. Much less speculative is the view that there is no afterlife, or at least not one in which we experience anything. We have ample evidence that our consciousness, necessary for experience, is dependent on our brains, which cease to function following death. If that is the case then we can, with reasonable confidence, even if not certainty, think that some fates *are* worse than death.[1]

Whether they believe in an afterlife or not, most people, I suspect, ultimately accept that death is not the worst thing that can befall us. One way to demonstrate this, although it would obviously be unethical to do so, would be as follows: Take those who doubt that there are fates worse than death, and strap them down in torture chambers. Then advise them that the torture will soon begin and will be delivered in a way that can continue for years, but that at any point they decide that they can take no more, they will be killed painlessly. If not everybody, then almost everybody will have a breaking point. Many of them would initially hold out hope of rescue. In due course, this would wear down and the near certainty of further torture would outweigh the increasingly remote hope of being rescued.

If death is not the worst thing that can befall one, then it must be prudentially rational to prefer death to those alternatives that are worse. Not all of these alternatives involve literal torturers. Malignancies block bowels, compress brains, and invade bones, growing relentlessly, and steadily eliminating any remaining positive quality of life. Degenerative neuro-muscular diseases gradually sap all control over one's body. Burns, whether intentionally or accidently inflicted, not only disfigure but also cause excruciating pain, sometimes over much of the body.

If it is sometimes rational to prefer death,[2] then those who fault suicide for always being irrational must be mistaken. It cannot be irrational to prefer the less bad over the worse. Indeed, in such cases it is irrational, all things being equal, not to prefer death.

Countervailing Considerations? The Morality of Suicide

That it is sometimes rational to prefer—and even to bring about—one's own death, does not mean that, even then, it is also morally permissible. This is because there might be other considerations that outweigh one's own interest in not living longer. Those who categorically oppose suicide cite a range of such considerations, the most important of which will be assessed here.

Sanctity of Life

One suggestion is that life is sacred. Although the most natural reading of this view is a religious one, there are also secular versions of it. The overarching idea is that (human) life has ultimate or overriding importance, such that additional quantities of life always override any quality-of-life considerations.

This view is hard to sustain and most people, when pushed, are unlikely to subscribe to it. Consider two possible courses your life could take. If it takes the first, you will live and be healthy until you are 80, at which point you have a stroke and die. If instead your life takes the second course, you will live and be healthy until you are 80, at which you'll have a stroke which does not kill you but reduces to you a vegetative state, in which you will

live for another five years until another stroke kills you at age 85. If additional quantities of life, no matter what their quality, always override quality-of-life considerations, then we should all prefer the second of the possible life courses. Yet (almost) everybody I ask prefers the first option, in which one dies at 80.

Perhaps, however, we should not interpret the "sanctity of life" as the view that additional quantities of life always override any quality considerations. If, instead, we understand it as the view that (human) life is *inviolable*—that we may never intentionally take[3] an innocent human life, including one's own—then we may prefer the shorter life without the additional merely vegetative component, on condition that we never *end* lives on the basis of such preferences.

However, anybody can *say* that human life is inviolable in this way. If they expect us to accept this view, a compelling reason for doing so needs to be provided. Why should we think that human life has sanctity in this sense?

Some answers to this question are religious. For example, it is sometimes suggested that humans are inviolable because they are created in God's image.[4] However, it is not clear why being created in the divine image, even if true, would always make it wrong to end a human life. One could as easily argue that if it is sometimes permissible[5] to end a non-human animal's life in order to spare it great suffering then *a fortiori* we should be permitted to release from such suffering a being created in God's image. In other words, does being created in the divine image make one's life inviolable or does it instead make suffering a stronger consideration in favour of shortening life?

Another possible religious explanation for why human life is inviolable is that though we hold our lives in trust, they actually belong to God and we are not free to end them. The problem, however, is that this is less an explanation and more an assertion. It is not clear what reason we have to accept it over rival assertions, including other religious ones, such as the claim that one's life is a gift from God. If it were a gift, at least in the traditional sense, one would not be obliged to keep it, especially if it ran counter to one's interests. Some religious people might argue against this, by saying that suicide amounts to a rejection of God's gift and that such ingratitude is wrong. However, we do not think, in other contexts, that discarding a gift that one may once have appreciated but which has since broken amounts to ingratitude.

Murder

It is also possible to understand the purported inviolability of human life in secular terms (by which I mean terms that *do not presuppose* religious claims, rather than ones that *reject* religious claims). Understood thus, intentionally taking an innocent human life amounts to murder.

Taking one's own life is certainly an instance of *killing*, but that is not enough to show that it is also *murder*. There is no contradiction in claiming that a killing is morally justified. "Murder," however, implies "wrongful killing" and thus to judge suicide to be murder one has to explain why, rather than assert that, self-killing is wrongful. What secular explanation could be provided for this?[6]

The most plausible explanations for why killing people is typically wrong do not work in cases where it is rational to prefer death. For example, if one says that killing is wrong because it deprives the victim of the good that she would otherwise have enjoyed, that would not apply in cases where death spares one the sort of bad that cannot be compensated by whatever good one is also deprived of by death. Similarly, if one says that killing people is wrong because it thwarts their interest in continued life, this does not apply in cases where there is either no longer such an interest or where interests in avoiding the evils of continued existence outweigh the interest in continuing to exist.[7]

Nor will it help if one thinks that killing is wrong because it violates a (negative) right to life—that is, a right not to be killed. Postulating a right not to be killed, far from ruling out all suicide, actually entails the

permissibility of suicide, at least in some situations.[8] This may seem surprising, but it makes eminent sense if one understands something about what rights are. Rights theorists disagree about whether rights fundamentally protect interests or whether they fundamentally protect choices, but either way, suicide is sometimes morally defensible.

If rights protect interests, then a right not to be killed is a protection of one's interest in not being killed. However, given that one no longer has an all-things-considered interest in continued life in those cases in which suicide is rational, one must be able to waive one's right in such situations if one's right is actually to serve one's interests. If one is forced, because one has a right not to be killed (even by oneself), to remain alive when life is no longer in one's interest, then the right no longer protects one's interests but instead undermines them.

The matter is even clearer if rights fundamentally protect choices. On this view, my right not to be killed actually protects my choice *whether or not* to be killed. Ordinarily, I choose not to be killed (because that is usually the rational choice). However, in those cases where it is rational to prefer death, I may choose not to continue living, and instead to take my own life.

If the best explanations for the wrongfulness of killing people are inapplicable in cases where suicide is rational, then although suicide in such cases is indubitably killing, it is not murder.

Unnatural

Another argument against suicide is that it is unnatural. It is not uncommon for people to argue that a practice is immoral because it is unnatural. However, the problem with arguments of this kind is that they need to explain both what exactly is unnatural about the practice and why that makes the practice immoral. Whereas it is usually possible to identify how a practice is unnatural,[9] it is notoriously difficult to explain why it is therefore immoral. This is exactly the problem faced by those objecting to suicide on grounds of unnaturalness.

One way in which suicide might be said to be unnatural is that it ends a life earlier than it would have ended if nature had taken its course. The person who takes his own life dies of unnatural causes. However, it is far from clear why this fact makes suicide wrong. Many life-saving medical interventions are unnatural in a symmetrical way. They ensure that a person dies *later* than he would have died if nature had been allowed to take its course. Yet very few people think that life-saving medical interventions are wrong because they lead to an unnatural life extension. If unnatural life extension is not wrong on account of its unnaturalness, then we are hard-pressed to suggest that unnatural life shortening is wrong because it is unnatural in the same sense.[10]

There is another way in which suicide might be said to be unnatural, namely that it runs counter to a natural instinct to preserve one's life.[11] So powerful is this instinct that people—as well as non-human animals—go to great lengths and endure many torments if that is necessary to preserve their lives. The life drive is indeed a deep, natural instinct. However, the loss or overriding of this instinct is no less natural than the instinct itself. Sometimes the loss or defeat of that instinct is irrational, in the sense of not cohering with what it would be rational to feel. In such cases the loss of the instinct is something to be regretted and, if possible, corrected. However, this is not always so. When it is rational to prefer death, it is better if the instinct to self-preservation is overridden or, perhaps best of all, lost entirely, as this removes an impediment to doing what best serves one's interests.

The more fundamental point here is that natural instincts should not always be followed. There are strong natural instincts towards sex and violence, but that does not mean that we should always act in accordance with them. We ought instead to exercise judgement in deciding when to follow and when to resist them. The same is true for the life drive and its absence. We need to decide when we should and should not be acting on the natural presence or absence of the instinct. Their mere naturalness imposes no moral imperative or prohibition.

Cowardice

Many people argue that suicide is immoral because they believe it to be cowardly. The objection is that suicide is the easy way out and that one should instead be courageous and continue to face life's burdens.

This objection is likely to appeal to those who have a crude view of courage, which maintains that it is always courageous to meet danger and adversity head-on. However, there are more sophisticated conceptions of courage, according to which embracing peril and hardship is sometimes foolhardy rather than courageous.[12] Running headlong into danger or confronting adversity when there is nothing to be gained from doing so is reckless rather than courageous. When suicide is rational—that is to say, when death is less bad than continued life—then, at least from the prudential perspective, there is no point in carrying on. When there is also no altruistic point to continue living, it is wise rather than cowardly to take one's own life.

Indeed, suicide is sometimes actually the courageous option. Given the powerful life drive, most people are inclined to cling to life even when it has ceased to be wise to do so. They do so not because they are courageous but because they cannot bring themselves to end their lives. In other words, they lack the courage to end it all. When one's life is not worth continuing, it takes great courage to override one's self-preservation instinct and to take one's own life.[13]

Although suicide is the more courageous option in such situations, I would not want to say that those who do not choose it are cowardly. This is because both options—suicide and a life of continued hell—require significant fortitude. There is no easy option here, even if one is *easier* than the other (and even if one could have substantial confidence which one were easier). The easier option will not be the same for every person, even if the different people are otherwise similarly situated. That is to say, for some people in a particular circumstance, continued life will be the easier option, while for others in the same circumstance, suicide will be the easier option. The easier option is not necessarily identical with the wisest one. One might be better off living but find suicide easier, or one might be better off dead but find continued living easier. All this provides further reason for those categorically opposed to suicide to desist from levelling the charge of cowardice against those who end their own lives. Not only is it false, it is also insensitive to the unenviable predicament of those driven to consider suicide.

Interests of Others

A more compelling candidate for a consideration that could countervail the prudential rationality of suicide is consideration for the interests of others. Suicide can have a serious impact on people other than the person who takes his own life. Most importantly, it can deeply affect family and friends, often for the rest of their lives. They are left bereft. Sometimes they will also feel a sense of guilt, misplaced though that often is. If the person who took her own life had fulfillable duties to these family members and friends—duties that she would have been able to discharge if she had remained alive—then suicide involves flouting her duties. For example, children may be deprived of the affection and rearing of a parent, or a man or woman may be deprived of the love and support of a spouse. Suicide might also prevent one fulfilling obligations to those beyond one's family and friends, although these obligations will often, but not always, be weaker ones.

It is clear, therefore, that suicide can sometimes be selfish. In such cases, the person who takes his own life either considers only his own interests or gives insufficient weight to the interests of others. However, considering the interests of others is not sufficient to rule out all suicide. This is because the problem of ignoring or discounting the interests of others is the flip side of another problem—ignoring or discounting one's own interests.

Thus, somebody contemplating suicide needs to consider both his own interests and the interests of those who would be adversely affected by his death. However, in paradigmatic cases of rational suicide, it is unlikely that the interests of others will outweigh one's own interest in avoiding what continued life would involve. This is partly because in such cases, one's own quality of life would be so appalling that it would typically be indecent to suggest that these are not decisive. It is also partly because when one's quality of life or prognosis is this poor one is unlikely, in any event, to be able to do much good for one's family, friends, and others. In other words, they will be deprived one way or the other. Either one's condition or one's death (for both consecutively) will deprive one's family and friends of the love, companionship, support and other goods one could provide if one were both alive and not in the appalling condition from which death is the only escape.

We should not pretend that there are not complicated situations where matters are less clear than they are in paradigmatic cases of rational suicide. However, the existence of the paradigmatic cases is sufficient to show that the interests of others cannot always rule out the moral permissibility of suicide. Sometimes the interests of others will simply not be strong enough to defeat the very powerful prudential interest in suicide.

It is also worth noting that the argument about selfishness can cut both ways. Just as suicides can be, and sometimes are, selfish it can also be said that *not* ending one's life can be selfish in some circumstances.[14] If, for example, an extra month of life would provide one with some minimal benefit, but would seriously set back the interests of those closest to one, perhaps by ruining them financially, then it seems it would be selfish to take the extra month.

Conclusion

Although I have argued that suicide is not always irrational or wrong, I do not deny that it often is either or both of these. When it is irrational, the person taking her own life is unlikely to realize this. Nor is it uncommon for suicide to be irrational. This is because suicidality is often associated with affective disorders in which emotional processing and decision-making are distorted. This should give significant pause to those contemplating suicide. How can they be sure that they are among those whose desire to end their lives is rational rather than among those whose inclination towards suicide is not?

The finality of (successful) suicide is another reason why those considering it should be especially careful that they are not making the wrong decision. Once one has taken one's life, there is no second chance to continue living (whereas a decision to continue living can typically be changed to suicide[15]).

However, neither of these reasons—fallibility and finality—are sufficient to render suicide irrational in all cases. Whereas many people mistakenly think that suicide is the least bad option for them, others are entirely correct that it is. That such a decision, once acted upon successfully, cannot be reversed, does not mean that, in those circumstances, it is not the correct decision.

Those who are suitably careful in deciding whether to end their lives will not act impulsively. Instead, they will deliberate carefully, over as extended a period as one's circumstances allow. If possible, they will seek the counsel of trusted family and friends.[16] An external perspective can be helpful in identifying one's own blind spots and biases. One's degree of confidence should also vary depending on one's circumstances. Those with terminal conditions where the suffering can be alleviated only by dulling consciousness are among the clearest cases in which suicide is rational. Suffering caused by depression is significantly more complicated. The suffering may be no less bad than the physical variety. However, it is much more difficult in such cases to discern when suicidality is a *symptom* of the pathology and when it is a *response* to the suffering caused by the pathology. It is also often harder to know whether the disease will still prove tractable (although I concede that the more that has been tried the less confidence somebody reasonably has).

Even when suicide is (prudentially) rational, it is not always moral. This is because the interests of other people also need to be considered. That said, the paradigmatic cases of rational suicide are also likely to be ones in which the interests of others cannot easily override the suicidal person's interest in ceasing to exist.

In English, we standardly say that people *commit* suicide. This verb is evaluatively laden—it embodies a negative judgement of suicide. One commits crimes or moral wrongs. One does not *commit* charity, or patience, or heroism. Suicide is no longer a crime in many legal jurisdictions (although it remains illegal in others). Where suicide is not illegal, either the verb "commit" suggests that suicide remains immoral or "commit" is merely a vestige of attitudes no longer held. To avoid confusion, those convinced that suicide is not always immoral, may prefer to eschew "commit" and speak instead of "carrying out" suicide. The latter is less elegant, but it is also less judgemental of those unfortunate enough to have reached a stage of life that is worse than death, and who are morally warranted in bringing about the latter.[17]

Notes

1. Epicureans hold that death can never be good or bad for the ones that die. Most will hold that, strictly speaking, it does not make sense to hold that continued existence could be *better* or *worse* than non-existence since those judgements require comparing a world where you exist with one where you don't. However, this does not matter for the purposes of my argument because Epicureans should grant the important point, namely that one should seek continued life when that life would be, on the whole, good and one should seek death when continued life would be, on the whole, bad. For more on this issue, see Jeff McMahan, "Death and the Value of Life", *Ethics*, 1988, pp. 34–38 and Travis Timmerman, "A Dilemma for Epicureanism", *Philosophical Studies*, 2019, pp. 241-257.
2. For more on the rationality of suicide see, for example, Richard Brandt, "The Morality and Rationality of Suicide," in Seymour Perlin

(ed.), *Handbook for the Study of Suicide*, New York: Oxford University Press, 1975, pp. 61–76; Margaret Pabst Battin, "The Concept of Rational Suicide," in *Ethical Issues in Suicide*, Englewood Cliffs, NJ: Prentice Hall, 1982, pp. 131–153.

3. There is a possible ambiguity here. To take a life may mean either (a) to perform some action that brings about the end of a life; or, in addition, (b) bringing about the end of a life by failing to act in some way. I suspect that (a) is the more natural interpretation. Some may deny that deaths brought about in the second way constitute suicide, a term they may wish to reserve for instances of (a). However, it is possible for somebody to think that both (a) and (b) are instances of taking a life. My arguments here do not presuppose a particular view about the scope of the word "suicide."

4. If being created in God's image were sufficient to make one's life inviolable, then killing in self-defence or as a punishment would be prohibited. Because many religious people think that capital punishment and killing in self-defence are sometimes permissible, they need to qualify the claim, and instead say that *innocent* humans are inviolable because they are created in God's image. That too is insufficiently qualified because it would rule out "collateral" deaths in just wars, at least in those cases where the deaths of the innocents are foreseen. I set aside these difficulties in order to address a more fundamental problem with the *imago dei* justification for human inviolability.

5. If not morally preferable or even obligatory.

6. The biblical prohibition in the "ten commandments" is, at least in the original Hebrew, against murder (לא תרצח) rather than killing (לא תהרוג), even though it is sometimes mistranslated. Thus, a religious argument against suicide cannot consist simply in citing the "sixth commandment."

7. Do the explanations for why killing people is wrong show that it is *wrong* to kill oneself where suicide is *irrational*? Some may respond that even in such cases suicide is not *immoral*. This is because they think that imprudent actions are not thereby immoral. These are more complicated matters that I shall not address here, except to note two possible lines

of response, which I shall not evaluate. First, it might be argued that even if prudentially irrational suicide is not also immoral, we ought not take our own lives in such cases, even though the "ought" here is a prudential rather than a moral one. Second, on some views, prudence is itself an important moral consideration, such that acting imprudently, at least when no altruistic point is served, is morally deficient.

8. For more on this, see David Benatar, "Assisted Suicide," Voluntary Euthanasia, and the Right to Life," in Jon Yorke (ed.), *The Right to Life and the Value of Life: Orientations in Law, Politics and Ethics* (Farnham: Ashgate, 2010), pp. 291–310.

9. There is one obvious sense in which suicide is *not* unnatural. It is an action performed by humans. Given that humans are part of nature and cannot act contrary to the laws of nature, suicide is natural in this sense.

10. This is an argument of David Hume's. See "Of Suicide," in David Hume, *Essays: Moral, Political, and Literary* (revised edition), ed. Eugene F. Miller (Indianapolis, IN: Liberty Classics, 1987), p. 583.

11. Thomas Aquinas, *Summa Theologica*, Part II, Q64, A5.

12. For example, Aristotle, *Nicomachean Ethics*, Book iii, Chapter 7.

13. There is thus some wisdom, and not merely a double entendre, in the quip that "seppuku (hara-kiri) takes lots of guts" (although I hasten to add that I am not endorsing suicide for the reasons that this ritual was usually performed).

14. John Hardwig, "Is there a duty to die?" *Hastings Center Report*, Vol. 27, No. 2, 1997, pp. 34–42.

15. There are circumstances where this is not the case. Among these are degenerative diseases in which one loses the ability to act, and thus one's opportunities for suicide are limited by the progression of the disease.

16. They must be trusted not only as reliable sounding boards, but also for not betraying one's confidence and preventing one's suicide if one is, in fact, rational.

17. I am grateful to Michael Cholbi and Travis Timmerman for their helpful comments on the first draft of this chapter.

33 Suicide and Its Discontents

Philip Reed

Most of us have at one time or another contemplated suicide. In my adult life, I went through a significant period of depression and thought about it a lot. When I was a kid, I recall suffering some setback and standing at the edge of my second-story bedroom window thinking about jumping. I was smart enough to know that I wouldn't have died if I had jumped, but I think what I was trying to express in that gesture was that I could commit suicide if I wanted to. That human beings can choose to end their own lives is clear. Recent philosophers have been especially interested in and impressed by the possibility of suicide and many believe that suicide is permissible. I will argue, though, that recent defenses of suicide have serious defects that can be traced to more basic assumptions.

In an essay that appears earlier in this volume, David Hume gives a famous defense of the permissibility of suicide. His argument is uncharacteristically (for him) bad. He contends that if suicide is unethical, it would have to be unethical on the grounds that it violates a duty to God, our neighbor, or ourselves. Before we analyze the argument further, why should we think that something could only be unethical if it violates one of these three kinds of duties? This is, as we will see, a narrow, peculiarly modern way to construe what ethics is. In other contexts, Hume does not take such a narrow conception of ethics. He is willing to criticize, for example, the religious practice of fasting, arguing that it is a kind of vicious behavior. But could fasting be a violation of a duty to God, our neighbor, or ourselves? Surely not, and Hume does not say that it is. Instead, he criticizes fasting on the grounds that it fails to help the person

live a good life. From prostitution to consensual cannibalism, there are lots of examples of things that you morally ought not to do that might not strictly violate a duty.

When Hume considers the possibility of suicide violating a duty to our neighbor, his discussion is astoundingly short-sighted. He immediately takes the issue of harming our neighbor to be an issue of harming "society" and the "public," and he argues that the act of suicide does no harm to these. We can for now grant Hume everything he says about what duties a person owes to society (e.g., that such duties are reciprocal, voluntary, and limited) and still see that he comes far short of establishing that suicide does not harm our neighbor or violate a duty to him. While society in the abstract may not be harmed by suicide, it's still the case that mothers and fathers, brothers and sisters, children, neighbors, and friends are preponderantly harmed when someone they love commits suicide. They suffer intense amounts of grief and sometimes guilt, as they lose permanently a person who matters to them. There may be some cases where a person commits suicide causing no harm to friends and family. In most cases, however, suicide does harm others, and, in most of these cases, a very strong case could be made that the person who commits suicide is violating a duty to the individuals who are harmed because the person fails to carry out his moral responsibilities to these individuals.

It might be said in Hume's defense that he means only to say that suicide does not *necessarily* harm others, even though there might be actual cases of suicide where others are harmed. However, when Hume makes pronouncements about the actual cases, he seems to generalize in a way that should strike you as at best cold and at worst shameful. He asserts that "most people" who are merely *tempted* to commit suicide are in a situation where they are genuine burdens on society, and so their suicides would be not only "innocent but laudable." "No man ever threw away life while it was worth keeping," Hume insists, assuming the prudential rationality of all suicidal acts. Imagine if Hume were your roommate. You explain to him that you're depressed and that you think you're a burden on your family. "Well," he replies, "suicide might be the solution to everyone's problems here." Of course, Hume did not have access to the field of mental health as it developed in the last century. He did not know, for example, that people who view themselves as burdens on others are almost never viewed that way by other people (Joiner 2007). He was, nevertheless, well-known as an astute observer of human behavior, patterns of thinking, and social dynamics. However, on this topic he is anything but. We must regard Hume's observation that people who commit suicide or think about it are "pernicious" members of society and genuine burdens on everyone else to be an enormous blunder.

The central argument that Hume makes in his essay defending suicide is that suicide does not violate a duty to God. It might seem suspicious that this argument is made by an atheist, since it's hard to see how you could violate a duty to someone who doesn't exist. Perhaps we can say, Hume is arguing that even if there were a God, suicide would not violate a duty to Him. But notice how Hume conceives of this possibly existing God. It is a Deistic God: a supreme power that at the beginning of time sets up the world to be governed according to laws of nature[1] and is indifferent about anything that happens as a consequence of these laws. Hume's view is that all events are subject to these universal laws, and suicide is no exception: because it falls under the laws of nature that God implemented to govern the world, it can't be something that God disapproves of. Hume writes: "Be it animate or inanimate, rational or irrational, 'tis

all a case: Its power is still derived from the supreme creator, and is alike comprehended in the order of his providence." All human actions are permitted by God, subject only to the physical laws that govern the universe.

A consequence of this view that Hume does not mention is that no action, considered in itself, could be displeasing to God. Consider cannibalism. Cannibalism, like suicide, is a natural event, subject to the laws of nature. God gave human beings the power to cannibalize and lawfully (subject to these physical laws) employ that power when they eat other people. It is no crime, says Hume, to intervene in nature in any capacity that is possible for me, so "where then is the crime of turning a few ounces of blood from their natural channels!" He is talking about suicide here, but the logic of his argument commits him to the view that he might be talking about you misdirecting your professor's blood into your own mouth. From God's (or the universe's) standpoint, it's just an intervention into nature. Of course Hume can still argue that cannibalism is wrong on other grounds (it's a violation of a duty to your professor), but he could not argue that cannibalism would violate a duty to God. Under the amoral, Deistic God that Hume puts forward, there are no actions whatsoever that God would consider wrong.[2]

Hume's argument presupposes a God that no major religion believes in or worships. Instead, it is common for people who actually believe in God to suppose that God not only creates the world and sets matter in motion but also gives commandments to human beings because He loves them. Theists overwhelmingly believe that God has at least some weak moral preferences about human choices. For such a God, it's not hard to see how suicide could violate a duty to him. Hume's God, meanwhile, gives no preference to human beings over oysters (he explicitly tells us), so of course (human) suicide wouldn't be anything God loses sleep over. In other places, Hume provides arguments to think that if there's a God, he is not the kind of being who gives commandments or who loves human beings. Obviously, an assessment of those arguments is beyond the bounds of this essay. And anyway Hume does not invoke those arguments here, which is curious because without them his polemic against suicide is a failure. All that Hume shows is that if theists abandon the understanding of God that they have and replaced it with a deist's portrayal of what God could be, suicide would not be wrong in the eyes of God.

Hume wrote his essay defending suicide at a particular period in Western history that was undergoing great change. The society around Hume was religious enough that he refrained from publishing the essay during his lifetime, since he knew his anti-theistic intentions would not be well-received (and they weren't when the essay was published after his death). Yet the culture had already begun to experience a significant shift away from traditional religion and morality, a shift that has been more or less completed by the present day. With respect to suicide, philosophers in the Enlightenment began to be more open to the idea of its moral permissibility in a way that was unprecedented. What happened between the time when Aquinas thought he could dismiss suicide in the matter of a couple of pages and the present day, when many philosophers now insist on a right to die? It was not merely a fading away of religion. The modern era, beginning in about the late sixteenth to seventeenth centuries, ushered in entirely new ways of thinking about both ethics and the human person.

In the premodern era, it was commonly accepted that human beings had a species-specific good that they had the potential to realize and that would make their life go well. Ethics was a matter of delivering the precepts necessary for achieving this good. In the modern era, however, the idea that human beings were meant to realize their good was gradually abandoned, and ethical precepts had to be adjusted accordingly. One particularly influential theory of ethics, in some ways initiated by Hume, was to see moral precepts in terms of how much happiness we could produce from our actions. "Happiness" was understood in terms of pleasure or desire-satisfaction. On this conception of ethics, a particular action is good or bad,

right or wrong, if the consequences are good or bad. Another influential modern ethical theory was the idea that our moral duties are delivered by reason. In these cases and others, ethics was no longer about becoming a certain kind of person, a person who needs to realize his or her species-specific good.

The dominant conception of the nature of human persons underwent an even more radical shift. The modern era sees human beings as discrete, autonomous individuals who act in order to realize whatever contingent preferences they happen to have, what we now call our "values." So what it means to live a good life in the modern era is simply to be satisfied by our subjective desires: if you enjoy playing video games, then you ought to do that, if you enjoy treating poor people's illnesses, then you ought to do that, and so on. This idea is captured well, for example, in the Declaration of Independence, where we are guaranteed the right to the pursuit of happiness. Your happiness is construed individually, based on your contingent desires, and limited only to the extent that whatever you choose cannot infringe on someone else's ability to pursue his conception of happiness. The Supreme Court Justice Anthony Kennedy interprets the Constitution to guarantee every individual the ability to "define one's own concept of existence, of meaning, of the universe, and of the mystery of human life." Many contemporary philosophers are commonly happy to endorse the central components of this conception of the nature of the human person and what makes a human life go well.[3] John Rawls, the most prestigious political philosopher of the twentieth century, contends that if someone is personally fulfilled by counting blades of grass his whole life, then his life does go well by doing just this thing (1971).

Our culture now accepts this hyperindividualism without much critical judgment. But if, for example, you've spent time in non-Western cultures, it is likely that you realize the extent to which our insistence on human beings as discrete, autonomous individuals pursuing their own personal versions of happiness is unique. It is true that we still have relationships and communities, but these are deeply impoverished by the fact that they are seen to be based almost entirely on the individual's preferences and willingness to continue them. You can join or quit any group (or "community") at will. We even tend to view our obligations to our own parents and siblings as imposing very few claims on us, which is why, for example, when we reach adulthood it is commonly expected of us that we will leave our hometown (and so our families, but also our friends and neighbors) in order to pursue our own personal fulfillment. It is also why, as another example, when our marriages become difficult and not personally fulfilling we end them through no-fault divorce.[4] Some of the effects of this unique experiment in human history have been very good and are appropriately celebrated, but other effects have been disastrous for our relationships, communities, and the living of worthwhile lives. Loneliness is now treated as an epidemic in most of the developed world. Rates of depression and of suicide are increasing significantly. The core elements of human happiness, such as meaningful community or a purpose larger than and outside of ourselves, seem to elude many of us at every turn.

Hume was among the first in a long line of philosophers from the Enlightenment to the present day to defend suicide as a natural outgrowth of the modern understandings of human nature and of ethics. The idea of quitting life is and should be open to us in the same way that the idea of quitting our hometown and our marriage is. Philosophers (e.g., in the existentialist tradition) now tend to emphasize the possibility of suicide, holding it out to us as a realistic option we must daily consider, because it follows from individual choice in all things. The permissibility of suicide then more or less follows from its possibility; individual choice is justified in virtue of simply being one's own choice. Just as we make every other significant choice for our lives, so too we should do so with respect to our deaths. If we believe our future suffering outweighs our future happiness, then it is right and fitting to end our lives.

A group of six of the most preeminent moral philosophers in the United States filed a brief in a Supreme Court case at the end of the twentieth century defending a "right to die" (Dworkin et al. 1997). Conceptualizing suicide as a right means buying into the notion that our choices are individually determined to maximize our preferences in a way that leads to our happiness.[5] Rights are claims that we use to prevent interference from others, to say nothing of obligations to them. Just as we have rights to use our own property as we please without harming others, so too with our lives. Who are we to challenge how an individual understands her own values and what choices can best make sense of those values?[6]

I don't mean to suggest that every philosopher since Hume defends suicide. There have been important exceptions, most notably Immanuel Kant. Kant thought that we have a moral duty to ourselves not to take our own lives. He said that the act of suicide rejects the possibility of ethical action and so the significance of ethics. It is therefore incoherent or self-defeating to think that it could be ethical to commit suicide; suicide is morally wrong because it destroys your agency. This is a clever and thought-provoking argument. It may be worth considering whether in the suicide debate, even granting modern assumptions, we are doing justice to the value of our lives compared to asking if we are getting enough out of them. However, Kant situated his ethical theory squarely within a framework of the modern conception of autonomous individuals, and the question is whether his position against suicide ultimately collapses because it depends on promoting an individual's understanding of how well his life is going (Brassington 2006).

If we reject the modern understandings of morality and the human person then suicide becomes difficult to justify. Suicide as we understand it today (as an individual act where one judges that one would be better off dead) was not at all common in the premodern era much less justified on that basis.[7] While suicide was always controversial, in no other time period do philosophers debate a "right" to commit suicide (i.e., whether it is permissible to engage in self-interested suicide), nor would it really even make sense to do so. Cases of self-killing in the ancient world (an act that was largely criminalized) were cases that had some political or social purpose, for example the achievement of a kind of heroic glory. But essentially no one thought that suicide was the best choice for a life judged to be filled with future suffering.[8] A significant amount of the premodern resistance to suicide came, of course, from religious sensibilities. But it had a deeper root, I would argue, in premodern conceptions of the human person and of ethics. I said above that this kind of account understands human beings as having a species-specific good that is achievable through ethical precepts. How exactly does this tell against suicide?

The best representative of this kind of premodern point of view is Aristotle.[9] Aristotle holds that human beings have a natural good that will make their life go well. In order to achieve this natural good, which Aristotle calls our flourishing (*eudaimonia*), we should not act to satisfy whatever desires we happen to have. Instead, living a good life requires stepping back from our desires and evaluating whether they are genuinely (objectively) good for us. We should act on the desires that enable us to develop our capacities and to acquire genuine goods such as friends, family, health, meaningful work, and worthwhile leisure activities and we should shun the desires that inhibit these. Aristotle says that virtues are what enable us to identify these goods and pursue them successfully. He believes, moreover, that this ethical project must be done cooperatively with others: human beings are fundamentally social creatures rather than isolated individuals. The uniquely human goods that we are capable of achieving cannot be achieved alone.

Perhaps this goes without saying, but all of the goods that are possible for human beings are prevented by suicide.[10] We cannot develop our capabilities and reach our species-specific good if we end our own lives. We do not flourish when we are dead. This is the necessary

context for understanding what Aquinas (who was a committed Aristotelian) means when he says that suicide is contrary to nature and to charity. It should be no wonder, moreover, that Aristotle rejects suicide as a violation to the community (1999, sect. 1138a). The disagreement between Hume and Aristotle on this point is revealing. Aristotle understands human beings as *belonging* to their civic community in a way that Hume and most modern philosophers do not. Hume observes that if an individual is living a miserable existence, then he is probably not contributing much to society anyway, so his suicide does society no harm. But Aristotle does not conceive of the injustice of suicide in terms of an individual's contribution to society, as if we could simply tally the utility of a person's occupation, tax revenue, or community service. Nor, according to Aristotle, does an individual's relationship to society exist on the basis of a tacit contract, meant to be mutually beneficial to self-interested individuals, as many other modern philosophers propose. Instead, Aristotle imagines that human beings are fundamentally interdependent and, therefore, the achievement of a community's good utilizes each part.

But why think this conception of the common good has any bearing on an individual's ability to achieve his good? In order to step back from our desires and evaluate them effectively, we need to have adequate self-knowledge as well as be able to imagine sufficient future possibilities. We need to understand how our lives could go better or worse. And this can only be adequately done, Aristotle holds, via robust social relationships. If you have ever been unsure about how good your philosophy essay was or how skillful you really are at painting, you have a sense of Aristotle's idea here: we need others to know who we are, what we can become, and what counts as good. Judgements about what is good or bad for us require a genuine community. It may seem as if talk about flourishing and living a good life seems too far away from the suicidal person, who sees no reason to go on at all much less live well. But one thing that such persons often lack is a sufficient perspective by which to judge what their future possibilities might mean for them, and part of the reason they lack this is that they largely try to imagine their future possibilities on their own.

One might object that suicidal persons have been harmed by their society or community, which is why they want to end their lives. But in saying that some have been let down, we are assuming appropriate norms of adequate community support. Our response to such individuals should not be to extend them a right to die, but to rebuild a meaningful community that might help them come to a better understanding of themselves and their future. Here, Aquinas offers a helpful corrective to Aristotle by emphasizing the virtue of mercy (*misdericordia*) whereby we respond unconditionally to the needs of another by recognizing the other's distress as our own (MacIntyre 1999). This is a far cry from the modern point of view, which tells people that they have to define their own concepts of meaning and the universe and then tells them they can end their lives if they fail.

Aristotle does say that flourishing may be impossible for you if your circumstances are bad enough. He mentions the Trojan king Priam, who suffered great misfortune at the end of his life, losing everything that mattered to him. Aristotle says that a good person will be able to bear misfortune well, and in extreme cases such as Priam, developing the virtues can prevent us, at least, from being miserable (1999, sect. 1101a). He might have added, moreover, as many philosophers do, that circumstances of suffering and affliction are opportunities for growth in virtue and bettering ourselves. Many of us in the modern era are accustomed to lives of comfort and privilege, which is historically anomalous. Modern suicide sometimes tries to preserve the fantasy that we should never face difficulty or struggle or dependence, even though these can be deeply instructive and might even, over time, contribute to our ability to flourish. Even in cases of a terminal illness, say, that robs almost completely our ability to flourish in the species-normal way, we too

often understand our lives only in terms of alleged indignities that accompany chronic disability or long-term dependence on others. The Aristotelian can affirm the notion that human well-being is vulnerable and fragile, but that we still can respond to our situations in more or less virtuous ways, being grateful, for example, that we can be loved by others (Lott 2016). In other words, even in cases where external circumstances greatly limit what goods we are capable of achieving, there are still relevant ethical precepts (virtues) that can enable us to live well under the circumstances (MacIntyre 1999).

We have all been influenced enough by modern sensibilities to know that our response to the grass-counter (and to the person addicted to drugs and to the person who dates a real jerk) is supposed to be "Who am I to judge?" But I think we also know deep down that this person makes an objectively bad choice for his life. The choice is unethical in so far as it prevents the person from realizing his species-specific good. I suggest that suicide is roughly in the same boat. The question is whether we will develop the premodern resources necessary to be honest with ourselves and each other in acknowledging suicide's discontents. If we see human persons as belonging to each other, as members of a community, attempting to realize together our species-specific ends, then the permissibility of suicide becomes far less intelligible.[11]

Notes

1. While Hume's argument has a structural similarity to Aquinas's, he is in fact not responding to Aquinas. For Aquinas, laws of nature are moral obligations that are parts of nature. For Hume, laws of nature are amoral, physical, deterministic laws that govern the universe. If Hume were intending to respond to Aquinas, he presumably would have tried to explain why laws of nature are the way he conceives them to be rather than the way Aquinas conceives them to be.
2. This criticism of Hume's essay is a common one, going back to the early nineteenth century. Even Thomas Holden (2005), who

recently aims to defend Hume's essay against its critics, acknowledges that this is a consequence of his view (but curiously does not regard it as an absurd consequence).

3. Some philosophers who define what is good for a person in terms of subjective desires and pleasures still distinguish the notion of a *meaningful* life as something different.

4. Using these as examples does not mean that every instance of leaving one's family or one's spouse are instances of individualism gone wrong.

5. It is common nowadays for philosophers and psychologists to divide the question about whether suicide is rational from the question of whether suicide is moral. This division is a peculiarly modern move (made possible in no small part by Hume), where a narrow construal of ethics is coupled with a narrow construal of rationality. It's rational to commit suicide, in this narrow sense of rationality, if there is a high probability that a person's future suffering would significantly outweigh her future happiness. I think that it's fairly obvious that a decision to deliberately end one's own life can be rational in this sense (though it is also rare among the actual cases of suicide). It could also be rational to cannibalize someone in the narrow sense. On a broader view of rationality, however, if someone ought not to do something because it is unethical, then these choices would not be rational.

6. There is, of course, a fairly strong consensus in the fields of mental and public health that suicide ought to be prevented. This does not, however, show that my story about modernity's embrace of the permissibility of suicide is incorrect. Mental and public health officials work against suicidal behavior on the grounds that it stems from mental illness. It is in fact confirmation of my understanding of modernity that the only way we can justify interfering with an individual's choice is to convince ourselves that the choice stems from illness and so does not truly belong to the individual.

7. The history of suicide is controversial; for some support for this line of thinking, see, e.g., Hecht (2013) and Durkheim (2006).

8. The most significant exception to the consensus against suicide in the premodern era was the ancient school of Stoicism. But even the Stoics do not seem to condone suicide out of despair or suffering.

9. See Aristotle (1999) and MacIntyre (2016).

10. Suicide can, of course, sometimes prevent some bads. However, it does so in a way that thwarts the person, being dead, from realizing what is good for him. In this respect, using suicide to prevent bad things is somewhat like aborting female fetuses in an effort to prevent them from experiencing discrimination against women.

11. I'm grateful to Jim Delaney, David Hershenov, John Keller, the editors of this volume, and my students in The Ethics of Killing in the spring of 2019 for helpful feedback on previous versions of this essay.

Bibliography

Aristotle. 1999. *Nicomachean Ethics*. Translated by Terence Irwin. 2nd edn. Indianapolis, IN: Hackett Publishing Co.

Brassington, Iain. 2006. "Killing People: What Kant Could Have Said about Suicide and Euthanasia But Did Not." *Journal of Medical Ethics: The Journal of the Institute of Medical Ethics* 32 (10): 571–574.

Durkheim, Émile. 2006. *On Suicide*. Translated by Robin Buss. New York, NY: Penguin.

Dworkin, Ronald, Thomas Nagel, Robert Nozick, John Rawls, Judith Jarvis Thomson, and Thomas Scanlon. 1997. "Assisted Suicide: The Philosophers' Brief." *New York Review of Books*, 27 March. www.nybooks.com/articles/1997/03/27/assisted-suicide-the-philosophers-brief/.

Hecht, Jennifer Michael. 2013. *Stay: A History of Suicide and the Philosophies against It*. New Haven, CT: Yale University Press.

Holden, Thomas. 2005. "Religion and Moral Prohibition in Hume's 'Of Suicide'." *Hume Studies* 31 (2): 189–210.

Joiner, Thomas. 2007. *Why People Die by Suicide*. Cambridge, MA: Harvard University Press.

Lott, Micah. 2016. "Agency, Patiency, and the Good Life: The Passivities Objection to Eudaimonism." *Ethical Theory and Moral Practice* 19: 773–786.

MacIntyre, Alasdair. 1999. *Dependent Rational Animals: Why Human Beings Need the Virtues*. Chicago, IL: Open Court.

MacIntyre, Alasdair. 2016. *Ethics in the Conflicts of Modernity*. Cambridge: Cambridge University Press.

Rawls, John. 1971. *A Theory of Justice*. Cambridge, MA: Harvard University Press.

34 An Irrational Suicide?

Jukka Varelius

I. Introduction

For over a year now, Ethan has had troubles with his studies. He finds most of the available courses far too abstract. This has compromised his motivation, resulting in several failed grades. His consequent anxiousness about his prospects turned his girlfriend's hopes of a bright future with him into bitter quarrels between the couple. Then Ethan's parents announced that, now that he is safely in college, they will get a divorce. Ethan has found all this quite depressing. Eventually, during yet another beery evening, he tells his roommate, Liam, that he has decided to kill himself. The kind of suffering my life is, Ethan says, I would just be better off dead. Liam had expected that something like this might be forthcoming. Yet he finds Ethan's idea of killing himself quite irrational.

Unfortunately, situations in which people end up killing themselves are not rare. According to the World Health Organization (2018), globally a person dies from suicide every forty seconds and suicide is the second-highest cause of death among 15–29-year-olds. According to Centers of Disease Control and Prevention (2018), the national suicide rate in the United States rose 25.4% from 1999 to 2016. Suicide has also drawn attention from philosophers for over two millennia (see, e.g., Pabst Battin 2015). Yet even defining the concept has turned out to be quite tricky. Does, say, a terminally ill patient who knowingly refuses vital therapy commit suicide? What about a soldier leaping on a live grenade so as to save her comrades? Due to questions such as these, some philosophers think that suicide may not be strictly definable at all.[1]

Also the other central question arising in connection with suicide, the question whether suicide is justifiable, remains debated. Some authors maintain that suicide can never be warranted whereas some others argue that it can sometimes be even obligatory (see, e.g., Cholbi 2010; Hardwig 1997). Many philosophers hold an intermediate position of one or another kind. Some maintain that suicide is permissible when one is tired of life, whereas some others think that suicide can be acceptable only in the cases of unbearably suffering terminally ill patients, for two examples.[2] Most centrally, the question whether suicide can be warranted relates to rationality and morality. The problem whether suicide can be rational is typically seen to concern the justifiability of killing oneself from the viewpoint of the suicide candidate. Assessments of the morality of suicide usually take the viewpoints of others into account too or focus on some particular kind(s) of impersonal perspective.

Consider that Ethan is serious about ending his life and that he would, say, take a lethal amount of drugs so as to kill himself, thereby permanently stopping his vital functions. That would, I take it, clearly be suicide.[3] Given that it would not be an exceptional suicide case and that cases similar to Ethan's might be of special interest to the primary audience of this volume, my concentrating on Ethan's predicament is, I assume, warranted. More precisely, I focus on the concern Liam has about Ethan's killing himself. As considerations of rationality and morality can overlap, the following reflections need not be morally irrelevant.[4] Yet the main question concentrated on below is whether it would be irrational of Ethan to commit suicide. I approach the question from a non-religious Western viewpoint. Some references to historical figures notwithstanding, I focus on what can be counted as contemporary views. Finally, I use the expression "to commit suicide" interchangeably with those of killing oneself and ending one's life.

II. Reasons for Considering Suicide Irrational and Ethan's Case

On the basis of lay attitudes towards killing oneself and philosophical research on suicide it is possible to distinguish three main grounds for thinking that ending one's life is irrational.[5] First, suicide is incomprehensible. Second, suicide is insane. Third, suicide is unreasonable.[6] Let us consider these three views in connection with Ethan's case.

II.1 Suicide Is Incomprehensible

As proposed, that Ethan would commit suicide would mean, roughly, that he would purposely act in a way that permanently stops his vital functions. Afterwards he might live in the memories of some people, but there would be no actual life for him anymore. Given that this much is clear, the view that Ethan's killing himself would be incomprehensible would plausibly rather concern his reason for wanting to end his life than what his killing himself would be about. Indeed, it has been maintained that the idea that someone would be better off dead is unintelligible. Two main grounds have been presented for the view. First, thinking that one would be better off dead presupposes knowing what it is like to be dead, but nobody has adequate experience of being dead (see, e.g., Clarke 1999; Devine 1978). Second, that one could be better off dead presupposes that a corpse has experiences, but corpses don't have experiences (see, e.g., Donnelly 1979).

However, from a non-religious perspective at least, death terminates one as an experiencing being. Accordingly, Ethan's view that he would be better off dead is based on his comparing his distressed existence with his altogether ceasing to have experiences (see also, e.g., Feldman 1994; Luper 2009). The latter would assumedly be something like falling into permanent dreamless sleep. Thinking what that would be like does not presuppose knowing what it is like to be dead—or that there is something it is like to be dead—nor believing that corpses have experiences (see also, e.g., Pabst Battin 1999). Hence, the two reasons for thinking that suicide is incomprehensible would both appear to be beside the point.

Given that many people have apparently endured much worse difficulties than Ethan is now facing, it could still be taken that it would be unfathomable of Ethan to now kill himself. Yet how one experiences things depends on such factors as one's temperament, personal history, and worldview. As these kinds of factors can vary from one person to another, objectively similar circumstances can give rise to subjectively dissimilar experiences (see also, e.g., Cassell 2004, ch. 3; cf. Wijsbek 2012). Looking at Ethan's predicament from a perspective that does not duly account for how his life feels for him would neglect the central reason why Ethan wants to end his life. Accordingly, whether suicide would be comprehensible in his case should plausibly be assessed from his viewpoint, not from those of other people possibly quite unable to see things his way. And looking at his life from Ethan's perspective, suicide would not be unfathomable.

II.2 Suicide Is Insane

The view that suicide is insane has two central interpretations. First, ending one's life is insane because, or when, it is impulsive. Second, suicide is insane because, or when, it is based on mental illness.[7] The impulsivity of suicide usually refers to shortness of the time taken to make the decision to kill oneself and/or to the paucity of the time between making the decision and acting on it. However, while up to 80% of suicide attempts have been estimated to be impulsive, it has been proposed that people seldom end their lives impulsively (see, e.g., Rimkeviciene et al. 2015). According to Thomas Joiner (2007), for instance, people who kill themselves typically work up to the act over a long period of time during which they so to speak habituate themselves to ending their life. Hence, even an apparently impulsive suicide need not necessarily be insane in the sense that it would not be grounded on thorough premeditation. Ethan has planned suicide for several months already and does not intend to act on his decision to end his life right away. Hence, were Ethan to carry out his suicide plan at some later stage, his ending his life would presumably be impulsive only if deliberate suicide presupposed planning for, say, at least a year ahead.[8] Yet there would not appear to be sufficient reason to deem all suicides that are not based on premeditation of such length impulsive.

Ethan's depression may be deep enough for him to count as mentally disordered, at least to a degree. The level of depression can make him perceive only negative possibilities, or at least significantly color his perception of his options, and lead him to see his bad prospects as more probable than they really are. Depression may also weaken one's ability to predict how well one is able to adapt to one's circumstances and to forecast how one will react to predictable future events. Accordingly, one's depression may compromise one's ability to adequately assess one's situation and undermine one's motivation to live (see, e.g., Brandt 1992: 328–332; Pabst Battin 1999: 16). Yet, by becoming aware of how it may affect his thinking, Ethan could assumedly at least weaken the effects his depression has on how he sees his circumstances. And, in any case, that one's conception of one's situation and prospects is as pessimistic as Ethan's need not necessarily mean that the conception is unrealistic.

Moreover, the distress one undergoes may also be the more agonizing for one the more one is in the throes of mental disorder. For the feelings one experiences when mentally disordered can be of disproportionate intensity. And being mentally disordered can make one unable to adopt a detached viewpoint to one's distress, for another example. For reasons

such as these, Ethan may now suffer even worse than he would were he in full mental health. Given that his desire to end his life is based on the suffering he undergoes, his being mentally disordered could thus provide Ethan with more rather than less reason to kill himself (see also, e.g., Hawton and Burgess 1998; Hardcastle and Stewart 2002). Hence, even if Ethan's suicide decision were insane in the sense of being based on or affected by mental disorder that as such would not necessarily make suicide irrational in his case.

II.3 Suicide Is Unreasonable

The view that suicide is unreasonable is usually based on one or more of the following five ideas. First, suicide is not natural. Second, death deprives one of life's goods (see, e.g., Bradley 2009).[9] Third, human life has inherent value that suicide eradicates. Fourth, ending one's life involves pursuing a good by destroying its purported beneficiary (see, e.g., Korsgaard 1996; Velleman 1999). Fifth, the desire to kill oneself is always dictated by circumstances: suicide is never what one really wants (see, e.g., Campbell 1999).

A natural death is usually conceived as one caused by severe disease or old age. Given that dying from old age appears preferable to dying as a result of such a non-natural cause as, say, violence, desiring a non-natural death can seem unreasonable. However, when intense distress deprives one of possibility to lead what one considers a life worth living, ending one's life does not seem unreasonable. Accordingly, the view that suicide is unreasonable because killing oneself is not natural raises the question why a non-natural death would always be unreasonable. That suicide interferes with what is considered the natural course of events does not qualify as a plausible answer. For such generally accepted things like, say, restoring the health of a seriously injured person can also interfere with the natural course of events. Hence, the mere fact that something interferes with what is seen as the natural run of things apparently does not make that something unreasonable (see also, e.g., Hume 1755).

Sometimes suicide is deemed unnatural because it is seen to conflict with natural human instincts. Yet although humans would appear to have a natural instinct to, say, violence, few maintain that people should always act according to it. In other words, it is not clear that natural instincts should always be obeyed. Moreover, as suggested by Ethan's case, people can apparently sometimes lose the instinct to live. That suicide is not natural might also mean that suicide is abnormal. If what is thereby claimed is that suicide is unusual, the claim is false, as unfortunately many people do end their lives. And, in any case, that something is unusual does not as such mean that it is unreasonable. If suicide is deemed abnormal in the sense of being rationally unacceptable, the view needs to be complemented with good reasons for why suicide would be rationally unacceptable.

Its depriving him of life's goods would presumably make suicide unreasonable in Ethan's case only if his life included enough good things to outweigh his suffering. Yet as Ethan sees his predicament, there are not enough good things in his life to outbalance his distress and no sufficient reason to believe that there ever will be. The position that a human life has inherent value that suicide would eradicate does not presuppose that an individual himself sees his life as valuable. However, even if a human life always had some value independently of what the person living it thinks, the prevalence of suicide suggests that the value can sometimes be outweighed by the suffering human existence can involve.

If Ethan's reason for killing himself were, say, that people would finally take him seriously, by ending his life he might destroy the purported beneficiary of the deed. At least he would no longer be around to be taken seriously thereafter. It has been proposed that several people who commit suicide tend to assume that even after death they continue to have experiences, to interact with others, and to play a causal role in the world (Pabst Battin 1999: 14). Yet, as explained, Ethan wants to kill himself because he wants his suffering to end. Because he would thereafter no longer

be around to experience things, his committing suicide would be a certain way for Ethan to achieve the goal. In other words, by ending his life Ethan would not act in a self-defeating way (see also, e.g., Clark 1998). Although some suicides would destroy the purported beneficiary of the act, not all of them involve the mistake (see also, e.g., Pabst Battin 1999: 14).

Ethan would not want to kill himself were he not undergoing overwhelming distress. Thus, death is not what he wants most. He would rather want a life free from undue suffering. Seen from that perspective, Ethan's ending his life does appear unreasonable. Yet, in formulating her desires a reasonable person takes her circumstances duly into account even when the circumstances are unfortunate. A gravely ill patient, for instance, would typically not want to undergo a risky, burdensome operation were she healthy. But that clearly does not entail that it would be irrational of her to have the operation under the circumstances she actually faces. Similarly, that Ethan would not want to kill himself were he not suffering gravely, or that life free from undue suffering is what he would want most, does not show that suicide would be unreasonable in his actual circumstances. In view of these considerations, suicide would not appear to be irrational in the sense of unreasonable in Ethan's case.

III. Would Suicide Be Rational in Ethan's Case?

However, as Ethan's central goal now is ending his suffering, whether it would be rational of him to commit suicide depends on whether dying is the only way of stopping his distress. Is it? Unfortunately, there are people who never seem to find their lives worth living. And some philosophers maintain that human life is always predominated by suffering. According to Arthur Schopenhauer (1788–1860), for instance, "the world is Hell, and men are on the one hand the tormented souls and on the other the devils in it" (Schopenhauer 2004: 48). If human existence can't be anything but distress, suicide would appear to be the way to avoid suffering.[10]

Yet if one is convinced that human existence must always be predominated by suffering, one's central problem would appear to lie with one's expectations towards life. Many people do manage to have lives they find worth living, some individuals are even very pleased with their existence.[11] Their assessment of their lives would not seem to be necessarily false. Neither have they all been lucky enough to avoid things that make life difficult. Indeed, several flourishing people have apparently endured even worse adversities than the ones now troubling Ethan. That suggests, not that Ethan's suffering is not overwhelming for him now, but that Ethan does not necessarily belong to the group of people whose whole lives are predominated by distress. Assumedly, his life could get better for him.

Accordingly, it would now be rational of Ethan to further consider the reasons behind his suffering. If the studies he is pursuing really are overly abstract for a person of his disposition, he would do well to, say, try a more practical major. By pursuing a career more suitable for him, he might also be able to reconcile with his girlfriend and perhaps even to avoid the kind of problems that destroyed the marriage of his parents. If his girlfriend is ready for good times only, perhaps Ethan would do both of them a favor by seeking a more mature relationship. Yes, all this might well sound overly speculative to Ethan, as desperate as he now is. Yet that the kind of possibilities remain open supports the view that suicide is not the only way for Ethan to get rid of his distress. Therefore, the answer to the question whether suicide would be rational in Ethan's case is no. Contrary to what Ethan now thinks, what he wants most—a life free of undue suffering—may well be achievable for him after all. This is not to say that suicide would always be irrational. Sometimes the prospect that a person can overcome the predicament that makes her want to die is very improbable (see, e.g., Brandt 1992; McCue 2017; Pabst Battin 1999). In such cases, committing suicide can be a more rational choice than desperately clinging on to false hope.

IV. Conclusion

Above we briefly considered the central contemporary lines of argument for the view that suicide is irrational in connection with a case of a young person who faces obstacles he finds grave enough to make him think that he would be better off dead. I proposed that the arguments do not show that suicide would be irrational in the person's case. Yet I also maintained that, as dying need not be the only way of ending his suffering, it would be irrational of the individual to commit suicide. As proposed, the considerations I presented do not imply that suicide can never be rational: some other cases can be importantly different from the one focused on above. On the other hand, as the justifiability of suicide depends on moral issues too,[12] even a rational suicide may not be warranted all things considered.[13]

Notes

1. For discussion on the definition of suicide and suicidal behavior, see, e.g., Beauchamp (1993), Cholbi (2011), Luper (2009), and Torisky (2015).
2. For discussion on different positions on suicide, see, e.g., Beauchamp (1993), Dworkin (2007), Luper (2009), and Pabst Battin (1996, 1999).
3. Accordingly, if a purported definition of the ordinary language meaning of "suicide" entails that Ethan's acting in that way would not be suicide that would arguably be an adequate reason to reject the definition. Yet the notion of suicide might also be used in, say, a metaphorical sense in which Ethan's acting in the above described way would not be suicide.
4. Indeed, some of the lines of thinking considered below have also been used in arguing for the view that suicide is immoral.
5. It has also been proposed that the concept of rationality does not apply to suicide because rationality is a future-oriented concept and suicide deprives one of a future (Cowley 2006). Yet Ethan's killing himself would be future-oriented in the sense that he would thereby aim to avoid the suffering that he believes continuing his life to entail. On the other hand, all considerations of rationality are not future-oriented (see p. 236).

6. Someone might also maintain, for instance, that ending one's life is insane because suicide is incomprehensible. The above classification is primarily expository.

7. Mental disorder is reported to be a causal factor in about 90% of suicides. Major depression is estimated to increase the odds of suicide by twenty times. The suicide rate of (untreated) bipolar patients – whose suicidal behavior reportedly occurs almost exclusively during severe major depressive episodes – is estimated to be 25 times higher than the same rate in the general population, see, e.g., Rihmer (2009), Stack (2014), and Windfuhr and Kapur (2011).

8. The case would be different were Ethan to first cancel his decision to end his life and then all of a sudden kill himself after all.

9. According to the ancient Greek philosopher Epicurus (341–270 BC), death is nothing to us "since when we exist, death is not yet present, and when death is present, then we do not exist" (Epicurus 1994: 29). The view is often objected to by reference to the idea that death deprives one of life's goods. For pertinent discussion, see, e.g., Bradley (2009) and Olson (2013).

10. One might also escape suffering by, say, inducing oneself into a coma. Yet such an option would not appear to be more rational for one than death.

11. Some people are also able to find meaning in the suffering they experience.

12. For discussion on the morality of suicide see, e.g., Cholbi (2011), Luper (2009), Pabst Battin (1996), and Section VIII of this volume.

13. FI thank Michael Cholbi and Travis Timmerman for their helpful comments

References

Beauchamp, Tom L. 1993. "Suicide." In Tom Regan, ed. *Matters of Life and Death: New Introductory Essays in Moral Philosophy*, 3rd edn. New York: McGraw-Hill, 69–120.

Bradley, Ben. 2009. *Well-Being and Death*. New York: Oxford University Press.

Brandt, Richard B. 1992. *Morality, Utilitarianism, and Rights*. New York: Cambridge University Press.

Campbell, Neil. 1999. "A Problem for the Idea of Voluntary Euthanasia." *Journal of Medical Ethics* 25(3): 242–244.

Cassell, Eric. 2004. *The Nature of Suffering and the Goals of Medicine*, 2nd edn. New York: Oxford University Press.

Centers of Disease Control and Prevention. 2018. *Vital Signs: Suicide Rising Across USA*. www.cdc.gov/vitalsigns/suicide/infographic.html. Accessed 26 October 2018.

Cholbi, Michael. 2010. "The Duty to Die and the Burdensomeness of Living." *Bioethics* 24(8): 412–420.

Cholbi, Michael. 2011. *Suicide: The Philosophical Dimensions*. Peterborough, ON: Broadview Press.

Clark, Michael. 1998. "Euthanasia and the Slippery Slope." *Journal of Applied Philosophy* 15(3): 251–257.

Clarke, David M. 1999. "Autonomy, Rationality and the Wish to Die." *Journal of Medical Ethics* 25(6): 457–462.

Cowley, Christopher. 2006. "Suicide Is Neither Rational Nor Irrational." *Ethical Theory and Moral Practice* 9(5): 495–504.

Devine, Philip E. 1978. *The Ethics of Homicide*. Ithaca, NY: Cornell University Press.

Donnelly, John. 1979. "Suicide and Rationality." In John Donnelly, ed. *Language, Metaphysics, and Death*. New York: Fordham University Press, 88–105.

Dworkin, Gerald. 2007. "Physician-Assisted Death: The State of the Debate." In Bonnie Steinbock, ed. *The Oxford Handbook of Bioethics*. New York: Oxford University Press, 375–392.

Epicurus. 1994. "Letter to Menoeceus." In Brad Inwood and L.P. Gerson, eds. *The Epicurus Reader: Selected Writings and Testimonia*. Indianapolis, IN: Hackett Publishing Company Inc., 28–32.

Feldman, Fred. 1994. *Confrontations with the Reaper: A Philosophical Study of the Nature and Value of Death*. Cary, NC: Oxford University Press.

Hardcastle, Valerie G. and Rosalyn W. Stewart. 2002. "Supporting Irrational Suicide." *Bioethics* 16(5): 425–438.

Hardwig, John. 1997. "Is There a Duty to Die?" *Hastings Center Report* 27(2): 34–42.

Hawton, Keith, and Sally Burgess. 1998. "Suicide, Euthanasia, and the Psychiatrist." *Philosophy, Psychiatry, and Psychology* 5(2): 113–126.

Hume, David. 1755. *Of Suicide*. Chapter 31 of this volume.

Joiner, Thomas. 2007. *Why People Die by Suicide*. Cambridge, MA: Harvard University Press.

Korsgaard, Christine M. 1996. *Creating the Kingdom of Ends*. Cambridge: Cambridge University Press.

Luper, Steven. 2009. *Philosophy of Death*. Cambridge: Cambridge University Press.

McCue, Robert E. 2017. "Would This Be Rational Suicide?" In Robert E. McCue and Meera Balasubramaniam, eds. *Rational Suicide in the Elderly*. New York: Springer, 23–32.

Olson, Eric T. 2013. "The Epicurean View of Death." *Journal of Ethics* 17(1–2): 65–78.

Pabst Battin, Margaret. 1996. *The Death Debate: Ethical Issues in Suicide*. Upper Saddle River, NJ: Prentice-Hall.

Pabst Battin, Margaret. 1999. "Can Suicide Be Rational? Yes, Sometimes." In James L. Werth, Jr., ed. *Contemporary Perspectives on Rational Suicide*. Philadelphia, PA: Brunner/Mazel, 13–21.

Pabst Battin, Margaret, ed. 2015. *The Ethics of Suicide*. New York: Oxford University Press.

Rihmer, Zoltán. 2009. "Suicide and Bipolar Disorder." In Carlos A. Zarate and Husseini K. Manji, eds. *Bipolar Depression: Molecular Neurobiology, Clinical Diagnosis and Pharmacotherapy*. Basel: Birkhäuser/Springer, 47–56.

Rimkeviciene, Jurgita, John O'Gorman, and Diego De Leo. 2015. "Impulsive Suicide Attempts: A Systematic Literature Review." *Journal of Affective Disorders* 171: 93–104.

Schopenhauer, Arthur. 2004. *Essays and Aphorisms*. London: Penguin Books.

Stack, Steven John. 2014. "Mental Illness and Suicide." In William C. Cockerham, Robert Dingwall, and Stella R. Quah, eds. *The Wiley Blackwell Encyclopedia of Health, Illness, Behavior, and Society*. https://doi.org/10.1002/9781118410868. wbehibs067.

Torisky, Eugene V. 2015. "Minimally Intentional Suicide and 'The Falling Man'." *Journal of Value Inquiry* 49(1–2): 69–79.

Velleman, J. David. 1999. "A Right of Self-Termination?" *Ethics* 109(3): 606–628.

WHO. 2018. *Suicide: Key Facts*. www.who.int/news-room/fact-sheets/detail/suicide. Accessed 26 October 2018.

Wijsbek, Henri. 2012. "The Subjectivity of Suffering and the Normativity of Unbearableness." In Stuart J. Youngner and Gerrit K. Kimsma, eds. *Physician-Assisted Death in Perspective: Assessing the Dutch Experience*. New York: Cambridge University Press, 319–332.

Windfuhr, Kirsten, and Navneet Kapur. 2011. "Suicide and Mental Illness: A Clinical Review of 15 Years Findings from the UK National Confidential Inquiry into Suicide." *British Medical Bulletin* 100: 101–121.

Part IX How Does Death Affect the Meaningfulness of Our Lives?

The Road Not Taken

Two roads diverged in a yellow wood,
And sorry I could not travel both
And be one traveler, long I stood
And looked down one as far as I could
To where it bent in the undergrowth;

Then took the other, as just as fair
And having perhaps the better claim,
Because it was grassy and wanted wear;
Though as for that, the passing there
Had worn them really about the same,

And both that morning equally lay
In leaves no step had trodden black
Oh, I kept the first for another day!
Yet knowing how way leads on to way,
I doubted if I should ever come back.

I shall be telling this with a sigh
Somewhere ages and ages hence:
Two roads diverged in a wood, and I,
I took the one less traveled by,
And that has made all the difference.

—Robert Lee Frost

Introduction to Part IX

Ask any layperson for an example of a philosophical question and there is a good chance they will say some variant of "What is the meaning of life?" It's ironic, then, that questions about meaning in life are largely ignored by contemporary philosophers. This section helps rectify that omission, and includes three contemporary philosophers' take on how (if at all) death affects the meaningfulness of our lives. Their chapters are preceded by excerpts from a classic text on this issue.

The initial text you will consider is a series of excerpts from Arthur Schopenhauer's magnum opus *The World as Will and Representation*. Schopenhauer's rich systematic philosophy defies any short summary, but it's worth noting that Schopenhauer is the father of pessimism, the view that human life consists of so much suffering and strife, without any ultimate meaning or compensating goods, that it's better not to have existed in the first place. Though it's a bit anachronistic to use the term pessimism (Schopenhauer himself didn't), he gave numerous arguments for a pessimistic view. Most notably, he argued we live in the worst of all possible worlds, that human life contains more pain than pleasure, and that even if it didn't, no amount of good in life can (morally) justify any amount of (undeserved) suffering. Schopenhauer's central argument is that human essence is, at bottom, willing or striving, which produces desire and need. Life consists in having those desires and needs either thwarted (which is bad for us) or satisfied (which only alleviates some badness temporarily). Once some desires or needs are satisfied, old ones reemerge or we develop new ones. But this cycle continues throughout our life with the bad outweighing the good. As Schopenhauer bleakly puts it, "All life is suffering."

The contemporary philosophical chapters on meaning are not so pessimistic. You'll first get to read Kathy Behrendt's paper, which seeks to answer the question "Does thinking about our death help us maximize the meaningfulness in our lives?" She shows that the answer to this question depends on how we accrue meaning in our lives. Suppose *additivism* is true, which is to suppose that we accrue meaning by engaging in a series of meaningful activities whose meaningfulness cannot be enhanced or diminished by whatever other activities one pursues in their life. On such a view, maximizing meaning requires generally not thinking about one's death, except in extenuating circumstances, since doing so might distract one from their ability to complete various meaningful activities. On the other hand, if meaning is accrued holistically on a pure whole-life view (e.g. achievementism, narrativism), then the meaningfulness of our lives is determined not just by the sum of meaningful events, but also by their connection with one another. On these views, thinking about one's death is generally good, as it allows one to ensure past hardships are redeemed, and optimal unity among one's life is achieved. Finally, one could accept middle-ground views (e.g. engagementism), where meaning is accrued non-cumulatively by engaging in meaningful projects, whether or not they're completed. Thinking about one's death may be neutral, as it needn't typically hinder or enhance one's ability to engage in such projects.

The next chapter, by Thaddeus Metz, explores how both mortal and immortal lives can be meaningful. Metz begins by considering, and rebutting, three arguments that mortal lives are necessarily meaningless. More precisely, one might be concerned that a mortal life precludes the possibility of justice being done, of making a permanent difference in the world, and of having a kind of moral freedom. In response, Metz argues that a finite life is compatible with justice being done, that we can have meaningful lives in unjust worlds, that finite changes in the world can suffice for meaning, and that mortality and moral freedom are not mutually exclusive. Finally, Metz ends the article by raising a problem for finite lives that seem very meaningful, such as Gandhi's. While they may have some non-zero sum of meaning accrued, the meaning in their lives is comparably trivial relative to an infinite life that contains infinite meaning. Metz worries that it's a pyrrhic victory to hold that, say, Gandhi's life wasn't meaningless, but it was practically meaningless in comparison to an infinite being's infinitely meaningful life.

This section ends with Michael Hauskeller's more optimistic chapter, where he argues that mortality does not *in any way* compromise people's ability to live meaningful lives. Early on Hauskeller considers Albert Camus' *Myth of Sisyphus*, which serves as the paradigmatic example of a meaningless life. For believing he was smarter than the gods, Sisyphus was condemned to continuously roll a giant boulder up a hill only to have it roll back down again ad infinitum. Hauskeller notes that Sisyphus' life seems meaningless because he is (a) engaging in a repetitive task (b) where his efforts are futile and so he (c) doesn't ever accomplish anything. Moreover, he is condemned to do this for an eternity. This shows that an immortal life can be meaningless too. In the rest of the chapter, Hauskeller considers how our mortal lives might also seem to be subject to (a)–(c) and argues that, in actuality, they are not. Contrary to (a), while typical human lives contain lots of repetition, it's a kind of repetition that can add meaning to our lives. Moreover, typical human lives contain many novel experiences as well. Contrary to (b) and (c), our efforts to accomplish goals are not futile. Our accomplishments can make the world better, and once they do, that cannot be changed even if the improvement is only temporary.

If you're interested in more readings on meaning in life and death, check out the following:

1. Susan Wolf's book *Meaning in Life and Why it Matters* (2010) Princeton University Press.
2. Thaddeus Metz's book *Meaning in Life* (2013) Oxford University Press.
3. Michael Sigrist's "Death and the Meaning of Life" (2015) *Philosophical Papers* 44 (1): 83–102.
4. Albert Camus' short story "The Myth of Sisyphus" (1942).

35 World as Will and Representation (excerpts)

Arthur Schopenhauer

Arthur Schopenhauer, *The World as Will and Representation*, 2nd edition, 1844, trans. R.B. Haldane and J. Kemp 7th edition (London: Kegan Paul, Trench, Trübner & Co., 1909) Supplements to the Fourth Book Chapter XLVI. 'On The Vanity And Suffering Of Life'

Awakened to life out of the night of unconsciousness, the will finds itself an individual, in an endless and boundless world, among innumerable individuals, all striving, suffering, erring; and as if through a troubled dream it hurries back to its old unconsciousness. Yet till then its desires are limitless, its claims inexhaustible, and every satisfied desire gives rise to a new one. No possible satisfaction in the world could suffice to still its longings, set a goal to its infinite cravings, and fill the bottomless abyss of its heart. Then let one consider what as a rule are the satisfactions of any kind that a man obtains. For the most part nothing more than the bare maintenance of this existence itself, extorted day by day with unceasing trouble and constant care in the conflict with want, and with death in prospect...

Life presents itself as a continual deception in small things as in great. If it has promised, it does not keep its word, unless to show how little worth desiring were the things desired: thus we are deluded now by hope, now by what was hoped for. If it has given, it did so in order to take. The enchantment of distance shows us paradises which vanish like optical illusions when we have allowed ourselves to be mocked by them. Happiness accordingly always lies in the future, or else in the past, and the present may be compared to a small dark cloud which the wind drives over the sunny plain: before and behind it all is bright, only it itself always casts a shadow. The present is therefore always insufficient; but the future is uncertain, and the past irrevocable. Life with its hourly, daily, weekly, yearly, little, greater, and great misfortunes, with its deluded hopes and its accidents destroying all our calculations, bears so distinctly the impression of something with which we must become disgusted, that it is hard to conceive how one has been able to mistake this and allow oneself to be persuaded that life is there in order to be happy. Rather that continual illusion and disillusion, and also the nature of life throughout, presents itself to us as intended and calculated to awaken the conviction that nothing at all is worth our striving, our efforts and struggles, that all good things are vanity, the world in all its ends bankrupt, and life a business which does not cover its expenses; – so that our will may turn away from it.

The way in which this vanity of all objects of the will makes itself known and comprehensible to the intellect which is rooted in the individual, is primarily *time*. It is the form by means of which that vanity of things appears as their perishableness; for on account of this all our pleasures and joys disappear in our hands, and we afterwards ask astonished where they have remained. That nothingness itself is therefore the only *objective* element in time, i.e., that which corresponds to it in the inner nature of things, thus that of which it is the expression.

... [O]ur life is like a payment which one receives in nothing but copper pence, and yet must then give a discharge for: the copper pence are the days; the discharge is death. For at last time makes known the judgment of nature concerning the work of all the beings which appear in it, in that it destroys them:

> And rightly so, for all that arises
> Is worthy only of being destroyed.
> Hence were it better that nothing arose.

Thus old age and death, to which every life necessarily hurries on, are the sentence of condemnation on the will to live, coming from the hands of nature itself, and which declares that this will is an effort which frustrates itself. "What thou hast wished," it says, "ends thus: desire something better." Hence the instruction which his life affords to every one consists, as a whole, in this, that the objects of his desires continually delude, waver, and fall, and accordingly bring more misery than joy, till at last the whole foundation upon which they all stand gives way, in that his life itself is destroyed and so he receives the last proof that all his striving and wishing was a perversity, a false path:

> Then old age and experience, hand in hand,
> Lead him to death, and make him understand,
> After a search so painful and so long,
> That all his life he has been in the wrong...

We feel pain, but not painlessness; we feel care, but not the absence of care; fear, but not security. We feel the wish as we feel hunger and thirst; but as soon as it has been fulfilled, it is like the mouthful that has been taken, which ceases to exist for our feeling the moment it is swallowed. Pleasures and joys we miss painfully whenever they are wanting; but pains, even when they cease after having long been present, are not directly missed, but at the most are intentionally thought of by means of reflection... In proportion as pleasures increase, the susceptibility for them decreases: what is customary is no longer felt as a pleasure. Just in this way, however, is the susceptibility for suffering increased, for the loss of what we are accustomed to is painfully felt. Thus the measure of what is necessary increases through possession, and thereby the capacity for feeling pain...

In general...the conduct of men towards each other is characterized as a rule by injustice, extreme unfairness, hardness, nay, cruelty: an opposite course of conduct appears only as an exception... How man deals with man is shown, for example, by negro slavery, the final end of which is sugar and coffee. But we do not need to go so far: at the age of five years to enter a cotton-spinning or other factory, and from that time forth to sit there daily, first ten, then twelve, and ultimately fourteen hours, performing the same mechanical labor, is to purchase dearly the satisfaction of drawing breath. But this is the fate of millions, and that of millions more is analogous to it...

And to this world, to this scene of tormented and agonised beings, who only continue to exist by devouring each other, in which, therefore, every ravenous beast is the living grave of thousands of others, and its self-maintenance is a chain of painful deaths; and in which the capacity for feeling pain increases with knowledge, and therefore reaches its highest degree in man, a degree which is the higher the more intelligent the man is; to this world it has been sought to apply the system of optimism, and demonstrate to us that it is the best of all possible worlds. The absurdity is glaring. But an optimist bids me open my eyes and look at the world, how beautiful it is in the sunshine, with its mountains and valleys, streams, plants, animals, &c. &c. Is the world, then, a raree-show? These things are certainly beautiful to *look at*, but to *be* them is something quite different. Then comes a teleologist, and praises to me the wise arrangement by virtue of which it is taken care that the planets do not run their heads together, that land and sea do not get mixed into a pulp, but are held so beautifully apart, also that everything is neither rigid with continual frost nor roasted with heat; in the same way, that in consequence of the obliquity of the ecliptic there is no eternal spring, in which nothing could attain to ripeness, &c. &c. But this and all like it are mere *conditiones sine quibus non* [conditions without which there is nothing – ed.]. If in general there is to be a world at all, if its planets are to exist at least as long as the light of a distant fixed star requires to reach them, and are not… to depart again immediately after birth, then certainly it must not be so clumsily constructed that its very framework threatens to fall to pieces. But if one goes on to the results of this applauded work, considers the players who act upon the stage which is so durably constructed, and now sees how with sensibility pain appears, and increases in proportion as the sensibility develops to intelligence, and then how, keeping pace with this, desire and suffering come out ever more strongly, and increase till at last human life affords no other material than this for tragedies and comedies, then whoever is honest will scarcely be disposed to set up hallelujahs.

Chapter XLIX. The Way of Salvation

There is only one inborn error, and that is, that we exist in order to be happy. It is inborn in us because it is one with our existence itself, and our whole being is only a paraphrase of it, nay, our body is its monogram. We are nothing more than will to live and the successive satisfaction of all our volitions is what we think in the conception of happiness.

As long as we persist in this inborn error, indeed even become rigidly fixed in it through optimistic dogmas, the world appears to us full of contradictions. For at every step, in great things as in small, we must experience that the world and life are by no means arranged with a view to containing a happy existence. While now by this the thoughtless man only finds himself tormented in reality, in the case of him who thinks there is added to his real pain the theoretical perplexity why a world and a life which exist in order that one may be happy in them answer their end so badly. First of all it finds expression in pious ejaculations, such as, "Ah! why are the tears on earth so many?" &c. &c. But in their train come disquieting doubts about the assumptions of those preconceived optimistic dogmas. One may try if one will to throw the blame of one's individual unhappiness now upon the circumstances, now upon other

men, now upon one's own bad luck, or even upon one's own awkwardness, and may know well how all these have worked together to produce it; but this in no way alters the result that one has missed the real end of life, which consists indeed in being happy. The consideration of this is, then, often very depressing, especially if life is already on the wane; hence the countenances of almost all elderly persons wear the expression of that which in English is called disappointment. Besides this, however, hitherto every day of our life has taught us that joys and pleasures, even if attained, are in themselves delusive, do not perform what they promise, do not satisfy the heart, and finally their possession is at least embittered by the disagreeables that accompany them or spring from them; while, on the contrary, the pains and sorrows prove themselves very real, and often exceed all expectation. Thus certainly everything in life is calculated to recall us from that original error, and to convince us that the end of our existence is not to be happy. Indeed, if we regard it more closely and without prejudice, life rather presents itself as specially intended to be such that we shall not feel ourselves happy in it, for through its whole nature it bears the character of something for which we have no taste, which must be endured by us, and from which we have to return as from an error that our heart may be cured of the passionate desire of enjoyment, nay, of life, and turned away from the world. In this sense, it would be more correct to place the end of life in our woe than in our welfare. For the considerations at the conclusion of the preceding chapter have shown that the more one suffers the sooner one attains to the true end of life, and that the more happily one lives the longer this is delayed.

… a certain awe, kindred to that which great suffering occasions us, is felt in the presence of every dead person, indeed every case of death presents itself to a certain extent as a kind of apotheosis or canonisation; therefore we cannot look upon the dead body of even the most insignificant man without awe, and indeed, extraordinary as the remark may sound in this place, in the presence of every corpse the watch goes under arms. Dying is certainly to be regarded as the real aim of life: in the moment of death all that is decided for which the whole course of life was only the preparation and introduction. Death is the result,... the added up sum which expresses at once the instruction which life gave in detail, and bit by bit; this, that the whole striving whose manifestation is life was a vain, idle, and self-contradictory effort, to have returned from which is a deliverance.

36 Death in Mind

Life, Meaning, and Mortality

Kathy Behrendt

Introduction: The Meaning Mandate

Many people wish to maximize meaningfulness in their lives. Let's call the impulse to do this the *meaning mandate*. My overriding question is: does thinking about our death help us fulfill the meaning mandate? I don't mean "help" in the sense of prompt us to drive safely and not stick forks into electrical outlets; basic self-preservation doesn't require deep philosophical reflection. By "thinking about our death" I mean dwelling on it reflectively. And by "death" I mean the fact of mortality, not the specifics of the event of your death.

One way of approaching the question is by considering how life accrues meaning. Does life involve separate segments of local meaning? Or is meaning global—a matter of relations between the parts of a life? Thaddeus Metz calls the first view the "pure part-life view" of meaning, and the second the "pure whole-life view" (2013, ch. 3). I will show that whether or to what extent thinking about your mortality contributes to fulfilling the meaning mandate will depend, in part, on which of these views you hold.

Part-Life Meaning: Additivism

"I imagine looking back, counting my achievements and failures, wondering 'What do they add up to after all?'" (Setiya 2014, 14). This is a sensible question from the viewpoint of what I'll call *additivism*. The additivist treats meaning in life as the sum of segments of meaning one enjoys throughout that life. You cook a meal, play with a child, volunteer at a shelter…. In theory, any activity could contribute to fulfilling the meaning mandate for the additivist, so long as it satisfies one condition central to any part-life view: that meaning and activity coincide. Since the meaning of any individual life-segment is not dependent on its relation to anything else, upon the part-life view, the activity has to be its own reward (see Sigrist 2015, 85–86). Fulfilling the meaning mandate is then regarded as a matter of amassing a large sum of such meaning-units. While meaningful experiences can be short or long, you can presumably stockpile more units by forgoing long-term projects. You can attend a thousand concerts in the time it would take you to compose your own symphony. And short-term, easily undertaken activity is less risky, since the meaning-payoff is immediate—an asset on this quantitatively driven model of meaning-accrual.

The implication of death for additivism is straightforward: death prevents us from maximizing meaning if there are further meaningful events or activities we could participate in. The only way actively to avoid this *too-soon problem* is to ensure that prior to death no further meaningful experiences are available to us. We could, for instance, take a psychotropic drug to wipe our memory and impair our cognitive capacity, and then lock ourselves into a sensory-deprivation tank and swallow the key. Death, in this circumstance, would be acceptable, since acquiring further meaning seems unlikely. But actively averting further meaning in order to prevent death depriving us of it is like "bulldozing one's house to ensure that no one can harm us by burning it down" (Luper 2013, 102). It's hardly a rational strategy for combating the threat death poses. Without such a strategy to hand, death will likely come too soon for the additivist, from the perspective of fulfilling the meaning mandate.

If death deprives us of more meaning in life, and there's no viable way to avoid this, we may be better off keeping death far from our minds. Thinking about it could interfere with the subjective fulfillment we otherwise get from our activities, which in turn may detract from their meaningfulness.[1] There might be times when thinking of death is of practical use; e.g., in the face of serious decline, it may be wise to do a hard accounting of how much meaning we stand to gain from continuing to live, relative to how much suffering we expect to endure. But in most circumstances, amassing meaning-units doesn't call for long-term planning, and so the temporal limit that mortality imposes on us doesn't bear contemplating. Death perpetually threatens the accumulation of more meaning in life for additivists, and there's little they can rationally do to circumvent this.

Additivism arguably has limited potential for realizing meaning in life. The more meaningful events and activities in life are typically thought to be those that provide deep subjective satisfaction and/or are objectively attractive.[2] And for these, "the success and satisfaction conditions are non-simultaneous with the actions to which they belong" (Sigrist 2015, 86). They take time before they yield meaning, and may fail to do so at all; the risk that they may fail perhaps enhances their meaningfulness (ibid., 100). And they can involve effort or sacrifice, which may also be integral; there is arguably a connection between meaningfulness and transcending our limits (Metz 2013, ch. 7.4.3). By contrast, the additivist, in the interest of maximizing quantity of meaning, seems reconciled to a life of activities with immediate payoff. There are different opinions about just what sorts of activities qualify, but the general thought is that the pursuit of quantity will detract from quality. Later, we will see a part-life view that tries to circumvent this problem.

Whole-Life Meaning

"What if my whole life has been wrong?" exclaims the protagonist of Tolstoy's novella, *The Death of Ivan Ilych*, on his deathbed (Tolstoy 1991, 164). Perhaps Ivan Ilych is expressing an additivist concern that now, at the end of his life, he lacks a sufficient quantity of individual meaning-units. But it is more likely that he is regarding life in its *entirety* as a distinct locus of meaning—distinct, that is, from its individual parts. Meaning attaches to the whole of life in a different way and for different reasons than it attaches to any part. And so, contrary to additivism, we cannot decide the meaning of events in isolation, treating each as a discrete unit. Rather, meaning in life concerns relations between events, and can only be determined by taking them together.

A number of considerations support this whole-life approach to meaning. One concerns the *shape* of a life. Two lives with an equal number of good and bad parts can differ in meaningfulness depending on how those parts are arranged.[3] For instance, the life with its good events distributed more toward the end is often thought preferable.[4] Likewise *variety* may contribute to meaning; on the additive version of the part-life view, just repeating a single, supposedly meaningful act, can technically yield a high aggregate-meaning score, though many people would take repetition to be a mark of a meaning-impoverished life (Metz 2013, 50–51). We cannot account for the effect that shape and repetition may have on meaningfulness in a life if we restrict our focus to individual parts of a life in isolation from one another. This is because shape and repetition are the product of relations amongst events. They only reveal themselves for what they are when we pull back from a narrow focus on individual life events, and look at the patterns that emerge when they are assembled together.

While these considerations reinforce the advantages of moving away from part-life approaches to meaning, they don't get to the heart of the whole-life approach. For that, we turn to several, more robust, whole-life views.

Whole-Life Meaning: Achievementism

"Your life has meaning just if, and to the extent that, you achieve the aims that you devote to it freely and competently" (Luper

2014, 198). Following Steven Luper, let's call this *achievementism*. Those aims may or may not include considerations of shape and variety, but the specifics are not always at issue. For achievementists, meaning lies primarily in accomplishing one's goals, whatever they may be (Luper 2014, 201). Even for those who insist that only certain goals are meaningful, the emphasis is less on the nature of the goals than it is on agency, accomplishment, and success (Sigrist 2015). Achievementism is usually tied to aspirations that propel us into the future, as Bernard Williams says about the sorts of desires that give meaning to life (Williams 1973). And "achievement" has active connotations; largely passive activities won't qualify, and nor will events outside our control, such as the sun rising (Luper 2014, 199). The active, future-driven and success-oriented nature of achievementism demands we take an interest in our life *as a whole* in order to set and achieve our goals. We need something resembling a life plan, though it needn't be fixed or rigid (Luper 2014), or always foregrounded in our consciousness.

Dwelling on mortality seems necessary in order to fulfill the meaning mandate, for the achievementist. Resources—including time—must be taken into account in order to construct a realizable life plan. But this model brings with it certain mortality-related risks including, once again, the too-soon problem. Death may arrive before aims are achieved, and so the thought of death can be not just a necessary tool, but also a source of anxiety for achievementists, as it was for additivists. The achievementist has greater power to combat this threat, however. While there may be no end to the meaning that death could curtail for the additivist, the achievementist's life plan can be made finite. Goals can be scaled to fit an estimated lifespan, leaving death nothing to dispossess one of in the end. By keeping in mind the limits that mortality imposes, the achievementist has the resources to "disarm" the threat of death coming too soon (Luper 2013), before meaning is maximized.

Disarming death by setting out, then accomplishing, a finite set of goals combats the too-soon problem. But it may plunge the

achievementist headlong into a *too-late problem*. Meaning is not a persistent good on this view; once a life plan is realized, the continuation of life does not add value to that achievement (Luper 2013, 108). Hence the successful achievementist runs the risk of living a portion of life devoid of meaning. Faced with a situation in which death is too late, we may fall into a state of malaise, eking out the rest of our days with no more meaningful aims to pursue or enjoy. Of course, death can come too late for the additivist as well, for instance, if she reaches a point where no further meaning-units are available to her. But as discussed, it's not rational for her to seek out such a state of affairs, and without active intervention, the additivist is more likely to end up in a situation where death comes too soon, while still in the midst of pursuing more meaning. By contrast, the achievementist actively works toward the possibility of exhausting life's meaning, since, for him, fulfilling the meaning mandate involves setting up a (in theory) reachable end-point.[5] Put this way, achievementism can look a little perverse: the overarching result of success on its terms may be a portion of life devoid of further meaning. Does this infringe on fulfilling the meaning mandate, though? That will be discussed in the next section.

Achievementists have a fraught relation with death. They ought to keep death in their thoughts, scaling their goals to fit their limited lifespan. Note, this is not because there is anything intrinsically good or meaningful about death; nothing in theory rules out that a longer life would be a more meaningful one, allowing for a richer set of achievements. Mortality is simply the temporal-biological constraint under which the life planner operates. Achievements are not made more meaningful by being constrained thus. And unless full achievement happens to coincide with death, the achievementist will be subject to either the too-soon or too-late problem, and their attendant anxiety or malaise. The achievementist, unlike the additivist, cannot cope with these problems by pushing death to the back of mind, since mortality must be kept in mind in order to construct a viable life plan.

Whole-Life Meaning: Narrativism

"Deciding when to die is not (despite the familiar saying) like deciding when to cash in one's chips… It is rather like deciding when and how to end a story" (David Velleman 1993, 346). This statement is a response to additive part-life views, which treat goods or meaning in life as incremental gains that can accumulate over time. The gambling metaphor suits additivists well, in that when faced with decline and wishing to maximize meaning, they must weigh the odds of increasing their meaning-stockpile against the losses incurred through hardship or suffering. But what, by contrast, is involved in fulfilling the meaning mandate by conducting oneself as the *author* of one's life? Here we encounter the narrativist view or *narrativism*.

Narrativism is closely related to achievementism.[6] It's a whole-life approach that seems to require active input on our part and an ongoing mindfulness of mortality. Whereas the achievementist specifically focuses on goals and their accomplishment, the narrativist is concerned with narrative relations—the way that events within a life affect one another and, in so doing, reconstitute meaning in life. This can happen even when the events in question aren't goals *per se* or parts of a life plan.

Consider: receiving an award in recognition of years of dedicated toil at some project, versus winning it because your name was drawn out of a hat. The additivist, taking both experiences in isolation, may view them as equally meaningful units to be added to the pile. Even the achievementist may have difficulty judging the first case as more meaningful if it was not the accomplishment of a consciously constructed goal as set out in a life plan. Whereas the enhanced meaningfulness of the first award is clearly apparent to the narrativist: it does not merely come after but *follows from* the work and effort that preceded it. The meaning of those earlier endeavours is then recast in light of what they have led to. A key idea emphasized by some narrativists is that events in life can *redeem* past hardships if

they are the genuine outcome of those hardships (Charles Taylor 1989; Velleman 1993). The ideal is a life in which events are optimally unified through a complex web of such interrelations, with events at one time in life altering and being altered by events at other times, to the point of realizing maximum possible meaningfulness overall.

As with achievementism, thinking about death is advisable on the narrative view; we sometimes can take an active (in this case, authorial) role in ensuring our past misfortunes are redeemed by later events, in order to maximize overall meaning in our life. Keeping the limitations of our temporal resources in mind will be crucial to this. A life story can realize optimal unity when as many struggles or bad experiences are redeemed and as many narrative loose ends are tied up as is possible within our limited lifespan.

The quest for optimal narrative unity means that the concern that death may come too soon or too late could also feature in the narrativist's consciousness, as it did in the achievementist's. Death comes too soon for the narrativist if hardships remain unredeemed, and too late if optimal narrative unity is secured well before life's end. However, the too-late problem takes on a different cast for the narrativist.

In the case of the achievementist, as discussed, it seems that the worst that can happen when death comes too late is malaise: if one's life plan is realized, continuing on in this state does not detract from the meaning achieved. There is no more meaning to be gained, but nor is any lost, and so, technically speaking, the fulfillment of the meaning mandate is undamaged; one achieves maximum meaning, then bides one's time until the end. Whereas for the narrativist, the too-late problem may undermine fulfillment of the meaning mandate, in that an optimally meaningful state once gained can then be lost.

To see this, consider how narrative relations work in stories. The overall meaning of events is not fixed until the end—prior to that, it can change depending on what happens later (the abandoned party and lost glass slipper is the catalyst for a royal wedding). This means that a state of optimal narrative unity, once secured, can subsequently be undone. A classical example of a life that surpasses its ideal end-point is King Croesus, who gained wealth, power, and personal satisfaction, only to have much of it taken away at the end. His story led Solon to proclaim that we must look to the end of a life before we deem it a happy one.[7]

In all, the fulfillment of the meaning mandate seems more precarious for the narrativist than for the achievementist, as not only the too-soon but the too-late problem conspire against it. Does this add an extra layer of gloom when it comes to pondering death, for the narrativist? Before drawing that conclusion, consider another substantive difference that mortality makes for the two views.

For the achievementist, as noted, life's temporal limit is simply a constraint we operate under in our attempt to fulfill the meaning mandate. Our goals are restricted by the estimated time we have for achieving them. The meaning of those achievements is not enhanced by the fact that there is a limit to them. By contrast, death can enhance overall meaning in life for the narrativist; death contributes to a robust notion of a complete life—one in which various events are interrelated to form a maximally meaningful whole (the way a good ending enhances the novel as a whole).[8] For every Croesus there may be a Perseus: someone whose life story has reached an end in which past hardships are redeemed, narrative loose ends tied up, and maximum satisfaction reached. This robust sense of completion that death allows is sometimes called *closure*, and it contributes to the meaning of life as a whole.

In sum, the achievementist and the narrativist both have reason to bear in mind life's finitude, in order to fulfill the meaning mandate on their own terms. The anxiety that death may come prior to this—i.e. too soon—may be acute in both cases. However, the problem of death coming too late is different for each. The too-late problem poses a more sinister threat for the narrativist, because fulfillment of the meaning mandate can be undone if a life outruns its state of maximal meaningfulness. But this heightened form of the too-late problem may be compensated by death also having a positive role to play for the narrativist; mortality allows for closure, which may enhance overall meaningfulness. Thinking about death may therefore be not just of practical use to narrativists; mortality can be appreciated in its own right. Where the achievementist regards death as a possible enemy to be disarmed, the narrativist can think of death favourably, as a potential ally in the quest to fulfill the meaning mandate.

Part-Life Meaning: Engagementism

"[T]he significance of projects for human life," writes Stephen Rosenbaum, "lies in the way they may or may not engage the natural capacities of the human, not in their completion" (1990, 37). One obstacle that prevented us from embracing a part-life approach to meaning was the additivist's impoverished vision of what is significant in life. As with any part-life view, meaning and activity coincide for the additivist. This is often thought incompatible with higher-order, more deeply meaningful endeavours, which typically don't yield meaning at all times during their pursuit, e.g., pursuits surrounding family, friendship, or work. If the part-life approach seeks to fulfill the meaning mandate by accumulating the most meaning-units, it will be less open to those complex, time-consuming endeavours for which meaning-payoff is apparently not immediate.

But part-life approaches are not necessarily caught in this position. It may be possible to avoid it by shifting the focus from a quantitative to a qualitative model: instead of treating meaning as something that can accumulate over time with the completion of more and more activities, meaning resides in full engagement in a project *at the time*. This remains a part-life view, because meaning and activity coincide; meaning is not a product of interrelations between different events or activities (contra the narrativist whole-life view), nor does it depend on activities' results (contra the achievementist). Let's call this version of the part-life view *engagementism*, in recognition of the fact that it places meaning in the moment, but without treating meaningful moments as cumulative. It is the cumulative aspect of additivism that drives it to rack up of meaning-units through short-term activities. Without this quantitatively structured picture of meaning, engagementists are freer to invest in long-term, arguably more meaningful activities, such as raising a family, cultivating friendships, or seeking solutions to climate change. All that is required is that they place the full weight of meaningfulness on engagement in the process, and not on any outcome.

Engagementism overcomes another obstacle faced by additivism, namely the too-soon problem and its attendant anxieties. That problem loomed large for the additivist because there are almost always more meaningful experiences to be had, and death is a perpetual threat to amassing as many as possible. But death does not pose this threat to the engagementist. To borrow an analogy, "when one becomes completely healthy, greater health is not possible"; complete engagement is a property like complete health, which, once obtained, cannot be augmented (Rosenbaum 1990, 27).[9] This means that no additional meaningfulness can be lost through death, since further meaningful moments would not increase one's meaning store. In the spirit of Epicurus, whose view on pleasure is the model here, engagementists who achieve meaningfulness in life can say that death is nothing to them, in the sense that there is no greater meaningfulness of which death can deprive them.

Does this entail that once meaningful engagement obtains, engagementists fall into the same too-late problem as the achievementists—eking out their days with no further meaning in life? Following the Epicurean model, the engagementist would contend that meaningfulness, though not cumulative, will persist. To use the analogy to hand, having obtained complete health, one can continue to possess it over an indefinite span of time. This is in contrast to the achievementists, for whom meaning reaches an end-point once goals are achieved, desires fulfilled, projects finished. Nor, it should be said, can meaningfulness once obtained be undermined by future events for the engagementist, as can happen for the narrativist—only in a whole-life view, in which meaning is a matter of relations between different events, can one event affect the meaning of another for better or worse.

Engagementism is challenging. We might question how realistic it is from a rational and psychological standpoint. Are people likely to engage in these more robustly meaningful pursuits for their own sake, without such things as goal-achievement or narrative closure as reasons for so doing? If simply being engaged in an activity is the apex of meaningfulness in life, why choose difficult or time-consuming projects? Yes, engagementists can in theory raise a family, cultivate friendships, or work against climate change. But would they in fact be motivated to do these sorts of things? Achievementists would point out that while some pursuits can be ends in themselves (art, gardening, conversation), in other cases, people "pursue their aims in order to *achieve* them" (Luper 2014, 201). Many social, career-oriented, and even personal endeavours are not consistently rewarding or meaningful throughout their pursuit; their meaning arguably depends in large part on their completion. Finally, it may be argued that the more significant a project is, the more likely we are to be invested in its outcome; one doesn't want merely to be engaged with friendship, family, or work, but also to be a *good* friend (parent, colleague). And being good at these things "involves caring about the many small and large accomplishments that go into [them]" (Sigrist 2015, 93). The concern here is that deep meaningfulness cannot be a product of the moment, however engaging it may be.

Some of these objections risk begging the question in favor of a whole-life view of meaning—one in which meaning depends on or is enhanced through relations across events, such as achieving long-term goals and/or redeeming investments of time, effort and sacrifice. Admittedly, this is a view of meaning that many are willing to presuppose. In light of this, engagementism is better regarded as aspirational: an approach to meaning in life that many do not emulate, but which might, in some respects, make things better for us if we did.

We've seen one considerable benefit already, namely that engagementism provides a workable means for curtailing anxiety about death coming too soon. More time does not enhance meaning within life when meaning is non-cumulative. This also has implications for thinking about death. Since death does not perpetually threaten fulfillment of the meaning mandate on the engagementist's terms, thoughts of mortality ought not to be anxiety-producing. This is in sharp contrast to the additive part-life view, with its insatiable impulse to fulfill the meaning mandate through accumulation of ever-more meaning-units—a project that death perpetually threatens. The best additivists could do to assuage anxiety about this was to reassure themselves that dwelling on death made little practical difference to fulfilling the meaning mandate. Whether this is sufficient to quell negative thoughts about death is another matter.

Engagementists have no need to suppress thoughts about death if they cause them no anxiety. But they have no practical reasons to dwell on mortality either, in contrast to the two whole-life views canvassed. The achievementist obligation to formulate life plans and keep them on track, and the narrativist impulse to ensure that hardships are redeemed and optimal unity realized, are absent when meaningfulness is not a matter of the complex relations across different parts of a limited lifespan.

In keeping with the Epicurean model, the engagementist can think about death with equanimity. There is no practical need to dwell on it, but no cause to avoid thinking about it either. Perhaps this doesn't reach the heights of positive thinking that the narrativist was open to: the prospect that life can in some deep sense reach closure, with the assistance of the right sort of death (one that ties up all narrative loose ends). But nor does it run the risk of failing in that regard. In a similar way it cannot fail in the achievementist's sense, since meaning lies in engagement with and not completion of an activity.

Final Thoughts?

> It makes me happy that men do not want at all to think the thought of death. I should like very much to do something that would make the thought of life even a hundred times more appealing to them.
>
> (Nietzsche 1974, §278)

Nietzsche wished to banish thoughts of death in order to allow people to focus on thoughts of life. If the previous analysis has revealed anything, though, it is that thinking about life and thinking about death are not necessarily opposed and may be inextricably enmeshed. Whether we regard death as a perpetual threat, an enemy to be defeated, a potential ally to be embraced, or a source, ultimately, of calm indifference, may be tied to our conception of life, specifically how we think life accrues meaning. How we conceive of the structure of meaning in life also affects the extent to which keeping mortality in mind will be useful or detrimental. The views that I have canvassed by no means exhaust the field. Nor do they all necessarily exclude one another.[10] But they do, it is hoped, provide some basis for further thinking about life and death together.

Notes

1. Provided subjective fulfillment is at least part of meaning, as many think; see note 2.
2. While some hold that meaning lies in the former and others in the latter, there are also hybrid views that treat meaning in life as a combination of subjective and objective factors; see Wolf (2010).
3. The debate is often framed more generally as concerning goods in life and not meaning alone, but can be and sometimes is transposed into a point about meaning-distribution; see Metz (2013, ch. 3.4).

4. See Metz (2013, 50–51) and Slote (1983). Cf. Velleman (1993, 332–335) and Luper (2013, 108) for discussion of alternative models of goods-distribution in life, such as constancy.

5. The notion of exhausting life comes from Luper (2013).

6. Narrative views are broad-ranging, and some of the more relevant ones talk less about meaning *per se* than about goods or well-being (the same can be said of whole and part-life discussions generally; see Metz 2013, 40). Nonetheless, there is considerable cross-fertilization. E.g. Charles Taylor's key point about redemption in narrative and making sense of one's life has been adapted by Velleman (1993) in discussing of modes of well-being, but also by others for the purposes of discussing meaning (Metz 2013, 46–47).

7. The anecdote comes from Herodotus; Solon's dictum is discussed by Aristotle (*Nicomachean Ethics*, 1100a ff.).

8. These ideas have their roots in MacIntyre (1984, ch. 15).

9. This point is made specifically in regard to the Epicurean view of pleasure, but Rosenbaum extends the argument to include meaning (1990, 37). Cf. Luper (2013, 113–114), who argues that the Epicurean values cannot avoid being cumulative.

10. Metz (2013) opts for a mixed-part and whole-life view, arguing that aspects of them are compatible.

Works Cited

Luper, Steven. 2013. "Exhausting Life." *The Journal of Ethics* 17.1: 99–119.

Luper, Steven. 2014. "Life's Meaning." In *The Cambridge Companion to Life and Death*, ed. Steven Luper. Cambridge: Cambridge University Press, 198–212.

MacIntyre, Alasdair. 1984. *After Virtue*. 2nd edn. Notre Dame: University of Notre Dame Press.

Metz, Thaddeus. 2013. *Meaning in Life*. Oxford: Oxford University Press.

Nietzsche, Friedrich. 1974. *The Gay Science*, trans. Walter Kaufmann. New York: Vintage Books.

Rosenbaum, Stephen. 1990. "Epicurus on Pleasure and the Complete Life." *The Monist* 73.1: 21–41.

Sigrist, Michael. 2015. "Death and the Meaning of Life." *Philosophical Papers* 44.1: 83–102.

Setiya, Kieran. 2014. "The Midlife Crisis." *Philosopher's Imprint* 14.31: 1–18.

Slote, Michael. 1882. "Goods and Lives." *Pacific Philosophical Quarterly* 63.4: 311–326.

Taylor, Charles. 1989. *Sources of the Self*. Cambridge: Cambridge University Press.

Tolstoy, L. 1991. "The Death of Ivan Ilych." In *Tolstoy's Short Fiction*, ed. and trans. Michael Katz. New York: W.W. Norton & Company, Inc., 123–167.

Velleman, J. David. 1993. "Well-Being and Time." In *The Metaphysics of Death*, ed. John Martin Fischer. Stanford: Stanford University Press, 329–357.

Williams, Bernard. 1973. "The Makropulos Case." In *Problems of the Self*. Cambridge: Cambridge University Press.

Wolf, Susan. 2010. *Meaning in Life and Why It Matters*. Princeton: Princeton University Press.

37 Meaning in Life in Spite of Death

Thaddeus Metz

I. Death Sucks, but Why, Exactly?

When we suppose that death is truly the end, virtually all of us in the western world[1] wish that neither we nor our loved ones would die. That is, if death essentially involves not merely the permanent disintegration of our bodies, but also of our selves, then pretty much everyone from Euro-American-Australasian cultures thinks that death would be undesirable, except insofar as death would be necessary to prevent a fate worse than it. Unless our only future is torture or some other sort of anguish, most are inclined to think that death is something to fear, hate, avoid, and mourn.

A common explanation of why death is bad for the person who dies is that it often deprives us of the possibility of living well in the future (e.g., Brueckner and Fischer 1986; Kagan 2012: 211–212). On this score, we point out that, say, a middle-aged person who has died will never experience the joy of seeing her daughter get married. Another, less frequent—but nonetheless powerful—explanation of why death is bad for one is that it consists of the permanent annihilation of a person, where a person is highly valuable entity (Benatar 2017). In the way that we have a sense of loss when a great artwork is destroyed in a fire, so we grieve the destruction of a self-aware being with a dignity. Sometimes philosophers and others, some of whom are addressed in this chapter, have a third explanation of why death is dreadful, which is that it renders our lives meaningless. Some contend that life is pointless if it will not continue forever, or, equivalently, that immortality is a necessary condition for a significant existence. The first rationale appeals to the *quality of life* we could have had, the second roughly invokes the intrinsic value of *human life itself*, while the third employs the concept of a *meaningful life*.

Focusing on the third rationale in this chapter, I argue that death is compatible with meaning. Although one usually has reasons of meaning to want to die much later than the norm for a human being, I contend that there is nothing inherent to life's ending that renders life meaningless.[2] In fact, I provide reason to doubt the view that an immortal life could have a much greater meaning by comparison with any mortal life. If death sucks, it is not because it always makes our lives insignificant, but for some other reason(s).

I begin by clarifying what philosophers tend to mean by speaking of "meaning in life" as a value (Section 2). Next, I expound and object to the position that death is sufficient for a life with no meaning (Section 3), after which I critically address the tempting view that, even if immortality is not necessary for life to be at all meaningful, it is necessary for a life with great meaning (Section 4). I conclude by briefly posing questions that philosophers of life's meaning are just beginning to address and that readers might consider if they want to contribute to the debates (Section 5).

II. The Value of Meaning in Life

When a philosophical approach to life's meaning comes up in conversation, people usually ask either "So what is the meaning of life (wise guy)?," or "What (the heck) are you talking about?" Before addressing the first question in the context of whether immortality is central to making life meaningful

(Sections 3 and 4), I here address the second question, about what we invariably have in mind when thinking about life's meaning.

Philosophers in the West disagree about what it means to describe a person's life as "meaningful." However, most currently writing on the topic at least share the view that this term (or a cognate word such as "significant") connotes a cluster of valuable properties such as: making sense of one's life; composing an interesting life story or narrative; living in ways that deserve reactions such as esteem or admiration; realizing purposes that are much higher than animal pleasures; or connecting positively to something beyond oneself. For most philosophers currently addressing life's meaning, when we think or speak about it, we have in mind at least one of these desirable features and quite often more than one as an "amalgam" (e.g., Thomson 2003: 8–13; Metz 2013: 24–35; Mawson 2016; Seachris 2019).

Philosophers also, by and large, agree about exemplars of what lacks meaning in a person's life. None of the following would confer any meaning on your life: chewing gum, taking a hot shower, watching sitcoms while eating ice cream, living the rest of one's life alone in a virtual reality, digging a hole and then filling it up and then digging a hole again and filling it up and so on indefinitely, blowing up the Sphinx for fun, killing one's innocent spouse for the insurance money, hating other people simply because of their race.

Some of these actions are worth doing, not because they would make your life more *important*, but perhaps because they would make it happier. If you believe that these actions could confer meaning on your life, then you have to tell a story that invokes some *further* condition, such as helping others or being rewarded for having made a sacrifice. Setting these kinds of conditions aside, the actions are meaningless, for lacking the kinds of valuable properties mentioned above, or so most philosophers believe.

Given the above understanding of what is involved in thinking about the meaning of a person's life, it is unlikely that whatever a person *finds* meaningful or whatever happens to

be "meaningful to" a person is in fact meaningful. Imagine a person found it meaningful to pray to the Flying Spaghetti Monster, a ridiculous creature that does not exist. Or suppose that a person deemed maintaining 3,732 hairs on one's head (Taylor 1992: 36), or "cultivating one's prowess at long-distance spitting or collecting a big ball of string" (Wolf 2010: 104), to be meaningful. These kinds of activities intuitively would *not* merit admiration, would *fail* to make for a good life story, etc. Most contemporary philosophers believe that meaning has an "objective" dimension; that is, we can be mistaken about what does or does not make our lives meaningful, which means that it is sensible to argue about the issue.

III. Does Meaning Require Immortality?

In this section I critically discuss three arguments that philosophers have advanced for thinking that death would be sufficient for a meaningless life. They are ones that have been particularly influential and should resonate with readers. In catchwords, they appeal to: obtaining justice; making a difference; and enjoying moral freedom.[3] After providing reason to doubt each of these rationales for thinking that meaning requires immortality, I argue directly against that conclusion, presenting reason to believe that a meaningful life is possible even if we all face death.

III.1 Obtaining Justice

Harking back some 2500 years to a book in the Hebrew Bible, one encounters the argument that, if everyone dies, then all our lives are meaningless because justice cannot be done. It is particularly prominent in Ecclesiastes, which means those who have gathered together. In this book, the speaker, Koheleth, repeatedly proclaims that "all is vanity," i.e., that everything is in vain or is futile, and that life is akin "to the pursuit of wind." One of his central rationales for this conclusion is that

the same fate is in store for all: for the righteous, and for the wicked; for the good and pure, and for the impure… That is the sad thing about all that goes on under the sun: that the same fate is in store for all.

(9.2–9.3; see also 2.14–2.16, 3.17)

If everyone dies, then we are saddled with our current lives in which people clearly do not get what they deserve, thereby robbing our lives of meaning (see also Walker 1989; Craig 2000). Life does seem to be nonsensical insofar as the upright, the courageous, the wise, the educated, and the hard-working suffer setbacks, whereas the wicked, the cowardly, the foolish, the ignorant, and the lazy flourish. It is even more absurd when, as Koheleth bemoans (2.12, 2.18–2.21), the latter get to enjoy the goods that the former had labored so hard to produce!

If we would forever survive the deaths of our bodies, then the scales could be rectified. In that case, God, an all-knowing and all-powerful moral judge, could compensate those who unjustly suffered hardships, reward those who had made sacrifices for others, and impose penalties on those who were evil. One could also imagine an impersonal force, akin to *karma* in South and East Asian thought, that would give people what they deserve after their selves have survived the deaths of their bodies.

It is hard to deny that there must be more to this life of ours if justice is going to be done in full. However, why believe that there must be an *eternity* beyond this life? If someone wrongfully breaks my arm, I deserve some compensation, but I do not deserve an infinite amount of it in the form of eternal bliss. In addition, the arm-breaker deserves some punishment, but also not an infinite amount in the form of eternal damnation.

The general point is that finite deeds undertaken on Earth seem to lack any infinite value or disvalue, and that deserved responses to them, i.e., ones that are proportionate or fitting, could also be finite.[4] In order for justice to be done, therefore, we do need more time beyond our 80 or so years as they tend to be on this planet, but we do not need to be immortal. Imagine that the content of

people's minds were uploaded into a computer upon their bodily deaths on Earth and then downloaded into new bodies on another planet. Why wouldn't another few hundred years there suffice to right the wrongs?

Another way to question this argument is to contend that it is precisely the presence of certain kinds of injustice that offers some of us a major opportunity to obtain meaning in our lives. Consider Nelson Mandela, who struggled for some 50 years against racist oppression (apartheid) in South Africa, succeeded in overturning it, and became the country's first democratically elected president. Not too shabby when it comes to meaning, one might suggest. From this perspective, undeserved harm does not render everyone's life unavoidably futile, but rather can be what gives some lives a point.

III.2 Making a Difference

Perhaps there is some consideration other than justice from which it follows that a meaningful life would have to be immortal. Leo Tolstoy, the famous Russian author of *War and Peace* and *Anna Karenina*, went through an existential crisis that he recounted in his work *My Confession*. Despite his success in terms of creativity, reputation, wealth, and family, he judged that his life would be meaningless if he were to die:

> Sooner or later there would come diseases and death (they had come already) to my dear ones and to me, and there would be nothing left but stench and worms. All my affairs, no matter what they might be, would sooner or later be forgotten, and I myself should not exist. So why should I worry about all these things? … "What is the meaning of my life?"—"None."
>
> (2000: 13, 15; first published in 1884)

Tolstoy's reasoning appears to be that life would be meaningless if nothing were worth doing and that nothing would be worth doing if it would not have an ultimate consequence for, or make a permanent difference to, the world. Since one could apparently make such an impact only if one's life did not end,[5] this rationale appears to support the idea that one must never die in order for one's existence to matter.

Tolstoy's rationale, articulated in the nineteenth century (but cf. Ecclesiastes 3.18–3.19), continues to have supporters, including William Lane Craig, an influential religious philosopher, who wrote of a mortal existence:

> The contributions of the scientist to the advance of human knowledge, the researches of the doctor to alleviate pain and suffering, the efforts of the diplomat to secure peace in the world, the sacrifices of good men everywhere to better the lot of the human race—all these come to nothing. In the end they don't make one bit of difference, not one bit. Each person's life is therefore without ultimate significance.
>
> (2000: 42)

Both Craig and Tolstoy are describing how they think life would be if we could not live forever (not how they believe life actually is).

Here is some reason to doubt that nothing is worth striving for if we are mortal. Imagine that there is a girl near you, say, your much younger sister, and she will get seriously burned if you do not do something to help her. Perhaps she will touch a hot stove, or fall into a bonfire, if you do not warn her or pull her away. And suppose that neither she nor you is destined to live forever. Is there truly no reason at all for you to prevent her from suffering? Would it not be worth making some effort to prevent her from experiencing intense pain and becoming disfigured?

Indeed, some critics try to strengthen the point: perhaps helping others is instead pointless on the supposition that everyone will live forever (Wielenberg 2005: 91–94; Hubin 2009; Maitzen 2009). Imagine that we could not die and that, upon the disintegration of our bodies, our selves would continue to live on in a better place. It is arguably *that* condition that would make it senseless to help anyone. If we cannot perish, then there is

no point in trying to save any of our lives! And if we will go to a better place, say, with God, then there is not even any point in trying to prevent our suffering, since God would be sure to compensate us for it later. By this bold reply, preventing burns, seeking peace, improving people's health, and the like make the most sense if this earthly life is all we have, if it is vulnerable to harm that will never be compensated, if it is delicate and precious. Actions that help mortal beings might not have "ultimate" significance, but nor is it true that "they don't make one bit of difference"; they are plausibly "in between" the extremes, such that they make some difference that has some significance.

III.3 Enjoying Moral Freedom

Consider now a third argument that philosophers have made for thinking that we must be immortal if our lives are to be at all meaningful. By this approach, we could not have certain mental faculties, which I sum up with "moral freedom," if we did not have an immortal soul. Even if it would be possible (*contra* Descartes) to have a mind that were material, specific kinds of meaningful mental states perhaps would not be. Immanuel Kant maintained, for instance, that if we were physical beings subjected to the laws of nature like everything else in the animal, vegetable, and mineral kingdoms, then we could not act according to reasons, could not be free, and would be incapable of acting morally. Instead, we would be causally necessitated to act at any given time by the prior state of the natural world, widely known as the thesis of "determinism."

For some thinkers, the only way we could transcend the material world and its deterministic causal laws is if we had some spiritual element that is independent of them and stronger than they are, viz., a soul. If our selves were constituted by an immortal, spiritual substance, then we could understand how it is invariably within our power to do the right thing, regardless of what might have happened before to us, where lacking such a moral freedom would render our lives meaningless. Such a view is suggested in the following passage by a theologian:

> The moral spirit finds the meaning of life in choice. It finds it in that which proceeds from man and remains with him as his inner essence rather than in the accidents of circumstance and turns of external fortune… (W)henever a human being rubs the lamp of his moral consciousness with moral passion, a Spirit does appear. This Spirit is God… It is in the "Thou must" of God and man's "I can" that the divine image of God in human life is contained.
>
> (Svenson 2000: 27–28)

The "I can," here, signifies a person's inherent ability to make the morally correct choice in any given situation. If we lacked that power, if it were beyond our control whether we do the right thing or not, then our lives would be senseless, so the argument goes.

One major way that critics have responded to this argument is to explain how the relevant kinds of action would be possible in a purely material world. Philosophers have striven to show that one could indeed act rationally, freely, and morally, in the important senses, if we were a part of nature in the way that everything else on Earth appears to be (e.g., Dennett 1984, 2003). Space precludes recounting these kinds of naturalist explanations, but it is worth keeping in mind how often the scientific method has been able to replace the spiritual with the physical. People used to believe that angels held planets in their orbits and gods were responsible for lightning, but these days cosmologists and meteorologists can identify the physical causes of these events, respectively. Perhaps the kinds of choices that we think make our lives important are analogous to these events, and it is plausible to expect that they too will be shown to have a material basis (if they have not already).

There is another way to criticize the present argument for thinking immortality is essential for meaning. That is to grant, for the sake of argument, that only a spiritual aspect of us could enable moral freedom, but to question whether it must persist forever in order to do so. Suppose, then, that only something utterly different from the natural world could intervene into it by making a moral choice and thereby changing the course of history. Grant, in particular, that it would have to be a powerful force in order not to be determined by the laws of nature. Even so, there is a gap between that idea and the concept of a soul, as something indestructible or at least destined to persist without end. It seems that a spiritual substance could influence nature without being influenced by it and yet not be the sort of thing that is eternal; just imagine that God were to assign it an expiration date.

Still more, suppose that indeed only an immortal soul could be powerful enough to overcome nature's causal laws. It still would not follow that *you*, as in your particular self, must never die. It is tempting to say that one just is one's soul, but that is a questionable view of personal identity. Normally, the idea is that a soul is an immortal, spiritual substance that contains one's psychological states but that need not; the soul you have could be emptied of any mental states, or it could even be taken over and possessed by someone else, perhaps by a demon. In these latter cases, you arguably would be gone, even though the soul that had once contained your mind were to remain. So, even if an immortal soul had to exist in order for moral freedom to be possible, there is still an argumentative gap to cross, of showing that the soul must forever contain your particular mind, and hence your particular self, as opposed to being either emptied altogether or filled with another personality. Why think that *your identity* must never come to an end in order for you to be able to act freely for a good moral reason while on earth?

There are additional arguments for thinking that life must be meaningless if we are not immortal (see note 3), but, rather than consider them here, I will now provide reason to doubt their conclusion. Here is an argument for thinking that, even if we are mortal, a meaningful life is possible, at least for many of us.

If we think of the (stereotypical) lives of Mother Teresa, Nelson Mandela, Albert Einstein, Charles Darwin, John Coltrane, and Pablo Picasso, they seem meaningful in virtue of the activities they performed, even upon imagining that they did not survive the deaths of their bodies (Baier 1997; Trisel 2004: 384–385; Wielenberg 2005: 31–37, 49–50; Norman 2006). Supposing for the sake of argument that none of these people exists any longer, most of us remain inclined to differentiate their lives, which exemplify morality, enquiry, or creativity (respectively), on the one hand, from lives devoted to long-distance spitting, creating a big ball of string, or living alone in a virtual reality, on the other. Meaning is present in the former cases, and absent in the latter ones. Reflection on the lives of those mentioned above indicates that we need not be immortal in order to realize ends higher than pleasure, to live in ways that merit admiration, or to lead a life story that is compelling.

It is not just that some little bit of meaning is available to mortal human beings, but that there is arguably enough available for some people to be aptly described as having lived "meaningful lives" on balance. Nobody's perfect. Einstein apparently held some prejudicial views in respect of Chinese people, Mother Teresa was reportedly stingy with painkiller, and Picasso is said to have repeatedly cheated on his lovers. Even so, all things considered, their contributions to the true (knowledge), the good (beneficence), and the beautiful (art), respectively, were so substantial as to make it plausible to describe their lives as "meaningful." And if they could achieve that, why can't we do something similar (even if not quite as grand)? Rather than sleep in or watch sitcoms, we could get an education, become wiser, work for a charity, rear children with love, cultivate a garden, or write poetry.[6]

This reasoning has convinced even many religiously inclined theorists of meaning. For example, one has said that it is "beyond reasonable doubt" that some meaning would be possible even if there were no soul (Quinn 2000: 58), while another remarks that it would be "incredible" (Audi 2005: 334) to think that no meaning would accrue from beneficent relationships in themselves (see also Cottingham 2003: 76–79; Mawson 2016: 5). There are some, perhaps Craig cited above, who will deny the intuition that Einstein's life mattered, on the supposition that Einstein is not in Heaven. However, the much more common reply these days from friends of immortality is to grant that it is not necessary for a life to be meaningful, but to contend that it is necessary for a *great* meaning in life.

IV. Does Great Meaning Require Immortality?

Among twenty-first-century philosophers of life's meaning, a large majority believe that a mortal and meaningful life is possible. However, there is still real debate to be had between those who believe that death is incompatible with meaning in some way and those who do not. Most of the debate is now about whether immortality would alone offer us a *greater* meaning than one available to a mortal life. After spelling out why some philosophers have thought that an eternal life could exhibit an ultimate meaning and a finite life could not, I aim to contribute to the debate by posing a problem for this position that needs to be addressed.

Although philosophers these days often speak of a "great" or "ultimate" meaning, they have not been clear and specific about what these terms mean. On the one hand, they might be making a quantitative claim, that we could have much more, perhaps an infinite amount, of meaning if we lived forever. On the other hand, they could be making a qualitative claim, that a higher type of meaning is alone available to an immortal life. In the following passage from a recent book on the meaning of life, T.J. Mawson mentions both in discussing what a world without a spiritual dimension could offer us:

(I)t might well be true that Gandhi's life is more meaningful than that of the wastrel even if there is no God. But, if there is no God, then there's some deeper or more permanent sort of meaning that even Gandhi's life lacked because *all* our lives lack it.

(2016: 5; see also 17, as well as Cottingham 2016; Swinburne 2016)

In a world without God—which, for Mawson, is also a world without a soul—we could not have a meaning that is "deep" or "permanent," as opposed to a "shallow or transient meaning" (Mawson 2016: 5), where a permanent meaning would presumably constitute a much larger amount than a transient one.

Indeed, Mawson contends that only an eternal life would have a potentially "infinite" amount of meaning (2016: 145). Suppose, as seems true, that meaningful actions or states have some kind of magnitude, i.e., come in degrees. For instance, helping an old lady cross the street would be meaningful, while liberating an entire country without much violence and destruction would be even more meaningful. We might not be able to assign specific numbers to meaningful conditions, but we nonetheless often have some rough idea of how to compare them. If so, then the amount of meaning available to an eternal life is potentially infinite, whereas that available to a finite life is not.

The argument is strong, but the problem is that it might "prove too much," as philosophers sometimes say. Recall that, in this section, we are evaluating the position that grants that a mortal and meaningful life is possible, but contends that an immortal life could alone have a great meaning by comparison. The trouble with the present rationale is that an infinite meaning would dwarf a finite meaning to such an extent that we could no longer plausibly describe the latter life as "meaningful" on balance. It would be like saying that a house can be big, even if it would be bigger were it to grow to be the size of a billion billion billion suns.[7]

To be sure, by the present reasoning, Gandhi's life would not be a "flat zero," but it would, compared to infinity, come about as close to zero as is mathematically possible for a non-zero number, and that arguably fails to capture the judgment that Gandhi's life was meaningful on balance absent a soul. Just as we would not describe someone's life as "happy" if it had only a smidge of happiness compared to what is frequently on offer, so we cannot plausibly describe someone's mortal life as "meaningful" if it has only a "small dollop" of meaning compared to infinity, "tending to nothing over time" (Mawson 2016: 144; see also 13, 154). Given the argument at the end of the previous section, approximating zero is not an accurate way to capture the lives of Mandela, Einstein, Picasso, and the like, or so I put forth for consideration.

V. Conclusion

The argument that an immortal life would have "too much" meaning, rendering us unable to capture the intuition that our mortal lives are capable of being meaningful, is not put forward as conclusive. It is only recently that philosophers have begun to consider a great, ultimate, or infinite meaning purportedly unavailable to persons who will die. As this sort of debate has just begun, many questions remain open for philosophers and their students to address, including: is it, upon reflection, coherent to describe a mortal Gandhi's life as "meaningful" compared to a life with an infinite amount of meaning?; might an eternal life not necessarily exhibit an infinite meaning, but rather a finite amount that would not render a mortal life more or less meaningless?; how else, besides quantitatively, might we understand the sense of "great" meaning that an immortal life would alone offer? For instance, a deep meaning sounds better than a shallow one, but what makes something a deep sort of meaning? May readers be moved to put their minds to these and related questions.

Notes

1. The qualification is important, as there are other traditions that do not seem to value being a distinct self, with the Hindu religion particularly salient.

2. I set aside the metaphysical issue of whether we are in fact immortal or not, and focus solely on how immortality or its absence would bear on the meaning in our lives.

3. Another argument that has been advanced is that meaning in life is a function of the maximally possible value for us, which would consist of a perfect relationship with a perfect being, i.e., God's pleasing us forever in Heaven (cf. Goetz 2012; Metz 2013: 106–138). Why think that anything less than perfect must be disqualified as a source of some meaning in life? (on which see Landau 2017).

4. You might be tempted to suggest that at least a mass murderer deserves eternal damnation, but that does not seem true, since if we all are immortal, then no one can ever be *killed*!

5. For doubt about this claim, see Metz (2013: 129).

6. Even if a mortal and meaningful life is possible, we usually (on grounds of meaning) have good reason to want to put death off for a long while beyond our expected 80 or so years, so that we can pursue all the more knowledge of ourselves and our world, intensify our relationships with persons and certain kinds of animals, create even better works of art, share them with others, and so on.

7. I first made this point in Metz (2017: 367), from which some of this phrasing is cribbed.

References

Audi, Robert. 2005. "Intrinsic Value and Meaningful Life." *Philosophical Papers* 34: 331–355.

Baier, Kurt. 1997. *Problems of Life and Death: A Humanist Perspective*. Amherst: Prometheus Books.

Benatar, David. 2017. *The Human Predicament*. New York: Oxford University Press.

Brueckner, Anthony, and John Martin Fischer. 1986. "Why Is Death Bad?" *Philosophical Studies* 50: 213–221.

Cottingham, John. 2003. *On the Meaning of Life*. London: Routledge.

Cottingham, John. 2016. "Meaningfulness, Eternity, and Theism." In *God and Meaning*, ed. Joshua Seachris and Stewart Goetz. New York: Bloomsbury Academic, 123–136.

Craig, William Lane. 2000. "The Absurdity of Life without God." Repr. in *The Meaning of Life*, ed. E.D. Klemke, 2nd edn. New York: Oxford University Press, 40–56. First published in 1994.

Dennett, Daniel. 1984. *Elbow Room: The Varieties of Free Will Worth Wanting*. Cambridge, MA: The MIT Press.

Dennett, Daniel. 2003. *Freedom Evolves*. New York: Viking Penguin.

Goetz, Stewart. 2012. *The Purpose of Life: A Theistic Perspective*. London: Continuum.

Hubin, Donald. 2009. "Empty and Ultimately Meaningless Gestures?" In *Is Goodness without God Good Enough?* ed. Robert Garcia and Nathan King. Lanham, MD: Rowman and Littlefield, 133–150.

Kagan, Shelly. 2012. *Death*. New Haven, CT: Yale University Press.

Landau, Iddo. 2017. *Finding Meaning in an Imperfect World*. New York: Oxford University Press.

Maitzen, Stephen. 2009. "Ordinary Morality Implies Atheism." *European Journal for Philosophy of Religion* 2: 107–126.

Mawson, T.J. 2016. *God and the Meanings of Life*. London: Bloomsbury Publishing.

Metz, Thaddeus. 2013. *Meaning in Life: An Analytic Study*. Oxford: Oxford University Press.

Metz, Thaddeus. 2017. "Meaning in Life." In *The Palgrave Handbook on the Afterlife*, ed. Benjamin Matheson and Yujin Nagasawa. New York: Palgrave Macmillan, 353–370.

Norman, Richard. 2006. "The Varieties of Non-Religious Experience." *Ratio* 19: 474–494.

Quinn, Philip. 2000. "How Christianity Secures Life's Meanings." In *The Meaning of Life in the World Religions*, ed. Joseph Runzo and Nancy Martin. Oxford: Oneworld Publications, 53–68.

Seachris, Joshua. 2019. "Meaning of Life: Contemporary Analytic Perspectives." In *Internet Encyclopedia of Philosophy*, ed. James Fieser and Bradley Dowden. www.iep.utm.edu/mean-ana/.

Svenson, David. 2000 [1949]. "The Dignity of Human Life." Repr. in *The Meaning of Life*, ed. E.D. Klemke, 2nd edn. New York: Oxford University Press, 21–30.

Swinburne, Richard. 2016. "How God Makes Life a Lot More Meaningful." In *God and Meaning*, ed. Joshua Seachris and Stewart Goetz. New York: Bloomsbury Academic, 149–164.

Taylor, Charles. 1992. *The Ethics of Authenticity*. Cambridge, MA: Harvard University Press.

Thomson, Garrett. 2003. *On the Meaning of Life*. Melbourne: Wadsworth.

Tolstoy, Leo. 2000. "My Confession." Translated by Leo Wiener. Repr. in *The Meaning of Life*, ed. E.D. Klemke, 2nd edn. New York: Oxford University Press, 11–20. First published in 1884.

Trisel, Brooke Alan. 2004. "Human Extinction and the Value of Our Efforts." *The Philosophical Forum* 35: 371–391.

Walker, Lois Hope. 1989. "Religion and the Meaning of Life and Death." In *Philosophy: The Quest for Truth*, ed. Louis Pojman. Belmont: Wadsworth Publishing Co., 167–171.

Wielenberg, Erik. 2005. *Value and Virtue in a Godless Universe*. Cambridge: Cambridge University Press.

Wolf, Susan. 2010. *Meaning in Life and Why It Matters*. Princeton: Princeton University Press.

38 Out of the Blue into the Black

Reflections on Death and Meaning

Michael Hauskeller

Out of the blue, into the black,
Once you're gone, you can't come back
—**Neil Young**

Much Ado about Nothing?

Few of us are entirely comfortable with the prospect of our own death, including those who believe in an afterlife. Whatever we may *believe*, as far as we *know*, death is going to end our existence, and our own non-existence is not only very hard to fathom ("How could *I*, the subjective centre of the world, ever *not* be, especially if the world continues to exist?"), but we also instinctively shy away from it and often fear it like nothing else. This may well be irrational, as Epicurus argued, because it seems impossible that our own death can be bad for us (or, more precisely, that our *being* dead can be bad for us), but that does not necessarily stop us from fearing it. Yet even if we are largely indifferent to our future non-existence, we may still be affected in other ways by the knowledge of our mortality. We may, for instance, wonder what the point of all our striving and caring is if whatever we do the outcome will always be the same: our life will end, and all we have built, all we have ever accomplished, all our knowledge and experience, all we have ever done or been, will end as well, perhaps not immediately, but eventually. If that is so, then why bother with any of it in the first place?

This is not a purely academic question. People can be seriously thrown off course by it. One well-known example is the great Russian writer Leo Tolstoy who, when he was forty years old, fell into a deep depression when contemplating the fact of his mortality.

Death is the ultimate reality, he felt, and for that reason life could only ever be a "stupid and evil joke" (Tolstoy 1882, 20). "Today or tomorrow," he writes in his *Confession*, "sickness and death will come (…) to those dear to me, and to myself, and nothing will remain other than the stench and the worms. Sooner or later my deeds, whatever they may have been, will be forgotten and will no longer exist. What is all the fuss about then? How can a person carry on living and fail to perceive this? That is what is so astonishing! It is only possible to go on living while you are intoxicated with life, once sober it is impossible not to see that it is all a mere trick, and a stupid trick!" (Tolstoy 1882, 21).

Tolstoy felt very strongly that if we seriously contemplate the reality of death, which few of us ever do while we are still fit and healthy, preferring to pretend that death is still far away or only comes for other people, we must come to the conclusion that none of what we do really matters, that "all the fuss," as he puts it, is ultimately about nothing at all. Whatever it is, we could just as well not do it because in the long run it won't make any difference anyway.

Universal Mortality

Now if that is true, our situation is truly hopeless because it is an undeniable fact that we are *all* going to die (whatever happens after), some sooner, some later, but without exception. For all we know, our death is the end for us, and nothing lasts forever, perhaps not even the universe itself. Consequently, we may be able to delay our death, but whatever we do we will not escape it. Even if we managed to figure out how to stop the aging process, as some biogerontologists believe we will soon be able to (e.g. De Grey and Rae 2008), we could still be certain that someday, however far in the future that day may be, *something* will kill us. Even if we found a way to exchange our carbon-based bodies for something more durable, or to upload our minds and selves to a computer and henceforth live a bodiless, virtual existence, largely unburdened by material constraints, we would still remain unable to survive forever: even such an existence would come to an end if its physical conditions were removed or destroyed, which is bound to happen eventually.

Radical life extension would, therefore, not solve the problem, which appears to be not that we die too early, but that we die at all. If the fact that we have to die makes it impossible for us to live a meaningful life, then a meaningful life is not possible for the simple reason that it is not possible *never* to die. All things that have a beginning in time also have an end in time. Accordingly, if a mortal life can never be meaningful, nobody will ever have lived a meaningful life, neither in the past nor in the future: not you or me, not Socrates, Picasso or Einstein, not Mother Teresa or Nelson Mandela. All lives, then, are equally pointless, equally meaningless.

But *why* would that be so? What are the reasons that lead people to believe that death, or the fact of our mortality, deprive our lives of meaning? What would be different if we no longer had to die at some point, or if at least our actions and achievements had a lasting effect on the history of a never-ending universe?— Let us suppose our life never ended. Whatever happened, to Earth, to the solar system, to the universe, our existence would not be affected by it. In that case we would have all the time in the world: we would never run short of it. Naturally, there would still be things that we could not do, but never because of a lack of time. We could be very patient and bide our time, doing nothing much at all for as long as we feel like it, then spend hundreds of years on perfecting a skill and the next few hundred years on learning and perfecting a different

one. We could make plans that require thousands of years for their execution and yet still be around to see them come to fruition. We could see not only our children grow up, but also our grandchildren and great-grandchildren, as well as *their* children, grandchildren, and great-grandchildren (provided people would still reproduce, which might no longer be considered necessary or expedient). If other people were immortal too, we could spend literally an eternity with the ones we love, or, if that is not what we want, we could instead have, successively, an infinite number of partners, lovers, and friends to enjoy life with. We would, of course, still have to decide what to do *now*, but many of the things that we decide *not* to do now we could still do at some time in the future because it would never really be too late for anything.

The Life of Sisyphus

Would such an immortal life be better than the mortal one we have now? Sure enough it would allow us to do things that we cannot do now, things that require more time than we currently have. So in *that* respect an immortal life would be better. (Note, however, that there may well be *other* respects in which such a life would be worse.) Would it also be more *meaningful* in the sense that it would be *less pointless* and that the things we do would *matter* more? To answer this question, let us take a look at what is often seen as the "perfect image of meaninglessness" (Taylor 1970, 20): the myth of Sisyphus. Because he deemed himself smarter than the gods, Sisyphus was condemned to push a large boulder up a hill, and to do so for all eternity, for the boulder, whenever Sisyphus reaches the top of his hill, inevitably rolls back down, so that he keeps having to start all over again. There is no hope that he will ever accomplish his task, and giving up is not an option. The relentless repetition that is his life will therefore never end.

Now if this is indeed a perfect image of meaninglessness, then we should expect that it throws into sharp relief the key features of a life lacking in meaning. There are three aspects of the situation that stand out. The first is the very *repetitiveness* of the action performed. Sisyphus does the same thing over and over again. There is no variation: take the boulder, push it up the hill, watch it roll down again, go after it, repeat. Then there is, secondly, the apparent *futility* of Sisyphus's laboring. It looks as if what Sisyphus intends to do is get the boulder up the hill. Since this intention is thwarted each and every time he tries it, nothing ever comes of what he is doing: he does not really *accomplish* anything, or so it may seem. Finally – and that is an aspect often overlooked – Sisyphus has to perform this repetitive fruitless task *for all eternity*. Clearly, this does not make things any better for Sisyphus. If anything, the fact that his meaningless life will never end makes matters worse for him. It is what makes his punishment so very cruel and hard to bear in the first place. Perhaps it does not exactly make his life more *meaningless*, but it certainly does not make it any *less* meaningless either. We can therefore conclude that an immortal life is not necessarily more meaningful than a mortal life. It seems that whether or not it is would very much depend on what that life is like. If it is very repetitive and never goes anywhere and if being so makes a mortal life meaningless, then an immortal life that has the same features is equally meaningless.

This does not necessarily mean that our having to die in no way affects our ability to live a meaningful life. It is theoretically possible that while even an immortal life *can* be meaningless, it does not *have* to be, whereas a mortal life is *always* meaningless, simply by virtue of being mortal. If mortal lives are necessarily repetitive and not leading anywhere, whereas immortal lives are *not* necessarily repetitive and may indeed lead somewhere, then only an immortal life can be meaningful.

Repetition

Now it is no doubt true that our mortal lives do seem rather repetitive. Like all living beings we tend to do the same things over and over again. Our days strongly resemble each other.

We get up, use the bathroom, have breakfast, go to work, come home, eat, sleep, and then we do it again the following day. Our life as a whole is equally predictable in its overall trajectory. We get born, grow up, find a job, a hobby, fall in love, marry (fall in love again, remarry), have children, get old, retire, and die. And our children will do the same, as will their children after them, and so on, ad infinitum. There is some variation in the detail, of course, but in terms of their general features most human lives are pretty much alike. For one thing, they are characterized by endless repetitions, and for another, they do not really lead anywhere, except to death. Our lives therefore seem, overall, just as pointless as the life of Sisyphus.

And yet, if we believe that this kind of repetitiveness stands in the way of our living a meaningful life, it is difficult to see how we can escape it by not dying. We would still have to get up in the morning and do various things that are necessary to keep us functional, and we would still be limited in the *kind* of things that we could do. In fact, the more time we have at our disposal the more likely it is that we will have to repeat at some point what we did before. An endless life in a finite world is necessarily a life of endless repetitions. And the kind of *variation* that an endless life promises, we can also have in a mortal life if we choose to. We can find a new job every few years, travel the world, change partners frequently, pick up new hobbies, pursue them for a while, and then drop them again, deliberately change our habits after some time or, even better, try not to develop any in the first place, be open to new experiences, be unpredictable, be unreliable. Since such a life would be far less repetitive, it should also, if repetition is indeed the problem, be more meaningful. It is, however, far from obvious that this would be the case.

It has been argued that repetition is bad for us because it "adds nothing in and of itself to lifetime welfare" and that what we need in order to add meaning to our life are, therefore, "new kinds of momentary benefits—for example, qualitatively new pleasures, new kinds of aesthetic experiences, different or deeper insights into the nature of things, etc." (Bramble 2015, 455). And yet, while it is true that too much repetition can easily be experienced as stifling, and a life that consists in nothing more than doing one and the same thing over and over and over again, like that of Sisyphus, can hardly be seen as meaningful, *too much change and variety* can be equally detrimental to meaning. As the Danish philosopher Søren Kierkegaard pointed out, meaning can be found in repetition, and even thrive in it. For Kierkegaard, it is precisely our willingness to embrace repetition that distinguishes the ethical life from (what he calls) the (merely) aesthetic life, which is a life devoted to the passions and the pleasures of the senses. The ethical life is preferable because it is more authentic: it allows us to be ourselves. Because, living ethically, we always have a hold in ourselves, we do not permanently have to chase the new to keep us entertained and hold boredom (and the emptiness of our lives that it reveals) at bay. We make our choices and we stand by them. This naturally leads to some repetition in our lives (which is, aesthetically speaking, the enemy of passion). Yet while the aesthetic self cannot endure repetition, the ethical self thrives off it and positively embraces it. "He who chooses repetition, he lives. He does not chase after butterflies like a child, or stand on tiptoe in order to glimpse the wonders of the world. He knows them. (…) He goes calmly about his life, happy in repetition" (Kierkegaard 1843, 4).

In truth, repetition contributes to a meaningful life just as much as variation does. Think of the seasons, think of our annual celebrations and family gatherings. Think of the pieces of music and the books that we return to throughout our lives, the food that reminds us of our childhood. They do not become less meaningful because they return, on the contrary. They gain their meaning through the repetition. Why would things have to change constantly to add meaning to our life? The aesthetic chase for the ever-new does not make our life more meaningful. It is true that crises of meaning can result from

a lack of newness in our lives, but they can also arise from an inability to appreciate the familiar pleasures and similar kinds of experience. They can result from a restlessness that propels us ever forward and actually prevents us from deepening our understanding of the world (simply broadening it instead) and, perhaps most importantly, from ever feeling truly at home in the world.

Futility

Where does this leave us? We have seen that a mortal life is not necessarily less meaningful than an immortal one, and that *if* it is, then it must be for some other reason than that it will end someday. Yet we have also seen that repetition is not altogether bad and does not have to undermine the meaningfulness of our lives either. But there is only one other feature we have so far identified that looks as if it could prevent our mortal lives from being meaningful, namely the ultimate futility of everything we do. Sisyphus works so hard to get his boulder up to the top of the hill, and it is all in vain; he never achieves his goal or for that matter makes any real progress. He may manage to get his boulder halfway up the hill, but he will soon be at the bottom again. Our own lives, however, are actually very similar, or so it may appear to us. That is what Tolstoy seems to have felt: that because in the long run nothing we do has any lasting effects on anything (even if what we do is write wonderful novels like he did or perform some other great deed, all of which will also be forgotten one day), because we always end up at the bottom again (said bottom being death and annihilation), and so does everything we have touched in our life, there seems to be no point in putting any effort into it. Why bother if whatever we do, whatever we achieve, whatever we change, whatever good we may bring about, will, in the long run, not have made any difference whatsoever. It would seem then that no matter what we do we could just as well not do it.

This worry obviously concerns not so much our own death, but rather the fact that, inevitably, even the things we have accomplished will disappear one day. It is the end of everything that results from our actions rather than our own personal end that seems to stand in the way of meaning here. This extended form of death is what makes our efforts futile. Our lives may have consequences that reach far beyond our individual demise, but they too will end one day, and at that point nothing we have ever done will matter anymore. In this sense what we do now is futile, and clearly we don't want our actions to be futile. Ideally, we want them to make a lasting impact. Without such an impact there does not seem to be much point in living.

Joshua W. Seachris calls this intuition the staying-power intuition (SPI), which he defines as the idea that, all else being equal, things that are worthwhile, significant, or meaningful last (Seachris 2011, 461). Actions that have no lasting consequences we call futile. Deep or cosmic futility is the futility that results from the presumed fact that, because of the way the world works, there is ultimately nothing that has any lasting consequences. But why do we have this intuition in the first place: that only what lasts is meaningful? Seachris argues that the naturalistic assumption that we are making when we consider the meaning of our lives threatened or undermined by the way we think the world is going to end can and should be understood as a narrative or "meta-narrative." In narratives, it always matters how they end. When we assess a story – emotionally, morally, aesthetically – the ending is particularly relevant. It not only matters to us what happens at the end, but also that it happens *at the end*. A bad ending is bad, just as a bad beginning is bad, but a bad ending is much worse than a bad beginning, precisely because it is a bad ending. A lot of sad things can happen in the course of a narrative, but they don't necessarily make the story as a whole a sad one. Yet a sad ending always makes for a sad story, and a happy ending for a happy story. Cosmic futility is a threat because we look at life as a whole from a narrative perspective. If we didn't—if we didn't care so much about how things end—we would not feel that our lives

can be rendered worthless by what happens or does not happen in the far future of the world, seemingly nullifying all the good things that are actually happening in the present, all our accomplishments and achievements.

Yet even if Seachris is right and we do have such a deeply ingrained narrative bias that makes us root for happy endings, which would explain why it matters to us how the things we have set in motion end, it would still be odd if the only possible happy ending were no ending at all. There must be a way for the ending of a life well-lived to be a *happy* ending and to still be an *ending*. Similarly, when the good consequences that my life may have had, my legacy as it were, finally come to an end, years, decades, or centuries after my death, their ending does not necessarily have to be an unhappy one. We should remember here that whatever happens in the future, none of it can affect what has already happened. What we have accomplished, we have accomplished. If we have changed the world for the better, we have changed it for the better, even if it lasted only for a while, because for a while it really *was* better. Nothing is going to change that. Happy moments will still be happy moments even if they don't last, and they will forever remain happy moments. The past is what it is. It cannot be changed by the future.

All this suggests that for our actions to be futile it is not sufficient that they have no lasting consequences. A lot depends on whether we *want* them to be lasting and *how* lasting we want them to be. Generally speaking, futile is an action whose intended goal is not accomplished. Accordingly, we cannot judge whether an action is futile or not if we don't know what goal it was intended to accomplish. If what I intend to accomplish by doing something is completely unrelated to the eventual fate of the universe, then what I am doing is not rendered futile by said fate. If I study hard to become, say, a decent philosopher, and I then, as a result, manage to become exactly that, then my labors have *not* been futile even if I eventually die or even if the whole solar system will perish in a few billion years, because that has got nothing to do with what I have or have not accomplished. Accordingly, we would only have reason to regard our actions as futile in light of the inevitable future destruction of our solar system, if we had a deep desire that what we do now will have an impact far beyond our own life span and even beyond the life span of our solar system. This, however, is rather unlikely. We may have some desire to be remembered after our death, mostly by our loved ones, and perhaps by others, for a while at least. But we don't usually have a deep desire to still have an impact on things a few billion years from now, and it would be a very odd desire to have indeed.

Even if our desires are more far-reaching, more world-changing in their ambition, we would (and perhaps, if we are wise, should) not seriously expect or even hope to make an everlasting impact. Let us suppose you could make the world a better place in some way, and you also desire to do so, but that at the same time you are aware that it is not going to last. The world will only be better for a decade or two and then revert to its previous, less desirable state. Would your plan, in that case, not be worth pursuing at all? No doubt, it would certainly be better if the world *remained* a better place, and the longer it remained a better place the better it would be, but it doesn't follow from this that being a better place only for a while is not better than never to have been a better place at all. There is no good reason to suppose that our inability to ensure that a particular state of affairs lasts forever makes it pointless to bring about this state of affairs in the first place.

Ultimate Significance

So what have we learned so far? We saw earlier that an immortal life can be just as repetitive as a mortal one, if not more so. We also saw that repetition does not necessarily stand in the way of meaning. Futility, on the other hand, does seem to threaten the meaningfulness of what we do. However, what is often *taken* for futility, namely the fact that *in the very long run* nothing we do is likely to make

much of a difference, is either not futility at all or not the kind of futility that can plausibly be said to undermine meaning. What may conceivably do that is the futility of an action that fails to achieve its purpose. Yet the fact that we have to die does not prevent us from achieving our purposes, unless our purposes are unreasonably ambitious. It is true that our life will be cut off at some point and in that sense does not lead anywhere beyond that point. Yet what we do in life does in fact lead to many things *in* life. Why should it have to lead to something that is no longer part of our life? As Thomas Nagel (1971) has argued, the chain of justifications ("I do this in order to achieve that") needs to come to an end somewhere, and there is no reason to think that it cannot be just as meaningful if it comes to an end within our given life span.

It has been argued, however, that in order to be MEANINGFUL our life also needs to have *ultimate significance*, and that a mortal life can never have that, no matter what it is like in other respects. What we need to lead a meaningful life is in fact the kind of immortality that only God can give us. "If there is no God," writes William Lane Craig, "then man's life becomes absurd" (Craig 1994, 40) precisely because if there is no God, then death is real, both for us and for everything else, including the universe itself, which is a horrible prospect. Without God there is no immortality for us, and without immortality no ultimate significance, because all the significance a mortal life can ever have is merely relative. What we do is relatively significant if it impacts on other events. But if the changes we bring about do *not change the final destiny of the universe* (because whatever we do, things will cease to exist someday), then they have no ultimate significance. Whatever we accomplish in life is then "utterly meaningless": "This is the horror of modern man: because he ends in nothing, he is nothing" (Craig 1994, 42). Clearly, though, more is needed for ultimate significance than just immortality. We could live forever and still be nothing in the sense that our existence still does not impact in any way on the final destiny of the universe. That is why God is needed who alone can make sure that we have a seat at the table that determines the universe's destiny. But then again, it seems strange and rather implausible to say that because we *end* in nothing, we *are* nothing. Why should only the eternal, the never-ending, count as *something*? This (essentially Platonic) assumption is especially implausible since all the somethings we have ever encountered and are ever likely to encounter are finite. As far as we know, everything that exists started to exist one day and will one day cease to exist. Out of the blue, into the black, this is our lot. This is what "being something" means: being something *in* time and therefore *for* a time. What is absurd is to expect and desire more than that. What makes our lives meaningful is not what comes of them (or *that* something comes of them), but the fact that we deeply care about what we do, that we are emotionally involved in our lives. The things we do are important to us, and that is enough to make our lives meaningful, even if nothing that we do actually leads anywhere (at least to nothing permanent, nothing that will stay). What matters not only in the first instance but *ultimately*, is that there are things that matter to *us*: "things worth achieving, doing or having, (…) things that bring joy, understanding, exhilaration or contentment to ourselves or to others" (Nielsen 1978, 157). That we cannot have those things forever does not in any way diminish their worth.

Bibliography

Bramble, Ben (2015): "Consequentialism about Meaning in Life", *Utilitas* 27/4: 445–459.

Craig, William Lane (1994): "The Absurdity of Life Without God", in: William Lane Craig, *Reasonable Faith: Christian Truth and Apologies*, Wheaton, IL: Good News Publishers/Crossway Books, 57–75. Reprinted in: *The Meaning of Life*, ed. E.D. Klemke, New York/Oxford: Oxford University Press 2000, 40–56.

De Grey, Aubrey & Michael Rae (2008): *Ending Aging. The Rejuvenation Breakthroughs That Could Reverse Human Aging in Our Lifetime*, New York: St. Martin's Press.

Kierkegaard, Søren (1843): *Repetition. An Essay in Experimental Psychology*, in: Søren Kierkegaard, *Repetition and Philosophical Crumbs*. Translated by M.G. Piety, Oxford: Oxford University Press 2009, 1–81.

Nagel, Thomas (1971): "The Absurd", *Journal of Philosophy* 68/20: 716–727.

Nielsen, Kai (1978): *Death and the Meaning of Life*. Reprinted in: *The Meaning of Life*, ed. E.D. Klemke, New York/Oxford: Oxford University Press 2000, 153–159.

Seachris, Joshua W. (2011): "Death, Futility, and the Proleptic Power of Narrative Endings", *Religious Studies* 47: 141–163. Reprinted in: *Exploring the Meaning of Life: An Anthology and Guide*, Chichester: John Wiley 2013, 461–480.

Taylor, Richard (1970): "The Meaning of Life", in: *Life, Death and Meaning: Key Philosophical Readings on the Big Questions*, ed. David Benatar, Lanham, MD: Rowman & Littlefield 2004, 19–28 (originally in Richard Taylor, *Good and Evil*, New York: Macmillan 1970).

Tolstoy, Leo (1882): *A Confession*, translated by Jane Kentish, London: Penguin Books 2008.

Index